INSIDE THE HUB

THE UNOFFICIAL AND UNAUTHORISED GUIDE TO TORCHWOOD SERIES ONE

INSIDE THE HUB

THE UNOFFICIAL AND UNAUTHORISED GUIDE TO TORCHWOOD SERIES ONE

STEPHEN JAMES WALKER

First published in England in 2007 by
Telos Publishing Ltd
61 Elgar Avenue, Tolworth, Surrey, KT5 9JP, England
www.telos.co.uk

Telos Publishing Ltd values feedback. Please e-mail us with any comments you may have about this book to: feedback@telos.co.uk

ISBN: 978-1-84583-013-7 (paperback) 978-1-84583-022-9 (hardback)

Internal design, typesetting and layout by Arnold T Blumberg
www.atbpublishing.com

Printed in the UK

1 2 3 4 5 6 7 8 9 10 11 12 13 14 15

British Library Cataloguing in Publication Data.
A catalogue record for this book is available from the British Library.

ACKNOWLEDGEMENTS

Thanks to my family for putting up with me spending huge amounts of time working on this book when I would otherwise have been spending it with them. Thanks to David J Howe, my fellow director in Telos Publishing, for all his support. Thanks also to Sarah Mowbray from BARB for permission to use the official viewing figures.

Stephen James Walker

TABLE OF CONTENTS

INTRODUCTION: WHEN EVERYTHING CHANGES

In 2005 – the forty-second year since it made its on-air debut, and the sixteenth year since it was last in regular production – the BBC's classic science-fiction drama serial *Doctor Who* returned to TV; and, somewhat to the surprise of most media pundits, but not to its many thousands of loyal fans worldwide, proved to be a huge success all over again. In fact, this new, updated series, masterminded by acclaimed scriptwriter Russell T Davies – previously best known as the creator of *Queer As Folk* – arguably brought *Doctor Who* even greater popularity than it had ever enjoyed before. It was watched by a phenomenal 7.95 million BBC One viewers on average over the course of its 13 weekly episodes, absolutely trouncing the main ITV competition in the battle for ratings in its key, early-Saturday-evening slot. Hundreds of thousands of BBC Three viewers also tuned in each week for repeats. After suffering years of neglect, and even distain, from successive teams of senior executives at the BBC, *Doctor Who* had suddenly become their biggest hit, and it seemed they couldn't get enough of it. Even before the first series had finished transmission, they had announced the commissioning of an hour-long special for Christmas 2005; a second full series and *another* Christmas special for 2006; and a *third* full series for 2007 – an unprecedented demonstration of commitment in today's highly competitive broadcasting environment. But even this was clearly not enough: on Monday 17 October 2005, news broke that, for the first time in its long history[1], *Doctor Who* was to spawn a full, 13-episode spin-off series: *Torchwood*, based around Captain Jack Harkness, one of the new regular characters introduced in 2005, as portrayed by actor John Barrowman.

Right from when that initial press announcement was made, I had a feeling that *Torchwood* was going to be my sort of series. For one thing, I have been a life-long devotee of *Doctor Who*, so naturally the prospect of a spin-off from it was instantly appealing. For another thing, the announcement indicated that *Torchwood* would be aimed at a more adult audience, and I have always enjoyed it greatly when the *Doctor Who* universe has been presented in a more adult light in other media – in fact, the adult-orientated New Adventures series of original novels published by Virgin Publishing between 1991 and 1999[2] still stands as one of my all-time favourite 'eras' of *Doctor Who*. Moreover, *Torchwood* was described as a 'sci-fi paranoid thriller, a cop show with a sense of humour' that would be 'dark, wild and sexy', and I have long been a huge fan of gritty and hardboiled crime fiction, and of the classic film noir productions that came out of Hollywood in the 1940s and 1950s. It was also characterised as '*The X-Files* meets *This Life*' – both of which series I absolutely loved.

Surely *Torchwood* couldn't fail to appeal to me, could it? Happily, when the 13-episode debut series eventually reached the screen, it didn't. In fact, I thought it was fantastic. It was

---

1 The only previous televised *Doctor Who* spin-off was *K-9 and Company*: 'A Girl's Best Friend', featuring Sarah Jane Smith (Elisabeth Sladen) and K-9, which was transmitted on 28 December 1981 and was effectively a pilot for a full series, although it turned out to be a one-off.

2 For their last two years, the New Adventures did not feature the Doctor himself, as Virgin had lost their licence to publish *Doctor Who* fiction; instead, they focused on the Doctor's one-time companion, introduced in the books, Bernice Summerfield.

not without its faults, of course; but then, what is? Over the course of its run, it was consistently my TV highlight of the week – and that included the week in which *Doctor Who*'s 2006 Christmas special, 'The Runaway Bride', was transmitted. But, more than that, I found myself becoming preoccupied with it; and I don't think that was just because I was writing this book. It's that sort of series: it gets under your skin, worms its way into your head and keeps you thinking about it long after each new episode has come and gone. In fact, the 'high-octane' exploits of Captain Jack and his team seem to have an almost addictive quality to them; and, judging from various online fan forums, even those who didn't much care for the series just couldn't stop watching it and talking about it.

But, more than that, *Torchwood* is an important series, for a number of different reasons. It has proved that the success of the new *Doctor Who* was not a 'one off', and that a new, British-made science-fiction drama series can win a big mainstream audience, not just a cult following as might at one time have been assumed; it has helped to boost the profile of BBC Three, and of digital programming more generally, by regularly attracting to it many viewers who in the past would doubtless have restricted themselves mainly to the major terrestrial channels; it has been in the vanguard of the use of new high definition TV technology for drama productions; it has given BBC Wales another major national hit, demonstrating the success of the ongoing regionalisation of the BBC's operations; and it has proved that the indefinable magic of *Doctor Who*, which has now endured for well over 40 years and made it arguably the most well-loved drama series of all time, still works even when its characters, concepts and values are carried across into a spin-off.

As will probably be apparent by now, any readers hoping for a damning indictment of *Torchwood* should look elsewhere: *Inside the Hub*, while not shying away from criticism where it is due, is essentially a celebration of the series, giving all the facts and figures, all the dates and details, but also, and more importantly, examining its appeal in depth, discussing the strengths – and weaknesses – of the 13 individual episodes and highlighting exactly what it is that makes *Torchwood* so special.

The basic structure of the text is as follows. Part One recalls the gradual build up of public excitement about the series during the period from October 2005 to September 2006 inclusive – that is, the year leading up to the month of its debut transmission – as steadily increasing amounts of advance information became available through press announcements, magazine articles, newspaper reports and the like. Part Two then takes up the story and covers in a similar fashion the period from October 2006 to January 2007 inclusive – the four months when the series was in regular transmission on BBC Three and BBC Two – completing a blow-by-blow account of the unfolding story of *Torchwood* as seen from the 'outside looking in' perspective of the viewing public. In Part Three, I then move on to describe 'the *Torchwood* format', presenting a behind-the-scenes account of the series' conception, discussing its storytelling and visual style, examining the debt of inspiration it owes to various 'fictional forerunners', and drawing on information gathered both from the episodes themselves and from the series' official websites in order to indulge in a little speculation about the history and set-up of Torchwood as an organisation. Part Four gives character profiles for the main Torchwood team members, again based on information gleaned both from the series and from other official sources. Part Five presents capsule biographies of the main cast and production team members. This then leads on to the most substantial section of the book, Part Six, which consists of a detailed guide to and analysis of the series' 13 episodes. Lastly there are five appendices, covering more peripheral matters: tie-in merchandise; the first three original novels based on the series; the *Torchwood Declassified* mini-documentaries; the series' ratings; and a brief overview of *Torchwood*-related websites.

In summary, I have aimed in this book to give a comprehensive overview of the phenomenon that is *Torchwood*, covering everything from its conception, commissioning and announcement right up to the end of its first series. Thankfully for its many fans – affectionately referred to as 'Woodies' by John Barrowman (although, probably coincidentally, the term was actually first coined by a contributor to the Torchwood.TV website) – its success has been such that there is now a second series to look forward to early in 2008.

I, for one, can hardly wait!

Stephen James Walker
3 February 2007

PART ONE:
THE EXCITEMENT BEGINS

CHAPTER ONE: BREAKING NEWS

FIRST ANNOUNCEMENT

In its initial, 17 October 2005 press release announcing the commissioning of *Torchwood*, the BBC said:

> Russell T Davies is to write a sci-fi paranoid thriller in a major new drama commission for BBC Three, it was announced today by Stuart Murphy, Controller of BBC Three.
>
> *Torchwood* is a 13-part drama series aimed at a post-watershed[3] audience and has an organic link to *Doctor Who*.
>
> '*Torchwood* is a British sci-fi paranoid thriller, a cop show with a sense of humour,' says Russell T Davies.
>
> 'It's dark, wild and sexy, it's *The X-Files* meets *This Life*. It's a stand-alone series for adult audiences, which will have its own unique identity.
>
> 'I have just begun working on the scripts with a team of writers and cannot wait to see the results.'
>
> Set in modern-day Cardiff, *Torchwood* stars John Barrowman as Captain Jack from *Doctor Who*; it's in the Christmas special and second series of *Doctor Who* that the story of Torchwood – a renegade group of investigators – is seeded.
>
> However, no stories will cross over between *Torchwood* and *Doctor Who*.
>
> The drama series is produced by BBC Wales and will be transmitted later next year.
>
> Stuart Murphy says: 'The renegades investigate human and alien crime, as well as alien technology that has fallen to Earth.
>
> '*Torchwood* is sinister and psychological – Russell was really keen to play with your head – as well as being very British and modern and real.
>
> 'But at the centre of the drama are warm, human relationships and the overcoming of adversity.'
>
> John Barrowman says: 'I'm absolutely thrilled about *Torchwood*. It's going to be a dark, wild and sexy roller-coaster ride.
>
> 'Working again with Russell T Davies, Julie Gardner and the BBC is like hooking up with family again. I can't wait to explore Captain Jack even more.'
>
> Murphy adds: '*Torchwood* is a massive coup for BBC Three, and a major commitment – it's the biggest drama we've ever had on the channel.
>
> 'It introduces a different tone into our drama, just as Russell's *Casanova* earlier this year brought warmth and humour.
>
> 'He's an absolute genius – you look at what he has done with *Doctor Who* – we said to him, "What would you do with a post-watershed sci-fi?" Its subject and tone is a perfect fit for BBC Three.'
>
> Filming on the 13 self-contained episodes will begin early next year in Cardiff; other writers so far confirmed include Chris Chibnall and P J Hammond.
>
> The executive producers are Russell T Davies and Julie Gardner, Head of Drama in BBC Wales.
>
> *Torchwood* follows the success of *Casanova* (which attracted a record audience for a

3 9.00 pm is regarded in British broadcasting as a 'watershed', after which the transmission of programmes with adult content is acceptable, on the assumption that most children will have gone to bed by then.

drama on the channel), *Bodies*, *Conviction* and *Outlaws*, with which the channel has begun to establish a reputation for cutting-edge British drama.

Torchwood is a BBC Wales commission for BBC Three.

This exciting announcement – of which, remarkably, no details at all had leaked out in advance – spawned stories in almost all the UK's national newspapers, and was also reported by many overseas and online news outlets. Little further information was forthcoming in these pieces, although a few additional quotes from BBC Three Controller Stuart Murphy were to be found in the *Independent* – which had some of the most detailed, and earliest, online coverage and, judging from hints dropped by Davies the previous week about a story imminently to be revealed in its pages, may at one point have been lined up for an exclusive on the news.

'The people have affairs with one another,' said Murphy. 'There will be sex and swearing, I assume. I'm quite relaxed about that; it will be post-watershed, and Russell can do it in a funny and sexy way.

'It's a renegade bunch of investigators who investigate real-life, normal crimes. They also look into alien happenings. They have been charged by the British government to find alien technology that has fallen to Earth, and they need to do it without the FBI and the UN knowing.'

Of the series' lead character, Captain Jack, the *Western Mail* quoted Davies as saying:

'We had a fantastic response to him [in *Doctor Who*] – he was larger than life, and it made sense for him to have his own show.

'We've been keeping these plans secret for many months now, but people have been saying, "Why don't you make a series with that character?"'

A news item on BBC Radio Wales, later used as the basis of an online report by BBC News, noted one point that the press release had missed, but that many of the newspapers had picked up on: that the word 'Torchwood' was an anagram of 'Doctor Who.' This item also featured a telephone interview with Davies, who elaborated:

'It's a modern series, an urban series, very much set on Earth – I don't want the term "science-fiction" to make people think we're off to Mars or anything like that! It's set in Cardiff. It's a Welsh series that I'm very, very proud of, with a lot of work, I hope, for a lot of Welsh actors and directors.

'It's going to be sexy, it's going to be funny. It's real people, in the modern day; real policemen using alien technology to solve crimes, and having a bit of trouble, and having a bit of a laugh along the way.

'*Doctor Who* has a completely different feel from this sort of thing. This is set in the same place every week … It's a different sort of fun from *Doctor Who* … They're two very distinct shows, at the end of the day …

'With *Doctor Who*, we often have to pretend that bits of Cardiff are London, or Utah, or the planet Zog, whereas this series is going to be "honest-to-god Cardiff."[4] We will happily walk past the Millennium Centre and say, "Look, there's the Millennium Centre."

'It's nice to be able to say this is the city, and this is how good it looks.'

In the same interview, Davies also explained how the title of the spin-off had been derived from a security measure:

'When we were making the first *Doctor Who* series, television pirates were desperate to get their

4 'Boom Town,' the eleventh episode of Davies's first *Doctor Who* series, had however been set in contemporary Cardiff, as well as recorded there.

hands on a tape. One of the people in the office had the idea of calling the tapes of episodes, as they went from Cardiff to London, *Torchwood*, instead of putting *Doctor Who* on them.

'I thought: "Oh, that's good, that's clever!" That ticked away at the back of my head for a good six months or so, and now here it is as a show!'

Whether or not television pirates really were desperate to get their hands on work-in-progress tapes of the new *Doctor Who* early in 2005 is open to debate. However, this concern, whether well-founded or not, was to have a lasting legacy, in the coining of the memorable *Torchwood* title.

THE WORD IS: TORCHWOOD

'Torchwood' is not only an anagram of 'Doctor Who' but also a word that can be found in the dictionary, where it is defined as[5]:

1. Any of several tropical American trees of the genus *Amyris,* especially *A. balsamifera*, having resinous wood that burns with a torch-like flame.[6]

2. The wood of any of these trees.

The earliest use of 'Torchwood' as the name of an on-screen organisation, however, came during 'Bad Wolf', the penultimate episode of the first new *Doctor Who* series, transmitted on 11 June 2005. In this, the Doctor's companion Rose is trapped in a sinister, futuristic version of the popular BBC game show *The Weakest Link*, in which questions are put to contestants by the Anne Droid – an android host modelled on, and voiced by, *The Weakest Link*'s regular presenter, Anne Robinson. One of the questions posed to a contestant named Broff is: 'The Great Cobalt Pyramid is built on the remains of which Old Earth Institute?' Broff answers: 'Touchdown.' The Anne Droid corrects him: 'No. Torchwood.'

As early as August 2005, some two months before the spin-off series was announced, eagle-eyed fans had already spotted a clue that the word 'Torchwood' might have some greater significance than its brief mention in 'Bad Wolf' would have suggested: the BBC was reported to have registered the internet domain name www.torchwood.org.uk. This immediately led to speculation that 'Torchwood' might be used as a recurring motif during the second *Doctor Who* series, in much the same way as the term 'Bad Wolf' had been used during the first. Earlier in 2005, bbc.co.uk – the BBC's online service – had launched www.badwolf.org.uk as one of a number of 'fictional' websites inspired by *Doctor Who* but separate from the main official website (others being www.whoisdoctorwho.co.uk, www.unit.org.uk and www.geocomtex.net), and the suspicion was that www.torchwood.org.uk would come to fulfil much the same function. Davies had already confirmed, in his 'Production Notes' column in Issue 359 of *Doctor Who Magazine*: 'There's another little something in the 2006 series. Not such a mystery, but a word for which the production team has plans. And we've been planning ahead – it's already been said on screen. And it's an anagram.' At that time, however, none of the magazine's regular readers could have realised the full significance of these comments.

On Sunday 16 October 2005, the BBC's main *Doctor Who* website advised readers to 'Prepare for a New Word Order' (an allusion, no doubt, to the fact that *Torchwood* was an anagram); then, on the stroke of midnight, this changed to a *Torchwood* logo, in the style of the new series *Doctor Who* logo. The excitement had begun!

5 Source: www.dictionary.com

6 As an in-joke in the *Torchwood* original novel *Another Life*, one of the characters has an *Amyris elemifera* as a pot-plant in his flat.

CHAPTER TWO: EARLY SPECULATION

After the BBC's initial announcement on 17 October 2005, there was a hiatus of a few weeks before the release of the next official *Torchwood* news – that James Hawes had been lined up to be the series' producer and Ed Thomas its production designer, and that one of the regular characters was to be called Gwen, as revealed by Russell T Davies in Issue 363 of *Doctor Who Magazine*. This allowed plenty of time for speculation to rage and rumour to circulate amongst *Doctor Who* fans eager to know more about the exciting new production.

A popular topic of discussion was whether or not any established *Doctor Who* characters other than Captain Jack would 'cross over' to the new series. Would there, for instance, be a guest spot for Prime Minister Harriet Jones (played by Penelope Wilton) – a character who made her debut as a back-bench MP in the Series One *Doctor Who* episode 'Aliens of London'? Or how about Henry van Statten (Corey Johnson), in view of his own interest in tracking down and collecting alien artefacts, as seen in 'Dalek'? Another character introduced in 'Dalek' who was hotly fancied by some to make a comeback in the spin-off was misguided genius Adam (Bruno Langley). Perhaps even the tenth Doctor (David Tennant) and his companion Rose Tyler (Billie Piper) would put in an appearance?

Delving further back in time to the classic *Doctor Who* series, characters tipped by some to return in *Torchwood* included Liz Shaw (Caroline John), Brigadier Lethbridge-Stewart (Nicholas Courtney) and the Doctor's old adversary the Master (portrayed most recently, in 1996, by Eric Roberts). Sarah Jane Smith (Elisabeth Sladen) and K-9 (voiced by John Leeson) were particularly strong favourites to turn up, after their guest-starring roles in the Series Two *Doctor Who* episode 'School Reunion'; although at the beginning of March 2006, stories began to circulate that one or both of them would soon be getting a spin-off series all of their own …

And what of the popular *Doctor Who* monsters? Would the Torchwood team find themselves up against the Daleks, perhaps, or the Cybermen? Or maybe some other established monster race, less familiar to *Doctor Who*'s new, 21st Century viewers, such as the Ice Warriors, the Yeti or the Sontarans?

The BBC's description of the spin-off as a post-watershed, adult-orientated drama led to much discussion about the extent to which swearing, graphic violence, nudity and scenes of a sexual nature would feature. In terms of earlier Russell T Davies series, would this be more akin to the frank, sexually-explicit *Queer as Folk*, or to the more restrained, albeit still provocative, *Casanova*? And, more frivolously, would viewers finally get to see Captain Jack's naked bottom – a shot of which had been censored by BBC executives from the Series One *Doctor Who* episode 'Bad Wolf'?

What would the new series' logo, title sequence and theme music be like? How many regular characters would there be? Would the advent of *Torchwood* prevent Captain Jack from returning in future episodes of *Doctor Who*? Would the official *Doctor Who Magazine* cover *Torchwood* as well; and, if not, would the series have its own regular publication? How could Captain Jack have got back to 21st Century Cardiff, when in *Doctor Who* he was last seen, in the episode 'The Parting of the Ways', stranded on a space station in the far future? Would *Torchwood* drain resources from *Doctor Who*, or cause the creative team to become over-stretched? And so it continued. No aspect of the new series, it seemed, was too inconsequential to provoke debate – some of it quite impassioned.

Most of this speculation, naturally enough, proved to be wide of the mark.

One rumour that was grounded in something more than mere speculation – although only in the sense that it was sparked by a press story that first appeared in the *Daily Star* on 19 October and was quickly picked up by a couple of other UK tabloids – was that young, Welsh opera-turned-pop-singer Charlotte Church would have a regular role in the new series as 'Face of a Devil … a raunchy, Satan-worshipping villain.' Again, however, this turned out to be untrue; the story in question had apparently been simply made up by the journalist, perhaps inspired in part by the fact that Church had been present at the press launch of the 2005 *Doctor Who* series. Another pop singer reported the following month to be taking a lead role in the series, possibly as Gwen, was Rachel Stevens, formerly of the group S Club 7 – but once more this proved to be baseless.

A rumour that actually had a basis in fact was that *Torchwood* might be repeated on BBC One after its BBC Three debut. John Barrowman himself hinted at this on 18 October during an appearance on the ITV chat show *Loose Women*. This was hardly a revelation, however, as it was established practice for BBC Three shows to be given a wider, terrestrial audience on BBC One or BBC Two if they proved a sufficiently big hit – as had happened, for instance, with Davies's *Casanova*, and with a new season of the comedy series *Little Britain*. And it was not long before the BBC's own *Doctor Who* website was stating as fact – albeit as an aside, in its 24 February 2006 announcement of the casting of Gwen – that *Torchwood* would indeed be repeated on BBC One after its initial BBC Three screening. (No mention was made at this time of the possibility that the terrestrial repeat might actually be on BBC Two rather than BBC One, as would eventually be the case.) Fan speculation then turned to the possibility that, following in the wake of another big science-fiction-themed adult drama success for the BBC in the form of Matthew Graham's series *Life on Mars*, *Torchwood* might even *debut* on BBC One, and be repeated on BBC Three subsequently. In this case, however, the speculation proved completely misguided; as the series had been commissioned by BBC Three in the first place, it was always odds on that it would debut on that channel.

As further official news began to emerge about the series, the rumour-mill began to wind down a little – but even some of the official announcements provoked fresh debate and conjecture, and it seemed that there would be plenty to keep the fans' curiosity piqued right up until the series was actually transmitted.

CHAPTER THREE: TOWARD PRODUCTION

SEEDING TORCHWOOD

Once *Torchwood* had been green-lit and announced, plans were made to foreshadow or – as the initial press release put it – 'seed' the new series by way of references to the Torchwood organisation in *Doctor Who*'s 2005 Christmas special, 'The Christmas Invasion', and its 2006 second series.

In 'The Christmas Invasion', written by Russell T Davies, the human race finds itself threatened by the alien Sycorax. Prime Minister Harriet Jones (Penelope Wilton) liaises with the British branch of UNIT – established in the classic *Doctor Who* series as the United Nations Intelligence Taskforce, although not named in full here – to try to combat this menace, but also keeps a second defensive option in mind, as the viewer gathers when she asks her military aide Major Blake (presumably seconded to UNIT from the British army): 'What about Torchwood? I know I'm not supposed to know about it. I realise that. Not even the United Nations knows. But if ever there was a need for Torchwood, it's now.' Blake replies that he can't take the responsibility, to which she retorts: 'I can. See to it. Get them ready.' Later, as the crisis escalates, the Prime Minister asks Blake for a progress report, and he tells her that, having lost a third of their staff (as a third of the world's population has fallen under the Sycorax's influence), Torchwood are 'still working on it.' She instructs that they be told to hurry up. Only in the closing minutes of the story does it become apparent exactly what Torchwood have been working on. As the Sycorax spaceship departs, the creatures' leader having been defeated in ritual combat by the Doctor, the Prime Minister is told that there is a message from Torchwood: 'They say they're ready.' She says: 'Tell them to fire.' In response to this, five bright green rays shoot up from different points around London and converge into one, which then streaks out from the Earth and destroys the Sycorax ship.

In summary, what the viewer learns from all this is that Torchwood is a secret, British-based, possibly military organisation, its existence supposed to be unknown to the United Nations and even to the British Prime Minister – although she does in fact know of it, and can actually command it; that it has a reasonable cadre of staff (given that it can remain operational even after having lost around a third of them); and that it has access to weapons technology that appears more advanced than could be developed by current human science, suggesting an alien origin.

The next, highly significant 'teasers' of information to be revealed about Torchwood came in the Series Two story 'Tooth and Claw'. The principal action of this episode unfolds in Torchwood House, an impressive but isolated residence in Scotland where Queen Victoria stops off *en route* from London to Balmoral in 1879, and where she is ultimately rescued by the Doctor and Rose from a band of murderous monks and a vicious werewolf. In the aftermath of these other-worldly events, the Queen determines to set up the Torchwood Institute, named after the House, as a first line of defence for her realm against any similar 'strange happenings' that might occur in the future – including any return visits by the Doctor himself.

As was often the case during Series Two of *Doctor Who*, the transmission of this episode was followed almost immediately by the coming online of a further new 'fictional' website – in this case, www.visittorchwood.co.uk – created by the bbc.co.uk team. This purported to describe a real Torchwood House, with only the website's disclaimer admitting, for the benefit of the uninitiated, that it was actually a fictional location featured in *Doctor Who*.

The home page of this website displayed a picture of Torchwood House nestling in the

Scottish Highlands – an image taken from 'Tooth and Claw' – and stated: 'Torchwood House is one of Scotland's great architectural treasures. Owned by the MacLeish family since the 1500s, it was purchased by the Crown in 1893. Famed for its beautiful grounds and stunning observatory, it was opened to the public in 1981. A real jewel of the Highlands, it has received over a million visitors since opening.' A moving line of black and white portrait illustrations along the bottom of the page depicted numerous 'Memorable MacLeishes,' starting with Lady Catherine (1502-1542), described as the 'family's first matriarch,' who 'died in a fire,' and ending with Sir Robert (1837-1839), the last of the line, and his widow Lady Isobel (1842-1893). These latter two characters were actually seen in 'Tooth and Claw', as played by Derek Riddell and Michelle Duncan respectively.

A second page, accessible from the home page, gave information supposedly for the benefit of potential visitors to the House, including details of opening dates, renovation work being undertaken, exhibitions and other attractions to be seen. It also featured links to two further pages, the first giving additional visitor information and the second relating to refreshments, and in particular the availability in the House's kitchens of a selection of deserts from the Millingdale Ice Cream range – complete with a link to yet another 'fictional' website, www.millingdaleicecream.co.uk, consisting of a home page (and accompanying musical jingle) and additional pages on, respectively, the company's history and its (in some cases decidedly strange) ice cream flavours.

Another page accessible from the Torchwood House home page was devoted to the building's most distinctive feature – the large observatory seen in 'Tooth and Claw'. By entering a password – 'Victoria' – those visiting this page were able to 'Scan for Heavenly Bodies', although attempts to 'View Lunar Surface' and 'Explore Solar System' were tantalisingly rebuffed. It was not until the end of June 2006 that the 'View Lunar Surface' function became 'active', although visitors were still unable to 'Explore Solar System', this having apparently been 'made unavailable by the Butler Institute.'

Yet another page advertised Torchwood House as a venue for holding wedding and civil partnership ceremonies, along with a further page of testimonials from happy couples who had supposedly done just that.

Perhaps the most interesting information accessible from the home page, however, was contained in a series of four pages devoted to the history of House. Referring to events described in 'Tooth and Claw', it said, in part:

'Although it was a house built to impress, much of it fell into disrepair during the time of Sir George MacLeish in the 1800s. An eccentric man, Sir George was fascinated by both the sciences and local folklore. He was good friends with Queen Victoria's husband Prince Albert … It was Sir George who built the famous Torchwood Observatory.'

Then, going beyond what was revealed in the televised story, the account continued:

'The House has a number of unique features. Its name comes from the wood used in the construction of the Great Staircase. Local legend said it was made from a gallows struck down by lightning (the Torched Wood), but recent studies have shown it to be *Amyris Elemifera*, which grows as a large tree in tropical areas such as Florida. Its oils are said to have excellent medicinal qualities. It is believed that one of Sir George's eccentricities was to have a number of the trees shipped over to Scotland, using the wood to rebuild the staircase.'

In fictional terms, therefore, it seems that Torchwood's name does ultimately derive from the tree referred to in the dictionary definition quoted in Chapter One of this book – although no doubt some would quibble over the canonicity of the information revealed by the Torchwood

House website.

The next *Doctor Who* episode, 'School Reunion,' also contained a reference to Torchwood, albeit a more peripheral one, when Rose's boyfriend Mickey attempts to obtain classified information from an Army Records website via a computer in a cyber café and finds his 'Access Denied' by Torchwood (something also seen in the downloadable online/mobile phone 'Tardisode' teaser for the episode).

Similarly, in 'Rise of the Cybermen,' there were two brief mentions: the first, a reference to a study published by the Torchwood Institute, in a news report heard on Rose's mobile phone; the second, an aside – 'How's it going at Torchwood?' – from Peter Tyler, a parallel world version of Rose's father, to a guest named 'Stevie' at his estranged wife Jackie's birthday party. This indicates that Torchwood also exists in the parallel world of 'Rise of the Cybermen' – and that adventure's concluding instalment, 'The Age of Steel' – and is apparently a less clandestine organisation there.

In 'The Idiot's Lantern,' a police officer mentions Torchwood in connection with the investigation into the fate that has befallen the victims of the alien being known as the Wire.

In 'The Satan Pit,' a far-future expeditionary team from Earth, sent to investigate a mysterious power source on a planet orbiting a black hole, is said by its commander to represent 'the Torchwood Archive.' (The two-parter's previous instalment, 'The Impossible Planet,' also had a sly reference of sorts to Torchwood, when the Doctor, noting the need for illumination, comments: 'A torch would do it ...')

In the quirky, humorous episode 'Love & Monsters,' the character Victor Kennedy – in truth an alien referred to as 'the Abzorbaloff' – has in his possession some Torchwood files on both the Doctor and Rose, although how he came by these is left unexplained. There is said to be some corruption of the files by the 'Bad Wolf virus' – interpreted by some fans as a reference to the computer virus that the ninth Doctor passed on to Mickey at one point, designed to remove all references to the Doctor from the internet.

'Fear Her' has an apparent mention of Torchwood – arguably the most difficult of all to catch – in a TV broadcast heard in the background of one scene, although it is possible that what the commentator actually says is '... torch would ...,' in reference to the Olympic torch as featured in that scene.

Even BBC Books' tenth Doctor spin-off novels got in on the act: in *The Feast of the Drowned* by Stephen Cole, Torchwood is mentioned by a senior US naval officer.[7]

However, it was in 'Army of Ghosts'/'Doomsday,' the climactic two-part finale to *Doctor Who*'s 2006 series, that Torchwood really came to the fore.

In 'Army of Ghosts,' the Doctor learns that the building known to the public as Canary Wharf, in London's Docklands, is in fact Torchwood Tower. This was built specifically to enable the Torchwood Institute to reach a 'hole in the world' – some sort of 'breach' or 'spatial disturbance,' detected as a 'radar black-spot' – 600 feet above sea level. It also, however, houses a lot of captured alien artefacts on its spacious floors. The organisation clearly has considerable resources at its disposal; and its leader, Yvonne Hartman (played by former *EastEnders* star Tracy-Ann Oberman), is seen to control a large team of scientists, soldiers (who carry machine

7 By a curious coincidence, a much earlier original *Doctor Who* novel, the 1880-set fourth Doctor Missing Adventure *Evolution* (written by John Peel and published underVirgin Publishing's *Doctor Who* Book imprint, 1994), featured a character, Ross, who described himself as '...a special agent working directly under the command and authority of Her Majesty Queen Victoria,' and who said that it was his job 'to investigate those matters that lie outside of the conventional.'

guns and wear black, grey and white camouflage uniforms and berets with a 'T' symbol on them) and other staff. Yvonne tells the Doctor that the weapon that destroyed the Sycorax spaceship the previous Christmas came from a Jathaa Sun Glider that ventured into Britain's airspace and was shot down. 'The Torchwood Institute has a motto,' she explains. '"If it's alien, it's ours". Anything that comes from the sky, we strip it down and we use it , for the good of the British Empire.' When Jackie points out that there is no British Empire, Yvonne simply replies: 'Not yet!' She confirms that Torchwood was established by Queen Victoria, and tells the Doctor: 'You're actually named in the Torchwood Foundation Charter of 1879 as an enemy of the Crown … Her Majesty created the Torchwood Institute for the express intention of keeping Britain great and fighting the alien horde.'

Five image files of animated graphics seen on Torchwood Institute computer screens in 'Army of Ghosts' were subsequently discovered by fans to be viewable online at www.millingdaleicecream.co.uk/restricted/ – a 'restricted' but accessible area of the Millingdale Ice Cream website mentioned above.

The series' closing story, 'Doomsday', confirms that there is indeed a Torchwood Institute in the parallel world that the Doctor and Rose visited in 'Rise of the Cybermen'/'The Age of Steel'.[8] The Doctor learns that there, the authorities in Britain – which is a people's republic governed by President Harriet Jones – discovered the Institute's shady activities and took it over. When Rose ultimately becomes trapped in the parallel universe at the end of 'Doomsday', she joins the organisation, possibly along with her 'father' Pete and friend Mickey, to continue defending the Earth against alien threats – an appropriate exit for this very popular companion.

THE PRODUCTION TEAM IS ESTABLISHED

As noted in the initial press release announcing the spin-off, Russell T Davies and BBC Wales's Head of Drama Julie Gardner would serve as executive producers on *Torchwood*, as they did on *Doctor Who*. However, the statement that James Hawes – one of the principal directors on *Doctor Who* – was to be the new series' producer proved premature. In February 2006, Issue 366 of *Doctor Who Magazine* confirmed reports from the previous month that Hawes had ultimately decided against taking on this role. Initial speculation was that this was due a clash of commitments resulting from a rescheduling, from January 2006 to later in the year, of the start date for recording on *Torchwood*. In Issue 367 of *Doctor Who Magazine*, however, Davies stated that it was in fact due to Hawes having concluded that he would prefer to continue working as a TV director – a job he loved – rather than step up to become a producer.

At the beginning of December 2005, the Internet Movie Database, at www.imdb.com, was the first source to reveal that Brian Minchin was to be a script editor on *Torchwood*; this was officially confirmed in Issue 366 of *Doctor Who Magazine*, which also reported that Helen Raynor, one of *Doctor Who*'s script editors, was to join him in that capacity.

On 24 February 2006, in a news item about the casting of Gwen (see below), it was revealed that

8 This raises an interesting question as to how Torchwood came to be established in the parallel world. Did Queen Victoria encounter the Doctor at Torchwood House here too? If so, this would seem to imply that the parallel universe has its own Doctor – although he cannot have been travelling with Rose Tyler, as Pete and Jackie Tyler in this universe did not have a daughter. If, on the other hand, the Time Lords essentially exist 'outside time,' as fans have often speculated, so that there is only one Doctor, not one in each parallel universe, then there must have been some other event that caused the parallel Torchwood to be formed.

the producer who had ultimately been assigned to *Torchwood* was Richard Stokes. The same report gave the name of a further writer, to join Davies, Chibnall and Hammond on the scripting team: Toby Whithouse, who was also contributing to the second series of *Doctor Who*.

Another addition to the news originally announced was that concept artist Matt Savage would be moving across from *Doctor Who* to *Torchwood*, where he would head up the art department. This was also confirmed in Issue 366 of *Doctor Who Magazine*.

March 2006 brought further news. Perhaps most significantly, it now became clear that Chibnall was to be not simply a writer for the series but also a member of its editorial team. Some months later, in an interview for Issue 342 of *Starburst*, Chibnall described his role as follows: 'My official title, I think, is going to be co-producer. I'm part of the team who are trying to realise Russell's vision of *Torchwood* and keep it moving in interesting directions. I work with the other writers, read outlines and drafts, see rushes, go to tone meetings, give notes on edits, etc. But Russell is the show's creator and, along with Julie Gardner, its executive producer – they're, thankfully, very hands-on across all the creative decisions on the show: policing, nudging and suggesting ways in which we can make things better.'

Asked how he had come to work on *Torchwood*, Chibnall replied: 'It was at the end of August 2005. I was about to go to France for a holiday with my family when I got an e-mail from Julie Gardner saying, "Can we meet? I've got a project I'd like you to think about." We met in the corner of a bar in London one Friday evening just before the August bank holiday, and she told me about the idea. At which point my jaw dropped. She told me a bit more about it and swore me to secrecy: it was all very cloak and dagger. Then, a couple of hours before I disappeared off on holiday, Julie e-mailed me Russell's outline for the series. It was a page and a half, [and] just extraordinary. [At] that point, I was just about to sign up to do a different show, but this was just impossible to refuse. So I said, "Yes, fine; however you want me involved, whatever I can do, I'm in." It all went quiet for a bit, and the next thing I knew, Julie was back on the phone going, "Would you like to be a sort of lead writer, after Russell?" At which point my jaw dropped again. And I said yes again.'

The other writers said to be confirmed as of March 2006 included Noel Clarke, Si Spencer and Helen Raynor. Raynor's script had started out as one of a number of 'over-commissions' – essentially, 'try out' scripts that had been commissioned to assess new writers or experimental ideas and that might ultimately prove unsuitable or surplus to requirements – but had been so well-received that it had been quickly accepted for production. Such 'over-commissioning' was fairly common practice on BBC series generally, but something that had not been done to a significant extent on the relaunch of *Doctor Who*. All these developments were duly covered in Issue 368 of *Doctor Who Magazine*, which also announced that the first block of episodes would be directed by Brian Kelly, and that the debut episode would be entitled 'Flotsam and Jetsam' (although this would later be altered to 'Everything Changes').

Shortly after this, some preliminary concept drawings for the Hub, the underground base of Torchwood (or, strictly speaking, of Torchwood Three, the Cardiff branch of the organisation) – set, in fictional terms, beneath the water tower fountain in the Roald Dahl Plass (commonly referred to locally as 'the Oval Basin'), near the Millennium Centre – were revealed, albeit briefly, in the documentary *Doctor Who Confidential*: 'One Year On', transmitted on BBC One on 15 April 2006.

Pre-production on the series was now in full swing.

PART ONE: THE EXCITEMENT BEGINS

TEAM TORCHWOOD TAKES SHAPE

After his popular debut in the 2005 series of *Doctor Who*, it was initially intended that Captain Jack would feature in the 2006 series as well. This plan was changed, however, after Christopher Eccleston decided to give up the role of the Doctor at the end of the 2005 series. With a new leading man arriving in the person of David Tennant, the *Doctor Who* production team felt that the focus of the 2006 series should be on the relationship between the Doctor and Rose, and how this changed as a result of the regeneration, and that to have Jack present on board the TARDIS as well would unduly complicate matters. Thus it was decided that Jack should take a 'sabbatical', and return instead in the 2007 series. This news was duly passed on to John Barrowman. Shortly after that, Russell T Davies and Julie Gardner took Barrowman out to dinner one evening. Barrowman feared that they were going to tell him that he was being dropped from *Doctor Who* altogether, but in fact they made him the offer of taking the starring role in the *Torchwood* spin-off – an offer he readily accepted, as he later recalled in a BBC press release of 13 October 2006:

'When Russell T Davies and Julie Gardner and I first sat down to talk about giving Captain Jack his own series, I was completely bowled over. It was a childhood dream to be a character in *Doctor Who*, so to have my own series was just unimaginable. I'm a grown man who gets to go to work every day and fight aliens, play with guns and kiss beautiful people – what more could I ask for?'

A major development in the lead-up to full production on the new series was the casting of the second lead character, Gwen. On 24 February 2006, a BBC press release headed 'Team Torchwood' revealed the character's surname to be Cooper and announced:

> Welsh actress Eve Myles has been confirmed to play Gwen Cooper – the lead female role in the new Russell T Davies drama for BBC Three, *Torchwood*.
>
> Eve will star alongside John Barrowman in the forthcoming 13-part drama that will be broadcast later this year.
>
> The British sci-fi crime thriller for adult audiences will follow the adventures of a team of renegade investigators, led by the enigmatic Captain Jack, played by John Barrowman.
>
> It will see the investigators scavenge alien technology in a very real world to solve crime; both alien and human.
>
> 'I'm thrilled to be playing the part of Gwen. To get the chance to do a 13-part series under the watchful pen of Russell is amazing,' says Eve.
>
> 'It's such a compliment to have been chosen for the part – I can't wait.
>
> 'I'm also looking forward to working with John. It'll be the perfect opportunity for the both of us to show everyone what we've got.'
>
> Eve Myles guest-starred in the first series of *Doctor Who* … and has recently finished filming *Soundproof* for BBC Two.
>
> Her credits also include a highly successful run at the National Theatre when she appeared alongside Michael Gambon in *Henry IV Parts I & II*.
>
> Russell T Davies says: 'I've admired Eve's work for years, and when she was able to guest-star in *Doctor Who* last year, it just confirmed to me that she was one of Wales's best-kept secrets.
>
> 'The part of Gwen in *Torchwood* was written specially for her – so it's a good thing she said yes!
>
> 'Eve and John Barrowman have already met up, and the combination is going to be

electrifying.'

John Barrowman adds: 'I'm really looking forward to working with Eve.

'We've had a good laugh on the occasions we've met and the fact that she's already been in *Doctor Who* means she knows what she's getting into.'

Head of BBC Wales Drama, Julie Gardner, says: 'We are delighted to announce the casting of Eve Myles in the central role of Gwen, alongside John Barrowman's Captain Jack in *Torchwood*.

'Eve is an intelligent and versatile actress, who has done exceptional work in a number of BBC dramas, including our local series *Belonging*.'

This announcement was repeated, almost verbatim, on the BBC's *Doctor Who* website, in a news item headed 'Leading actress for new series announced'. This also brought the added bonus of a publicity photo of Barrowman and Myles together – the first official *Torchwood* image to be published.

As mentioned in the press release, Myles had previously guest-starred in *Doctor Who* – as Gwyneth, a young woman with psychic abilities in the Series One episode 'The Unquiet Dead'. This, along with the similarity between the names 'Gwyneth' and 'Gwen' and the fact that 'The Unquiet Dead' was, like *Torchwood*, set in Cardiff (albeit, in the former case, in the 19th Century), immediately led fans to speculate that there might be some link between the two characters, or that they might even be one and the same person, with Gwyneth having been somehow transported to, or reincarnated in, the 21st Century. Hints had also been given, in an online commentary to 'The Christmas Invasion' on the BBC's *Doctor Who* website, that the dimensional rift in Cardiff referred to in 'The Unquiet Dead' (including as the source of Gwyneth's psychic abilities) and the later Series One *Doctor Who* episode 'Boom Town' (where its epicentre was established to be in Roald Dahl Plass), would be of considerable significance in *Torchwood*, accounting for Captain Jack's presence in the city in the first place. And Barrowman had, perhaps rather mischievously, commented in an earlier interview, 'Gwen is not what you think.' Some fans even picked up on the idea that Gwen might prove to be a reincarnation of Gwen the Great, otherwise known as Guinevere, the Queen Consort of the legendary King Arthur – speculation that was fuelled by the inclusion of a space probe named Guinevere in 'The Christmas Invasion', and by the nicknaming of the new *Doctor Who/Torchwood* production facility as Camelot – the idyllic home of Queen Guinevere and King Arthur. No doubt this speculation would have been even more intense had it been publicly known at the time that Davies's initial working title for the new series had been *Excalibur* ...[9]

The identities of two more of the regular Torchwood team members were revealed in a BBC press announcement on 24 April 2006: Toshiko Sato, played by Naoko Mori, and Owen Harper, played by Burn Gorman.

Doctor Sato had previously appeared in the Series One *Doctor Who* episode 'Aliens of London'. There she had been introduced as a scientist at the Albion Hospital in London, charged with examining what was thought to be an alien whose spaceship had crash-landed in the Thames – although the Doctor soon revealed that the creature was actually a pig, augmented with alien technology. Given Sato's apparent medical background, it came as a surprise to some fans that the BBC press release described her as 'the member of the team who

9 See Chapter Nine for further details.

specialises in all things computer, surveillance and technical'. The press release went on to quote Russell T Davies as saying: '[Mori] was absolutely brilliant [in "Aliens of London"] and we wanted to bring her back.'

Unlike Sato, Harper was a new character, described in the press release as 'the raw but charming medic of the group'. Of Gorman, Davies said: 'Burn was just dazzling in last year's [BBC serialisation of Dickens'] *Bleak House*, and attracted our attention immediately. We beat a path to his door. He's one of the UK's brightest new talents, and I can't believe how lucky we are to get him for *Torchwood*.' Quoted on the website of *SFX* magazine on 17 October 2006, Richard Stokes added: 'There were a lot of names flying on e-mail between me, Julie, Russell and Chris Chibnall when we were first talking about casting this character. We were talking about someone Welsh to start with, and we were talking about other names, and then Andy Pryor, our casting director, mentioned Burn, and all of us had completely fallen in love with him during *Bleak House*.'

The name of the fifth *Torchwood* regular was first made public not, as usual, via a BBC press release but through a report dated 8 May 2006 in the *South Wales Argus* newspaper. This revealed that the Torchwood receptionist, Ianto, was to be played by 25-year-old Welsh-born actor Gareth David-Lloyd. 'I'm really excited,' David-Lloyd was quoted as saying. 'This is going to be different from anything else I've done before.' It was reported that the actor would feature in all 13 episodes of the forthcoming series. Ianto's surname, Jones, was revealed for the first time in a news item in Issue 373 of *Doctor Who Magazine*, published on 17 August.

The sixth and final member of the *Torchwood* team to be announced, also in the news item in Issue 373 of *Doctor Who Magazine*, was Suzie Costello, played by Indira Varma – although, as viewers would later discover, the suggestion that she was to be a regular was misleading; intentionally so on the BBC's part, to ensure that her death in the series' opening episode would come as a shock to viewers.

CHAPTER FOUR: INTO PRODUCTION

Although a date of January 2006 had initially been mooted for the start of recording on *Torchwood*, it soon became apparent that production would actually begin a few months later than that. Russell T Davies, in an interview published on 21 March 2006, told the US Sci-Fi Channel's Sci Fi Wire website that the cameras were expected to start rolling in May, with a view to the debut UK transmission of the series beginning in October. This would ultimately prove to be correct.

The main production base for *Torchwood* was to be a huge facility set up specifically to house both *Doctor Who* and this spin-off – plus, it later transpired, the second spin-off, *The Sarah Jane Adventures*. It was initially nicknamed Camelot, but later formally designated Upper Boat after the area where it was situated, just off the A470 road near Pontypridd, South Wales. Consisting of six large studio spaces arranged in two units, plus some 45 offices accommodating around 60 production and 75 art department staff, it took six months to plan before construction work eventually got underway on 6 February 2006. Studios 1 and 2 were completed to schedule on 6 March, and the Torchwood Hub was the first major standing set to be erected. Work on the set lasted for approximately 11 weeks – around five weeks to construct the basic metal framework and another six to paint and dress it.

By this point, *Torchwood* was already being offered, alongside *Doctor Who*, to potential purchasers outside the UK. On 6 April, at a media conference in Cannes in the South of France, Canadian broadcaster CBC, which was already a co-production partner on *Doctor Who*, announced that it had signed a deal to take on a similar role on the spin-off series. What this meant, in effect, was that CBC had purchased up-front, in advance of production, the right to screen the series in Canada; and in return had no doubt obtained it on more favourable terms than other overseas purchasers.

The cast began rehearsals for the first recording block on *Torchwood* in the latter half of April, with a read-through for the first two episodes taking place on Wednesday 26 April. Recording itself then got under way on Monday 1 May, and the first exterior location work to be spotted by fans took place on 4 May, in Charles Street in Cardiff's city centre, with the group's distinctive customised vehicle making its first public appearance. Much of the early recording was carried out on location, in part because the Hub set was still being completed.

On 1 June, the www.torchwood.org.uk spin-off website 'went live' for the first time, although the only content at this stage was a screen with the name of the organisation and a red, flashing 'Access Denied' message.

Part of the first read-through and some of the recording for the debut episode – specifically, the scenes of Gwen trying to gain access to Torchwood by posing as a pizza delivery girl – were shown in the 'Welcome to Torchwood' episode of the BBC Three *Doctor Who Confidential* documentary series, first transmitted on Saturday 2 July. Also in this programme, John Barrowman was briefly interviewed and shown being given a 'sneak preview' of the Hub set by producer Richard Stokes; and the *Torchwood* production team were seen in a tone meeting from April considering issues such as exactly how secret an organisation Torchwood is; how much violence and blood the series would contain; and how much nudity it would feature – or, in a nutshell, to what extent its post watershed content would differ from *Doctor Who*'s pre-watershed, family-orientated content. Davies noted: 'It's a chance to tell all the sort of science-fiction stories, and great drama stories, that we can't in *Doctor Who*. I mean, I absolutely love *Doctor Who*, but there is a limit to certain stories – how far you can go – stories of possession, or violence, or sexuality. And we've got all sorts of writers and all sorts of design teams clamouring to do more adult stuff.'

On 24 July, BBC Three's autumn schedule was officially unveiled by the BBC, and *Torchwood* was described as being its 'centrepiece' – a clear demonstration of confidence in the series. Stuart Murphy's successor Julian Bellamy was quoted as saying: '*Torchwood* is just the kind of cutting edge, ambitious drama of real scale that we're seeking on BBC Three, and I'm delighted to be unveiling it at my first BBC Three launch as Controller.' The accompanying press pack revealed little in the way of new information, but gave the following neat summary of the series' premise:

> *Torchwood* follows the adventures of a team of investigators as they use alien technology to solve crimes, both alien and human. This new British sci-fi crime thriller, from Russell T Davies, follows the team as they delve into the unknown. They are fighting the impossible while keeping their everyday lives going back home.

One notable point about these latest press releases was that they avoided making any mention of the series' origins as a *Doctor Who* spin-off, suggesting perhaps a desire to see it stand on its own merits, and/or a confidence in its ability to do so. The connection was certainly not forgotten by the press themselves, however, when they followed up on the story over the next few days. The MediaGuardian website quoted Julie Gardner as saying, 'You are going to get blood and snogging in *Torchwood* that you wouldn't have got in *Doctor Who*', while Jane Tranter, the BBC's Controller of Drama Commissioning (under whom Davies and Gardner worked in the BBC's hierarchy), was reported to have observed, '*Torchwood* builds on some of the myths and legends that have been present in *Doctor Who*, but it's a completely different show in every way, in terms of the tone and audience it's going for. It's alien hunters in Cardiff, not travelling in time and space.' Gardner's comments in particular were picked up in a number of subsequent newspaper reports.

Of perhaps greatest interest to fans was that the material made available to the press at this time included a number of new publicity photographs – including one of a Weevil, the first of the series' monsters to be publicly revealed.

The Upper Boat facility was officially opened by Welsh Enterprise Minister Andrew Davies on 27 July, although production of *Torchwood* had of course been in full swing for some weeks by that point, and had also begun on the *Doctor Who* Christmas special for 2006, 'The Runaway Bride'.

Issue 372 of *Doctor Who Magazine*, published on 20 July, summarised all the latest *Torchwood* news, including the identities of three more writers – the team of Dan McCulloch and Paul Tomalin, whose script had initially been another of the 'over-commissions', and Cath Tregenna – and two more directors – Colin Teague (whose involvement had been announced a few weeks earlier) and Alice Troughton (no relation to actor Patrick Troughton, who played *Doctor Who*'s second Doctor).

The script by Si Spencer had by this point been dropped from the production schedule, as had one – entitled 'Virus' – by Andrew Rattenbury. It also appeared for a time that the confirmation of Noel Clarke's involvement as a writer would prove premature: rumours had started to circulate that his script had been postponed to the (potential) second series of *Torchwood*, as it had been judged 'too big' (i.e. too expensive to produce) for the first. In the event, however, Clarke's story was included in the first series after all.

In mid-August, a promotional DVD of trailers for a number of BBC Three's new autumn shows was made available by the BBC to a select group of journalists and industry insiders. This included a 57-second trailer for *Torchwood* that drew a highly favourable response from those who saw it – the retail website www.sendit.com commented '[It] rocks!' – and raised still further the level of expectation for the series. In addition, at around the same time, BBC Worldwide produced a DVD for potential licensees featuring clips from a number of different BBC shows, including *Torchwood*; included was a 73-second clip of the scene of Gwen's initial encounter with a Weevil in the debut episode.

The press pack and promotional DVD were seized upon by some of the leading genre magazines, such as *Dreamwatch*, *TV Zone* and *SFX*, to form the basis of news items and short preview articles. These, however, generally contained little or nothing in the way of fresh information. Indeed, so few additional details were officially released about *Torchwood* in late August and September that even the publication of a single new publicity photograph could become a source of excitement and discussion amongst fans – as occurred when a new edition of *Broadcast* magazine hit the shelves in the last week of September and featured a previously-unseen photograph of the character Carys being taken over by the alien gas entity from 'Day One' (although it was not identified as such at the time). This photograph illustrated a short interview with Will Cohen of the Mill TV effects house, in which he revealed that some episodes of *Torchwood* would contain up to 100 digital effects shots, ranging from simple sky replacements in 3-D environments, through matte-paintings, to the creation of animated creatures such as the pterodactyl living in the roof of the Hub – the first mention of this creature in print.

As October began, however, the information drought would finally end, and a veritable flood of new publicity material would start to be made available in the lead-up to the series' debut transmission …

PART TWO: THE SERIES AIRS

CHAPTER FIVE: TOWARD TRANSMISSION

The BBC's advance publicity campaign for *Torchwood* began in earnest at the beginning of October 2006. During a programme break at 8.30 am on the first day of the month, BBC One broadcast an approximately three second teaser trailer of the distinctive 'T' logo in red – the first on-screen trailer for the series. This was then repeated on numerous occasions over the course of the following week, during programme breaks on BBC One, BBC Two and BBC Three, sometimes reportedly in a pink-hued version.

The debut transmission date for the series had still not been confirmed at this point – a mere three weeks or so ahead of time. This was quite deliberate: as John Barrowman explained in a 3 October radio interview on BBC Wales's *Good Evening Wales* programme, the BBC was concerned that if the date was revealed too far in advance, this would give the rival ITV network an opportunity to schedule stronger competition against the series. Within a day of that interview airing, however, eagle eyed fans had spotted that – possibly a little earlier than the BBC had intended – adverts for *Torchwood* had started to appear on the sides of buses in major towns and cities, featuring a publicity photograph of Captain Jack holding a gun, and giving a date of 22 October.

Also at the beginning of October, the first of a series of four 30-second trailers began to be seen in cinemas nationwide. These had been given a PG rating by the British Board of Film Classification (BBFC) on 22 September, having been submitted for classification by the distributors, Carlton Screen Advertising.

The promotion of TV programmes in such places as on buses and in cinemas was still a relatively new phenomenon in the UK – only a handful of other series, including Channel 4's *Lost* and the BBC's *Robin Hood*, had previously been accorded similar treatment – and the fact that the BBC was willing to pay for such advertising for *Torchwood* was a clear indication of the priority they were giving to the series.

On Friday 6 October, the BBC press office issued information on programme highlights for the week of 21 to 27 October inclusive, including *Torchwood*. This maintained – somewhat implausibly, in the face of the aforementioned bus adverts – that the programme was still 'unplaced' in the schedules, with date and time of transmission to be determined. It did, however, elaborate a little on the details previously released:

> Created by award-winning writer Russell T Davies, the high-octane sci-fi thriller follows a team of modern-day investigators as they use alien technology to solve crime both alien and human.
>
> Separate from the Government, outside police jurisdiction and beyond the United Nations, the Torchwood Institute sets its own rules. Based in Cardiff, the Torchwood team delves into the unknown, battling against the impossible in a highly volatile underworld of savage aliens and monsters whilst trying to maintain their everyday lives.
>
> Enigmatic Captain Jack Harkness is the ever-watchful leader of the Torchwood team. Gwen Cooper is initially an outsider, whose first, chance meeting with Torchwood at the scene of a brutal murder sparks within her a burning curiosity to get to the truth. She is intrigued by Torchwood and her life changes when she is catapulted into an unfamiliar and exciting world.
>
> Second in command to Captain Jack is Suzie Costello, the hard-working hardware

specialist who catalogues and strives to understand the alien devices the team comes across. Owen Harper is the arrogant, brilliant medic and Toshiko Sato specialises in all things computer, surveillance and technical. Ianto Jones, meanwhile, cleans up after the team and gets them everywhere on time.

This press release also indicated that (unlike *Doctor Who*) the series was being made in HD (high definition), and officially confirmed for the first time the opening episode's title, 'Everything Changes'.

Also on 6 October, the BBC anonymously – under the user name 'mattypeteUK' – placed on the YouTube video sharing website a 31-second clip entitled 'Crime Scene', with the description 'Something weird I saw from a car park'. This intended 'viral video'[10] consisted of some shaky, indistinct footage shot from the vantage point of a deserted multi-storey car park overlooking a crime scene akin to, but curiously not quite the same as, the one that Gwen would observe at the beginning of 'Everything Changes', where a lone hooded figure briefly revives a murder victim using a metal glove.

On 7 October, a 30-second trailer similar to that previously screened in cinemas began to appear on TV as well, on both BBC One and BBC Three. It was first shown at 7.49 pm on BBC One, in the programme break between the end of the debut episode of *Robin Hood* and the start of the first in a new series of *Strictly Come Dancing*. It elicited much excited comment amongst fans and, perhaps inevitably, was soon to be found posted on YouTube. Also on this date, the 57-second trailer from the BBC promotional DVD was illicitly uploaded to YouTube.

On 8 October, a slightly different, approximately five-second teaser trailer was spotted on BBC Two, again featuring the 'T' logo but with faint images of the faces of the Torchwood team in the background; again, this was then repeated on several occasions over the next few days, mainly on BBC One and BBC Three.

8 October also saw the BBC7 radio station launch a competition to win pairs of tickets to preview screenings – in HD – of 'Everything Changes' in cinemas in 'secret locations' in four different cities: London, Cardiff, Glasgow and Manchester. Those wishing to enter had simply to e-mail BBC7 with the name of the actor who plays Captain Jack Harkness. This competition announcement was notable for asserting that the series would debut on both BBC Three *and* BBC One on 22 October. The same thing was reported in Issue 375 of *Doctor Who Magazine*, published on 12 October, which also stated that BBC Three would show the first and second episodes back-to-back, with subsequent episodes following weekly, while BBC One would present only the first episode and then defer a complete run of the series until early 2007. This was indeed the intention at one point, the thinking being that it would give the series the strongest possible launch and also, by encouraging BBC One viewers to switch over to BBC Three at the end of the first episode in order to catch the second, boost the profile and ratings of the digital channel. However, the idea of 'Everything Changes' being given a debut transmission on BBC One at the same time as on BBC Three was eventually dropped in a late change of plan by the BBC schedulers. The reason for this change was the subject of some speculation in an article on the website of the industry journal *The Stage*, which put forward three possible explanations:

10 This term refers to a video that gains widespread popularity through internet sharing, typically through sites such as YouTube and e-mails, blogs and instant messaging.

1) *Torchwood* is brilliant, and the various sectors of the BBC are fighting over having a piece of the next hot thing.
2) *Torchwood* is a bit of a let down, and the various sectors of the BBC are figuring how best to get mileage out of the show before the audience at large realises.
3) Going out on BBC One would put the first episode in a head-to-head collision with the final *Prime Suspect*, and battening down the hatches and retreating to BBC Three is the best option for preserving a healthy rating for a show that deserves to be seen. Certainly the words ratings and juggernaut can be attached to *Prime Suspect*.

The realist in me suspects (and hopes) that it's a combination of 1 and 3. I desperately want *Torchwood* to be good. For all my love of *Doctor Who*, it's like the lover who you adore beyond all else but you know they have faults that will always be forgiven unconditionally. Could *Torchwood* be the new, exciting, dangerous other woman who might have what it takes to tempt me from the well-worn path?

'There's been a battle in the BBC,' confirmed John Barrowman in an interview previewed on *SFX* magazine's website the following week, 'because Peter Fincham, Controller of BBC One, as soon as he heard people talking about [the series] and as soon as he started seeing snippets of it, he told BBC Three, "I'm taking it!" And then we have to be loyal to BBC Three, because they're the ones who commissioned it in the first place, and we have to do it for them. BBC Three are huge supporters of *Who* and of *Torchwood*, so we have to do it. And y'know what? £30 for a freeview box and you get the damn thing! It's not even *that* at Tesco!'

The schedulers ultimately decided that it would be unfair to those viewers without access to digital channels to give them only the opening episode on BBC One and then make them wait until the new year to see the rest; far better, they felt, to repeat the whole series on a terrestrial channel, BBC Two, only a few days behind the initial BBC Three transmissions.

On 9 October, there was a long-awaited development as the BBC's new official *Torchwood* website at www.bbc.co.uk/torchwood (as distinct from the 'fictional' Torchwood organisation website at www.torchwood.org.uk) presented for the first time some actual online content – for those willing to search for it. Previously, this site had simply displayed the same flashing 'Access Denied' sign as seen on the 'fictional' one (which remained unchanged for the time being). Now, however, by clicking on the link for the 'Text Only' version of the site and then entering a 'secret' pass number – 221006, derived from the debut transmission date – it was possible to access a further link to another, 31-second 'Crime Scene' video. This was very similar in style and content to the previous one posted on YouTube, and supposedly shot at the same time but from a different, ground level vantage point. At the end of the clip, the voice of a woman – supposedly the person shooting the footage – could be heard crying out 'Torchwood!' as she was apprehended. Again, this was similar to, but did not quite match, action that would be seen in the opening minutes of 'Everything Changes'.

At 10.00 pm on 10 October, a new 30-second TV trailer made its debut on BBC Three between episodes of *I'm With Stupid* and *EastEnders*. This included a lot of previously-unseen clips, with – to use Julie Gardner's phrase – more 'blood and snogging' than the first trailer. In line with the usual pattern, it was subsequently repeated numerous times, on BBC One, BBC Two and BBC Three. Later the same night, at 00.20 am, a third 30-second trailer, although this time only slightly different from the first, appeared on BBC Three between episodes of *Family Guy* and *Nighty Night*. Short trailers for the series had also by this point started to air on most of the BBC's national radio stations.

Also on the evening of 10 October, a new, 29-second BBC-produced viral video appeared on YouTube, posted by 'sands2007' – apparently a genuine YouTube user rather than a BBC pseudonym – under the title 'Up the Alley' and with the description: 'Sent to me by The Inner Peace. Do not pull in Cardiff on a night out!' This consisted of what purported to be some silent, high-viewpoint CCTV footage of a man being led by a woman along a dark alley, apparently having sex with her against the wall (although the picture broke up and rolled at this point) and suddenly disappearing in a flash of light, with the woman then walking away. Like the previous viral videos, this was similar to, but not entirely consistent with, action that would be seen in one of the forthcoming episodes – in this case, 'Day One'. A place, date and time caption at the bottom of the CCTV image stated 'T-WOOD SUN 22-10-06 21:59:29' at the start, with the seconds then ticking down to 21:59:59 as the clip progressed – a reference to the date and time of the debut transmission of 'Day One'. The mysterious 'Inner Peace' apparently also e-mailed the same clip to a number of fan websites[11].

Later on the morning of 11 October, the second 'Crime Scene' video, previously accessible only by entering the pass number on the 'Text Only' version of the official website, became more easily reached via a simple link, immediately below the 'Access Denied' wording – which had by this point ceased flashing – on the website's front page. This link disappeared later in the day, but the clip remained accessible using the pass number as before and, at the same time, the 'Up the Alley' clip was added alongside it.

On 12 October, just before 1.00 pm, the *Torchwood* official website went properly 'live', in a choice of two formats: an impressively slick Flash version; and a somewhat simpler HTML version, both designed for bbc.co.uk by Backflip Ltd. A veritable feast of new material was presented, including: publicity photographs and short character sketches of all the Torchwood team members (including Suzie Costello, perpetuating the suggestion that she was to be a regular); panoramic 'virtual tours' of their workstations and other areas of the Hub; a video tour of the Hub; another slightly different 30-second trailer, ending with the caption 'Begins 22nd October'; the five-second teaser trailer; and a short video interview with Russell T Davies. In theory, certain features of the site were not viewable by those outside the UK, for 'rights reasons'. In practice, however, this restriction could be fairly easily circumvented by any non-UK web-surfer with a little technical knowledge – or simply by using the 'hidden' url address www.bbc.co.uk/torchwood/holder.swf. In addition, some areas of the site, including a page called 'Episode Guides', displayed only a caption stating that an update was scheduled for a later date. Again, however, it did not take long for enterprising fans to discover some of the information in hidden url addresses behind these barriers. The BBC subsequently removed the information from their servers, but this was a classic case of shutting the stable door after the horse had bolted, and before the day was out, titles and brief descriptions of all 13 episodes of the series had been disseminated widely on the internet.

Mobile phone users, meanwhile, were able to obtain a trailer, wallpaper and some general information about the series by texting 'Torchwood' to 81010.

Racking up the excitement still further, at 8.00 pm on 12 October yet another trailer, this one a generous 57 seconds in duration, was broadcast virtually simultaneously on BBC One, BBC Two and BBC Three.

12 October also saw news breaking that *Torchwood* would be complemented by a 13-part mini-documentary series, *Torchwood Declassified*, from essentially the same team as was

11 See Appendix E for information about *Torchwood*-related websites.

responsible for the similar *Doctor Who Confidential* programmes. Each entry in the series would be around ten minutes long and available to view not only on BBC Three but also on the official website – as would brief 'catch up' highlights of each episode of *Torchwood* itself.

On 13 October, the BBC press office issued some further information, consisting mainly of a short interview with John Barrowman. The official website meanwhile featured a competition to win tickets for the 18 October preview screenings of 'Everything Changes'. A similar competition was also run on BBC Radio 1, on the Jo Whiley show. In addition, another slightly different teaser trailer made its debut on TV, alternating the red 'T' logo with the blue and white BBC Three logo and giving the series' officially confirmed start date – 22 October.

Although the date had now been confirmed, fans were still left in some uncertainty as to the actual time of transmission. The *Radio Times* website and other online sources were listing it as 9.00 pm, but the waters were muddied on the evening of 15 October when it was announced as 10.00 pm at the end of a number of screenings of the trailers on both BBC One and BBC Three. This was discovered the next day to be incorrect, and although there was some speculation that it had been another, last-minute attempt to confuse the ITV opposition, in truth it had been a simple error. 9.00 pm was indeed the start time, and any remaining confusion was dispelled on 17 October when the TV listings magazines for the following week began to appear on newsagents' shelves. Subsequent episodes would, however, debut at 10.00 pm – the usual slot for BBC Three first run dramas.

The week leading up to 22 October saw a number of interviews with cast and production team members appearing in the press. Some journalists had by this point seen preview copies of 'Everything Changes', and initial reactions were generally very favourable. The BBC's own *Radio Times* featured *Torchwood* on its front cover and included an interview with Davies, a double-page photo spread of the main area of the Hub interior with explanatory captions by production designer Ed Thomas, and brief character profiles of the Torchwood team. It also recommended the series as one of 'Today's Choices' for Sunday viewing, as would be the case on a number of other occasions in subsequent weeks.

18 October saw the excitement building to fever pitch as the previously-announced public preview screenings took place. BBC Wales also hosted a formal press launch starting at 7.00 pm at St David's Hotel, Cardiff Bay, where a screening of 'Everything Changes' was followed by a question and answer session with Davies and all five regular cast members, and an after-show party. Non-transferable invitations to this event had been sent out to a select contingent of journalists at the beginning of the month. Amongst the guests in attendance were Jane Tranter, Julie Gardner, David Tennant, Billie Piper, Noel Clarke, *Doctor Who* producer Phil Collinson, writers Chris Chibnall, Steven Moffat, Matthew Graham, Mark Gatiss, Gareth Roberts and P J Hammond, music composer Murray Gold and BBC Wales Controller Menna Richards.

In its 6.30 pm bulletin, the BBC Wales *Wales Today* news programme carried a report on the launch event, including clips from the first episode, pre-recorded interviews with Eve Myles and John Barrowman and a live interview with Davies from outside the St David's Hotel. Barrowman commented: '*Torchwood* is a show that is like nothing else you've ever seen on BBC television. It's a science-fiction show that will involve human stories, human nature, it'll involve aliens, a lot of blood and gore, and quite a bit of sex. It's about relationships, so that's one of the main things we delve into.' Davies also likened the series to BBC spy drama *Spooks*, in that they both juxtapose their central characters' extraordinary working lives with their ordinary home lives.

To the intense frustration of those fans who had missed out on winning tickets in the BBC's competitions, it later became apparent that none of the four public preview screenings had had anything like a capacity audience. The Glasgow one had been particularly poorly attended, with reportedly fewer than 30 people present. Given that the BBC had stated in advance that all the available tickets had been snapped up, this led to speculation that there must have been some sort of a mix-up over the allocations. Those fans who *had* been lucky enough to secure tickets, however, were generally full of praise for 'Everything Changes', many commenting that it had been 'better than expected,' notwithstanding that their expectations had been high to start with.

Also on 18 October, the BBC press office put out some further information about the series, including in particular interviews with Eve Myles, Gareth David-Lloyd and Indira Varma – the latter of which maintained the pretence that Suzie Costello was to be a regular in the series, quoting Varma as saying: 'Suzie gets on well with everybody and she really knows her stuff. I think she's slightly threatened by Gwen, because Captain Jack is so passionate about her, but she does also see that she's probably the most talented of the lot. It's very strange for Suzie ...'

At 10.50 pm on the same date, BBC Radio 1 ran, as part of the Colin Murray show, a short documentary entitled *Is Anybody Out There?*, about secret government departments investigating UFOs. This was narrated by Eve Myles and featured producer Richard Stokes commenting on public suspicions regarding conspiracies and cover-ups, but otherwise had little to do with *Torchwood* itself, being more in the nature of a loosely-related tie-in.

The most important development on 19 October occurred late in the afternoon when the BBC made available to view online, via the *Torchwood* official website, an approximately ten-and-a-half-minute preview 'trailer' for the *Torchwood Declassified* mini-documentary series. While this repeated some of the material from the 'Welcome to Torchwood' episode of *Doctor Who Confidential*, it also included some new interviews with production team and cast and showcased numerous clips, mainly from 'Everything Changes'.

Also on 19 October, a further press screening of 'Everything Changes' was held, at 8.00 pm in the Smeaton Room, 1 Great George Street, in London's West End. Radio 4's *Front Row* programme meanwhile included a short item on the series, and BBC7 presented a slightly longer feature interviewing some of those who had won tickets to the preview screenings in their earlier competition – all of whom bar one were very complimentary about the debut episode.

On 20 October, BBC One's *Breakfast* programme featured an approximately three minute pre-recorded interview with Barrowman, illustrated by a number of previously-unbroadcast clips. The rival GMTV's *Entertainment Today* also had a short clip of Jack introducing Gwen to the rest of the team from 'Everything Changes'.

21 October brought a live radio interview with Barrowman on Jonathan Ross's morning show on BBC Radio 2; an interview feature with Davies in *The Times*'s *The Knowledge* magazine (also reproduced on the newspaper's website, Times Online); and (almost all positive) preview pieces in many of the other national newspapers. Subscribers had also started to receive their copies of the new issues of the genre magazines *Starburst* and *SFX*, both of which featured *Torchwood* on their front cover and in articles inside.

Taken as a whole, the many and varied – and in some cases innovative – techniques adopted to publicise the on-air debut of *Torchwood* represented a quite phenomenal promotional effort.

While this was in part a reflection of the BBC's desire to raise the profile of its digital programming more generally – the eventual switch-over to digital-only transmissions itself being the subject of an ongoing public information campaign across all terrestrial channels at this point – it was also, without question, a considerable show of faith in what the cover of *TV & Satellite Week* described as 'the sexy new *Doctor Who* spin-off'. Whether or not that faith was well-placed, only time would tell.

CHAPTER SIX: INTO TRANSMISSION

A RATINGS TRIUMPH

Will 22 October 2006 one day be as significant and celebrated a date for *Torchwood* fans as 23 November 1963 is for *Doctor Who* fans? No doubt this will depend in part on the spin-off's longevity, but it could scarcely have had a more successful launch: when the overnight viewing figures became available the following day, they revealed that the debut double bill was a record-breaker[12]. The UK Press Association reported the news as follows:

> *Doctor Who* spin-off *Torchwood* pulled in a record audience for its debut last night, the BBC said today.
>
> The BBC Three show was watched by an average of 2.4 million viewers – the highest [rated] homegrown non-sport programme ever shown on a digital channel.
>
> A second episode screened back-to-back won an audience of 2.3 million.
>
> The ratings are believed to be second only to an episode of US series *Friends*, broadcast on Sky One in 2000, which attracted 2.8 million viewers.
>
> …
>
> The BBC described the ratings as 'absolutely phenomenal.'
>
> BBC Three Controller Julian Bellamy said: 'I'm delighted that last night's *Torchwood* was such a big hit.
>
> 'It's an incredible achievement to be the highest rated show ever on BBC Three and one of the most watched programmes on a digital channel.'

The reference here to an episode of *Friends* winning an audience of 2.8 million viewers on Sky One in 2000 was somewhat misleading. A new BARB ratings system was introduced in 2002, so figures from before that time are not strictly comparable with those from later years – the pre-2002 system in fact significantly overstated numbers of viewers by comparison with the post-2002 system. The BBC's internal magazine *Ariel*, in its own story of 23 October, reported more accurately:

> The previous highest rating for a digital programme on any channel, excluding football matches, was the episode of *The Simpsons* with Ricky Gervais, which was watched by 2.2 million.[13]
>
> *Torchwood* was also the third most watched show on any UK network in its time slot between 9.00 pm and 9.50 pm, beaten only by ITV1's *Prime Suspect* and Channel 4's screening of *The League of Extraordinary Gentlemen*. It tied for third place with BBC One drama *Wide Sargasso Sea*[14], also on 2.4 million viewers.

Even on these initial, overnight figures it was clear that *Torchwood* had achieved an astounding early success. One particularly encouraging aspect was that they clearly showed that most of

---

12 For more detailed discussion of the series' ratings, see Appendix D.

13 The episode of *The Simpsons* in question actually achieved a rating of 2.29 million viewers on Sky One on 23 April 2006.

14 This drama, produced by former *Doctor Who* script editor Elwen Rowlands for BBC Wales, had first been transmitted on BBC Four on 9 October, so the BBC One screening on 22 October was actually a repeat.

those who had watched 'Everything Changes' had been sufficiently impressed to stay on for 'Day One' as well. In fact, the very small drop in ratings from 2.38 million for the first episode to 2.33 million for the second could be accounted for entirely by a reduction from 200,000 to 150,000 in the number of viewers aged four to 15 (most of whom would, presumably, have been at the upper end of that range), as the other 50,000 were no doubt sent off to bed by their parents at 10.00 pm. And the average audience share actually increased from 12.6 percent for 'Everything Changes' to 13.5 percent for 'Day One'. When, at the beginning of November, the figures were adjusted upwards to include those who had recorded the episodes rather than watched them live, the news was even better: 'Everything Changes', with 2.52 million viewers, and 'Day One', with 2.50 million, now stood in second and third places respectively in the all-time ratings league for digital channels, beaten only by a Manchester United -v- Arsenal football match screened in 2004 by Sky Sports 1, which had attracted 2.77 million viewers. It seemed, then, that the huge promotional campaign mounted by the BBC in advance of the series' debut had paid off most handsomely.

A WEEK OF TRANSMISSIONS

The morning of 22 October had seen the advance publicity continuing, with short preview pieces appearing in many of the Sunday newspapers. Most of these pieces had been positive, but a rare exception was the coverage in the *Sunday Express*, which even railed against the series in its editorial column:

> What has happened to the BBC? For decades parents could trust the quality of its programmes, but not any more. Tonight a new 13-part TV drama series begins that features plenty of same-sex kissing, erotic aliens and gory death scenes – not material most families would choose to watch.
>
> Not according to BBC bosses, who say the content is fine and are leaving it to parents to decide whether to let children tune in. They say the programme, *Torchwood*, will go out after the 9.00 pm watershed and that adult audiences expect this sort of entertainment.
>
> But that's hypocritical – the drama is a spin-off from *Doctor Who* and will be heavily repeated. It can't fail to attract curious young viewers. This exercise is nothing more than a cynical attempt to cash in on a genuine family show. The BBC should be ashamed.

The BBC was no doubt mindful of the possibility of criticisms such as these, and the continuity announcement at the start of 'Everything Changes' alerted viewers to the fact that there was 'strong language' in the episode, while that at the start of 'Day One' warned of 'scenes of a sexual nature.'

The versions of 'Everything Changes' and 'Day One' screened in this debut double bill (and in its BBC Three and BBC Two repeats during the week that followed) were slightly different from the 'standard' master tapes that would be used for subsequent, single episode repeats and for DVD and overseas sales, in that the next episode trailer at the end of 'Everything Changes' was captioned 'Coming Up ...' rather than 'Next Time ...'; there were no closing credits at the end of 'Everything Changes'; the usual opening sequence with Captain Jack's voiceover was omitted from 'Day One'; and the closing credits at the end of the latter episode covered the former as well (although with some omissions – see Part Six of this book for further details). This was done in order to reduce the gap between the conclusion of the action in 'Everything Changes' and start of that in 'Day One' – the two episodes being bridged only by a short trailer promoting a number of BBC Three's autumn season shows – and thus minimise the risk of viewers deciding to change channels at that point.

Some viewers were disappointed that a large 'BBC Three' logo – technically known as a digital on-screen graphic (DOG) – remained in vision in the top left hand corner of the picture throughout the two episodes, at some points even partly obscuring characters' faces or significant pieces of action. This, however, was standard practice for drama programmes on BBC Three, and would be maintained for the remainder of the series. Less expected was the fact that the sound appeared to be slightly out of sync with the picture for some of the time. This was corrected on later screenings; and the BBC Two repeats of 25 October provided a first opportunity to see the episodes DOG-free.

Virtually simultaneously with the debut BBC Three transmissions, the two episodes were also broadcast in HD on the BBC HD channel, although in this case the 'standard' master tapes were used, probably because no edited versions equivalent to the BBC Three ones had been prepared in HD format. BBC HD also screened, immediately after 'Day One', a new 87-second trailer for the whole series, including numerous previously unseen clips from later episodes. At this point in time, however, BBC HD was still operating essentially on an experimental basis – its transmissions were restricted to certain regions of the UK and not generally advertised, and only around 100,000 viewers were capable of receiving them. This meant that few people actually saw the debut episodes in HD. Some of those who did, though, commented on various shortcomings in the picture quality. These were due largely to difficulties encountered by the production team with the Panasonic HD cameras used for the early production blocks, which had prompted them to switch to a different brand, the Sony HDW-750P, for subsequent recordings. This latter type of camera produced much better-received results, as producer Richard Stokes later noted in an interview for *Producer* magazine dated Spring 2007: 'It was fairly robust in fairly extreme weather. We had storms, rain, cold and extreme heat. We had a very hot summer when we were [recording], and inside the studio it got to about 45 degrees plus. We thought the actors were going to fall over in front of the cameras! The picture is extraordinary. I think I would try and do any new show that I do in HD now, because I think the richness of colour, the detail in the picture, what the director of photography can do with the lights and the mood and the feel, what you can end up doing in the grade when you actually put the final polish on it, it's all so good that if you're using the right equipment, and people who know how to use the equipment, you can get results that are head and shoulders above standard definition.'

The double bill of episodes had its first, late night BBC Three repeat at 1.00 am on Monday 23 October, pulling in an average of around 150,000 viewers (presumably for the most part different individuals than those who had tuned in earlier, although doubtless a small number wanted a chance to see the episodes again and had not recorded them the first time). This was immediately followed by a previously-unseen 30-second trailer for the third episode, 'Ghost Machine', and then by another double bill: the first two episodes of *Torchwood Declassified*, receiving their debut transmission. Many fans were disappointed that the mini-documentaries were being shown in such an unfavourable slot, where they would be bound to receive very low ratings – in fact, they had only around 30,000 viewers apiece. Most elected to record them rather than watch them live, or else catch up with them on the official website, where they became available to view later the same day, or on subsequent repeats.

Two further BBC Three repeats of the double bill of episodes, this time without *Torchwood Declassified*, came within a few hours of each other, at 10.30 pm on Tuesday 24 October and at

1.10 am on Wednesday 25 October respectively. The former of these won a very respectable average audience of almost 500,000, although the latter understandably failed to break the 100,000 viewer mark.

The evening of 25 October brought the first terrestrial transmission of the double bill on BBC Two. Starting a couple of minutes later than the scheduled 9.00 pm, it was prefaced by a slightly more strongly-worded 'adult content' warning than had been given on BBC Three. The following day, the overnight ratings indicated that the episodes had drawn a very creditable average audience of 2.8 million viewers, representing an audience share of 12.9% and making *Torchwood* the second highest-rated BBC Two programme of the day (losing out on the top spot by only a very small margin to a short nature programme that immediately preceded it), and twenty-third in the all-channel chart. When the audience appreciation figure came in later in the week, it was an excellent 80.

'Everything Changes' had its first (non-HD) 'single episode' airing, complete with closing credits, on BBC Three at 9.00 pm on Friday 27 October, immediately followed by a repeat – at a more civilised hour – of the opening episode of *Torchwood Declassified*. 'Day One' then had its own first (non-HD) 'single episode' screening on the same channel at 10.30 pm. On the overnight figures, 'Everything Changes' pulled in just short of 250,000 viewers on this occasion, representing a 1.5% share of total viewer numbers at that time, and 'Day One' almost 200,000, a 1.7% share.

Wrapping up the week's transmissions, the two episodes appeared as a double bill once more, and for the final time, at 12.50 am on Saturday 28 October, followed by a repeat of the second *Torchwood Declassified* mini-documentary, plus the first (but not the last) BBC Three screening of a slightly-re-edited, 90-second version of the series trailer that had previously been shown only on BBC HD. Ratings this time were low, as was to be expected from the late night slot and from that fact that this was the seventh airing the episodes had received within the space of a week.

Tallying up the ratings for each of the seven separate screenings, and making the safe assumption that the audience each time was made up largely of new viewers, it can be concluded that both 'Everything Changes' and 'Day One' were seen by around six million different individuals within the space of the week – a very considerable achievement, exceeding what all but the most optimistic could have expected in advance.

EARLY PRESS REACTION

Brief reviews of the debut double bill of episodes appeared in a number of the national newspapers and/or on their websites on Monday 23 October – although these tended to focus on 'Everything Changes' rather than 'Day One', suggesting that, in line with journalists' usual practice, they had been prepared ahead of transmission, on the basis of the single episode preview DVD sent out by the BBC press office. The Media Guardian website commented: 'This looks promising: it's slick, quick and a tiny bit scary. Not much humour yet, which was the lovely thing about *Doctor Who*. But it's early days; don't jump quite yet.' *The Times*'s Caitlin Moran was also impressed, although she seemed to have been won over primarily by the charms of the leading man: 'To be fair, you don't have the second episode of your new series based on an alien who lives off human orgasmic energy unless you want your audience to have certain thoughts. To wit: Captain Jack Harkness being incredibly sexually charismatic is enough.' The *Daily Telegraph*, on the other hand, headed its review 'Rubbish from Space' and opined that the show was 'surprisingly bad'. Iain Heggie of the *Scotsman*, who actually filed his review in advance on 21 October, was also less than impressed: '[The Torchwood team] are very annoying to work with. They overact yoofy scorn about Gwen's ignorance way beyond what is necessary. This is obviously cold calculation on the part of the BBC about its demographic, since there's nothing the average teen likes better than over-acted scorn. They're also a scary bunch of rule-flouters who try out the aliens' toys for their own selfish ends ... So far, the show is hovering in moral ambivalence about the team's twattish behaviour. I not very eagerly await PC Gwen Cooper sorting them out in future episodes.'

The BBC press office, meanwhile, continued its publicity offensive, releasing a lengthy interview with Burn Gorman as part of its advance programme information for the week of 11 to 17 November, which also included brief details of the forthcoming episode 'Small Worlds'. 'I'm obsessed by sci-fi,' commented Gorman, '... but I wouldn't have wanted to be in a ... sci-fi show unless it was something unusual, and *Torchwood* is extraordinary. It is one of the most ambitious, exciting television series I've ever been involved in. The marriage of science-fiction and crime drama based on Earth I don't think has ever been done before. The set will blow your mind. It's like the Bat Cave times 100; it's just extraordinary. It's not every day you shoot an alien after breakfast, get snogged by a huge Welshman before lunch and resuscitate Blake from *Blake's 7*[15] before dinner! It's literally the job of a lifetime.'

WEBSITE UPDATES

As 'Everything Changes' was receiving its 22 October debut transmission on BBC Three, the flashing red 'Access Denied' graphic that had for over four months been the only thing to be found at the 'fictional' Torchwood organisation website, www.torchwood.org.uk, was finally taken down and replaced with substantive content. Now identified as the Torchwood Institute System Interface, this resembled the *Torchwood* official website in that it could be accessed in either an impressive Flash form or a simpler HTML version, described here as the 'Hi-Tech Interface' and the 'Lo-Tech Interface' respectively.

The 'Hi-Tech' version presented what appeared to be a blue-toned, electron-microscope-type image of some kind of spore moving in liquid – very similar to images seen on screens on the Torchwood Hub set – with a blue, bar-code-like column of short horizontal lines scrolling down the left hand side and a number of index-card-like windows, labelled 'Nodes', floating over the rest of the picture. By clicking on the side column, it was possible to bring up further Nodes on the first two 'case files' – 'Everything Changes' and 'Day One'. Clicking on any of the Nodes caused it to stop moving, come to the fore and display the information it contained. This information took a variety of forms, including case notes by members of the Torchwood team, photographs and other images related to the cases, text-message exchanges, e-mail correspondence, PDF documents and even a few short video clips – including extracts from the 'Crime Scene' and 'Up the Alley' viral video teasers. Some of the Nodes gave, or at least hinted at, background details regarding Torchwood and its operations that would not be revealed in the TV series itself.[16]

Clearly a great deal of work had gone into the design of this website; and the content would be steadily built upon, with the addition of many more Nodes of information, on a weekly basis as the series progressed. Virtually all the same information was also accessible via the 'Lo-Tech'

15 This was a reference to actor Gareth Thomas, who had played the lead in the BBC's 1970s sci-fi series *Blake's 7* and who guested in *Torchwood* in the 'Ghost Machine' episode.

16 Some of these details are discussed in later sections of this book.

version of the site, although naturally presented in simpler form, without the slick graphics.

On 23 October, the *Torchwood* official website, www.bbc.co.uk/torchwood, also underwent an update. Not only were the first two standard *Torchwood Declassified* programmes added to it, as previously mentioned, but a number of new cast and crew video interviews were made available, and brief details of the first two episodes were given. Again, further content would be added each week during the course of the series' run.

Taken together, the *Torchwood* official website and the 'fictional' Torchwood Institute System Interface comprised a highly impressive online complement to the series itself. It is safe to say that no previous BBC production – not even *Doctor Who* itself – had ever had such attention, and no doubt money, lavished on its official websites: indeed, few others had even had their own websites. This was another clear indication of the high priority that the BBC was according to *Torchwood*.

THE PRODUCTION WRAPS

While the BBC was celebrating the extraordinary ratings success of *Torchwood*'s debut episodes, back in Cardiff there was still a couple of weeks' recording to be completed on the twelfth and thirteenth episodes before production could finally wrap at the beginning of November. This meant that the cast and crew were in the fortunate position of knowing that the series had had a fantastic reception from the viewing public before they had even finished working on it. The wrap party, held on the evening of Saturday 4 November after the last day of work on set, was reportedly a very happy affair.

And by that time, rumours were starting to buzz amongst fans that, although no public announcement had been made, *Torchwood* had already been recommissioned by the BBC for a *second* series, which it was assumed at that time would air in the autumn of 2007.

CHAPTER SEVEN: THE SERIES IN PROGRESS

Starting with 'Ghost Machine', a regular pattern was established for *Torchwood*'s weekly transmissions. Each episode would debut at 10.00 pm on BBC Three on the Sunday and have a terrestrial airing at 9.00 pm on BBC Two on the Wednesday. There would also be five BBC Three repeats – the first in the early hours of the Monday morning, the second on the Tuesday evening, the third in the early hours of the Wednesday morning[17], the fourth on the Friday evening, and the fifth in the early hours of the Saturday morning – making seven screenings in total. The latest *Torchwood Declassified* mini-documentary would generally be shown after both the first and the last of these repeats.[18] Other BBC Three repeats would be scheduled from time to time – for instance, a triple bill of the first three episodes was shown on 4 November, and again in the early hours of 5 November.

Initially, a 30-second trailer for the following week's episode would debut shortly after the first BBC Three transmission – sometimes later the same night – and would then have a number of further airings during the course of the week, in programme breaks on BBC One, BBC Two and BBC Three. Later, however, these trailers became less and less frequent, and they were not seen at all for the episodes from 'They Keep Killing Suzie' onwards. Sometimes, although again only for the early episodes of the series, an audio trailer would also run on the BBC's national radio stations.

After the spectacular success of the heavily-publicised debut pairing, the ratings for each new episode would settle down to a norm of just over a million for the initial BBC Three transmission and just over two million for the BBC Two transmission, with around five hundred thousand viewers catching it on the BBC Three repeats. There would thus be a fairly consistent total weekly audience of around four million viewers – an extraordinarily impressive figure, far surpassing any previously achieved by a BBC Three-originated programme.

Radio Times presented another *Torchwood* feature in its edition for the week of 28 October to 3 November, promoting 'Ghost Machine'. Similar to the previous week's item on the main area of the Hub interior, this consisted of a double-page photograph of Jack's office with explanatory captions by Ed Thomas. In later weeks, however, the magazine's coverage of the series would be more low-key; and although disappointing to some fans, this was not really surprising, given that *Torchwood* was a post-watershed BBC Three drama rather than a prime-time BBC One family show like *Doctor Who*, which had a *Radio Times* article to accompany every episode.

At 7.45 pm on 31 October, a special episode of *Torchwood Declassified*, essentially a very heavily re-edited and extended, 13-minute version of the preview 'trailer' previously viewable only via the *Torchwood* official website, received its debut airing on BBC Three. Like the other episodes of the mini-documentary series, this would be repeated on a number of occasions over the following weeks.

On 2 November, the BBC press office issued its latest batch of advance programme information, which covered the episode 'Greeks Bearing Gifts' and presented a lengthy interview with the last of the Torchwood team cast members to be featured in such a release:

---

17 This repeat was dropped for 'They Keep Killing Suzie' and 'Random Shoes', reducing the total number of screenings within those weeks to six.

18 The sixth, ninth and tenth *Torchwood Declassified* episodes were repeated after the penultimate BBC Three screenings of the episodes they accompanied, rather than the last. The seventh and eighth episodes were not repeated at all during the week of their debut transmission.

Naoko Mori. 'I'm a bit of a geek myself,' Mori was quoted as saying. 'I love computers and gadgetry or anything technical. I always have to have the latest thing – I'm Japanese, so it's in the blood ... I've always wanted to do a science-fiction thing and an action thing – they're on my list of things to do before I die – and with *Torchwood*, I've managed to tick both boxes. There's a lot of running around with guns, and there's all that sci-fi stuff, but there's also really good drama with great characters and storylines.'

In a further batch of advance programme information released a week later, the BBC press office revealed for the first time the full title of the series' eighth episode, 'They Keep Killing Suzie'. This had been previously abbreviated to 'They Keep Killing' in order to preserve for as long as possible the surprise that Suzie would be making a further appearance.

The following day, 10 November, saw John Barrowman taking a guest slot on the *Friday Night With Jonathan Ross* show on BBC One. *Torchwood* was the main subject of discussion, and a clip from 'Cyberwoman' was shown. This was just the first of several promotional appearances that Barrowman would make during November and early December, in the short period between him finishing work on *Torchwood* and starting rehearsals in earnest for his starring role in the Christmas pantomime *Jack and the Beanstalk* in Cardiff. Others were on *Sunday AM* (BBC One, 12 November), *This Morning* (ITV1, 17 November), *Something for the Weekend* (BBC Two, 19 November), *BBC Breakfast* (BBC One, 22 November), *Loose Women* (ITV1, 29 November) and *Eight Out of Ten Cats* (Channel 4, 1 December).

From the 19 November transmission of 'Countrycide' onwards, *Torchwood* faced some potentially threatening new digital broadcast opposition. This came from Sky One who, in a multi-million pound deal, had secured the rights to screen the third season of the hit US drama series *Lost* (previously a Channel 4 acquisition), and started doing so in the same Sunday night slot as BBC Three had *Torchwood*. In the event, however, *Lost* failed to make any significant impact on *Torchwood*'s ratings, and by the second episode of its short run had actually fallen below the BBC show in the TV charts, although it later overtook it again on a couple of occasions.

Adding fuel to the rumours that *Torchwood* had already been re-commissioned for a second series, the icWales website reported on 25 November:

> The Director General of the BBC believes Wales has set a benchmark for the other regions to aspire to with its popular series of *Doctor Who* and *Torchwood*.
>
> Mark Thompson said the BBC Wales-produced dramas were a fine example of the 'sexy and modern' programmes the regional offices should be making for the network.
>
> *Doctor Who*, penned by Swansea writer Russell T Davies, is soon returning to BBC One for a third series and has won a clutch of awards.
>
> A spin-off show *Torchwood* ... pulled in more than two million viewers when it made its debut on BBC Three last month.
>
> Mr Thompson believes both series will run and run.
>
> 'Menna Richards (BBC Wales Controller) and her team here in Wales are flying at the moment,' said Mr Thompson, who visited Broadcasting House in Cardiff yesterday.
>
> 'I'm sure we will be seeing more series of both *Doctor Who* and *Torchwood*.
>
> 'There's a lot of admiration and a bit of jealousy elsewhere in the BBC because of the success here.'
>
> Mr Thompson said there had been a debate for many years about whether a Wales-produced drama could be a success if it was screened nationwide.

> He believes that with its stunning aerial shots of Cardiff and its fast-paced scenes, *Torchwood*, starring John Barrowman and Welsh actress Eve Myles, is the perfect solution.
> 'We wondered whether Wales could be portrayed as modern and forward-looking, and *Torchwood* is the answer. It's obviously Welsh and it's sexy, modern and fantastic.'

On 27 November, the BBC press office released its final batch of advance programme information for *Torchwood*'s first series, covering the episodes 'Combat', 'Captain Jack Harkness' and 'Apocalypse' (later to be retitled 'End of Days'). This gave the first hint that the series was to end as it had begun, with a double bill of episodes on the same evening.

At the end of November, a whole host of official BBC publicity photographs from *Torchwood* appeared online, in very high quality, in the gallery section of the Sparklies.org website, where they were soon joined by some similar shots from various episodes of *Doctor Who*, including the then forthcoming Christmas special 'The Runaway Bride'. These images were all removed a few days later, however, presumably at the BBC's insistence.

John Barrowman and Naoko Mori were both in the news on 4 December, when they took part in the Royal Variety Performance – Barrowman singing a solo number and Mori appearing as a cast member of *Avenue Q*, the West End show she had recently joined.

On 11 December, icWales ran another *Torchwood* report, speculating further on the prospects for a second series of episodes:

> Rival BBC channels are fighting for the chance to screen a second series of Cardiff-based sci-fi hit *Torchwood.*
> It has not been officially confirmed that a second series of the *Doctor Who* spin-off will be commissioned. But the team behind the city-set show, starring John Barrowman and Eve Myles, is already working on scripts for the next series at BBC Wales' Llandaff headquarters.
> And both BBC Two and BBC Three are fighting for the right to screen it first – with writer Russell T Davies pushing for a slot on BBC One.
> At the moment the 45-minute episodes are screened several times a week, first on digital channel BBC Three on Sunday nights and second on the mainstream BBC Two. The result has been a viewing-figures bonanza for the broadcaster with up to 4 m people watching it every week over the different showings.
> It is the biggest draw on BBC Three and is regularly one of the best-watched non-sport programmes on digital television.
> But insiders at the BBC say that the mainstream BBC Two has been so impressed with the drama and its stunning Cardiff backdrop that the channel is fighting for the chance to screen it first.
> An insider told the Echo: 'Nothing's been confirmed, but the big question is not if it will be re-commissioned, but which channel is going to screen it.'

Although the first series of *Torchwood* was rapidly drawing to a close, it seemed increasingly certain that this would not be the last that the viewing public would see of Captain Jack and his colleagues inside the Hub.

CHAPTER EIGHT: THE SERIES ENDS... AND A SECOND IS CONFIRMED

On Tuesday 12 December 2006, official confirmation of a second series of *Torchwood* – and the channel on which it would be broadcast – finally arrived, in the form of a BBC press release that read, in part:

> BBC Three's *Torchwood* is back for a second series, but this time it will premiere exclusively on BBC Two as confirmed by Jane Tranter, Controller of BBC Fiction, and BBC Two Controller Roly Keating …
>
> Roly Keating said: 'Inventive, intelligent and unpredictable, *Torchwood* is a brilliant piece of 21st Century fantasy drama. I'm delighted that its second series will be premiering on the channel.'
>
> Julian Bellamy, Controller of BBC Three, said: 'Breaking all records on BBC Three is no mean feat and we've been proud to help build *Torchwood* into one of the most talked-about and eagerly-anticipated series of recent years.'
>
> Jane Tranter said: '*Torchwood* is a modern and innovative drama that has truly captured the imagination of its audience, and we are very excited that there will be more of the adrenaline-fuelled, action-packed adventures of our team of Torchwood heroes.'
>
> Russell T Davies said: 'The whole team is bristling with ideas and we are delighted that Cardiff is going to be home to more monsters and mayhem.'
>
> *Torchwood* will be executive produced by Julie Gardner and Russell T Davies.
>
> [Recording] is due to start in Cardiff in Spring 2007 and the series will hit screens later next year.

This announcement was naturally met with considerable delight by *Torchwood* fans. The promotion of the series to BBC Two for its second year was also a clear recognition of its success in the BBC's eyes. Although not mentioned in the press release, the series would however continue to be repeated on BBC Three, maintaining its presence on the channel that had originally commissioned it, as confirmed by Julie Gardner during a BBC Radio Wales phone-in programme on 22 December.

While thoughts were already turning to the second series, the last few episodes of the first had still to be transmitted; and, due largely to the fact that this coincided with the Christmas holiday period, there were now some changes from the established pattern.

The BBC Three debut screening of 'Combat' was scheduled to start half an hour earlier than usual, at 9.30 pm, on Christmas Eve; and – mirroring the way the series had opened – the last two episodes, 'Captain Jack Harkness' and 'End of Days', went out as a double bill, with a single, combined set of closing credits at the end, on New Year's Day. This being a Monday, it marked the first occasion that *Torchwood* episodes had debuted on a day other than Sunday – a late change of plan, as up until a week or so before the Christmas schedules were fixed, it had been intended to go out in its usual slot, on New Year's Eve. All three episodes received, as usual, several BBC Three repeats over the days following their initial screenings – and a *Torchwood Declassified* mini-documentary relating to each was also aired on a couple of occasions – but again generally in different slots than in previous weeks. The repeats of 'Captain Jack Harkness' on Thursday 4 January and of 'End of Days' on Friday 5 December were particularly notable, in that they constituted their first screenings in their 'standard', single episode form, with individual closing credits and a 'Next Time' teaser at the end of the former.

The BBC Two transmissions were also slightly disrupted over the festive season, although they remained on Wednesdays, with 'Combat' going out at 10.00 pm, an hour later than usual, on 27 December, and 'Captain Jack Harkness' and 'End of Days' appearing as a double bill beginning at 9.00 pm on 3 January.

Somewhat surprisingly, given that this story arc appeared to have reached a natural conclusion in 'Army of Ghosts'/'Doomsday', the *Doctor Who* Christmas special 'The Runaway Bride', transmitted at 7.00 pm on Christmas Day, contained a number of further tie-in references to the Torchwood Institute. The Doctor's 'stand-in' companion, Donna Noble, tells him that she works as a temporary secretary at a security company called H C Clements – the sole proprietor of which, he quickly discovers, is Torchwood. Infiltrating the company's headquarters, the Doctor, Donna and her fiancé Lance gain access to a secret underground base bedecked with the familiar Torchwood logo. 'H C Clements was bought up 23 years ago by the Torchwood Institute,' says the Doctor. 'Torchwood was destroyed,' he adds, suggesting that he may not know about the other branches such as the one in Cardiff, 'but H C Clements stayed in business. I think someone else came in and took over the operation.' This 'someone else' later turns out to be the Empress of the Racnoss. The secret base, it transpires, extends below the Thames Flood Barrier – 'Torchwood snuck in and built this place underneath,' explains the Doctor – and has at its heart a tunnel leading down to the centre of the Earth – 'Very Torchwood.' The base is taken out of action at the end of the story, when the Doctor floods it with water from the Thames in order to destroy the Empress's children.

Almost immediately after the closing credits of 'The Runaway Bride' had finished rolling[19], there came a 30-second trailer for the New Year's Day double-bill screening of 'Captain Jack Harkness' and 'End of Days', presenting numerous clips from the two episodes. That the *Torchwood* finale on BBC Three was considered worthy of receiving a prime-time Christmas Day trailer on BBC One arguably speaks volumes for the high regard in which the series is held by the BBC. The same trailer was repeated a number of times over the subsequent week, marking a return to the level of promotion that had accompanied the early episodes of the series.

On 26 December, the series' first five episodes were released by 2 Entertain on DVD, along with a number of 'extras', and did brisk business in the post-Christmas shopping spree. The first three original novels based on the series also started to appear in shops at around this time, although the official publication date was not until 11 January, and they too sold very well – so much so, in fact, that they went to a reprint on the strength of pre-orders alone.[20]

1 January brought news, via a report in the *Sydney Morning Herald*, that *Torchwood* would make its Australian debut on ABC – the channel that screened *Doctor Who* – during the course of 2007. Nine days later, it was announced via a press release in New Zealand that the series was amongst a major package of programming acquired from BBC Worldwide Australasia by TVNZ – a long-time broadcaster of classic *Doctor Who*, but not of the new series, which airs instead on Prime – and would likewise be screened there later in the year. The terrestrial channel Cuatro in Spain was the next overseas broadcaster to take the series, as announced in a 16 January report on the website of the industry journal *Variety*. Given that the series had been pre-sold to CBC in a co-production deal, it was also odds-on that it would appear in

19 They were separated only by a 30-second trailer for *The Sarah Jane Adventures*: 'The Invasion of the Bane'.

20 See Appendix A for further details of tie-in merchandise.

Canada sometime during 2007. At this point, however, the BBC had still not succeeded in striking a deal for *Torchwood* to be shown by a US network, although efforts were continuing. Rumours suggested that the Sci-Fi Channel, which had enjoyed considerable success with *Doctor Who*, was interested in picking up the spin-off. A potential problem, though, was that the series' content was of a more adult nature than the Sci-Fi Channel would normally broadcast, raising the prospect that some episodes might have to be dropped, or at least edited to make them suitable in the network's eyes, if an agreement was to be reached. A complication arose in Australia, too, at the end of January, when it became clear that the *Sydney Morning Herald* had rather jumped the gun with their announcement at the beginning of the month. It now seemed that ABC would not be screening the series after all, but that Seven Network and Network Ten were both interested in doing so, and were reportedly in a bidding war for the rights.

Fans in the UK, meanwhile, would not have long to wait for Captain Jack's next appearance – this time not in *Torchwood*, but in his original series, *Doctor Who*. Russell T Davies confirmed via various public statements that the former companion of the ninth Doctor would meet up with the tenth in a number of episodes toward the end of Series Three. Reports soon began to surface that Jack would feature strongly in the closing two-parter, scripted by Davies himself, and might also appear in the preceding, eleventh episode, tentatively entitled 'Utopia', again by Davies. Finally, it seemed, Jack was to get his craved-for appointment with 'the right kind of Doctor'.

In an interview published on the website of the *Metro* free regional newspaper on 24 January 2007, John Barrowman looked ahead to his return to *Doctor Who* – and gave a few hints of what might lie in store for viewers in the second series of *Torchwood*:

> John Barrowman says he can't wait to play a 'sassier' Captain Jack when he returns to *Doctor Who* this year.
>
> The star of the sci-fi show's spin-off *Torchwood* is due to start [recording] the final three episodes of the third series of *Doctor Who* and is looking forward to playing 'the other side of Captain Jack'.
>
> 'In *Torchwood* he's a little darker, slightly more moody and more focused,' the 39-year-old revealed.
>
> 'But in *Doctor Who* he's slightly more fun and I think that's because he's not the leader of the pack, the Doctor's the leader, so he's a little more light-hearted.
>
> 'He's more childlike and he's a lot sassier.'
>
> The actor is also due to start [recording] the second series of *Torchwood* in the spring – and says he hopes the hit drama will go even further this time.
>
> 'What I would like to see is that we become edgier and we push the limit a little more on the adult aspect of everything.
>
> 'In the first series we played it safe a little bit and this second series, I hope that we will go further.'

PART THREE: THE TORCHWOOD FORMAT

CHAPTER NINE: CONCEPT AND STYLE

GENESIS OF A SERIES

The essential elements of the *Torchwood* concept were summarised up-front in the early press announcements: it would be 'a British sci-fi paranoid thriller, a cop show with a sense of humour', concerning 'a renegade team' who 'investigate human and alien crime, as well as alien technology that has fallen to Earth'. Russell T Davies had first conceived the idea for a series of this kind around 2002, while working with Julie Gardner on the BBC Three drama series *Casanova* and before being invited to revive *Doctor Who*. His initial working title for the series was *Excalibur*, and at that point he envisaged it essentially as a cross between a science-fiction series and a realistic crime drama. Another early working title is reported to have been *Psychic Cops*, although this has not been substantiated.

'I'd been watching shows like *Buffy* [*the Vampire Slayer*] and *Angel*,' explained Davies in an interview published in the 21-27 October 2006 edition of *Radio Times*, 'and I said to Julie Gardner, "Why don't we make a series like that?"' What Davies had in mind, and wished to emulate, was the way these American series juxtaposed monsters and other extraordinary phenomena with the ordinary, everyday lives of their lead characters.

'Russell pitched me the idea for *Excalibur*,' recalled Gardner in an interview published in Issue 343 of *Starburst*, dated November 2006, 'and the starting point was, there's an alleyway at night that is a crime scene, [and] what's unusual about it is that the police are the wrong side of the crime tape, because a very sexy team of people stride onto the scene and begin to investigate using alien technology.' This scene, which Davies considered pivotal, would ultimately open the series' debut episode.

It was not until 2005, however, that Davies took his idea any further. This was when Stuart Murphy, the then Controller of BBC Three, decided in the wake of the phenomenal success of the new *Doctor Who* to invite him to devise a major new science-fiction series for the channel, for transmission in a post-9.00 pm slot.

It was Davies himself who, in his formal pitch for the series, took his earlier *Excalibur* idea and proposed making it into a *Doctor Who* spin-off. While this could perhaps be seen as inevitable, given Davies's long-time devotion to *Doctor Who*, it was certainly a characteristically astute move, not least because it guaranteed that there would be a buzz of interest and excitement about the series right from the word go, and would even be a pre-existing audience for it – in that it would be bound to carry across at least a proportion of *Doctor Who*'s regular adult viewers and established fan-base. The challenge would then be to hold onto that audience throughout the 13 week run; which would be largely down to the appeal of *Torchwood* itself. And by choosing to centre the series around Captain Jack Harkness – a character with proven popularity, played by an actor with real star quality and a reputation very much in the ascendancy – Davies again ensured that the battle was half-won. Without the *Doctor Who* connection, and without the established popular lead character, it would have been a far more difficult prospect for the new series to have generated publicity and won a good-sized audience from the outset.

As mentioned in Chapter Three, Davies's initial pitch document for *Torchwood* ran to one-and-a-half pages. In his interview for Issue 342 of *Starburst*, Chris Chibnall recalled: 'Anybody who wants a master class on how to pitch a TV series should read that document: so clear and brilliant.'

The series was quickly commissioned, and the ongoing storyline and the content of the 13 individual episodes were then developed through a process of collaboration, mainly between Davies, Gardner, Chibnall and script editors Brian Minchin and Helen Raynor. As Chibnall told *Starburst*: 'We had a storylining session [for *Torchwood*] at the beginning of January 2006, where we threw around ideas. From that, we got the shape of the series. For a lot of the episodes, we had a basic premise, which we then discussed with individual writers.'

'I created the characters and the settings and other things like that,' Davies told *Western Mail* journalist Hannah Jones in an interview published on the icWales website on 21 October 2006. 'They're my inventions – Captain Jack, Gwen, Ianto and Toshiko. I set up what they sound like and what they're capable of and what kind of world they inhabit. Then there are the background stories and the sort of world they live in. All of that is mine. Within that, you're telling the story of the week, and out of 13 episodes, I came up with nine or ten rough outlines of scripts. Like in one written by Catherine Tregenna, we go back to 1941 – that idea came from a one line suggestion from me. But she's got the hard job of filling in 56 pages of dialogue. It's only then that the thing really starts coming alive.'

'Russell said "It's got to be a real world,"' noted Raynor in an interview for Issue 344 of *Starburst*. 'Which is great. But in terms of early ideas we talked about with the writers, that tended to mean slightly gritty, underbelly, almost Inspector Rebus-type territory.[21] In the early stages, we kind of ping-ponged a bit between ideas that were kind of real-world investigative – they could almost have been an episode of *Spooks* – and ideas that were incredibly fantastical – like alien races living in Cardiff and not having contact with anyone. They were episodes that could have been set on a spaceship; they were literally removed from what the show was.'

In a video interview posted on the *Torchwood* official website, Davies commented: 'A lot of [the series] was in my head already. I'd had a lot of time to think about *Torchwood* before writing it, which is always good, so that the base was there, a lot of it spinning off that *Doctor Who* episode "Boom Town". We'd use under the water tower … I mean, I actually live on the bay front in Cardiff; you just look out of the window and think, "What a great setting." So that was there. A lot of it was planned far in advance. We'd worked with Eve Myles on *Doctor Who* and loved her, so we actually signed her about six months even before an episode was written. It was just like, we promised it to her, and said, "Please come and do this." We did the same obviously with John Barrowman as Captain Jack.'

Davies's own first series *Doctor Who* episode 'Boom Town' did indeed provide much inspiration for *Torchwood*, in that it developed the premise of the dimensional rift in Cardiff – established in the earlier episode 'The Unquiet Dead' as a portal through which alien entities can potentially reach the Earth – and also the theme of the Doctor trailing 'unfinished business' in his wake when he departs in the TARDIS at the end of each of his adventures, leaving those who remain behind to deal with the consequences.

Unlike on *Doctor Who*, however, Davies would be the credited writer on only one of the new series' 13 episodes and co-writer on one other (which he later described as an 'emergency measure'), and would not generally be heavily involved in the scripting process.

The time between the series being commissioned and reaching the screen was exceptionally short for a current TV drama series. 'Tell me about it!' joked Raynor in her *Starburst* interview. 'It was like somebody fired a starting gun and everybody just started writing at the same time. Again that's difficult, but you have scripts coming in in parallel, rather than one after another.

21 Inspector Rebus is the lead character in a series of gritty, and enormously popular, crime novels by Ian Rankin. These novels have also been adapted into a TV series starring Ken Stott, transmitted on ITV1 from 2000 onwards.

So, we'd have the writer of episode eight saying "What happens in episode four?" and I'd be saying "It doesn't exist yet!" … People [can] move a lot faster [on *Torchwood*] than [on] other shows because [Davies], who is driving the script, can also kick-start the production. I don't know how we would have done it otherwise …

'The ones that were [recorded] early kind of found their feet by bumping up against the edges of what the editorial parameters were. Whereas with later episodes, we could say very successfully, "This sort of character is particularly at home in this world," or "This sort of story doesn't get the most excitement [out] of what the show is.

'There is a very strong editorial hand behind it. It's not a sprawling, hierarchical, traditional series structure – there's a very clear line of communication between Russell and Julie and Chris, the script editors and the producer.'

As regards the tone of the series, producer Richard Stokes was quoted in Issue 368 of *Doctor Who Magazine* as saying: '[This series is] much darker [than *Doctor Who*] – both in style and in look. I'm discussing style with directors, the design team, Russell T Davies and Julie Gardner all the time, and we keep talking about a noir style, lots of shadows. *Doctor Who* famously sends the kids round the back of the sofa; I want the grown-ups there too. The tradition of horror films … has filtered through to American television for many years, and we should do a bit more of that here …

'Its themes are more adult – which is not about lots of swearing and gratuitous violence – it's about exploring more adult themes and sides of humanity you may not want your kids to watch. That's not to say we don't have a laugh on the way …

'Like all the most memorable shows in this genre, it's about us; who we are and what we're doing to ourselves and each other. *Doctor Who* taps into a yearning for adventure in all of us, and *Torchwood* will, similarly, touch on universal truths in the human condition.'

These thoughts were echoed by Davies in his later interview on the official website: 'The overall tone of *Torchwood* is dark. It's delving into those areas of the human soul and human nature and human awfulness that it wouldn't be our place to do on *Doctor Who* … *Torchwood* is there not just to look at the dark stuff but at the sexual drives, the lusts, the passions – but, of course, passion being so strong, it can take a wrong direction, and become a bitter and twisted thing. So it's there … with some big science-fiction devices in it, but always coming back to square one, which is to look at people, to look at us, us now: western people in 21st Century cities, what our lives are like … A lot of the stories that come up – the crimes that they solve or the problems they encounter – are very much out there in the real world: they go to clubland, they go out to the country, they go into people's houses. We meet really ordinary people whose lives become something extraordinary because of contact with something alien.'

As with *Doctor Who*, however, Davies was keen that *Torchwood* should have an optimistic slant, as he told journalist Matt Wolf in an interview published in *The Sunday Times* on 15 October 2006: 'I think pessimism is easy. It's very sixth-form to say the world is terrible and we're all going to die. Though *Torchwood* is a much darker world than *Doctor Who*, it is all about optimism. I think, if you put people in terrible circumstances, some – not all, but some – will find a way out. I think that is the point of fiction, to be optimistic and to shape an ending. That's why it exists in the first place.'

FOR ADULTS ONLY?

Although sometimes wrongly described – even by people who've worked on it – as a 'children's series', *Doctor Who* has always been aimed at a family audience. Up until the 1980s, the BBC had a long and distinguished track-record of popular family programming, but this then became something of a 'lost art' as the channel controllers, apparently finding rather quaint and outmoded the idea that families might gather round their TV sets to watch programmes as a shared experience, preferred to allocate their budgets to shows like the flagship soap-opera *EastEnders* and other ratings big-hitters.[22] One of Russell T Davies's biggest achievements in successfully reviving *Doctor Who* in 2005 was to prove wrong the many critics and commentators who argued that traditional family audiences were gone for good and could not be recaptured in the modern, multi-channel TV environment of the early 21st Century.

Unlike a children's series, a family series must work on more than one level in order to achieve a broad appeal. *Doctor Who* has always done this admirably, combining a relatively superficial action-adventure story, intended to excite the kids, with a deeper and more thoughtful subtext, designed to engage the interest of the teenagers and adults.[23] The trick to this type of programming – which is by no means easy to pull off – is to avoid patronising adult viewers or insulting their intelligence but at the same time to steer clear of including anything that would be unsuitable or unduly disturbing for children. So whereas it is regarded as appropriate to include, say, a certain amount of non-realistic violence, or mildly horrific material of a fantastical nature, it is considered unacceptable to feature, for instance, scenes of vicious domestic conflict (the stock-in-trade of soap operas) or the use of household implements as weapons – and indeed the BBC has guidelines that programme-makers are expected to adhere to in this regard.

Torchwood was conceived from the outset as a series that would be aimed at an adult, post-watershed audience. As such, it would have no need to cater for younger viewers, and could indeed present material that would be over the heads of and/or decidedly unsuitable for children – including, potentially, material of a strongly violent, horrific or sexual nature or featuring expletive-laden dialogue. It would thus have a narrower audience-base and appeal, and a more limited ratings potential, than *Doctor Who*.

In his initial BBC Radio Wales interview about the spin-off, Davies was asked by the presenter: 'Would it be mean to call it *Doctor Who* for grown-ups?' Laughing, Davies responded: 'I'm not allowed to call it that.' This could perhaps be seen as an allusion to the fact that, as discussed above, *Doctor Who* is itself intended for 'grown ups', as well as for children, and is indeed hugely popular with viewers of *all* ages. It may also, though, have been indicative of a tricky dilemma that the BBC faced: to what extent should they attempt, or permit, cross-promotion between *Doctor Who* and *Torchwood*, given that the latter had a narrower intended audience than the former? On the one hand, it would be pointless to ignore the links between the two series, given that the Torchwood Institute was such an important element of *Doctor Who* in 2006, and that Captain Jack would be returning to the parent series in 2007. It would also be counterproductive, given that – as observed above – one of the advantages of producing a spin-off, as opposed to a brand new series, is that it can capitalise on the popularity of the parent. On the other hand, however, the BBC would not want to be accused of upsetting children – or, even more undesirably, encouraging them to watch (or to pressurise

22 One possibly unintended consequence of this was that when families *did* come together round their TV sets in the 1980s and 1990s, it was often to watch programmes that were arguably not entirely suitable for the younger family members – *EastEnders* being, perhaps, the prime case in point.

23 In the new, Russell T Davies-produced *Doctor Who*, the appeal has been broadened still further, through a conscious effort to capture a previously-neglected female audience, in part by giving the stories greater emotional depth.

their mums and dads to allow them to watch) a series that was patently unsuitable for them – by creating such a close association between the parent and the spin-off that *Doctor Who*'s younger viewers were made to feel that they were seriously 'missing out' in being excluded from seeing *Torchwood*.

Davies commented on this dilemma in Issue 373 of *Doctor Who Magazine*: '[*Torchwood*] has a slight problem in that it's an adult show, and we don't want kids to feel that they have to watch it. Nonetheless, it is going to have that *Doctor Who* inheritance. The Torchwood Institute was written all through Series Two, so it isn't coming out of the blue. That's branding, basically. I cannot emphasise enough the importance of branding. I'm saying that quite proudly. I'd be very cynical about a programme that's just branding, all commerce, saleability, demographics ... but I'm saying that knowing that also we produce the best drama in the world.'

It later emerged that Julie Gardner had at one point issued a directive to the production team that *Torchwood* was not to be spoken about publicly in the same context as *Doctor Who*. Although this rule was subsequently broken – including by Gardner herself, as Davies pointed out in the online commentary to *Doctor Who*'s Series Two finale 'Doomsday' – it was further evidence of a degree of sensitivity felt over this issue. As mentioned in Chapter Four, the BBC's press releases promoting *Torchwood* as part of BBC Three's autumn schedule for 2006 notably made no mention of its *Doctor Who* roots. And while Panini's *Doctor Who Magazine* continued to report *Torchwood* news, the BBC's children's comic *Doctor Who Adventures* understandably made no mention of the new series at all.

Asked in his 18 October 2006 interview for BBC Wales's *Wales Today* programme what advice he would give to parents whose children were curious about *Torchwood*, Davies replied: 'I think you've just got to be honest. And actually, kids know their television better than anyone else. They know what a nine o'clock show is. So I think, just say, "It's a nine o'clock show." They know; they know they're not supposed to watch it.' In an interview published the following day on the BBC News website, he went even further, explaining that he had deliberately ensured that there was swearing early in the first episode so that no-one could be confused as to the type of series they were watching: 'It's saying very clearly, if you are watching with a child, get out of the room.'

Ultimately, though, the spin-off would always be linked to the parent series in the minds of all the viewing public – and, reinforcing this, in press coverage – and, regardless of the rights and wrongs of the matter, many young *Doctor Who* fans would no doubt find a way to sample the 'forbidden fruit' of *Torchwood*.

VISUAL STYLE

In describing the world in which the *Torchwood* stories take place, Russell T Davies, Julie Gardner and other members of the production team tend to use certain words time and time again: dark, gritty, sexy, urban, glamorous and 'real'. These intentions are very much reflected in the series' visual style. Take, for instance, the costumes. Dark colours – blacks, greys, browns and dark blues – predominate, and certainly the clothes of the five Torchwood regulars are stylish, sleek and sexy, while also being tailored to reflect the characters' individual functions and personalities. The set designs by Ed Thomas draw on a very similar colour palette, and have an urban, contemporary, realistic look. The exception to this rule is the elaborate, three-storey-high Hub interior set – conceived from the outset as a key feature of the series – as Thomas explained in a video interview on the *Torchwood* official website:

'There are all sorts of different architectural styles within it. So you've got the Victorian railway tunnel, and you've got more modern elements like ... the interrogation room, which is cast concrete. From early conversations with Russell, we decided that we wanted different architectural styles and that we wanted it to have a real history to it, as Torchwood has. So with each individual person that requires [an individual] area, you have to introduce parts of their personality into that ... You've got Captain Jack's office, which is slightly stuck in the '40s, a little bit period, a little bit deco ... Captain Jack's living accommodation is below his office, very much a confined area that he's used to sleeping in[24], feels like the inside of a spaceship or a jet plane.'

However, despite the use of a number of different architectural styles, the Hub still conforms to the dark, gritty, 'lived in' look of the rest of the production, and has an almost 'industrial' feel to it, with metal and concrete structures and water pooled in the base. And even in Jack's office, as Thomas told the *Radio Times* of 28 October to 3 November 2006, 'There are hints of Victoriana and the '40s with a bit of art deco influence, but we wanted those to fade away and the modern tech and computers to stand out.'

The opening scene of 'Everything Changes' takes place at night, in a dingy alley beside a multi-storey car park, in the pouring rain. This sets the tone for much of the rest of the series' location work. Indeed, for a BBC drama production, *Torchwood* features an unusually large amount of location material shot at night. 'Yeah, there's been quite a bit of night shooting ...' commented Chris Chibnall in his interview in *Starburst* Issue 342. 'It varies according to the demands of the story. The first three episodes are quite night-heavy, but Peter Hammond's, for example, takes place mostly in daylight. We have to be slightly careful, as shooting in the height of summer means you have [fewer] night hours to [record] in, but that's just one of the many logistical factors in producing the show. Everybody's main concern is that the show looks as beautiful as possible, whether it's day or night.'

While it might perhaps seem almost paradoxical to describe the impersonal, threat-filled urban locations of *Torchwood* as 'beautiful', the way in which they are shot – the action replete with images of the breathtaking modern architecture of the Roald Dahl Plass and punctuated by sweeping, panoramic views of the cityscape captured from a helicopter – does indeed make them appear alluring and glamorous.

Taken together, the dark, muted, almost monochrome tones, the sharp, sexy costumes, the gritty, urban look and the glamorous metropolitan locations of *Torchwood* almost inevitably invite comparison with the style of classic film noir – the low-budget, black-and-white American crime films of the '40s and '50s in which grim, compelling human dramas are played out in smoky, shadow-filled rooms and on the mean streets of the big city – except that in *Torchwood*'s case, the big city in question is not Los Angeles, but Cardiff.

'WELSHNESS'

Whereas in *Doctor Who* Cardiff has often doubled for other places, primarily London, in *Torchwood* it is unashamedly itself.

'I think Russell was very keen to make Cardiff a real place in this series,' commented producer Richard Stokes in *SFX* Issue 150, dated December 2006. 'I think we've taken it much further than even he thought we could do, the reason being that we invested a bit of money in the budget for the first episode to get up in a helicopter, both at day and at night, and we shot three hours' worth of rushes, which we're able to use across the entire series. John Barrowman

24 In fact, as revealed in the episode 'Ghost Machine', Jack no longer sleeps.

saw the first episode and said we'd managed to make it look like LA! … The geography of this city is really important.'

'I wanted it to look like a city does in an American show,' explained Davies in an interview published on the BBC News website on 19 October 2006. 'They aren't ashamed about putting what they've got on the screen. That's what I wanted to achieve.'

'Cardiff gives us stunning locations and a perfect template on which to explore life in a modern city,' noted Chibnall in his *Starburst* interview. 'It looks fantastic: we got some great helicopter footage of the city, which really gives a new perspective on the place. Working in Cardiff has [also] meant we've had access to a great pool of talent, in terms of writers and actors and crew.'

For the cast, too, the series' setting was an important factor. 'Cardiff is actually one of the biggest characters in *Torchwood*,' said Eve Myles in a *Wales Today* interview of 18 October 2006. 'It just shows it in the best possible light.'

Although only two of the five regular team members – Gwen and Ianto – are Welsh, almost all the supporting and guest characters are 'locals', considerably reinforcing what has been described as the series' 'Welshness'. The Welsh accent has traditionally been greatly underrepresented in mainstream TV drama productions – certainly in comparison with other regional and national accents, such as Scottish and Irish – but *Torchwood* makes a valiant attempt to redress the balance.

BBC Wales Controller Menna Richards perhaps put it most succinctly when, speaking at the series' 18 October press launch, she described *Torchwood* as Davies's 'love letter to Cardiff'.

CHAPTER TEN: FICTIONAL FORERUNNERS

While much about *Torchwood* is fresh and new, it also follows in the wake of, and owes a certain debt of inspiration to, many other popular TV series, both British- and American-made – mostly in what is sometimes described as the 'telefantasy' vein.[25] Discussed in this chapter are some of the most notable of these fictional forerunners.

THE X-FILES

Russell T Davies's initial description of *Torchwood* as '*The X-Files* meets *This Life*' was to remain, in some ways, very apt – even though he and his team later 'moved slightly away from that,' as Julie Gardner put it in an interview in Issue 343 of *Starburst*.

The X-Files, an American series created and overseen by Chris Carter for his 10/13 production company and broadcast initially on the Fox network, ran for nine seasons between 1993 and 2002 and spawned a spin-off movie in 1998. Like *Torchwood*, it involved a team of agents working for an organisation – in this case, the FBI – investigating crimes that could not be solved by conventional means and that often had other-worldly features.

The two lead characters for most of the series' run were agents Fox Mulder (David Duchovny) and Dana Scully (Gillian Anderson). As time went by, additional regulars were introduced, including FBI Assistant Director Walter Skinner (Mitch Pileggi), to whom Mulder and Scully reported; the sinister Cigarette Smoking Man (William B Davis); and Mulder's conspiracy theorist, internet geek friends Langley (Dean Haglund), Byers (Bruce Harwood) and Frohike (Tom Braidwood), collectively known, after a newsletter they produced, as the Lone Gunmen (which subsequently became the title of a single-season spin-off series). Toward the end of *The X-Files*' run, as Mulder's appearances became increasingly sporadic, a new leading male agent was introduced in the person of John Doggett (Robert Patrick), partnered by a new female agent, Monica Reyes (Annabeth Gish).

Mulder, who as a boy had witnessed his sister being apparently deducted by aliens, was a firm believer in UFOs and paranormal phenomena, and determined to discover 'the truth' behind a conspiracy involving alien plans to infiltrate and colonise the Earth. The scientifically-minded, medically-qualified Scully, on the other hand, was initially a sceptic, preferring to believe that the mysteries they encountered had more mundane explanations. Later, though, Scully underwent something of a role reversal: after years of working with Mulder, she became more open to and accepting of 'extreme possibilities', while Doggett fulfilled the function of the sceptic in the team.

The X-Files was a huge hit all over the world, and a groundbreaking series in a number of respects. Unlike almost all previous US genre TV, it was cynical in tone, eschewed tidy resolutions and took a decidedly jaundiced view of 'the establishment'. In the introduction to their book *X-Treme Possibilities* (Virgin Publishing, 1997), authors Paul Cornell, Martin Day and Keith Topping put it like this:

> With the American psyche turning increasingly against its own government, against all

25 Writer Phil Tonge, in an online article about BBC telefantasy, gives the following succinct definition of this term: 'Telefantasy is a term originally coined by French writers who wanted to avoid long-winded sub-categories for programmes such as say *The Avengers* ... Basically, if a programme contains elements of SF, horror, the supernatural, mythology and/or surrealism, then it can be deemed to be "telefantasy".'

> authority, nobody, in the 1990s, can tell an American citizen what to believe. The skies are full of UFOs/black helicopters, containing aliens/UN troops who do experiments on/wilfully destroy herds of cattle. The American public has become thoroughly alienated, shocked that the betrayals of Watergate haven't stopped: Irangate, Whitewater, many other revelations that power is in the hands of people as mortal as those they govern. Their nation, the one that has always believed in freedom and democracy, is being ferociously shown the realities of power and capitalism. That these terrible things have happened cannot be the fault of the public themselves: it's the fault of those in power. Not those fallible Presidents and their parties, who are just as much victims of the real world as the public are. The real people in power. Those whose presence in government makes America such a scary place. The conspiracy. *The X-Files* is the product of a nation looking for such people to blame.

In characterising *Torchwood* as a 'sci-fi paranoid thriller, a cop show with a sense of humour,' Davies could just as easily have been describing *The X-Files*. Paranoia was *The-Files*' stock-in-trade, with layer upon layer of conspiracy and intrigue being exposed as the ongoing storyline unfolded. In Jack Harkness and Gwen Cooper, *Torchwood* has its own 'Mulder and Scully' characters, investigating similar types of cases and fulfilling similar roles in the narrative, with – at least in the early part of the series – a similar underlying sexual tension. Even Gwen's introduction as a 'new girl', initially suspicious of Jack, mirrors the way that Scully first comes to work with Mulder at the start of *The X-Files*. Neither series, however, focuses solely on its male and female leads; the other regulars essentially 'take it in turn' to have occasional episodes revolving around their characters – although even more so in *Torchwood* than in *The X-Files*. In this sense, *Torchwood* is a more of a true 'ensemble cast' series. This approach was perfected in, and to some extent pioneered by, the classic US comedy series *Cheers* (Paramount 1982-1993), which had a male and female lead pair – initially Sam (Ted Danson) and Diane (Shelley Long), then Sam and Rebecca (Kirstie Alley) – but also a group of other regulars – including 'Coach' (Nick Colasanto), Carla (Rhea Perlman), Norm (George Wendt), Cliff (John Ratzenberger), Frasier (Kelsey Grammer) and 'Woody' (Woody Harrelson) – who would each come to the fore in particular episodes. This is mirrored in *Torchwood* in the way that, for example, Ianto features strongly in 'Cyberwoman' and Toshiko takes centre stage in 'Greeks Bearing Gifts', while the central pair of Jack and Gwen (the 'Sam and Diane' figures) continue to feature strongly.

THIS LIFE

This Life was a BBC Two drama series broadcast in two seasons in 1996 and 1997, with a one-off reunion special transmitted at the end of 2006. Initially conceived by BBC Two Controller Michael Jackson and then developed by producer Tony Garnett and writer and former trainee solicitor Amy Jenkins, it focused on the frenetic lives, stormy relationships, emotional crises and fraught careers of a group of five recently-qualified solicitors who also shared a house in Southwark, South London. Joe Ahearne, who would later go on to direct for the new *Doctor Who*, was one of the series' writers and directors. An article on the BBC's h2g2 website notes:

> For its time, the show had a fresh and radical approach to life. It showed life for what it was and included sexually explicit scenes, violence, drug taking and drunkenness, all of which were portrayed realistically. Perhaps the biggest shock to those who believed the

> show marked the end of civilization was the explicit scenes of gay sex. From the very start, gay characters … played key roles in the show [and] … homosexuality was portrayed as a normal part of life.

The 'biggest shock' comment here alludes to the fact that the series was criticised by some, particularly in the more reactionary sections of the British press, for the frank nature of its adult content. A commentator in the *Daily Mail*, for instance, was 'appalled at the drugs, booze and, worst of all, simulated sex between homosexuals.'

While *Torchwood* is generally less explicit in its treatment of adult material, and has thus avoided the sort of controversy that surrounded *This Life*, there is nevertheless a clear similarity between the two series in the way that the professional lives of the regular characters are juxtaposed and intertwined with their personal lives – as alluded to in the 24 July 2006 press notice about BBC Three's autumn schedule, with its observation that the Torchwood team are 'fighting the impossible while keeping their everyday lives going back home.'

This Life was not the first series to focus on a group of attractive young colleagues who also have personal attachments and entanglements. The US series *thirtysomething* (ABC, 1987-1991), which also revolved around a group of young(ish) professionals with complicated personal lives, was arguably a direct forerunner. Other US series to adopt a somewhat similar model include, perhaps most notably, *ER* (NBC, 1994-), and more recently *The Practice* (ABC, 1997-2004), *CSI: Crime Scene Investigation* (CBS, 2000-) – as referenced in a joke in 'Everything Changes' – and *House MD* (Fox, 2004-). Where *This Life* broke new ground, however, was in the degree of emphasis it placed on the characters' personal issues, and in the realism, candour and emotional honesty with which it treated them. This has since been echoed in other post-watershed British TV dramas, such as Russell T Davies's own *Queer as Folk* (Channel 4, 1999) and Toby Whithouse's *No Angels* (Channel 4, 2004-2006). *Torchwood* can be seen as following in a similar vein.

BUFFY THE VAMPIRE SLAYER

No discussion of the 21st Century revival of *Doctor Who* or of *Torchwood* would be complete without acknowledging the debt they owe to *Buffy the Vampire Slayer* – not least because Russell T Davies has himself cited the US series as a notable influence, and a standard-setter for contemporary TV drama in the telefantasy vein. Created by writer/director Joss Whedon, initially for a 1992 movie of the same title, *Buffy the Vampire Slayer* debuted in 1997 and ran for seven seasons – the first five on the WB and the final two on UPN – before coming to an end in 2003. The series followed the life and adventures of Buffy Summers (Sarah Michelle Gellar), a teenager fated to battle against vampires and a variety of other supernatural foes, aided by her circle of high school friends – sometimes referred to collectively as 'the Scooby gang' – and a spiritual Watcher (Anthony Stewart Head). Many of the stories arose out of the fact that Buffy's home town, Sunnydale, is the site of a Hellmouth – a portal through which demons and other supernatural creatures can pass to Earth from the underworld. This of course has a clear parallel in *Torchwood* in the siting of the Torchwood Hub over the epicentre of the dimensional rift in Cardiff – a key aspect of the series.

The killing off of an apparent regular, Suzie Costello, in *Torchwood*'s opening episode mirrors the fate of the character Jesse (Eric Balfour) in the second episode of *Buffy the Vampire Slayer*. Joss Whedon had at one point actually wanted Jesse to be featured in the title sequence for the first two episodes of his series, to help convince viewers that he was to be an ongoing character, and it was only the prohibitive cost of producing a different title sequence for those episodes that ruled this out. This serves as a clear precedent for the way that Suzie was presented in the pre-publicity for *Torchwood.*

But it is not so much in its use of similar plot motifs – further examples of which are discussed in the Episode Guide later in this book – as in its overall storytelling and visual style that *Torchwood* owes a clear debt to *Buffy the Vampire Slayer* – and even more so to that series' own popular spin-off, *Angel* (the WB, 1999-2004). (Some fans have even commented that the font used for the *Torchwood* logo resembles that used for the *Angel* logo.) Whereas *Buffy the Vampire Slayer* was aimed primarily at a teenage audience and leavened its horror with humour and pastiche, *Angel* had a somewhat older target audience and was accordingly more adult in approach and darker in tone, paying homage to classic film noir as much as to the horror movie genre.[26] This is very much paralleled in the relationship between the family-orientated *Doctor Who* and the darker, adult-orientated *Torchwood.*

SPOOKS

Another series referenced by Russell T Davies himself in discussing *Torchwood* is the BBC One spy drama *Spooks* (broadcast in the USA as *MI-5*). This made its debut in 2002 and has had a run of five seasons at the time of writing, with a sixth commissioned for 2007. Like a number of the other series discussed in this chapter, it is recalled by *Torchwood* in the way that its central characters – another 'ensemble cast' team – face the dilemma of balancing their exciting and out-of-the-ordinary professional lives as members of a secret agency with their relatively mundane private lives. It also has a similar adult, realistic style, with slick production values and 'high octane' storylines. Like *Buffy the Vampire Slayer*, it killed off an apparent regular character, Helen Flynn (Lisa Faulkner), in its second episode, provoking considerable controversy – and providing a further precedent for the killing off of Suzie Costello in 'Everything Changes'.

CAPTAIN SCARLET AND THE MYSTERONS

Captain Scarlet and the Mysterons – often referred to simply as *Captain Scarlet* – was one of Gerry Anderson's famous 'Supermarionation' puppet shows of the 1960s, which ran over 32 episodes on the ITV network. It later spawned a remake, *Gerry Anderson's New Captain Scarlet* (2005-), realised through the use of CGI effects rather than puppetry. These series are worth mentioning as fictional forerunners of *Torchwood* for one key reason: the central character, Captain Scarlet, is a member of a secret organisation tasked with defending the Earth against alien attacks and, having been 'duplicated' by the Mysterons in the opening episode, is 'indestructible' – incapable of being killed. As such, Captain Scarlet is an obvious forerunner of Captain Jack.[27]

DOCTOR WHO

It might perhaps be considered trite to cite *Doctor Who* itself as a fictional forerunner of

26 When the two series were released on DVD in the UK, episodes of *Angel* generally received higher BBFC ratings than those of *Buffy the Vampire Slayer*; indeed, one episode of the spin-off was even rated 18, whereas the highest that any episode of the parent series was rated was 15.

27 There are other immortals to be found in telefantasy, perhaps most notably the lead character of the *Highlander* series, spun off from a successful films franchise, but these generally have no other similarities to Captain Jack.

Torchwood, given that the latter was actually conceived as a spin-off of the former. However, the debt owed by the spin-off to its parent goes far beyond the simple carrying across of a couple of characters – most notably, of course, Captain Jack. For one thing, the two series are clearly intended to be set in the same fictional universe; so just as references to the Torchwood organisation were to be found liberally sprinkled throughout *Doctor Who* from the first Christmas special onwards, effectively 'trailing' the spin-off, so references to aspects of *Doctor Who* crop up repeatedly in *Torchwood* (see the Episode Guide later in this book for further details). More than that, however, the two series share the same ethos, in that the universe they inhabit is a dangerous place, in which a flawed and divided humanity needs to be constantly on its guard against the threat of attack or infiltration by alien entities, and in which fear of the unknown is quite definitely justified. This is quite unlike much of American TV science-fiction, which – as perhaps best exemplified by *Star Trek* – posits an essentially civilised and well-ordered universe, with the human race standing as a bastion of truth and justice against the forces of evil; although, as mentioned above, *The X-Files* is a clear exception to this rule – perhaps because it is rooted as much in the horror genre as in science-fiction.

Torchwood is, in essence, very similar in concept to *Doctor Who*'s UNIT. Introduced in the 1968 story *The Invasion* and most recently featured in the 2005 Christmas special *The Christmas Invasion*, UNIT – the United Nations Intelligence Taskforce – is an organisation of military and scientific personnel tasked with investigating 'the odd, the unexplained, anything on Earth … or even beyond'[28] – a remit that has often seen it defending the Earth against alien incursions and invasion attempts. Captain Jack fulfils a dramatic function similar, in many ways, to that of the third Doctor in the UNIT stories of early 1970s *Doctor Who*. Both are 'outsiders', co-opted by their respective organisations to provide expertise beyond that normally available on contemporary Earth, and both are somewhat maverick in their respective approaches. And the UNIT stories of the early 1970s could themselves be said to have been a sort of British forerunner of *The X-Files*, with the Doctor – certainly a UFO 'believer'! – and his sceptical assistant Liz Shaw (Caroline John)[29] in the Mulder and Scully roles, and their 'boss' Brigadier Lethbridge-Stewart playing a part akin to that of FBI Assistant Director Walter Skinner. At the risk of overstretching the analogy, the Doctor's regular Time Lord adversary the Master could even be seen to have been *Doctor Who*'s equivalent of *The X-Files*' Cigarette Smoking Man. A number of the original *Doctor Who* novels, and some spin-offs such as the independent dramas *Auton* (BBV, 1997) and *Daemos Rising* (Reeltime, 2004),

28 This description of UNIT's remit was given by Brigadier Lethbridge-Stewart (Nicholas Courtney), commanding officer of the British branch, in the 1970 *Doctor Who* story 'Spearhead from Space'.

29 It seems more apposite here to cite Season 7 companion Liz Shaw than Season 8-10 companion Jo Grant (Katy Manning), not only because Liz, as a scientist, was a more 'Scully-like' character, but also because Season 7 seems to have served as a particularly rich source of inspiration to Russell T Davies. Some prime examples: Davies's debut *Doctor Who* episode, 'Rose', clearly owes a debt of inspiration to Season 7's opening story, 'Spearhead from Space', and not just in its reuse of the Nestenes and Autons; the Mars probe disaster of 'The Christmas Invasion' recalls that of 'The Ambassadors of Death', with the probe in each case being drawn inside a gigantic alien spaceship and losing contact with mission control in England until the aliens make a transmission; the destruction of the aliens behind the Doctor's back by Prime Minister Harriet Jones at the end of 'The Christmas Invasion' mirrors the action taken by Brigadier Lethbridge-Stewart at the end of 'Doctor Who and the Silurians'; and the 'parallel world' storyline of 'Rise of the Cybermen'/'The Age of Steel' and 'Army of Ghosts'/'Doomsday', featuring alternative versions of some of the series' regulars, repeats an idea from Season 7's closing story, 'Inferno'.

later suggested that UNIT held a cache of alien artefacts and possibly even a number of live aliens – recovered in the aftermath of invasion attempts and the like – in storage, again foreshadowing aspects of *Torchwood*.

All this might possibly be thought to beg the question why Russell T Davies did not simply centre his spin-off series on a Welsh-based branch of UNIT, rather than introduce Torchwood as a different organisation with a similar function. One reason he might have decided against using UNIT is that the 'fictional' UNIT website – www.unit.org.uk – launched by bbc.co.uk after the broadcast of the 2005 *Doctor Who* episode 'Aliens of London' apparently drew a complaint from the United Nations to the effect that their name, abbreviation and emblem were reserved for official use only. This meant that although the BBC could still use the UNIT name, it could no longer spell out that UN meant United Nations. This could perhaps have been seen as an impediment to basing a whole series around UNIT.

More likely, however, Davies simply wanted the organisation featured in the spin-off to be a 'home grown' one. At the time when UNIT was first introduced in *Doctor Who*, the United Nations was viewed by most members of the British public in a generally positive light, as an idealistic organisation acting in the best interests of humanity as a whole, above petty national concerns. Whenever UNIT was depicted as being at odds with the British establishment or regular Army – in stories such as 'The Invasion', 'Spearhead from Space', and 'The Claws of Axos' – it was always UNIT that was shown to have the moral high ground, while the national authorities were portrayed as courting disaster through the pursuit of parochial interests. Since that time, however, a succession of real-world events have arguably led to the United Nations' reputation becoming distinctly tarnished, so that most members of the British public now hold a decidedly more cynical view of the organisation. It would be much more problematic now than it was in the 1970s to portray the members of a UN-affiliated organisation in a heroic light in a TV series, and the decision to base *Torchwood* around a purely British group – 'separate from the Government, outside the police, beyond the United Nations,' as described by Captain Jack in 'Everything Changes' – can thus be considered a very shrewd one.

For those who regard the Big Finish-produced *Doctor Who* audio dramas as canonical, the picture is complicated still further by the existence of the Forge, created by writers Cavan Scott and Mark Wright and first featured in their play 'Project: Twilight' (2001). This organisation, formed around the beginning of the 1900s, is tasked with studying and experimenting with extraterrestrial material and technology and applying it to the security interests of the United Kingdom – an idea very similar to that underlying Torchwood. The agents of the Forge sometimes use the code phrase 'for King and country' – which can perhaps be seen to have been echoed in the protestations of Yvonne Hartman, head of the Torchwood Institute in the 2006 *Doctor Who* TV story 'Army of Ghosts'/ 'Doomsday', on being converted into a Cyberman: 'I did my duty, for Queen and country'. It certainly seems possible that the Forge was one source of inspiration that Russell T Davies – known to be a fan of the Big Finish audio dramas – drew on in his conception of Torchwood.

OTHER TELEFANTASY FORERUNNERS

While no other British telefantasy series has featured an organisation as similar to Torchwood as *Doctor Who*'s own UNIT, a number have centred around groups responsible for investigating out-of-the-ordinary types of crimes or supernatural incidents and can be seen as forerunners of a less direct kind. The following are some of the prime examples.

In the late 1960s and early 1970s, Lew Grade's ITC Entertainment production company made for the ITV network a number of film series that could be loosely described as involving teams of investigators and crime-fighters with special remits, and sometimes even special powers. Of these, *Department S* (1969-70), although very different from *Torchwood* in its style and approach, is the one with the closest similarities to it in terms of its basic premise. The eponymous Department's investigations are carried out by a small team of agents effectively led by a charismatic and libido-driven 'outsider' hero – Jason King (Peter Wyngarde), seen by some as an influence on the depiction of the third Doctor in *Doctor Who* – and concern a succession of strange mysteries 'too baffling' for the minds of its parent body, the international police organisation Interpol. The series spawned its own spin-off, *Jason King* (1971-72).

Doomwatch was the brainchild of Kit Pedler and Gerry Davis – former *Doctor Who* writers and creators of the Cybermen – and ran on BBC One for three seasons between 1970 and 1972. It focused on the investigations of a group of Government scientists – the Department of Observation and Measurement of Scientific Work (aka Doomwatch) – into new ecological and technological threats to the world, and was arguably the first TV series to deal seriously with 'green' issues. The team is led by the highly principled Spencer Quist (John Paul), and other regular or semi-regular members include Tobias 'Toby' Wren (Robert Powell), John Ridge (Simon Oates), Colin Bradley (Joby Blanshard), Anne Tarrant (Elizabeth Weaver) and Fay Chantry (Jean Trend). Amongst the subjects covered are pollution, genetic engineering, biological weapons and culture shock. As in *Torchwood*, the characters' private lives are also dealt with in the stories: Quist is wracked with guilt over his past involvement in atomic weapons tests; the team are faced with having to cope with Wren's death after he is killed during an investigation in the first season finale 'Survival Code'; a romantic relationship develops between Quist and Tarrant; and Ridge is seen to undergo a drastic mental breakdown. The series gave rise to a spin-off feature film of the same title from Tigon British Film Productions in 1972, and was later revived for a one-off TV movie, produced by Working Title for Channel 4, in 1999.

The Ωmega Factor, created by Jack Gerson, was a BBC Scotland production transmitted over ten episodes on BBC One in 1979, and has sometimes been characterised as a British forerunner of *The X-Files*. Its subject matter is succinctly described in an article on the Wikipedia website – www.wikipedia.org – as follows:

> The series concerns a journalist called Tom Crane (James Hazeldine), who finds that he possesses psychic powers which in turn bring him to the attention of the team of scientists who comprise Department 7, a secret 'need to know only' government offshoot investigating paranormal phenomena and the potential of the human mind. The phenomena explored include hypnosis, brainwashing, extra-sensory perception, telekinesis, poltergeist[s], out-of-body experiences and spiritual possession.

There are clear parallels between the types of phenomena investigated by *The Ωmega Factor*'s Department 7 – the members of which include psychiatrist Dr Roy Martindale (John Carlisle) and physicist Dr Anne Reynolds (former *Doctor Who* companion actress Louise Jameson) – and the cases that come within Torchwood's purview. Like Torchwood, the clandestine Department 7 operates outside normal Government authority, and is known about only by the Prime Minister and some senior colleagues. *The Ωmega Factor* was also a series aimed very much at adults, and indeed incurred the wrath of self-appointed TV 'watchdog' Mary Whitehouse.

Coming right up to date, *Sea of Souls*, another post-watershed BBC Scotland drama production for BBC One, is a more direct forerunner, and indeed some of its behind-the-scenes team have gone on to work on *Doctor Who* and *Torchwood*. Created by writer David Kane and broadcast in three seasons of hour-long episodes (some two-part stories, some one-part) between 2004 and 2006, it concerns the lives and investigations of a team headed by the initially sceptical Dr Douglas Monaghan (Bill Patterson) at the Parapsychology Unit of Clyde University – a fictional academic establishment in this instance, rather than a police- or government-related one. Other members of the team include, in the first season, Megan Sharma (Archie Panjabi) and Dr Andrew Gemmill (Peter McDonald) and, in the second and third seasons, Justine McManus (Dawn Steele) and Craig Stevenson (Iain Robertson). Amongst the phenomena the team have investigated are telepathy, clairvoyance, reincarnation and voodoo magic. At the time of writing, production of a mooted fourth season is still unconfirmed.

CHAPTER ELEVEN: TORCHWOOD – THE ORGANISATION

TORCHWOOD HISTORY

The Torchwood Institute's foundation and initial purpose are clearly established in the *Doctor Who* story 'Tooth and Claw': it is set up in 1879 by Queen Victoria with the aim of protecting her realm against 'strange happenings' and visitations of an alien nature – including from the Doctor himself. Nothing more is then seen of it, however, until the events leading up to the Battle of Canary Wharf, a century and a quarter later, as depicted in the story 'Army of Ghosts'/'Doomsday'. What happened in the intervening period?

Certainly Torchwood was neither seen nor heard of in *Doctor Who* during the Doctor's many battles with would-be alien invaders of the Earth during the 1970s or 1980s. Was it effectively moribund at that point in time? Or was it so concerned to maintain its secrecy that it kept a low profile and allowed UNIT and the conventional armed forces to take the lead in combating the various threats that arose? Another possible explanation is that the time-line in which Torchwood exists did not actually come into being until the tenth Doctor became involved in the events of 'Tooth and Claw', and it would not therefore have been possible for his earlier incarnations to have encountered the organisation. Russell T Davies, however, has stated that it was not his intention to suggest such a time paradox. In the *Doctor Who Confidential* episode 'Welcome to Torchwood', he said: 'We can presume … that it's always been there, throughout the many years of Doctor Who's life when he lived on Earth working for the United Nations. It's very much like the FBI and the CIA not telling each other what they're doing. I think the key to that is that, actually, the Doctor is officially the enemy of Torchwood.' This explanation is also reflected in an exchange of dialogue between the Doctor and *Torchwood*'s Yvonne Hartman in 'Army of Ghosts'.

David Tennant added: 'The Doctor remains blissfully unaware that this place exists until, in ["Army of Ghosts"], he lands the TARDIS there and discovers that there's this huge organisation … [that] is basically harvesting and reusing alien technology that falls to Earth or is shot down … to make Britain an empire again … He thought he knew Earth, and the ways of the human race, inside out, and yet there's this whole thing going on that he knows nothing about.'

It does indeed seem possible that Torchwood could have been set up even without the Doctor's intervention in 'Tooth and Claw', as it is seen to exist also on the parallel Earth of 'Rise of the Cybermen'/'The Age of Steel' and 'Army of Ghosts'/'Doomsday', where presumably its foundation must have resulted from a different set of circumstances.

In 'Everything Changes', Jack tells Gwen: 'This is Torchwood Three. Torchwood One was London, destroyed in the Battle. Torchwood Two is an office in Glasgow; very strange man. Torchwood Three, Cardiff. Torchwood Four has kinda gone missing, but we'll find it one day.' The lack of any mention of a base in the Scottish Highlands suggests that – contrary to what some fans had assumed – the Torchwood Institute was not established in the place after which it was named, Torchwood House. This would be consistent with information given on the Torchwood House website, which states that the House was in fact shut up in 1879 (after the events of 'Tooth and Claw'), eventually purchased by the Crown in 1893 – some 14 years later – and opened to the public in

1981.[30] It is not explained how the numbers of the different Torchwood bases were allocated, but if they reflect the chronological order of establishment, this would mean that the original was actually in London – which would make sense, given that this was the capital and administrative centre of Queen Victoria's Empire. It must then have relocated to Torchwood Tower in Canary Wharf after the spatial anomaly seen in 'Army of Ghosts'/'Doomsday' was discovered in that location, 600 feet above sea level, some years later – just as Torchwood Three was built at the epicentre of the dimensional rift in Cardiff. Or perhaps the four bases (assuming Jack was not simply joking about there being a fourth one that has 'kinda gone missing') were established more or less simultaneously. Certainly it seems likely that the first three were all set up in the Victorian era, in view of the Victorian-style architecture of the secret underground railway system that links them together, as mentioned by production designer Ed Thomas and others in behind-the-scenes interviews.[31] The words 'Torchwood Three' can also be seen carved into the Victorian-style stone arch at the entrance to the Hub's boardroom, although the date of establishment beneath them remains tantalisingly unreadable in the televised episodes. To speculate even further, it could conceivably have been the events of the *Doctor Who* episode 'The Unquiet Dead', in which the rift was briefly opened in 1869 by the gas-dwelling Gelth, that alerted Queen Victoria to the anomaly in Cardiff, albeit that those events occurred a decade or so earlier; a note by Ianto on the Torchwood Institute System Interface website suggests that the events of 1869 were known to Torchwood from contemporary newspaper reports. Clearly the rift continued to give rise to 'strange happenings' after that time, even though it was supposedly closed at the end of 'The Unquiet Dead'.

But if the Cardiff branch of Torchwood was established in the Victorian era, has it been active ever since, or was it at one time effectively dormant? If a Torchwood team had been present in 2006, then surely this would have become apparent in the *Doctor Who* episode 'Boom Town', when the Doctor materialised the TARDIS beside the water tower fountain in that year – bringing Jack to Cardiff for the first time – and the rift was opened for a short while again, allowing energy to pour through? It seems likely that the Hub would have required extensive repair work in the wake of those events, which caused large fissures to open up across Roald Dahl Plass and presumably threatened it with destruction. Indeed, Jack implies in 'Everything Changes' that it was only after that point that the Hub's invisible lift was constructed. So is it, in fact, possible that Torchwood Three was revived, after a period of inactivity, as a direct result of the events of 'Boom Town'?

If there was indeed a period of inactivity, it may have begun at some point after 1952, judging from a diary extract to be found on the Torchwood Institute System Interface, which implies that Torchwood Three was active and had a cheroot-smoking leader – presumably someone other than Jack – at that time.

While this would in principle hold up as a coherent history of Torchwood Three, certain other information presented on the Torchwood Institute System Interface would suggest a more complicated scenario: Jack – looking the same age as in *Torchwood* – can be clearly

---

30 In this slightly speculative chapter, I am treating information presented on the BBC's *Doctor Who*- and *Torchwood*-related 'fictional' websites as canonical, on the basis that it is approved by the series' production teams. However, I will indicate clearly where details are drawn from such sources, for the benefit of those readers who would prefer to disregard them and rely on the TV episodes alone.

31 The tunnel entrance to this disused railway system is seen being used as a firing range in the episode 'Ghost Machine'.

glimpsed at the edge of a photograph printed in a newspaper or magazine dated 12 January 1971; another diary, which from its style and presentation would seem to have been written sometime during the 1980s, mentions someone who appears to be an 'alien catcher' and who matches Jack's description; and a Torchwood leaflet dated 1990 contains a picture of a Weevil, which, on the assumption that these creatures appear only in Cardiff, suggests that Torchwood Three must have been its source.

There is also the question of how the Hub was not discovered and made public during the construction of the Roald Dahl Plass and the water tower fountain, particularly given that the latter actually extends down through the base. This, if nothing else, would suggest that there must have been some Torchwood intervention there at the end of the 1990s, to ensure that their secrets were preserved.

But if Jack did arrive in, say, the mid-1950s when he returned to Cardiff from the far future, why did he not then contact the Doctor when the TARDIS materialised there in 2006, given that he would have known in advance that it was going to do so? Was it perhaps for fear of what might happen if he were to meet the younger version of himself who was accompanying the Doctor at that time? (The catastrophic consequences of such a meeting were seen in the *Doctor Who* episode 'Father's Day', when Rose encountered herself as a baby.) Could this in itself account for why Torchwood Three played no part in the events of 'Boom Town'?

It would seem that, following the demise of the Time Lords, time travel is now an even more hazardous and paradox-ridden business than ever before ...

TORCHWOOD ADMINISTRATION

How does the Torchwood Institute function as an organisation now, in *Torchwood*? The fact that there are a number of different branches – recently reduced by one with the destruction of Torchwood One – suggests that there must be some superior authority to which they all answer. Jack is the leader of Torchwood Three, but presumably someone must have appointed him to that position. In 'Everything Changes', he states that Torchwood is 'separate from the Government, outside the police, beyond the United Nations,' but ducks the question as to who exactly *is* in charge.

Obviously Jack's team must derive their authority from somewhere. They are able to commandeer the crime scene at the beginning of 'Everything Changes' – the police deferring to them on the basis of 'orders from above' – and are also able to displace the army in investigating the crashed meteor in 'Day One', seemingly by simply asserting that they represent Torchwood. They are actually called in by the police to examine the death of a man in a cell in 'Small Worlds', and to investigate another crime scene in 'They Keep Killing Suzie'. Normally this would suggest some form of Government backing – the security service MI5, for instance, operates with the authority of the Home Secretary and in accordance with a number of Acts of Parliament – but as Torchwood is 'separate from the Government', perhaps it is more akin to an independent agency, established by statute, with specific legal powers.

If public authorities such as the police and the army – and even, as seen in 'End of Days', Cardiff Hospital – know of Torchwood, then presumably the press and the public do too, not least because its name is boldly displayed on its buildings, vehicles and stationery. Both Mary (or the alien possessing her) in 'Greeks Bearing Gifts' and Eugene in 'Random Shoes' manage to uncover information about Jack's team; and in 'They Keep Killing Suzie', Ianto reports that as many as 2,008 people have in the past been given an amnesia-inducing drug to make them forget what they have learned about it. This suggests that what is secret about Torchwood is not its existence as an organisation but its remit and the nature of its operations. Admittedly Gwen seems not to have even heard of Torchwood at the start of 'Everything Changes', but this could just mean that its existence is unpublicised, rather than that it is secret. Some supporting evidence for this is to be found in the 'Tardisode' online trailer for 'Army of Ghosts', in which a journalist offers his editor a 'scoop' on Torchwood's history and activities, but is apprehended by Torchwood operatives before the story can be published. Again this recalls the status of MI5 and the other security services – organisations whose existence is public knowledge, but whose functions and procedures are shrouded in the strictest secrecy. In 'Greeks Bearing Gifts', Jack even challenges the Prime Minister over the fact that Torchwood operations have apparently now become part of the regular security briefings given to the Leader of the Opposition.

If Torchwood is indeed some sort of independent statutory body, then it could be funded by the Treasury out of tax revenue. There are certainly indications that its finances are limited: in 'Everything Changes', Jack alludes to costings; and in correspondence recorded on the Torchwood Institute System Interface, Ianto chides Owen for excessive and inappropriate use of a 'Torchwood credit card'. In fact, Torchwood Three seems to be somewhat less well-resourced than the lavishly-appointed Torchwood One was, notwithstanding the – no doubt expensive – IT terminals and other equipment dotted around the Hub. Jack's comment to Gwen at the end of 'Everything Changes' to the effect that Suzie's death leaves a 'vacancy' for her to fill could be taken literally to imply that there is an upper limit of five on the number of operatives in Torchwood Three. Could this be due to a limited staffing budget? Gwen does not ask about such mundane matters as salary and pension entitlement when Jack offers her the job, but presumably these would have to be worked out at some point – assuming that Gwen is not simply seconded to Torchwood from the police force on her existing terms and conditions, as could perhaps be inferred from the scene in 'Day One' where she encounters her former police colleague, PC Andy, and he appears to be under the impression that she has been transferred, or possibly promoted, to a 'special ops' unit. (She tells her boyfriend Rhys the same thing in the opening pre-titles sequence of the episode, but this could be dismissed as simply an example of her 'pulling the wool over his eyes' if it were not for this corroboration.)

Another possibility is that Torchwood funds its own operations, either in part or in full, by using the alien tech that it acquires, or 'inventions' derived from it. While the morality of this would be questionable, it could also help to explain why Torchwood One was apparently so much more affluent than Torchwood Three; perhaps Torchwood One was more willing, or eager even, to exploit the alien tech for commercial gain. Then again, the explanation may lie simply in the different status of the two branches: in a transcript of an 'online counselling session' on Ianto's area of the Torchwood Institute System Interface, he refers to Torchwood One as the 'head office' and to Torchwood Three as 'little more than a monitoring station'.

But perhaps there is a more radical answer to all these questions regarding Torchwood's administration and funding. Could it be that, in the *Doctor Who/Torchwood* universe, the Queen is not simply the symbolic figurehead that she is in our universe, but that she continues to exercise some degree of real power, alongside the Government? (Certainly there are some differences between the two universes; it is established in the *Doctor Who* story 'Battlefield' that Britain has a King rather than a Queen in the late 1990s – albeit only for a brief period of time, judging from later stories such as 'Army of Ghosts'/'Doomsday'.) If so, it could well be that Torchwood is still answerable to, and funded by, the sovereign, as presumably was the case when it was first set up by Queen Victoria back in the late 1800s. Lending some support to this theory, a report on the Torchwood Institute System Interface about the devastation wrought on

Torchwood One in the Battle of Canary Wharf states: 'The recommendation that has gone to Her Majesty for her consideration is the immediate closure of Torchwood One, together with the formation of a steering committee to fully examine future options.' This would certainly suggest that the Queen does have some significant degree of control over Torchwood's operations.

Will the definitive answers to some of these conundrums be finally revealed in *Torchwood*'s second series? It remains to be seen.

CHAPTER TWELVE: TORCHWOOD TIMELINE

In what year is *Torchwood* set? No specific date is given in the transmitted episodes, but there are a number of clues.

In *Doctor Who*, it is firmly established that 'Rose' is set in 2005 and 'Aliens of London' in 2006. The events of 'Boom Town' take place about six months after that. 'The Christmas Invasion' sees the newly-regenerated Doctor and Rose back on Earth again on Christmas Eve and Christmas Day, probably also in 2006. 'School Reunion' takes place the following year, thus probably in 2007. 'Rise of the Cybermen'/'The Age of Steel' is set on 1 February, probably in the same year – albeit in a parallel universe, where it is possible that the dates are different. 'Love & Monsters' almost certainly takes place in 2007, because Elton Pope states that two years have passed since the events seen in 'Rose'. 'Army of Ghosts'/'Doomsday', though, is more difficult to date. Pete Tyler states that three years have passed in the parallel universe since the events of 'Rise of the Cybermen'/'The Age of Steel'. Assuming that he is being precise to within, say, three months, this could mean that 'Army of Ghosts'/'Doomsday' is set sometime between the winter of 2009 and the spring of 2010. Yvonne Hartman, however, speaks of the destruction of the Sycorax spaceship, as depicted in 'The Christmas Invasion', as having occurred 'on Christmas Day', which would appear to mean the previous Christmas Day; unless the 'Christmas Day' of the Sycorax's attack, as an event of huge global significance, has now entered common parlance in the same way as, say, '9/11', making it unnecessary to specify the year. Jackie Tyler, meanwhile, states that she is 40 years old, whereas her alternative universe counterpart would by this point have been 43 (had she not been converted into a Cyberman), given that in 'Rise of the Cybermen'/ 'The Age of Steel' she was seen celebrating her fortieth birthday (and trying to pass it off as her thirty-ninth!) The weight of evidence would therefore seem to suggest that the dates in the parallel universe do not correspond directly to those in the *Doctor Who*/*Torchwood* universe, and that 'Army of Ghosts'/'Doomsday' is probably set just a few months after 'Love & Monsters', in the autumn of 2007.

In 'Everything Changes', Jack refers to the Sycorax spaceship hovering over London on Christmas Day, although – like Yvonne Hartman – he does not specifically say that it was the previous Christmas Day. He also mentions the Battle of Canary Wharf, as depicted in 'Army of Ghosts'/'Doomsday'. From this it is possible to conclude that 'Everything Changes' is probably set toward the end of 2007. It is likely to be no earlier than the last week of September, judging from the fact that it is completely dark outside when a clock in the fake tourist information office at the Hub's front entrance gives the time as 8.35 pm – unless, of course, the clock has been wrongly set.

'Cyberwoman' would seem to take place not long after 'Army of Ghosts'/'Doomsday', given the direct links it has to that story, which again would suggest a probable late 2007 or early 2008 dating.

In 'Ghost Machine', Owen is seen referring to a 2006 Cardiff telephone directory, but this could be just an out-of-date edition that happens to have been kept in the Hub. More persuasive is the fact that 66 years are said to have elapsed since 1941, which reinforces the late 2007 or early 2008 dating.

The waters are somewhat muddied, however, in 'Greeks Bearing Gifts'. This opens with a sequence set in 1812, which ends with a soldier being killed. The man's long-buried skeleton is later examined by the Torchwood team, and Toshiko states that it has been in the ground for 196 years and 11 or 11-and-a-half months. This would seem to imply that the episode is set sometime between the very end of 2008 and the very end of 2009. Does this mean that 'Army of Ghosts'/'Doomsday' really was set in the winter of 2009 after all? Given what has been established previously, it would seem more likely that there is an error in Toshiko's calculation. She is later said to have joined Torchwood three years earlier, which would be around 2004 if the date is now 2007 – in which case she would already have been a Torchwood operative (presumably, like Ianto, assigned to Torchwood One at that point) when she was called in to examine what appeared to be an extraterrestrial creature in 'Aliens of London' – or around 2006 if the date is now 2009 – in which case her assignment in 'Aliens of London' could have pre-dated (and perhaps led on to) her job with Torchwood.

In 'They Keep Killing Suzie', a period of three months is said to have passed since the events of 'Everything Changes'. The most likely date for this episode is therefore, once again, late 2007 or early 2008, although – on the alternative theory – it could possibly be early 2010.

In 'Random Shoes', the character Eugene Jones dies shortly after selling his alien eye in an eBay auction. The start date of this auction, as shown in a graphic recorded on the Torchwood Institute System Interface website, is '14 Oct 06'. The graphic looks nothing like the eBay page format of 2006, however, so it seems likely that it follows some future redesign, and that the information given is erroneous due to some sort of system glitch. Support for this theory is to be found in the fact that the line of text immediately below reads 'Starting bid: £75.00', whereas it is clearly established in the episode that the actual starting bid was £2.50. There is also an obvious spelling mistake on the page – 'Learn how your [sic] are protected' – and the category in which the item is said to be listed – 'Computing > Software > Graphics/Multimedia > Digital Photo Imaging' – seems completely inappropriate, although this could have been simply a mistake on Eugene's part when he submitted the listing. At any rate, none of these questionable details is seen on screen in the episode itself – although the listing page format is the same, and various other aspects of auction are likewise inconsistent with the way that eBay worked as of 2006 – so it seems safe to discount them. Eugene states that his father left the family on the evening after the final of the Interschool Maths Competition 1992, and later implies that this event took place 14 years earlier, which would also be consistent with a 2006 dating. It is however possible that the final of the 1992 competition was delayed and actually took place in 1993, or – perhaps more likely – that the 14 year interval mentioned is only approximate. If the final took place around, say, the end of December 1992 and 'Random Shoes' was set around the beginning of December 2007, then the period between the two would indeed be just less than 15 years. A flyer seen in the episode refers to a lecture taking place on 'Thursday 27th', with no month or year given. This would on first consideration seem to suggest an April 2006, July 2006, September 2007, December 2007, March 2008, November 2008 or August 2009 dating. However, it has long been established that dates in the *Doctor Who*/*Torchwood* universe do not fall on the same days of the week as in ours[32] – and further solid evidence of this is presented in 'Captain Jack Harkness', in the form of a poster indicating that 20 January 1941 is a Saturday, whereas in our universe it was a Monday – so this is actually of no real assistance.

In 'Out of Time', pilot Diane Holmes states that she and her two passengers took off on 18 December 1953. No date is given on screen for their arrival in modern-day Cardiff, but it is clearly just before Christmas. When Owen and Diane visit the airfield to discuss booking a flying lesson for Diane, the date 'Friday the 29th' is mentioned, presumably meaning 29

32 The first clear indication of this came as early as in 'The War Machines' (1966), when the date of 'C-Day' was clearly stated as Monday 16 July 1966. In our universe, 16 July 1966 fell not on a Monday but on a Saturday.

December, or just possibly 29 January if the flying school is booked up a long way in advance. In our universe, 29 December falls on a Friday in 2006, and 29 January falls on a Friday in 2010, but again this is probably not the case in the *Doctor Who/Torchwood* universe. A number of documents on the Torchwood Institute System Interface website strongly suggest that it is in fact December 2007. In particular, there is an air traffic control report dated 18 December 2007 about a plane suddenly appearing on the radar as if from nowhere. Although not explicitly stated, it seems likely that this is Holmes's plane, the Sky Gypsy.[33] The reliability of the Torchwood filing system is again called into question, however, as two vintage newspaper reports relating to the disappearance of the plane, which were clearly published in December 1953, are rubber stamped with the dates 21 December 1963 and 26 December 1963 respectively – probably an error on the part of whichever Torchwood clerk entered them into the records back in 1953.

Leaving aside its rather haphazard filing, the same website gives the best indication yet of a specific dating for *Torchwood* in its records relating to two of the characters featured in 'Combat': a short newspaper notice of the death of Dan Hodges; and an obituary, by his former business partner Ben Frost, of Mark Lynch. These both give the year of death as 2007.[34] Bearing in mind that the preceding episode, 'Out of Time', takes place around Christmas time, this suggests that 'Combat' is probably set at the very end of December 2007.

In the novel *Border Princes*, 1978 is stated to be 29 years earlier, and 1899 to be 108 years earlier, both also supporting a 2007 dating.

The best conclusion to be drawn from all this seems to be that – although there is a certain amount of contradictory evidence – the events of the first series of *Torchwood* most probably take place over a period of four months or so between about late September 2007 ('Everything Changes') and about January 2008 ('Captain Jack Harkness'/'End of Days').

---

33 If 29 December is a Friday then, in our universe, 'Thursday 27th' – the date seen on the flyer in 'Random Shoes' – would have to be in either June or July. As this seems unlikely – unless, perhaps, the *Torchwood* episodes are screened in a different order than the events within them occur – it suggests that the months in the *Doctor Who/Torchwood* universe actually have different numbers of days than in ours, which would help to account for the many discrepancies seen over the years.

34 Reportedly, when these documents first appeared on the website, the year of death was given as 2006, but this was quickly changed.

PART FOUR: CHARACTER PROFILES

CHAPTER THIRTEEN: MAIN CHARACTERS

CAPTAIN JACK HARKNESS (JOHN BARROWMAN)

Captain Jack is first seen in the 2005 *Doctor Who* story 'The Empty Child'/'The Doctor Dances'. He is encountered by the ninth Doctor and Rose in London in 1941 – the time of the Blitz – where he has assumed the guise of an American flight officer voluntarily attached to the Royal Air Force's 133 Squadron. It soon transpires that he is a one-time human Time Agent from the 51st Century, who has had a two year period of his memory wiped by the Agency and whose motivations are initially far from altruistic.

John Barrowman gave the following description of the character in a 2005 press release from the BBC: 'He's a rogue Time Agent, and he knows he's done something in his past and he's not sure what it is or whether it is good or bad, because his memory has been erased. But he's also an intergalactic conman, and he starts off by trying to con the Doctor and Rose. He tries to sell them something in order to get money, because that's what he does. He has conned a lot of people in the past. His method is to sell people things that are not what he says they are – and then once he has got the money, he runs.'

During the course of his introductory adventure, Jack comes to realise the error of his ways, and he ends 'The Doctor Dances' as a hero when he proves willing to sacrifice his own life to stop a German bomb from detonating at the site of the action. Jack in turn is rescued by the Doctor and becomes a member of the TARDIS crew. His journeys in the Doctor's ship include visits to Cardiff in the 21st Century, as seen in the episode 'Boom Town'; to Raxacoricofallapatorius (home world of the Slitheen); to Kyoto, Japan in the 14th Century; and ultimately to Satellite 5 in the year 200,100, as seen in 'Bad Wolf'/'The Parting of the Ways', where he is killed in a battle against the Daleks, only to be resurrected by Rose, who has temporarily acquired godlike powers.

When the Doctor and Rose depart at the end of 'The Parting of the Ways', Jack is left behind, apparently the only person to have survived on Satellite 5. In the subsequent *Children in Need* special, broadcast on 18 November 2005, the newly-regenerated tenth Doctor and Rose both appear to be aware that Jack is still alive, and the Doctor says that he will be busy 'rebuilding the Earth' after the destruction wreaked on it by the Daleks. It is possible, though, that the Doctor really thinks that Jack is dead and is simply keeping this unpleasant fact from Rose, who may have no memory of what occurred between when she absorbed the time vortex and when the Doctor drew it out of her.

Jack was created by Russell T Davies, who in his brief format document for the new *Doctor Who* series initially named him 'Captain Jax' and noted: '[He] is revealed to be a futuristic soldier from another world ... Out of his English disguise, Jax is everything the Doctor's companion should be – or so it seems to Rose. Lively, funny, sexy and arrogant, he struts about, armed to the teeth with laser-guns, bandying interstellar information with the Doctor.'

Davies decided upon the surname 'Harkness' at a later date. It was one that he had used before for characters in his TV series (specifically *The Grand* and *Century Falls*), and was originally taken from the witch Agatha Harkness created by Marvel Comics' supremo Stan Lee and artist Jack Kirby for the *Fantastic Four* comic book series in 1970.

When it came to finding an actor to play the role, the choice of Barrowman was an easy one to make, as casting director Andy Pryor explained in an interview in Issue 376 of *Doctor Who Magazine*: 'The idea of that character just presented this most startling possibility of John, who, for me, is the perfect person for the role. He's incredibly contemporary in many ways, but still has that matinee idol look, and delivery, and he's ironic and self-aware enough to play around with that, and turn that on its head. I knew that he had the wit to pull that off. It must have been one of the easiest decisions in the history of casting, let alone [*Doctor Who*], because he came into the audition and charmed the pants off us all, made us howl with laughter, and read the scenes brilliantly. Happily enough, that afternoon we had a meeting with [Head of Drama] Jane Tranter, who, within five minutes of watching John's audition tape, was like, "Wow! Yes! Absolutely!"'

Although the character as eventually seen on screen matched Davies's initial description fairly well, Barrowman noted in a 2005 interview by Adam McGechan for Issue 72 of the New Zealand-published *Doctor Who* fanzine *TSV* that he had had a lot of influence in the way the part was developed: 'The first episode was already written, but they asked me, "What do you want to do?" I didn't want [Jack] to be an asshole; I wanted him to be likeable. But I wanted him to first come off with this bad impression. I'm glad that when people saw that episode, everyone … said, "Oh, we don't like him!" It was great, because I didn't want them to like him right off at the beginning! They thought he was too full-on and too devious. But he had a purpose and he was trying to get something, and he was trying to achieve something, and in order to do that, he had to be full-on. And then, as the episodes went on, they were like, "Yeah, we kinda like him, with his quirkiness," which is exactly what I wanted to add in. So they allowed me to do that, and I played with it a lot.'

Elements of Barrowman's own personality and performance were then picked up by Davies and reflected in the writing of the subsequent episodes of the 2005 *Doctor Who* series.

Captain Jack was thus firmly established as a bold, fearless, devil-may-care hero. As Davies put it in the 'Welcome to Torchwood' episode of the *Doctor Who Confidential* documentary series: 'He is one of those sort of marvellous characters it's lovely to write, because he'd say absolutely anything in any situation … Captain Jack absolutely does not care.'

In the same programme, Steven Moffat, writer of 'The Empty Child'/'The Doctor Dances', added: 'Captain Jack is sort of everything the Doctor isn't. He's the space hero that the Doctor isn't. He's glamorous; he's military; he's almost entirely driven by his libido. He's capable of being sexually attracted to anything. But it's not that he's bisexual, or heterosexual, or pansexual: it's that he wouldn't understand what any of those things meant. There are other life-forms out there and there are dating opportunities, and that's all that he understands. It doesn't occur to him, probably, that Rose Tyler, and probably the Doctor himself, are a bit more limited in their choice of companion for dinner. I don't think he's noticed. I think he just thinks, "Well, it's warm, it's got a pulse; does it have a phone number?"'

Quoted in a BBC press release of 13 October 2006, Barrowman went even further, quipping: 'It doesn't have to have a pulse for Jack to fancy it. And if it's got a zip code, he'll sleep with it.'

'There are various secrets about his life yet to come out,' noted Davies in *Doctor Who Confidential*. 'Various things that have happened to him off-screen since we saw him in *Doctor Who* that have yet to be fully explained, that we are actually going to take a long time to explain as well. So there's a lot more of Captain Jack's story still to come.'

Speaking on stage at the London Film and Comic Convention on 2 July 2006, Barrowman gave a few hints as to what might be revealed in *Torchwood*. Referring to Captain Jack's reaction on being left behind by the ninth Doctor and Rose at the end of 'The Parting of the Ways', he said: 'Two people that you've … changed yourself for and … you know, become a better person for, and they turn around and they ditch ya! … So, yeah, Jack's a bit angry. And also, the Doctor does not believe in bringing people back to life. So there's going to be a whole conflict thing when we meet again. Plus I don't know what [the Doctor] looks like [following his regeneration] ... You've got to remember that – Jack doesn't know what he looks like.'

In response to other questions from the audience, Barrowman added:

'The thing about playing Jack is I'm a hero. How many times in your everyday life do you get to be a hero to somebody? I'm a hero to a lot of young people and a lot of middle-aged people and a lot of older people, [or] Jack is, and that's great, because I've created Jack. I was given the script and the dialogue, but I've made him this British iconic hero, which I think is fantastic ...

'There's a lot of stuff in *Torchwood* that you will be told about Jack by the other characters. Jack becomes a lot darker. He still has a good sense of humour, and he's still very witty, very dry, very cutting with his dialogue, but he does become a bit darker, a bit more mysterious, because he doesn't want to give himself away right off the bat.'

Contrasting Torchwood Three – Captain Jack's team – with Torchwood One – the Torchwood group seen in the 2006 *Doctor Who* story 'Army of Ghosts'/'Doomsday' – Barrowman told *SFX* magazine, in an interview previewed on their website on 18 October 2006: 'Remember what Torchwood One did. They collected anything that was found, and we have remnants of that [stored in the Hub] – although Torchwood One disappeared, it no longer exists, destroyed in the Battle of Canary Wharf. They became imperialistic. But we're not like that. Jack is for the greater good ... Jack is obviously the hero, the glue that keeps Torchwood together, and the decision maker.'

In his interview for the BBC's 13 October 2006 press release, Barrowman elaborated further on the character's situation in *Torchwood*:

'Jack's not a time traveller, he's a Time Agent, and he can only travel through time with the assistance of someone like the Doctor. Now, Cardiff has this rift in it, and so it's one of the places the TARDIS is likely to return to, so Jack is just waiting. He never leaves, he never sleeps.

'Jack gets on with everyone in Torchwood, but the only person who knows anything about him is Gwen. Gwen comes in and she brings something new to the team – she brings heart. And, for some reason, Jack starts to reveal things to her.

'Every now and then there are major in-house battles. There are always tensions bubbling away, because they're facing life-or-death situations every day. Sometimes Jack gets very angry because the team don't understand why he's doing what he's doing. But Jack has seen Earth's future and he knows that the 21st Century is when it all changes – and they've got to be ready.'

At the outset of *Torchwood*, 'Everything Changes' brings a major new revelation about Jack: that, following his resurrection in 'The Parting of the Ways', he now cannot die. Small wonder that he is so determined to meet up with the Doctor again, to find out what has caused this. (It appears that he does not know exactly how he came to be resurrected after his extermination by the Daleks.)

Scarcely less remarkable than Jack's immortality is the fact that he was once pregnant – or so he says in 'Everything Changes', although it is possible that he is joking. His taste buds are sufficiently sensitive to enable him to detect traces of the hormone oestrogen as a pollutant in Cardiff's rain. Also in this episode, the viewer sees for the first time that Jack's drink of choice is water[35] – although he does resort to alcohol on a couple of occasions later in the series, after

35 In a section of dialogue omitted from the transmitted episode, but included in a deleted scene viewable on the series' first DVD release, Jack tells Gwen that he needs to keep hydrated as he may need to travel home 'at any moment'. Gwen also recalls being told this by Jack in the *Torchwood* original novel *Another Life*.

particularly harrowing experiences.

In 'Day One', Jack is seen to be able to transfer vital energy to people by kissing them, causing them to glow in the process. When the possessed Carys says that she wants to 'feel alive' he comments: 'I've got a surplus of "alive". I'm giving it away.' This is presumably another after-effect of his resurrection in 'The Parting of the Ways', and recalls the way in which the Doctor saved Rose's life in the same episode by drawing the time vortex energy out of her with a kiss.

In the following episode, 'Ghost Machine', Jack tells Gwen that he doesn't sleep – although whether he means that he is physically incapable of doing so or that he simply chooses not to or is prevented from doing so in some way is a moot point. Subsequently, in 'Small Worlds', he appears to be attempting to sleep at one point, but experiences a nightmare-like flashback to a time when he witnessed the deaths of a group of soldiers on a train in Lahore, India, in 1909.

In 'Cyberwoman', it becomes clear that although Jack cannot die, he can sustain injuries short of death, as he is left with a bruised lip at the end of the episode. There are also hints that his past may hold some even darker secrets, as Ianto says to him: 'You like to think you're a hero, but you're the biggest monster of all.'

In 'Small Worlds', the full complexity of Jack's personal timeline becomes apparent. Judging from a letter dated January 1908 recorded on the Torchwood Institute System Interface website, his experiences in Lahore occurred during the period before he met the Doctor, when he was operating as a con artist; the letter refers to a plot to steal a consignment of diamonds from a diamond mine. Intriguingly, however, the letter begins 'Hey boss', suggesting that Jack was working for someone else at that time. Also to be found on the same website are three letters sent to Jack by his one-time lover Estelle. The first of these is dated 18 February 1944 and suggests that Estelle has only recently parted company with Jack. This is curious, given that Jack left Earth with the Doctor and Rose in 1941. The second letter, in which Estelle indicates that she has recently received a short note from Jack, is strangely dated '18th June 1944?', but the question-mark probably indicates nothing more than that Estelle failed to keep track of the exact date while she was – as the letters confirm – working as a Land Girl in the countryside during that period of the War. To add to the mystery, the website identifies the correspondence as 'Letters from Estelle Cole, 1942'. This however is doubtless simply a mislabelling – particularly given that the third letter is a much later one, dated 18 August 2004, in which Estelle says that she thinks she has glimpsed Jack, looking the same as he did during the War, 'outside a pound shop in Newport multistory [sic]'. One possible way of making sense of these dates is to assume that when Jack returned to Earth from the year 200,100, after the events of 'Bad Wolf'/'The Parting of the Ways', it was to a time before 1944, which would mean that he was immortal at the point when he first met Estelle 'in London, at the Astoria Ballroom, a few weeks before Christmas' – casting a rather different light on the vow they apparently once made to be with each other until they died. This was certainly writer Peter J Hammond's belief, as he commented in the 'Away with the Fairies' episode of *Torchwood Declassified*: 'I think she never knew that he did live forever, and her idea that they would grow old and die together was a lie on his part, but a very sad lie. And then taking her in his arms when she's an old lady, and dead, and he wasn't there for her, I think is a very moving moment. And he's left alone.'

In 'Countrycide', there is further evidence of a very dark aspect to Jack's past when he tells a wounded man: 'A long time ago, I was pretty good at torture … I had quite a reputation as the go-to guy. My job demanded it at the time, you see.' It is, though, possible that he is lying about this, or at least exaggerating, simply in order to scare the man into telling him what he needs to know.

Toshiko discovers in 'Greeks Bearing Gifts' that she is unable to read Jack's thoughts with the aid of the telepathy-inducing pendant she has acquired from her lover Mary (who is an alien in human form), and tells him: 'It was like you were … dead.' And when Mary asks him 'What are you?', he can only reply 'I don't know.'

In 'Out of Time', Jack tells John, a man from 1953 who has been unwillingly transported to 21st Century Cardiff: 'I was born in the future, lived in your past. My time has gone too.' The full extent of his discontent with his situation also becomes apparent here where he describes himself as 'a man … out of his time, alone and scared.' Also in this episode, a further aspect of Jack's invulnerability is revealed when he appears completely unaffected by poisonous car exhaust fumes that have a lethal effect on John.

'Combat' confirms that, as seen in 'Cyberwoman', Jack can sustain painful injuries short of death. Here, he is clawed by a Weevil, and left with bloody scratch marks across his chest.

In 'Captain Jack Harkness', when he finds himself back in 1941, Jack comes face-to-face with the American officer whose identity he adopted – confirming that his *real* name has yet to be revealed. The date is Saturday 20 January, and Jack tells Toshiko that his namesake is due to die in action the following day. He says: 'I took his name, falsified his records, so it seemed he was still alive.' This creates a small mystery of its own, as in 'Everything Changes', Gwen's police colleague Yvonne tells her that the only Captain Jack Harkness mentioned in official sources: '… disappeared, vanished off the records, presumed dead … [in] 1941, at the height of the Blitz; on the morning of January 21st 1941, Captain Jack Harkness failed to report for duty.' If Jack altered the records to remove details of his namesake's death in action, why did he not go further and indicate that he had transferred to a new posting, rather than simply leave it to be assumed that he had disappeared? Wouldn't his apparent failure to report for duty in Cardiff – which hardly supports the assertion that 'it seemed he was still alive' – have caused problems for him when he started to serve in London later the same year, before beginning his travels in the TARDIS?[36] And given that he did serve in London later in 1941, why are no details of this uncovered when Yvonne carries out her check? How, too, can all this be reconciled with the fact that he also apparently served in London in late 1943 and early 1944, when – according to the letters on the Torchwood Institute System Interface – he first met Estelle Cole from 'Small Worlds'?

It is possible that further light will be shed on this period of Jack's life in future episodes. For the time being, though, the only semi-plausible explanation that presents itself is that, sometime after the original Jack's service records were changed by *Torchwood*'s Jack, they were changed again by someone else. If so, could that 'someone else' have been the sinister Bilis Manger, in furtherance of his plot against the Torchwood team in 'Captain Jack Harkness'/'End of Days'? That might also explain why two contemporary documents preserved on the Torchwood Institute System Interface strangely suggest an incorrect date for the original Jack's death in action. A telegram informing Jack's mother – 'Mrs E Harkness' – of his heroic demise,

36 The Doctor notes in 'The Empty Child'/'The Doctor Dances' that the year is 1941, but no precise date is given. The Blitz attacks on London effectively ended on 10 May 1941, and the characters in the story do not seem to be dressed for winter weather, so the most likely dating is April or early May 1941. It has been previously suggested by some fans that the story must take place later in the year, because the RAF's 133 Squadron, to which Captain Jack is attached, was not actually formed until August 1941. However, 'Captain Jack Harkness' definitively confirms that – in the *Doctor Who*/*Torchwood* universe, unlike in ours – the Squadron was in existence as early as January 1941.

which it says occurred 'yesterday', is date-stamped 5 January 1941, while a newspaper report indicating that he was killed 'last week', is dated 7 January 1941. Could these inaccurate accounts have been planted by Bilis for some reason? Maybe so.

'Captain Jack Harkness' also sees Jack giving an intriguing hint about his early life, presumably in the 51st Century, when he tells his namesake that as a boy he went to war against 'the worst possible creatures you can imagine'. Could this be a reference to the Daleks, perhaps, given that he clearly knows of them and even recognises their ships when he sees them in 'Bad Wolf'?

Rounding off the first series of *Torchwood*, 'End of Days' sees Jack's immortality put to the ultimate test as he faces off against the ferocious Abaddon – and brings about the beast's destruction when it is overwhelmed by his surfeit of life-force. Jack is left comatose – in fact, seemingly dead – for a number of days, but is ultimately revived by, fittingly, a kiss from Gwen. This comes just in time for him to vanish from the Hub after a mysterious wheezing, groaning sound is heard …

It seems that, where Jack is concerned, the more the viewer learns about him, the more mysterious he becomes. 'You can peel away the layers of Jack's enigma,' noted Catherine Tregenna, writer of 'Out of Time' and 'Captain Jack Harkness', in an interview for *Starburst* Issue 345, dated January 2007, 'but he is not defined. There's no bible lying around with him all worked out, and that is really creative. Russell has very strong ideas about him that we might not know – if fact, Russell is like Captain Jack in a way – but it makes him a very intriguing presence.'

GWEN COOPER (EVE MYLES)

In an early interview in the *Western Mail*, Eve Myles succinctly described the character of Gwen Cooper: 'Gwen starts off as a police officer in Cardiff and then gets involved in the Torchwood team. She's a very down-to-earth girl, kind and generous, but extremely ambitious, feisty, intelligent and witty. But she's also very human – she's really the girl next door. Because I'm playing her, I put a lot of me into it and I take a lot of my own characteristics.'

Russell T Davies, in the *Doctor Who Confidential* episode 'Welcome to Torchwood', commented: 'Gwen Cooper is an ordinary Cardiff policewoman, with an ordinary life, ordinary boyfriend, ordinary flat, who comes across extraordinary events happening. She just looks at a situation and thinks further, and thinks around it, and takes action. She's very independent, as well. Where her bosses would be saying, "No, don't," she will cross that line and say, "I'm going to investigate further." So she's destined to join this team!'

'The audience will see Torchwood through Gwen's eyes,' explained Myles in an interview for a BBC press release of 18 October 2006. 'She introduces the world into Torchwood and, for the first time, life in Torchwood is explained … and then Jack introduces me to the Weevil. It's almost like the audience is trying to take it all in and so is Gwen …

'The thing with Gwen, which is a running thread with her all the way through, is that she's incredibly inquisitive, and if she needs to get to the bottom of something, she will do it, she will always cross that safety barrier, she'll always go further.

'Her skill is bringing Torchwood back from thinking that the human race and everyday life [are] about numbers, statistics and alien technology, what we can find, what we can scavenge, how we can use it to protect the human race. Gwen brings them back home.

'There's a connection made straight away with Gwen and Jack, and it's Jack who invites her into Torchwood, because he takes a liking to her. They just connect very well. It's almost instinctive, and you think these guys could work really well together.

'Gwen is incredibly honest and trustworthy and she will always do what she thinks is right. She will always question Jack. In her eyes, Jack isn't always right, and that is what he loves about her, that she will always question him and push him. Nobody ever challenges him, and he thinks it's a great thing for [him], because he needs somebody like that by his side, to tell him when he's right and when he's wrong, and how he should work in Cardiff in [2007].'

The brief character profile published on the *Torchwood* official website describes Gwen as 'passionate and determined' and states that she would be 'the first (sometimes only) Torchwood member to see the human side to any situation.'

Gwen is, in short, the 'heart' of the Torchwood team, who empathises strongly – and sometimes goes further than that. As Myles commented to *Radio Times*: 'Gwen's in a long-term relationship, but she can't help herself. The team are all incredibly individual and talented – she finds them all very sexy. It's a very sexy world.'

It is to Jack himself that Gwen is initially attracted. There seems, though, to be a slight cooling of their friendship after the events of 'Small Worlds', and it is to Owen that she turns in the wake of the horrendous experience she goes through in 'Countrycide'.

'[Gwen] starts to have an affair,' noted Davies in an article in *The Times*'s magazine *The Knowledge*, published on 21 October 2006. 'She has a lovely boyfriend at home, [but] she has this extraordinary job at Torchwood that she can't talk about. She starts to have this affair with someone at work because it's the only way she can share what's going on. It's a very human situation. I'm very pleased with that storyline, because it's told in a very adult manner. There are powerful scenes of lust and anger and hurt and the joy you get out of the initial stages of having an affair.'

'She's having to live two separate lives,' agreed Myles in an interview published on the *SFX* magazine website on 23 October 2006. 'It's kind of like Clark Kent and Superman. She's got a boyfriend at home she's been with for years and years and years, and then she's got a group of alien investigators she works with, and he knows nothing about it. Y'know, he thinks I work for special ops – aka filing! – for South Wales Police, whereas I'm chasing all sorts all over countryside, cities, towns. And she changes, she evolves throughout the entire thing. That's what's so interesting about her. It's a new world for her and she's having to change with this new world; she's having to keep up with it. She's sometimes having to take over, and … she's riding a different wave every single day, and she's learning every day, she's trying to compromise every day. So it's constantly hard for her, but she wouldn't change it for the world; it's what she does.'

By the time of 'Random Shoes', things seem to have soured somewhat between Gwen and Owen, and they indulge in a certain amount of sniping and arguing. Matters really come to a head, though, in 'Combat', when she learns that he has had a brief relationship with Diane Holmes in the preceding episode, 'Out of Time', and they agree to call off their affair.

Gwen has by this point become more assimilated into the murky world of Torchwood. She tells her boyfriend, Rhys, about her affair with Owen, but only because she needs to assuage her conscience by hearing him say that he forgives her, and not without first slipping him an amnesia-inducing drug so that he will have no memory of her confession. Rhys lapses into a drugged sleep without giving her the forgiveness she craves, and she is left distraught.

It is nevertheless clear that Gwen is still very much in love with Rhys, and in 'End of Days' it is her feelings for him that enable the sinister Bilis Manger to manipulate her, along with the rest of his team, into betraying Jack and opening the rift. When disaster is averted, though, it is Gwen who sits with the seemingly-dead Jack and ultimately revives him with a kiss.

TOSHIKO SATO (NAOKO MORI)

Toshiko 'Tosh' Sato is first seen in the Series One *Doctor Who* episode 'Aliens of London', where she is credited as 'Doctor Sato' and entrusted with the task of examining what is believed to be an alien creature – but turns out to be a pig augmented with advanced technology.

In *Torchwood*, viewers learn that she is actually a brilliant expert in computers, surveillance equipment and all types of gadgetry, and is dedicated to her work on Captain Jack's team. She is intense and driven, and doesn't suffer fools gladly. 'It's the perfect job for Tosh,' noted Naoko Mori in an interview published in a BBC press release of 3 November 2006. 'She's at the cutting edge of technology, and with Torchwood, she's always coming across new things. She loves the challenge of trying to work things out.'

'[She is] sharp-witted,' agreed Chris Chibnall in an interview for Issue 342 of *Starburst*, 'but a little more reserved than the other Torchwood members. That reserve soon gets stripped away, mind ...'

'She seems to be a bit square and quiet,' acknowledged Mori in her press release interview, 'but she's actually just a very private person. She's more of a thinker than a feeler, but that doesn't mean she doesn't feel; she just doesn't share it. She keeps her private life private, and work is work. But work is the biggest thing – she loves her job, as everyone in the team does.

'It's like a hothouse [environment]. They're all cooped up in the Hub but also in this secretive, underground world that they can't share with anyone else outside. So it's very intense and intimate.'

Tosh initially has a crush on Torchwood medic Owen Harper, but this is not reciprocated.

In 'Greeks Bearing Gifts', details of her background, initially made public in the 3 November press release, are confirmed when the alien-possessed Mary recounts what she has found out about her, supposedly from the internet: 'Born in London, 1975, moved to Osaka when you were two, then back to the UK in 1986. Parents in the RAF. Grandfather worked at Bletchley Park.[37] Very impressive. University, blah, blah. Snapped up to Government science think-tank when you were 20. Recruited to Torchwood three years ago.' Tosh's loneliness causes her to embark upon an ill-fated relationship with Mary, which ends when the latter turns out to be a ruthless killer and is sent into the heart of the sun by Jack. This affair leaves Tosh distraught, but she picks herself up and returns to her work, which remains her principal focus.

OWEN HARPER (BURN GORMAN)

In his interview for Issue 342 of *Starburst*, Chris Chibnall outlined the character of the London-born Dr Owen Harper as follows: 'Owen's got a medical background – the autopsy room in Torchwood is his domain ... He brings an edge, an energy and a sense of mischief to the team. He looks great in a white coat – and Owen's black leather jacket.' In addition to these qualities, Owen is headstrong, insolent and sometimes thoughtless, and likes to live the fast life. He has an impressive intellect, but is also aware of this fact, and tends to believe that he is unquestionably right in whatever approach he takes to a problem. This arrogant streak can often lead him into trouble. He is a chancer – or, as Russell T Davies has put it, 'a geezer' – and a cynic.

'Owen has a temper and an attitude,' noted Burn Gorman in an interview for the 21-27 October 2006 edition of *Radio Times*. 'He's incredibly inappropriate. But he's also bloody hard-working and has an open mind. And he's loyal to the last.'

37 Bletchley Park was a secret code-breaking establishment in the Second World War.

In an interview released by the BBC press office on 24 October 2006, Gorman commented in greater depth on Owen's role and character:

'Owen has got the best job in the world. He is a quick-witted lad who is a trained doctor who worked in Cardiff A&E. One day, he was headhunted by a 21st Century alien crime-fighting team as a medic. How do you say no to that? You get a gun, you get to drive fast cars and you get to chase aliens. Owen is living the dream, without a doubt.

'He has a great amount of admiration for Captain Jack, who is, without doubt, the boss. In a sense, in this strange world that Owen has been brought into, he looks up to Jack as a beacon of guidance. If you can imagine some of the stuff he is seeing ... it would blow your mind. But Jack, he's somebody who you just know tells the truth, no messing about. So Owen looks up to Jack as a mentor, if not as an uncle figure.

'He has to keep an eye on alien life forms, whether that be plants or the aliens that come in to Torchwood or are held at Torchwood in one way or another. Owen investigates what these alien life forms, and the technology they bring with them, can add to our life in the 21st Century ...

'He's also a sensible lad; he's not an idiot. If he likes someone, he's going to go for it. But, unfortunately, he's not averse to breaking the rules in terms of making advances on people who have long-term partners. He's just living for the moment.

'Owen never talks about his family – you suspect that there are skeletons in the closet and that this job allows him, in many ways, to vent his frustration and anger. There is a certain loneliness that emanates from Captain Jack, but also from Owen. Really, you're on your own.'

At the end of 'Countrycide', Owen begins a relationship with Gwen that continues over the next few episodes. It is clear, though, that the sexual aspect of this is what matters to him, and that he feels no deeper connection with his colleague. It is not until 'Out of Time' that he finds himself falling in love, not with Gwen but with the beautiful, intelligent and highly independent Diane Holmes, a famous aviator from the 1950s who has fallen through the rift and ended up in modern-day Cardiff. When Diane leaves him at the end of the episode to try to get back through the rift, Owen is revealed to have a more vulnerable side. Shorn of his usual cockiness, he is seen to be – as scriptwriter Catherine Tregenna puts it in the 'Time Flies' episode of *Torchwood Declassified* – 'a frightened boy.'

In 'Greeks Bearing Gifts', Owen uses the Hub's computer to access details of a body – later revealed to be one of the alien-possessed Mary's victims – that he examined while he was a doctor at Cardiff Hospital. The date of the case is given as September 2001, and he later recalls in his thoughts that he had been qualified for only six months at that point, suggesting that he qualified around March 2001.[38]

Following on from the events of 'Out of Time', Owen is in a very dark emotional place in 'Combat', and he ultimately attempts suicide by allowing himself to be attacked by a Weevil. He is saved by Jack, but could hardly be described as grateful. In 'End of Days', his open defiance of Jack leads to him being – to his considerable distress – dismissed from Torchwood. However, desperate to be reunited with Diane, and having been tricked into believing that this

38 It is unclear exactly when Owen was recruited to Torchwood. A short exchange of dialogue edited out of 'Everything Changes' before transmission, but included in the deleted scenes package on the series' first DVD release, suggests that it must have been at around the same time as, or more likely later than, Toshiko, as she recalls that he wept on first joining; although he claims that he was actually suffering from hay fever. This would imply that he has been with the organisation for less than three years.

can be achieved by the opening of the rift, he returns to the Hub and shoots Jack down, thinking that he has killed him. The two men are ultimately reconciled when Jack revives at the end of the story and tells Owen that he forgives him. Owen thus regains his place as a member of the Torchwood team.

The *Torchwood* novel *Slow Decay* reveals that Owen hails from Plaistow in London's East End; he decided to train as a doctor after his father died suddenly at home one day from an aortic aneurysm; and he lost his virginity at the age of 15 in a stationery cupboard at school.

IANTO JONES (GARETH DAVID-LLOYD)

'Ianto is Torchwood's receptionist and unofficial butler,' comments Chris Chibnall in an interview for *Starburst* Issue 342. '[He] quietly keeps the team together, most often through coffee and takeaways.'

'He's a sort of Alfred to Jack's Batman, if you like,' observed Gareth David-Lloyd in a BBC press release of 18 October 2006. 'I think he probably feels a little on the outside of things to begin with, and he might feel that his talents aren't being used to their full potential. But as the series progresses, he develops personal relationships with the other members of the team and becomes gradually more integrated. He loves Torchwood, he's fascinated by it and he constantly wants to be better at the job and make even more important contributions to the work they do … He puts up a bit of a front at first – he's this quiet, reliable, very smart guy, who's always in a suit. But I think it's a hard exterior he puts up to cover something that's probably a bit more vulnerable and a bit more childlike underneath.'

Although courteous, efficient and unflappable on the surface, Ianto has – as the *Torchwood* official website puts it – 'hidden depths of anguish and darkness' lurking within him. The reason for this is revealed in 'Cyberwoman': his girlfriend Lisa was part-converted into a Cyberman during the creatures' recent invasion attempt, at which time it seems they were both working at Torchwood One in London, and he is desperate to find a way of curing her, even if this means placing the lives of all his colleagues – and possibly the whole world – in danger. When Lisa is killed by the other members of the team at the end of the episode, Ianto is left grief-stricken, although Jack allows him to keep his job.

In 'Countrycide', Ianto is even allowed to join his colleagues on mission to the Brecon Beacons – apparently a rare opportunity for him to work outside the Hub – although he finds the experience a harrowing one and comes close to losing his life at the hands of the local cannibal community.

Any resentment he might have felt toward Jack following the death of Lisa in 'Cyberwoman' has clearly dissipated by now; and indeed, judging from a rather curious conversation they have about a stopwatch at the end of 'They Keep Killing Suzie', it seems that they may even have begun a sexual relationship. Clearly Owen suspects that they are more to each other than simply colleagues: when Ianto asserts, in 'Captain Jack Harkness', that Jack needs him, he retorts: 'In your dreams, Ianto. Your sad wet-dreams where you're his part-time shag, maybe.'

Even the fiercely-loyal Ianto, though, betrays Jack at one point in 'End of Days', when, having been encouraged to do so by a 'phantom' of Lisa, he joins with the others in opening the rift. He is forgiven by Jack at the end of the story, when they exchange a hug and a kiss.

The name 'Ianto Jones' was first coined by Russell T Davies for his 2004 drama serial *Mine All Mine* – in which the role was also taken by David-Lloyd.

SUZIE COSTELLO (INDIRA VARMA)

Suzie is second-in-command to Jack in Torchwood Three. She is the team's hardware specialist, and fascinated by all the alien tech that they acquire. 'Suzie was the second person to be part of Torchwood,' commented Indira Varma in a BBC press release dated 18 October 2006. 'She's been in it the longest and she is probably the most passionate about it, or intense. She lives for it, quite literally … Everyone else goes home to boyfriends and music and life but Suzie doesn't have anything, apart from a couple of dead flies! You could say that she's quite sad. But you could also say that she's incredibly ambitious and cares most about saving the world … She sees herself as being the one who's the least frivolous. She hasn't got time for stupid little jokes and things like that, because she is trying to save the world from aliens. The others have fun and go out, and I think they're a little less conscientious in their work and mistakes happen …'

It is Suzie's obsession with her work that ultimately proves to be her downfall: at the end of 'Everything Changes', she takes her own life after she is revealed to have carried out a number of murders simply in order to test out an alien glove with the power to temporarily resurrect the dead.

This, though, is not the end of her story. In 'They Keep Killing Suzie', it transpires that she has laid an elaborate plan to ensure that, in the event of her death, her colleagues are manipulated into using the resurrection glove on her, thus restoring her to life and enabling her to escape – and to kill her hated father *en route*. Although her plan succeeds, Jack tracks her down and kills her 'for the last and final time' by shooting her repeatedly in the chest and then instructing Toshiko to destroy the resurrection glove, which has been keeping her alive by channelling Gwen's life-force into her.

RYHS WILLIAMS (KAI OWEN)

Gwen's live-in boyfriend Rhys is an affable, down-to-earth man who works as a transport manager.[39] He is kept in the dark by Gwen about her new job at Torchwood and is under the impression that she has transferred to a police 'special ops' unit where her duties include filing. As time goes by, he becomes increasingly irritated by her antisocial working hours and general secretiveness about what she is doing, and they have a major falling-out over this at the beginning of 'Combat'. He nevertheless remains unaware of her affair with Owen as, although she does tell him about it at one point later in the same episode, she also slips him a dose of Torchwood's amnesia-inducing drug beforehand. His life comes under threat in 'End of Days', and Gwen stuns him and places him in a cell in the Hub for his own protection. This is all to no avail, however, as the malevolent Bilis Manger releases him and then stabs him twice in the midriff, killing him. Fortunately, these events are reversed when the rift is opened at the climax of the story, and Gwen is delighted to find Rhys back in their flat again, once more blissfully unaware of what has occurred.

39 In dialogue from an unused version of a scene from 'Everything Changes', Gwen tells Jack that the company Rhys works for is: 'Luckley's the printers. It's not very exciting, but he's not stupid.'

PART FIVE:
BIOGRAPHICAL DATA

CHAPTER FOURTEEN: MAIN CAST

JOHN BARROWMAN (CAPTAIN JACK HARKNESS)

John Barrowman was born on 11 March 1967 in Glasgow, Scotland. He grew up in his native city until, when he was aged eight, his family emigrated to live in the USA, in the Illinois town of Aurora, just south of Chicago. He had always been keen on performing – both acting and singing – and pursued this interest during his education at Joliet West High School, Illinois, where he appeared in a number of student productions between 1983 and 1985. An early job was as a musical entertainer in a Nashville, Tennessee theme park called Opryland. He returned to the UK in 1989, initially to study Shakespeare at a London university, and his theatrical career really took off when he won a role opposite Elaine Paige in *Anything Goes* in London's West End. He also started gaining TV work during the 1990s, including as a regular presenter on the BBC children's series *Live and Kicking* (1993). Roles in the American series *Central Park West* (1996) and *Titans* (2000) followed, and more theatre work, including in a couple of productions on New York's Broadway. His starring roles in the theatre have come mainly in musicals, such as *Chicago*, *Sunset Boulevard*, *Miss Saigon*, *Evita*, *Beauty and the Beast* and *Phantom of the Opera*, although he has also had a number of non-singing parts, including in productions of *Rope* and *A Few Good Men* (2005). On the big screen he has appeared in *De-Lovely* (2004), a biography of composer Cole Porter, and in Mel Brooks' *The Producers* (2005). He has sung on a number of original-cast soundtrack recordings of musicals, and has also released three solo CDs: *Aspects of Lloyd Webber* (1998), *Reflections from Broadway* (2000) and *John Barrowman Swings Cole Porter* (2004). When, in 2004, his agent was approached by casting director Andy Pryor about the possibility of him playing Captain Jack in the new *Doctor Who*, he was eager to take on the role – and was in fact the first regular to be cast in the series. So popular did he prove as Captain Jack that he was soon offered the opportunity to star in his own spin-off series, *Torchwood*. He appeared in pantomime – *Cinderella* at the Wimbledon Theatre – over the 2005/06 Christmas holiday season, and early in 2006 could again be seen on TV, in the variety shows *The Magic of Musicals* for the BBC and *Dancing on Ice* for ITV. He also had a stint as presenter of the ITV morning talk show *This Morning*, standing in for regular host Phillip Schofield. Later in 2006, he was one of the judges on the BBC show *How Do You Solve a Problem Like Maria?*, about the search for a newcomer to star in a revival of the musical *The Sound of Music*, and then went into rehearsals at the New Theatre, Cardiff, for the Christmas 2006/07 pantomime *Jack and the Beanstalk*, in which he was to take the starring role of – coincidentally – Jack. On 2 November, he received the Entertainer of the Year award from the Stonewall gay rights organisation. 4 December then saw him singing on stage as part of the Royal Variety Performance, with a 12 December broadcast on BBC Two allowing his contribution to be enjoyed by a much larger audience. On 22 December, BBC Radio 2 broadcast the special *John Barrowman – A Musical Christmas*. Rounding off the year, on 27 December he entered into a civil partnership with Scott Gill, his partner of 16 years, at a ceremony in Cardiff attended by family members and friends, including the other Torchwood team regulars and Russell T Davies.

EVE MYLES (GWEN COOPER)

Eve Myles was born in 1978 in the small South Wales mining village of Ystradgynlais. In addition to playing Gwyneth in the *Doctor Who* episode 'The Unquiet Dead', her TV credits prior to *Torchwood* included parts in *Score* (BBC Wales, 2001), *Tales from Pleasure Beach* (BBC

Wales, 2001), *EastEnders* (BBC One 2003), *Colditz* (ITV1, 2005) and, most notably, a regular starring role in the BBC Wales drama series *Belonging* (2000-). She had a role in the movie *These Foolish Things* (2006), and on stage she has appeared in a Royal Shakespeare Company production of *Titus Andronicus* (2003) and at the National Theatre in *Henry IV, Part I and II* (2005).

NAOKO MORI (TOSHIKO SATO)

Naoko Mori was born in 1975 in Nagoya, Japan. Her family moved to New Jersey, USA, when she was four, and it was there that she learned to speak English. They relocated again when she was 11, to Surrey in the UK. There she started taking singing lessons, and soon decided to pursue a career in the theatre. At the age of 17, she became the first Japanese national to play a lead in London's West End, when she had a stint as Kim in *Miss Saigon*, opposite John Barrowman. Prior to her appearances in *Doctor Who* and *Torchwood*, she was best known for playing Mie Nishi-Kawa in the medical drama *Casualty* (1993-94) – which marked the start of her TV career – and Sarah (aka 'Titicaca') in the comedy series *Absolutely Fabulous* (1995-2003), both for the BBC. She also won parts in a number of other series, including *Thief Takers* (ITV1, 1997), *Bugs* (BBC One, 1998), *Psychos* (Channel 4, 1999), *Judge John Deed* (BBC One, 2001), *Spooks* (BBC One, 2002), *The Smoking Room* (BBC Three, 2004) and *Hiroshima* (BBC One, 2005), and in the movies *Spice World* (1997) and *Topsy-Turvy* (1999). From 20 November 2006 she could be seen in the role of Christmas Eve in the ribald puppet show *Avenue Q* at the Noel Coward Theatre; she also appeared in the show's Royal Variety Performance segment on 4 December.

BURN GORMAN (OWEN HARPER)

Although born in Hollywood, California, Burn Gorman was brought up in England from an early age by his British parents. He has since pursued parallel careers as an actor and a musician. He began acting in the theatre, and he has gone on to notch up numerous stage, radio, television and film credits. His TV work includes roles in *Coronation Street* (ITV1, 1998), *A Good Thief* (ITV1, 2002), *Funland* (BBC Three, 2005) and – most notably – as Guppy in *Bleak House* (BBC One, 2005). On film he has had parts in, amongst others, the gangster movie *Layer Cake* (2004), the comedy/drama *Colour Me Kubrick* (2005) and the light-hearted fantasy *Penelope* (2006). As a musician, he has performed at venues around the world and accompanied stars including Neneh Cherry and Groove Armada. He has also worked on videos for the Streets, is an expert breakdancer, and in 2003 won a BBC OneXtra award as Human Beatbox Champion.

GARETH DAVID-LLOYD (IANTO JONES)

Gareth David-Lloyd was born in the Welsh town of Bettws, Newport in 1981. He was educated locally at Monnow Junior School, Bettws Comprehensive School and Coleg Gwent, Cross Keys. After taking acting lessons at the Risca Leisure Centre, he joined the Dolman Youth Theatre and Gwent Young People's Theatre. In 2003 he moved to London in order to gain greater experience, and won minor TV parts in *Absolute Power* (2003), *Casualty* (2003) and *The Genius of Beethoven* (2005) for the BBC and *Rosemary & Thyme* (2004), Russell T Davies's *Mine All Mine* (2004) and *The Bill* (2005) for ITV. He also took on some further stage roles, including as Sebastian in *Twelfth Night* and Macheath in *The Threepenny Opera*. Ianto in *Torchwood* is, however, his highest-profile role to date. While recording the series, he was also studying for a part-time degree in Philosophy with the Open University.

INDIRA VARMA (SUZIE COSTELLO)

Indira Varma was born in 1973 in the English city of Bath, of Indian and Swiss descent. She joined the Musical Youth Theatre Company and then went on to win numerous TV and film roles. Her TV credits include *Psychos* (Channel 4, 1999) (appearing alongside Naoko Mori), *Other People's Children* (BBC One, 2000), *The Canterbury Tales* (BBC One, 2003), *The Quatermass Experiment* (BBC Four, 2005) and regular roles as Sasha in *Attachments* (BBC Two, 2001) and as Niobe in *Rome* (HBO, BBC, RAI, 2005). Her films credits include *Kama Sutra: A Tale of Love* (1996), *Sixth Happiness* (1997), *Bride and Prejudice* (2004) and *Basic Instinct 2* (2006).

KAI OWEN (RHYS WILLIAMS)

Kai Owen's TV work prior to *Torchwood* included parts in *Treflan* (S4C, 2002) and *Casualty* (BBC One, 2003) and the starring role of David 'Shiner' Owen in the six-part serial *Rocket Man* (BBC One, 2005). He has also appeared in a number of plays in the theatre, including *Portrait of the Artist as a Young Dog* (2004), *A Chorus of Disapproval* (2006) and, perhaps most notably, co-starring as Ronnie in *Life of Ryan … and Ronnie* (2006).

CHAPTER FIFTEEN: PRINCIPAL CREATIVE TEAM

RUSSELL T DAVIES (SHOWRUNNER, EXECUTIVE PRODUCER, WRITER)

Russell T Davies was born in Swansea, South Wales, in 1963. (He in fact has no middle name: he starting using 'T' as an initial in the 1980s in order to distinguish himself from an actor, journalist and broadcaster also named Russell Davies.) He studied English Literature at Oxford University, and graduated in 1984. His TV career began with posts as a floor manager and production assistant at the BBC, where in the late 1980s he also trained as a director and gained a presenting credit on *Play School* (1987). He produced the children's series *Why Don't You ...?* for BBC Manchester from 1988 to 1992, during which time he also started to work as a writer, gaining credits on *The Flashing Blade* (1989), *Breakfast Serials* (1990) and *Chucklevision* (1991). His writing career moved up a gear when he was responsible for the acclaimed BBC children's serials *Dark Season* (1991) – which he also novelised for BBC Books – and *Century Falls* (1993). In 1992, he moved from the BBC to Granada, where he produced and wrote for the popular children's drama *Children's Ward* (1992-1996). He also started to gain writing credits for family and adult programmes, including *Cluedo* (1993), *Families* (1993), *The House of Windsor* (1994) and *Revelations* (1994). He worked briefly as a storyliner and writer on the hugely popular *Coronation Street* (1996) and contributed to Channel 4's *Springhill* (1996). It was at this time that he had his first professional association with *Doctor Who* – having been a long-time fan of the series – when he wrote the New Adventures novel *Damaged Goods* (1996) for Virgin Publishing. The following year, he was commissioned to contribute to the ITV period drama *The Grand* (1997), and ended up scripting the whole series after a number of other writers dropped out. He subsequently left Granada and joined a company called Red Productions, where he had a major success as creator, writer and producer of *Queer as Folk* (1999/2000), a ground-breaking two-season drama series for Channel 4 about a group of gay men in Manchester, which also spawned a US remake. Since then, his career has gone from strength to strength, with writer and executive producer credits on *Bob and Rose* (2001) and *Mine All Mine* (2004) for ITV and *The Second Coming* (2003), *Casanova* (2005) and of course *Doctor Who* (2005-), *Torchwood* (2006-) and *The Sarah Jane Adventures* (2007-) for the BBC. He is now frequently cited as one of the most influential and powerful people in the British TV industry.

JULIE GARDNER (EXECUTIVE PRODUCER)

Julie Gardner was born in South Wales, near Neath, in 1969. Having gained a degree in English at London University, she began her working life as a teacher of English to secondary school pupils in Wales. In her mid-twenties, however, she decided that this was not the career for her, and she successfully applied for a job at the BBC, as the producer's secretary on the series *Our Friends in the North* (1996). She quickly ascended the ladder of promotion to script reader in the Serial Drama Department, then to script editor and then to producer, working on shows including *Silent Witness* (1996), *Sunburn* (1999) and *The Mrs Bradley Mysteries* (2000). In 2000, she left the BBC and took up a post as development producer at London Weekend Television. There she was responsible for dramas including a controversial modern-day retelling of Shakespeare's *Othello* (2001) and *Me and Mrs Jones* (2002). She was working on further ideas at LWT when, in 2003, she was head-hunted to become Head of Drama at BBC

Wales. The new *Doctor Who* series, on which she took an executive producer credit, was one of her first responsibilities in that role; and it was natural that she would take a similar interest in *Torchwood*. Other projects she has overseen at BBC Wales include *Casanova* (2005), *Girl in the Café* (2005) and *Life on Mars* (2005). On 21 September 2006 it was announced that she had been promoted to the post of the BBC's Head of Drama Commissioning, and would have special responsibility for implementing a cohesive independent drama strategy across the UK. She would however remain as Head of Drama, BBC Wales, for the foreseeable future, and would continue as executive producer of *Doctor Who*, *Torchwood* and *The Sarah Jane Adventures*.

RICHARD STOKES (PRODUCER)

Richard Stokes trained in picture editing at film school and gained early experience as third assistant director on some corporate videos. He then joined the BBC as a researcher, initially for light entertainment shows, before, in the mid-1980s, being recruited to BBC One's flagship soap opera *EastEnders*. He remained on *EastEnders* for several years, advancing to script editor, series editor and ultimately producer. After this, he produced *Murder in Mind* (2001-2002) and popular medical drama *Holby City* (2002), and then became an executive producer on the latter, on *The Inspector Lynley Mysteries* (2004) and on some single films, including *Magnificent 7* (2005). He narrowly lost out to Phil Collinson for the post of producer on *Doctor Who*, but was later offered *Torchwood* instead, which he readily accepted.

CHRIS CHIBNALL (CO-PRODUCER, LEAD WRITER)

Chris Chibnall is a long-time *Doctor Who* fan who was raised in Lancashire and began his TV career as a football archivist and occasional floor manager for Sky Sports. He then took a succession of administrative jobs with different theatre companies including, between 1996 and 1999, the experimental group Complicite. He subsequently became a full-time writer, initially for the theatre, with credits including *Gaffer!* – a single-actor piece about homophobia in football, first staged in 1999 – and *Kiss Me Like You Mean It* – which premiered at the Soho Theatre in 2001 and has also been staged in a number of European venues, including Paris under the title *Un Baiser, Un Vrai*. On the strength of his play scripts, he was invited by the BBC to develop a period drama series for them. This became *Born and Bred* (2002-2005), which he not only created but also contributed to as consultant producer and lead writer throughout its four seasons. His other TV writing credits include episodes of *All About George* (2005) and *Life on Mars* (2006).

BRIAN MINCHIN (SCRIPT EDITOR)

Brian Minchin was born in Aberystwyth, Wales, in 1987. He has worked as script editor on BBC Wales's *Belonging* (2005) – starring, amongst others, Eve Myles – and as assistant producer or producer on a number of low-budget films, including *Down* (2003), which he also co-wrote, *Work in Progress* (2004) and *Dead Long Enough* (2005).

HELEN RAYNOR (SCRIPT EDITOR, WRITER)

After graduating from Cambridge University in the mid-1990s, Helen Raynor began her career in the theatre, as an assistant director and director for a number of companies, including the Bush Theatre, the Royal Shakespeare Company and the Royal Opera House. She then joined the BBC, where she became script editor of BBC One's daytime serial *Doctors* (2002-2004). This led on to a post as one of the two script editors on the new *Doctor Who* (2005-). She has also gained credits as a writer for the theatre (*Waterloo Exit Two*, Young Vic, 2003), for radio (*Running Away With the Hairdresser*, BBC Radio 4, 2005) and for TV (*Cake*, BBC One, 2006).

PETER J HAMMOND (WRITER)

Peter J Hammond – sometimes credited as simply P J Hammond – took a course in art at the Hammersmith College of Arts and Crafts, studied drama at Goldsmith's College and penned a number of plays for BBC radio before beginning a long and distinguished career as a writer of popular British TV. In the 1950s and 1960s he contributed scripts to a considerable number of series, many of them police dramas or thrillers, including *Dixon of Dock Green* (1955), *Z Cars* (1962), *Thirty Minute Theatre* (1966), *Ramshackle Road* (1968) and *Special Branch* (1969). He also served as script editor of *Z Cars* for a year, in 1969/1970. In the 1970s, his credits included episodes of the popular telefantasy series *Ace of Wands* (1971-1972), the soap opera *Emmerdale Farm* (1972) and the hard-hitting police series *The Sweeney* (1975) for ITV, and the nursing drama *Angels* (1975) and the police series *Target* (1977) for the BBC. More recently he has written for *Lame Ducks* (1984), *The Bill* (1992), *Dangerfield* (1996), *Wycliffe* (1997-1998) and *Midsomer Murders* (2001-), amongst others. He came close to contributing to Season 23 of the classic *Doctor Who* series in the mid-1980s, but his story, *Paradise Five*, was ultimately rejected. His most celebrated work came on the atmospheric ITV telefantasy series *Sapphire & Steel* (1979-1982), of which he was the creator and lead writer.

TOBY WHITHOUSE (WRITER)

Toby Whithouse grew up in Southend, Essex, where he also attended art college before switching to train in acting. After some seven years as a jobbing actor – during which time he appeared as a regular in the BBC series *The House of Elliot* (1993) and won a number of stage roles, including in London's West End in a production of Neil Simon's *Laughter on the 23rd Floor* (1997) – he turned his hand to writing. His first major script credit was on the ITV series *Where the Heart Is* (1997). He subsequently contributed to the BBC Two series *Attachments* (2000), produced by a company called World Productions, for whom he went on to create the highly successful Channel 4 series *No Angels* (2004-). He became involved in the new *Doctor Who* owing to a long-time friendship with executive producer Julie Gardner, and was commissioned to write the episode 'School Reunion' for the second series. This led on to his commission for *Torchwood*. In addition to his writing work, he continues to take occasional acting roles, such as in the movie *Bridget Jones's Diary* (2002) and the TV series *Holby City* (2000, 2004) and *The Virgin Queen* (2005).

PAUL TOMALIN AND DANIEL McCULLOCH (WRITERS)

Paul Tomalin and Dan McCulloch were introduced to the *Torchwood* production team by Paul Abbott and Hilary Bevan Jones of Tightrope Productions. Tomalin graduated from the University of East Anglia with a BA degree in Film and English and spent the following year writing several short film scripts. One of these, *Grandma*, was made in 2002, by his and producer Nick Tanner's own Obsessive Films company, giving him his debut credit as both writer and director. McCulloch was production runner on the TV play *The Girl in the Café* (2005) and post-production secretary on the mini-series *To the Ends of the Earth* (2005).

CATHERINE TREGENNA (WRITER)

Cath Tregenna hails from Wales. She started out as an actress, winning minor parts in the film

Y Mapiwr (1995) and the BBC series *Satellite City* (1996), before turning to writing. She developed (from an idea by former *Doctor Who* director Matthew Robinson) and wrote for the BBC Wales courtroom drama series *The Bench* (2001-); and, in addition to *Torchwood*, her other writing credits include episodes of the BBC One series *Casualty* (2003-2006) and *EastEnders* (2003) and the play *Art and Guff*, which debuted at London's Soho Theatre in March 2001.

JACQUETTA MAY (WRITER)

Jacquetta May was born in 1960 in the county of Kent and, after studying at Bristol University, first made her mark as a stage actress in a variety of roles, including some at the National Theatre, over a ten year period. She then came to wider attention in the regular role of Rachel Kominski in *EastEnders* on BBC One between 1991 and 1993. Other TV credits include roles in *Crocodile Shoes* (ITV1, 1994), *Dangerfield* (BBC One, 1996), *Home Farm Twins* (BBC One, 1999), *Peak Practice* (ITV1, 2000), *I'm Alan Partridge* (BBC Two, 2002), *Holby City* (BBC One, 2003), *Silent Witness* (BBC One, 2005) and *The Bill* (ITV1, 2006). She has also appeared in the feature films *The Naked Cell* (1987) and *Get Real* (1998). As a writer she has contributed episodes to *Where the Heart Is* (ITV1,1997), *Shades* (ITV1, 2000) and *New Tricks* (BBC One, 2006).

NOEL CLARKE (WRITER)

Noel Clarke is best known to *Doctor Who* fans as the actor who played the Doctor's companion Mickey Smith – sometime boyfriend of Rose Tyler. He was born in 1975 in the Ladbroke Grove area of London, where he was also brought up and educated. He studied drama at GCSE level at school and began to take an interest in writing when he attended sixth form college, where he took an A Level in Theatre Studies. His first significant role as an actor, as the lead in the Channel 4 series *Metrosexuality* (1998), came about after the director spotted him while he was working as a swimming pool lifeguard to supplement his income as a student on a Media degree course at North London University. He also worked around this time as a fitness instructor, an assistant manager of a gym, and a DJ. He even tried out as a rapper. Subsequent TV work – with him sometimes credited as Noel Anthony Clarke – included roles in *The Bill* (2000), *Judge John Deed* (2001), *Waking the Dead* (2001), *Casualty* (2001), *Doctors* (2003), *Holby City* (2004) and *A Touch of Frost* (2004). He also had a regular part as Wyman in the last two seasons, plus a special, of the BBC's revival of *Auf Wiedersehen, Pet* (2002-2004). He made his theatre debut at the Oval Theatre in *Talking About Men* (2001), and came to wider attention in a Royal Court Theatre production of *Where Do We Live* (2002), for which he later won the prestigious Laurence Olivier award for Most Promising Newcomer. Also in 2002, he became a founding member of a writing collective called Three Scoops Entertainment and gained his first credit as a co-writer, as well as a producer and actor, on the short comedy-drama film *Licks*. A more major project was his feature film *Kidulthood* (2006), which he both wrote and, again, acted in. This was a hard-hitting, semi-autobiographical piece about a group of 15-year-old boys growing up in West London. His episode of *Torchwood* gives him his first credit as a TV scriptwriter.

BRIAN KELLY (DIRECTOR)

Brian Kelly has previously gained directorial credits on, amongst other programmes, *Barmy Aunt Boomerang* (BBC One, 1999), *Hope and Glory* (BBC One, 1999), *Teachers* (Channel 4,

2001), *Taggart* (ITV1, 2002), *Monarch of the Glen* (BBC One, 2003), *55 Degrees North* (BBC One, 1994) and *Sea of Souls* (BBC One, 2005, 2006).

COLIN TEAGUE (DIRECTOR)

Colin Teague's directorial credits include the feature films *Northwest One* (1999), *Shooters* (2002), *Spivs* (2004) and *The Last Drop* (2005), all of which apart from *Shooters* he also co-wrote, and episodes of *London's Burning* (ITV1, 2002) and *Holby City* (BBC One, 2003-2006). He is also the director of the one-hour introductory special of *The Sarah Jane Adventures* (2007).

JAMES STRONG (DIRECTOR)

James Strong's first TV credits were as a documentary maker, on *Critical Mass* (Carlton, 1998), *World in Action* (ITV, 1998/99), *My FC* (Channel 5, 2000) and *Crimewatch UK* (BBC One, 2000). He then moved into directing comedy and drama programmes, including *Otis Lee Crenshaw* (Channel 4, 2000), *Jack Dee's Happy Hour* (BBC One, 2001), *Doctors* (BBC One, 2000/01), *Nothing but the Truth* (ITV1, 2001), *Blood on her Hands* (ITV1, 2002), *Mile High* (Sky One, 2002), *Holby City* (BBC One, 2002-2004), *Casualty* (BBC One, 2004), *The Good Citizen* (BBC One, 2004), *Rocket Man* (BBC One, 2005) and *Doctor Who*: 'The Impossible Planet'/'The Satan Pit' (BBC One, 2005). He both wrote and directed the comedy short *Sold* (2002) and the TV dramas *Lady Jane* (ITV1, 2003) and *Billie Jo* (ITV1, 2004).

ALICE TROUGHTON (DIRECTOR)

Alice Troughton has directed numerous episodes of *Doctors* (2003-2004), *Holby City* (2004-2005) and *EastEnders* (2006) for the BBC and *No Angels* (2006) for Channel 4. She also directed her own comedy short screenplay *Doris the Builder* (2004).

ANDY GODDARD (DIRECTOR)

Andy Goddard began his career as a writer and director on the award-winning short film *Little Sisters* (1997), *Yabba Yabba Ding Ding* (Film Four 1999), *Kings of the Wild Frontier*: 'New Found Lands' (STV, 2000) (co-written with Ian Rankin) and *Rice Paper Stars* (BBC Scotland, 2000). He then focused increasingly on directing rather than writing, and was responsible for episodes of *G4CE* (CBBC, 2001), *Stacey Stone* (CBBC, 2001), *Taggart* (ITV1, 2003), *Casualty* (BBC One, 2003), *The Bill* (ITV1, 2003-2004), *Twisted Tales* (BBC Three, 2004), *Murphy's Law* (BBC One 2004-2005), *Hex* (Sky One) and *Wire in the Blood* (ITV1 2005-2006).

JAMES ERSKINE (DIRECTOR)

James Erskine started his career in the independent films sector, receiving his first directorial credit on the comedy short *The Invitation* (2001). He produced and co-directed the TV documentary series *The Human Face* (BBC Two, 2001) and *Ruby Does the Business* (BBC Three, 2004), wrote, produced and directed *EMR* (2004), produced and directed *Closing the Deal* (2005), and wrote and directed the drama segments of *7/7: Attack on London* (Channel Five, 2005). He has been a semi-regular director on the medical drama *Holby City* (BBC One, 2002-).

ASHLEY WAY (DIRECTOR)

35-year-old Cardiff-born Ashley Way started out as an assistant director on a number of largely-Welsh-based film projects. These included *The Proposition* (1997), *Hooded Angels* (2000) and *Berserker* (2001) and a series of fantasy-orientated subjects directed by David Lister: *The Fairy King of Ar* (1998), *Dazzle* (1999), *The Meeksville Ghost* (2001), *Askari* (2001) – for which he also co-wrote the script and acted as associate producer – and *The Sorcerer's Apprentice* (2002). He wrote and directed the 2003 movie *Hoodlum and Son*. His TV credits include the South African-produced children's puppet series *Filligoggin* (2000) (co-directed with David Lister), the Eve Myles-starring *Belonging* (BBC Wales, 2000-) and two episodes of the medical drama *Casualty* (BBC One, 2005-2006). His first contact with the *Doctor Who* world came when he directed the special interactive episode 'Attack of the Graske' in 2005. He then went on to direct the 13 online 'Tardisode' trailers for the Series Two episodes. His most recently-transmitted project is the S4C production *Calon Gaeth* (2007).

EDWARD THOMAS (PRODUCTION DESIGNER)

Edward Thomas took a foundation course in art and design after leaving school, and then studied at the Wimbledon School of Art, from which he graduated with a BA (Hons) degree in 3-D Design, specialising in theatre. He began his career as a designer on a wide variety of commercials and a number of theatrical productions, including *Turandot* for the Royal Opera Company at Wembley Arena, *Under Milkwood* for the Dylan Thomas Theatre Company and Shakespeare's *Twelfth Night* and *Cymbeline* for the Ludlow Festival. This was followed by work on numerous feature films, including over a dozen South African productions in the early 1990s and *The Mystery of Edwin Drood* (1993), *Resurrection Man* (1998), *Darkness Falls* (1999) and *The Meeksville Ghost* (2001). He also gained credits on a wide range of TV shows including, for BBC Wales, *Jones*, *The Coal Project* and, of course, *Doctor Who* (2005-) and *Torchwood* (2006-). He has sometimes been credited as Edward Alan Thomas or simply as Ed Thomas, and is represented by the Creative Media Management agency.

PART SIX: EPISODE GUIDE

TORCHWOOD – SERIES ONE (2006/2007)

SERIES CREDITS[40, 41]
Created By: Russell T Davies
Producer: Richard Stokes, Sophie Fante (1.09)[42]

MAIN CAST
John Barrowman (Captain Jack Harkness)
Eve Myles (Gwen Cooper)
Burn Gorman (Owen Harper)
Naoko Mori (Toshiko Sato)
Gareth David-Lloyd (Ianto Jones)
Kai Owen (Rhys Williams) (1.01, 1.02, 1.03, 1.04, 1.06, 1.10, 1.11, 1.13*)[43]
Indira Varma (Suzie Costello) (1.01, 1.08)

PRODUCTION TEAM
Co-Producer: Chris Chibnall

1st Assistant Director: Peter Bennett (1.01, 1.02), Nick Rae (1.03, 1.05, 1.07, 1.10, 1.12, 1.13), Nick Brown (1.04, 1.08), Jon Williams (1.06, 1.11), Nael Abbas (1.09), Daf Arwyn Jones (1.09)
2nd Assistant Director: Stefan Morris (1.01, 1.02), Lynsey Muir (1.03, 1.05, 1.07, 1.10, 1.12, 1.13), Guy de Glanville (1.04, 1.08), James DeHavilland (1.06, 1.11), Daniella Bowen (1.09)
3rd Assistant Director:[44] Lynsey Muir (1.01, 1.02), Rhian Salisbury (1.03, 1.04, 1.06, 1.07, 1.08, 1.09, 1.11), Nick Britz (1.09), Paul Bennett (1.10, 1.12, 1.13)
Runner: Glen Coxon (1.03, 1.04, 1.06, 1.08, 1.11, 1.12, 1.13), Llywarch Davies (1.04, 1.06, 1.07, 1.08, 1.11, 1.12, 1.13), Joney Lyons (1.06, 1.09, 1.11, 1.12, 1.13), Michael Green (1.09)
Location Manager: Paul Davies
Location Scout: Nicky James (1.04, 1.08), Christian Reynish (1.04, 1.08), Iwan Roberts (1.09)
Unit Manager: Geraint Havard Jones (1.01, 1.02, 1.03, 1.04, 1.06, 1.07, 1.08, 1.09, 1.10, 1.11, 1.12, 1.13)
Production Co-ordinator: Carmelina Palumbo

---

40 Where an episode number (or more than one) appears in brackets after a person's name in the listing, this means that they were credited only on the episode (or episodes) indicated. Otherwise, the person concerned was credited on all 13 episodes.

41 On their debut transmission, the series' first two episodes, 'Everything Changes' and 'Day One', were presented in a double bill, in slightly edited form, with the credits for both episodes presented together at the end of 'Day One'. Similarly, the last two episodes, 'Captain Jack Harkness' and 'End of Days', were initially shown as a double bill compilation, with a combined set of credits at the close of 'End of Days'. The credits for those cast and production team members marked * in the listing were omitted from these compilation versions but included in the 'standard' single episode versions as seen in repeats and in the series' DVD releases.

42 Richard Stokes given sole producer credit in *Radio Times* for the entire series, including episode 1.09.

43 Not credited on screen for episode 1.05, but credited in *Radio Times* and does appear in the episode, although without dialogue. His only speaking scene in the episode was deleted before transmission, but is due to be included in the extras on the Series One: Part Two DVD set.

44 Paul Bennett was 3rd Assistant Director on 1.05, but not credited on screen.

Assistant Production Co-ordinator: Kate Powell (1.01*, 1.02*, 1.03, 1.04, 1.07, 1.08)
Production Secretary: Margarita Felices (1.01, 1.02, 1.03, 1.04, 1.06, 1.07, 1.08, 1.09, 1.10, 1.11, 1.12, 1.13), Kirsty Jones (1.11, 1.12, 1.13)
Script Secretary: Helen Pugsley (1.01, 1.02, 1.04, 1.06, 1.07, 1.08, 1.09, 1.10, 1.11, 1.12, 1.13), Claire Thomas (1.03, 1.04, 1.06, 1.08, 1.09, 1.10, 1.11, 1.12, 1.13)
Contracts Assistant: Kath Blackman (1.01*, 1.02*), Beth Britton (1.03, 1.04, 1.06)
Accounts Assistant: Debi Griffiths (1.07, 1.08, 1.09, 1.10, 1.11), Beth Britton (1.07, 1.08, 1.10, 1.11, 1.12), Kath Blackman (1.08, 1.09, 1.10, 1.11, 1.12, 1.13), Charlotte Cole (1.12, 1.13)
Continuity: Llinos Wyn Jones (1.01, 1.02, 1.04, 1.06, 1.08, 1.11), Vicky Cole (1.03, 1.07), Suzanna Binding[45] (1.05, 1.10, 1.12, 1.13), Sally Hope (1.09)
Script Editor: Brian Minchin (1.01, 1.02, 1.03, 1.04, 1.05, 1.06, 1.08, 1.09, 1.10, 1.11, 1.12, 1.13), Helen Raynor (1.07)
Camera Operator: Gareth Hughes (1.01, 1.02, 1.03, 1.04, 1.07, 1.08), Jenny Budd (1.05, 1.10, 1.12, 1.13), Richard Mahoney (1.06, 1.11), James Moss (1.09)
Camera Assistant: Mani Blaxter Paliwala (1.01, 1.02, 1.03, 1.04, 1.07, 1.08), Steve Davies (1.06, 1.10, 1.11, 1.12, 1.13), Gareth Coop (1.09)
Focus Puller: Duncan Fowlie (1.01, 1.02, 1.03, 1.04, 1.07, 1.08), Alwen Hughes (1.06, 1.10, 1.11, 1.12, 1.13), Chris Reynolds (1.09)
Grip: Dai Hopkins (1.01, 1.02, 1.03, 1.04, 1.06, 1.07, 1.08, 1.10, 1.11, 1.12, 1.13), Dave Logan (1.09)
Boom Operator: Jeff Welch (1.01, 1.02, 1.03, 1.04, 1.07, 1.08), Tam Shoring (1.06, 1.11), James Drummond (1.09), Kevin Staples (1.10, 1.12, 1.13)
Gaffer: Dave Fowler (1.01, 1.02, 1.03, 1.04, 1.07, 1.08), Mickey Reeves (1.05, 1.10, 1.12, 1.13), George Vince (1.06, 1.09, 1.11)
Best Boy: Steve Slocombe (1.01, 1.02, 1.03, 1.04, 1.07, 1.08), Suzanne Sanders (1.06, 1.09, 1.11), Llyr Evans (1.10, 1.12, 1.13)
Stunt Co-ordinator: Garry Connery (1.01, 1.02), Lee Sheward (1.01*), Tom Lucy[46] (1.03, 1.04, 1.06, 1.07, 1.08, 1.11, 1.12, 1.13), Roderick P Woodruff (1.09)
Stunt Performers: Curtis Rivers (1.01*, 1.02*, 1.03), Jo McLaren (1.01*, 1.03), Maxine Whittaker (1.02*), Gary Hoptrough (1.03), Crispin Layfield (1.03), Will Willoughby (1.04)
Chief Supervising Art Director: Stephen Nicholas
Supervising Art Director: Keith Dunne
Assistant Art Director: Nadia Dand (1.10)
Art Department Production Manager: Jonathan Marquand Allison[47]
Art Department Operations Manager: Adrian Anscombe (1.01, 1.02, 1.03, 1.04, 1.06, 1.07, 1.08, 1.09, 1.10, 1.11, 1.12, 1.13)
Art Department Director: Matthew Savage (1.01, 1.02, 1.03, 1.04)
Associate Designer: Matthew Savage (1.07, 1.08)
Art Department Co-ordinator: Matthew North (1.01, 1.02, 1.03, 1.04, 1.06, 1.07, 1.08, 1.09, 1.10, 1.11, 1.12, 1.13)
Design Assistants: Ben Austin (1.01*, 1.02*, 1.03, 1.04, 1.07, 1.08, 1.10), Al Roberts (1.01*, 1.03, 1.04, 1.08, 1.10), Rob Dicks (1.02*, 1.07)

---

45 First name misspelt 'Suzanna' on 1.05.

46 Credited on double bill compilation version of 1.12 and 1.13, but not on 'standard' single episode versions.

47 Credited as 'Jonathan Allison' on 1.05, 1.06, 1.09, 1.10, 1.11, 1.12 and 1.13 (including the double bill compilation version of the latter two).

Story Board Artist: Shaun Williams (1.10)
Standby Art Director: Dafydd Shurmer (1.01, 1.02, 1.04, 1.06, 1.08, 1.11), Leonie Rintler (1.03, 1.07) , Jon Howes (1.05, 1.10), Cathy Featherstone (1.09), Alison Brown (1.12, 1.13)
Standby Props: Brian Patrick Henry (1.01, 1.02, 1.03, 1.04, 1.07, 1.08), Andy Harris[48] (1.06, 1.10, 1.11, 1.12, 1.13), Matt Bacon (1.09), Keith Pitt (1.09)
Standby Carpenter: Will Pope (1.01*, 1.02*, 1.03, 1.04, 1.06, 1.07, 1.08, 1.10, 1.11, 1.12, 1.13), Gareth Thomas (1.09)
Standby Rigger: Keith Freeman (1.01*, 1.02*, 1.03, 1.04, 1.06, 1.07, 1.08, 1.10, 1.11, 1.12, 1.13), Neil Ruck (1.09)
Standby Painter: Clive Clarke (1.09), Julia Challis (1.10, 1.11, 1.12, 1.13)
Concept Artists: Ian Bunting (1.01*, 1.02*, 1.03, 1.04, 1.07, 1.08), Peter McKinstry (1.01*, 1.02*, 1.03, 1.04, 1.07, 1.08)
Designer: Julian Luxton (1.01, 1.02, 1.04, 1.08), Penny Harvey (1.03, 1.05, 1.07, 1.09, 1.10), Kay Brown (1.06, 1.11), Julie Signy (1.12, 1.13)
Property Master: Nick Thomas (1.01, 1.02, 1.03, 1.04, 1.07, 1.08), Stuart Woodisse[49] (1.06, 1.09, 1.10, 1.11, 1.12, 1.13)
Production Buyer: Ben Morris (1.01, 1.02, 1.04, 1.08), Catherine Samuel (1.03, 1.07), Zoe Hewitt (1.06), Blaanid Maddrell (1.10), Phil Clarke (1.13*), Holly Handel (1.13*)
Props Buyer: Catherine Samuel (1.09), Zoe Hewett (1.11), Phil Clarke (1.12), Holly Handel (1.12)
Props Chargehand: Dewi Thomas (1.06, 1.09, 1.10, 1.11, 1.12, 1.13)
Props Fabrication Manager[50]: Barry Jones (1.06, 1.09, 1.10, 1.11, 1.12, 1.13)
Props Storeman: Carlie Malik (1.01, 1.02, 1.03, 1.04, 1.07, 1.08)
Specialist Props Maker: Mark Cordory (1.01, 1.02, 1.03, 1.04, 1.06, 1.07, 1.08, 1.11, 1.12, 1.13)
Props Maker: Penny Howarth (1.01*, 1.03, 1.04, 1.07, 1.08, 1.10, 1.11, 1.12, 1.13), Nick Robatto (1.02*, 1.06, 1.10, 1.11, 1.12), Mark Cordory (1.10)
Practical Electrician: Albert James (1.11)
Construction Manager: Matthew Hywel-Davies
Construction Chargehand: Scott Fisher (1.01*, 1.02*, 1.03, 1.04, 1.06, 1.08, 1.09, 1.10, 1.11, 1.12, 1.13)
Scenic Artist: John Wally (1.11), John Pinkerton (1.11)
Graphics: BBC Wales Graphic Design
Costume Supervisor: Debra Haggett (1.01, 1.02, 1.03, 1.07), Charlotte Mitchell (1.04, 1.06, 1.08, 1.09, 1.11, 1.12), Bobby Peach (1.05, 1.10, 1.13)
Costume Assistants: Bobby Peach (1.01, 1.02, 1.03, 1.04, 1.07, 1.08, 1.11, 1.12*), Sam Benbow (1.01, 1.02, 1.03, 1.07), Sara Morgan[51] (1.04, 1.08, 1.10, 1.11, 1.12, 1.13), Dan Summerville (1.09), Maxine Brown (1.09), Marie Jones (1.10), Maria Franchi[52] (1.10, 1.12, 1.13), Charlotte Mitchell (1.13)
Make-up Supervisor: Claire Pritchard, Sarah Astley-Hughes (1.09)

---

48 Surname misspelt 'Hams' on 1.06.

49 Surname misspelt 'Woodisse' on 1.06 and 1.09.

50 Title given as 'Fabrication Manager' on 1.10, 1.11, 1.12 and 1.13 (including the double bill compilation version of the latter two).

51 First name misspelt 'Sarah' on 1.04 and 1.08.

52 Credited on the double bill compilation version of 1.12 and 1.13 but not on the 'standard' single episode version of either.

Make-Up Artists: Sarah Astley-Hughes (1.01, 1.02, 1.03, 1.04, 1.06, 1.07, 1.08, 1.10, 1.11, 1.12, 1.13), Kate Roberts (1.01, 1.02, 1.03, 1.04, 1.06, 1.07, 1.08, 1.10, 1.11, 1.12), Hayley Watkins (1.09, 1.11, 1.12, 1.13), Ellen Rhian[53] (1.09, 1.13), Anwen Hughes (1.09), Vicky Owen (1.09, 1.11)
Casting Associate: Andy Brierley (1.01, 1.02, 1.03, 1.04, 1.06, 1.07, 1.08, 1.09, 1.11, 1.12, 1.13), Kirsty Robertson (1.11, 1.12, 1.13)
Assistant Editor: Matt Mullins
Post Production Supervisors: Helen Vallis, Chris Blatchford
Post Production Co-ordinator: Marie Brown (1.01, 1.02, 1.03, 1.04, 1.06, 1.07, 1.08, 1.09, 1.10, 1.11, 1.12, 1.13)
On-Line Editor: Matthew Clarke (1.01, 1.02, 1.03, 1.04, 1.06, 1.07, 1.08, 1.09, 1.10, 1.11, 1.12), Jon Everett (1.09, 1.10, 1.11, 1.12, 1.13), Mark Bright (1.13)
Colourist: Jamie Wilkinson (1.01), James Bamford (1.02), Mick Vincent (1.03, 1.04, 1.05, 1.06, 1.07, 1.08, 1.09, 1.10, 1.11, 1.12, 1.13)
Visual Effects Co-ordinator: Kim Phelan (1.01*, 1.03, 1.04), Natalie Stopford (1.02*, 1.07)
3D Artist: Nicholas Hernandez* (1.01, 1.04, 1.05, 1.07, 1.13), Jean-Yves Audouard (1.01*, 1.07, 1.13), Jean-Claude Deguara (1.01*, 1.04, 1.05, 1.07, 1.13), Neil Roche (1.01*, 1.04, 1.07, 1.13), Nick Webber (1.02*), Paul Burton (1.02*), Andy Guest (1.02*, 1.13), Adam Burnett (1.07)
2D Artist: Simon Holden (1.01*, 1.03, 1.07), Joe Courtis (1.01*, 1.03, 1.04, 1.13), Sara Bennett (1.02*, 1.04, 1.07, 1.13), Bronwyn Edwards (1.02*, 1.07), Astrid Busser Casas (1.03), Charlie Bennett (1.04, 1.07), Russell Horth (1.13)
Digital Matte Painter: Alex Fort (1.01*)
Dubbing Mixer: Tim Ricketts (1.01, 1.03, 1.04, 1.05, 1.06, 1.07, 1.08, 1.09, 1.10), Peter Jeffreys (1.02, 1.11, 1.12, 1.13)
Supervising Sound Editor[54]: Doug Sinclair
Sound Editor: Paul McFadden (1.01, 1.02, 1.03, 1.04, 1.06, 1.07, 1.08, 1.09, 1.10, 1.11, 1.12, 1.13)
Sound FX Editor: Howard Eaves (1.01, 1.02, 1.03, 1.04, 1.06, 1.07, 1.08, 1.09, 1.10, 1.11, 1.12, 1.13)
Senior Production Accountant: Endaf Emyr Williams (1.01, 1.02, 1.03, 1.04, 1.07, 1.08, 1.10, 1.11, 1.12, 1.13)

Casting Director: Andy Pryor CDG
Production Accountant: Ceri Tothill
Sound Recordist: Jeff Matthews (1.01, 1.02, 1.03, 1.04, 1.06, 1.07, 1.08, 1.09, 1.11), Dave Baumber (1.05, 1.06, 1.10, 1.11, 1.12, 1.13)
Costume Designer: Ray Holman
Make-Up Designer: Marie Doris
Music: Murray Gold, Ben Foster (1.02, 1.03, 1.05, 1.06, 1.07, 1.08, 1.09, 1.10, 1.11, 1.12, 1.13)
Visual Effects: The Mill (1.01, 1.02, 1.03, 1.04, 1.05, 1.07, 1.08, 1.09, 1.12, 1.13)
Visual Effects Producers: Will Cohen (1.01, 1.02, 1.03, 1.04, 1.07, 1.08, 1.09, 1.12, 1.13), Marie Jones (1.01, 1.02, 1.03, 1.04, 1.07, 1.08, 1.09, 1.12, 1.13)
Visual Effects Supervisor: Dave Houghton (1.01, 1.02, 1.03, 1.04, 1.07, 1.08, 1.09, 1.12, 1.13)
On-Set Visual Effects Supervisor: Barney Curnow (1.01, 1.02, 1.03, 1.04, 1.07, 1.08, 1.09, 1.12, 1.13)
Special Effects: Any Effects (1.01, 1.02, 1.03, 1.04, 1.05, 1.06, 1.07, 1.09, 1.11, 1.12, 1.13)

---

53 Name spelt 'Elin Rhiannon' on 1.13 (and on the double bill compilation version of 1.12 and 1.13).

54 Title given as 'Sound Supervisor' on 1.10, 1.11, 1.12 and 1.13 (including the double bill compilation version of the latter two).

Prosthetics: Neill Gorton (1.01, 1.02, 1.04, 1.06, 1.07, 1.08, 1.11, 1.13*), Rob Mayor (1.04, 1.06, 1.11, 1.13*) and Millennium Effects (1.01, 1.02, 1.04, 1.06, 1.07, 1.08, 1.11, 1.13*)
Prosthetics Supervisors: Martin Rezard (1.04), Pete Hawkins (1.04)
Production Manager: Catrin Lewis Defis (1.03, 1.05, 1.07, 1.10), Debbi Slater (1.04, 1.08), Marcus Prince (1.04, 1.06, 1.08, 1.11), Kaela Langan (1.12, 1.13)
Editor: William Webb (1.01, 1.02), Mike Hopkins (1.03, 1.07), Mike Jones (1.04, 1.08), Bobby Sheikh (1.05, 1.10), Richard Cox (1.06, 1.11), Phil Hookway (1.09), Nick Ames (1.12), Elen Pierce Lewis (1.13)
Production Designer: Edward Thomas
Director of Photography: Mark Waters (1.01, 1.02, 1.03, 1.04, 1.06, 1.07, 1.08, 1.11), Ray Orton (1.05, 1.10, 1.12, 1.13), Simon Butcher (1.09)
Associate Producer: Marcus Prince (1.01, 1.02), Terry Reeve (1.03, 1.04, 1.05, 1.06, 1.07, 1.08, 1.09, 1.10, 1.11, 1.12, 1.13)
Production Executive: Julie Scott
Assistant Producer: Sophie Fante (1.01, 1.02, 1.03, 1.04, 1.05, 1.06, 1.07, 1.08, 1.10, 1.11, 1.12, 1.13)

Executive Producers: Russell T Davies, Julie Gardner

A BBC Wales Production in association with the Canadian Broadcasting Corporation

EPISODE GUIDE

In the episode guide that follows, no details are given for transmissions on the BBC HD channel, as these are regarded as having been essentially on a test basis, the channel having yet to be formally launched at the time. In general, however, each episode debuted on BBC HD at the same time as it did on BBC Three. The first two episodes were shown in their complete, 'standard' versions on BBC HD, as opposed to the edited versions used for the double bill screenings on both BBC Three and BBC Two.

Those cast members marked + were not credited in the BBC's listings magazine *Radio Times*.

All references here to credits in *Radio Times* relate to the listings for the Wednesday evening BBC Two transmissions; there were no detailed listings given for the BBC Three debut screenings.

The episode durations quoted are those of the original BBC Three broadcasts, unless otherwise indicated. These were generally a couple of seconds shorter than the full versions of the episodes on the BBC's master tapes, and on the series' DVD releases, as each episode tended to be cut into very slightly by the preceding and/or following continuity caption and announcement. In addition, the preceding continuity caption was generally faded into the start of the episode, rather than there being a clean cut, so the timings are necessarily approximate.

Readers who have yet to see the episodes may wish to bear in mind that this guide is a comprehensive one that contains many plot 'spoilers'.

1.01 – EVERYTHING CHANGES

WRITER: Russell T Davies
DIRECTOR: Brian Kelly

DEBUT TRANSMISSION DETAILS

BBC Three	BBC Two
Date: 22 October 2006.	Date: 25 October 2006.
Scheduled time: 9.00 pm.	Scheduled time: 9.00 pm.
Actual time: 9.00 pm.	Actual time: 9.02 pm.

Duration: 50' 39" (Complete episode duration: 51' 09")[55]

ADDITIONAL CREDITED CAST

Guy Lewis (Young Cop); Tom Price (PC Andy), Jason May (SOCO[56]), Rhys Swinburn (Body[57]), Olwen Medi (Yvonne), Gwyn Vaughan-Jones (DI Jacobs), Dion Davies (Officer), Jams Thomas (Hospital Porter), Paul Kasey (Weevil), Mark Heal (Security Guard), Gary Sheppeard+ (Pizza Lad), Gwilym Havard Davies+ (Man[58]), Cathryn Davis+[59] (Woman[60])

PLOT: Cardiff policewoman Gwen Cooper is shocked when, after arriving at a crime scene, she sees a team of mysterious strangers from an organisation called Torchwood briefly resurrect a murder victim through the use of alien technology. She eventually tracks them down to their secret base, the Hub, below the Roald Dahl Plass. The team's leader, Captain Jack Harkness, introduces her to its other members – Owen Harper, Toshiko Sato, Suzie Costello and Ianto Jones – and tells her that their job is to capture aliens, scavenge their technology and protect the Earth in the 21st Century, when 'everything changes'. He drugs her to make her forget what she has seen, but she manages to make her way back to the Roald Dahl Plass, where she regains her memory after discovering that Suzie has allowed her obsession with her work to turn her into a murderer, and that Jack cannot be killed.

QUOTE, UNQUOTE

- Captain Jack: 'Tell me, what was it like when you died? What did you see? John, tell me what you saw.'
  John Tucker: 'Nothin'. I saw nothin'. Oh my god, there's nothin''

- PC Andy: 'CSI Cardiff, I'd like to see that. They'd be measuring the velocity of a kebab.'

55 On this episode's debut transmission, in a double bill with 'Day One', the closing credits were removed. Its first (non-HD) transmission in its 'standard' form, complete with closing credits, was at 9.00 pm on BBC Three on 27 October 2006.

56 Spelt out as 'Scenes of crime officer' in *Radio Times*.

57 Named as 'John Tucker' in the dialogue of the episode.

58 Named as 'Colin' in the dialogue of the episode.

59 Surname misspelt 'Davies' on the debut transmission version at the end of 'Day One'.

60 Named as 'Linda' in the dialogue of the episode.

- Gwen: 'I'm getting tired of following you.'
  Captain Jack: 'No you're not; and you never will.'

- Captain Jack: 'The 21st Century's when it all changes, and you gotta be ready.'

- Suzie: 'How can you do any other job after this one? Cause it gets inside you. You do this job for long enough, and you end up thinking … How come we get all the Weevils and bollocks and shit? Is that what alien life is – filth? But maybe there's better stuff out there; brilliant stuff, beautiful stuff, just … they don't come here. This planet's so dirty, that's all we get: the shit.'

- Captain Jack: 'Something happened to me a while back. A long story, and far away. But I was killed, and then I was brought back to life, and ever since then, I can't die … One day I'll find a Doctor, the right sort of Doctor, and maybe he can explain it, but until then …'

DOCTOR WHO REFERENCES

- Jack wears an RAF great-coat of World War Two vintage, like the one he had when he first appeared in the *Doctor Who* story 'The Empty Child'/'The Doctor Dances'.

- Gwen traces Torchwood through a Jubilee Pizza takeaway outlet. In the *Doctor Who* story 'Dalek', a pizza box bearing the same company name and logo was seen in Van Statten's base in Utah, USA, in the year 2012 – which presumably implies that Jubilee Pizza is a successful global franchise in the *Doctor Who* universe. (The use of the name in 'Dalek' was a homage to the *Doctor Who* audio play 'Jubilee', which provided much of its inspiration and was the work of the same writer, Rob Shearman.)

- A severed right hand is seen floating in a jar of preservative fluid in the Hub. The implication of this and later episodes is that it is the Doctor's hand, which was cut off in a fight with the Sycorax Leader in the *Doctor Who* special 'The Christmas Invasion' (although, as the Doctor had only recently regenerated at the time, he was able to regrow it).

- The Hub set contains numerous other artefacts first seen in *Doctor Who*. Although these are not all seen on screen in 'Everything Changes', behind-the-scenes features in *Radio Times* and elsewhere indicate that they include: various weapons such as Cyberman guns and Sycorax staffs; the binoculars that Captain Jack was seen using in 'The Empty Child'; television sets from Magpie Electricals as featured in 'The Idiot's Lantern'; magna-clamps like those in the possession of Torchwood One in 'Army of Ghosts'/'Doomsday'; and 3-D glasses similar to (but not quite the same as) those used by the Doctor in the latter story. There is even a piece of coral described by production designer Ed Thomas as Captain Jack's ongoing attempt at growing a TARDIS!

- Captain Jack implies that a possible explanation for the area of invisibility – the 'perception filter' – beside the water tower fountain is that the TARDIS previously materialised there and its 'dimensionally transcendental chameleon circuit … welded its perception properties to a spacio-temporal rift'.

- The spacio-temporal rift running through Cardiff was previously featured in the *Doctor Who* stories 'The Unquiet Dead' and 'Boom Town', and is an important element of *Torchwood.*

- Captain Jack refers to the Sycorax spaceship hovering over London in 'The Christmas Invasion', and to the Battle of Canary Wharf with 'a Cyberman in every home', as seen in 'Army of Ghosts'/'Doomsday'.

- Captain Jack tells Gwen about his death and resurrection, as seen in 'The Parting of the Ways' in *Doctor Who*, and refers – albeit obliquely – to the Doctor.

ALIEN TECH

- There is in Torchwood's possession a metallic glove of alien origin that can resurrect the dead – but only temporarily, for about two minutes. It works best on those whose death has been violent, and/or who have been killed with a particular alien knife, also in Torchwood's possession, to which it is presumably linked in some way.

- The Hub evidently contains much alien tech, scavenged by Torchwood.

- As he did in *Doctor Who*, Jack wears on a leather wrist-strap an electronic device, presumably of alien origin, that will be used throughout the series for a variety of purposes, including scanning and the remote control of various different types of equipment – including, in 'Everything Changes', the lift that ascends from the Hub to emerge invisibly in Roald Dahl Plass.

- Toshiko has 'borrowed' from Torchwood an alien device that allow her to scan the pages of a book without opening it and then download the images onto her computer.

- Owen has similarly 'borrowed' an aerosol-type spray – also presumably alien – that makes him irresistibly attractive.

- The drug that Jack gives Gwen to induce amnesia may possibly have an alien origin, although he says that he concocted it to his own 'recipe'.

'BLOOD AND SNOGGING'

- The murder victim in the alley in the opening scene is lying in a pool of blood.

- A hospital porter is killed when a Weevil bites his neck, causing copious amounts of blood to spurt out.

- Gwen affectionately kisses her boyfriend, Rhys.

- Owen, with the aid of the alien spray, seduces and kisses a young woman – and subsequently her boyfriend – at a local bar.

- Suzie shoots Jack in the forehead, then – when this fails to kill him and his injury instantly heals – commits suicide by shooting herself under the chin.

CONTINUITY POINTS

- The Torchwood team drive a black SUV, which is actually a heavily customised Range Rover. It has the licence plate CF06 FDU – which does not officially exist.

- A couple of hundred alien Weevils live in the sewers beneath Cardiff. Their real name and planet of origin are unknown, owing to their inability to communicate. Every so often, one comes to the surface, goes rogue and attacks.

- The events of the episode take place mid-week, as Gwen's colleague Andy is making plans for Friday at the beginning of the episode, and later Toshiko is intending to ensure that the caretaker's body is found the following Tuesday, which she implies is in five days' time.

- Alien 'flotsam and jetsam' washes up in Cardiff because of the rift in space and time that runs through the city.

- There is a pterodactyl living in the roof of the Hub.

PRODUCTION NOTES

- Made with 'Day One' as part of Block 1 of production.

- This episode had the working title 'Flotsam and Jetsam', which was dropped only after recording had been completed. An earlier working title is reported to have been 'The Valley of Death'.

- The *Torchwood* theme music is closely based on a piece of incidental music used in the *Doctor Who* episode 'Army of Ghosts', which can be found on the CD *Doctor Who: Original Television Soundtrack* (Silva Screen, 2006).

- This episode, unlike the others in the series, has no teaser scene before the opening title sequence. Although one was written and recorded, which took the form of a flash-forward to Gwen and Jack talking on the roof of the Millennium Centre at the end of the story, it was cut before transmission. It is included amongst the deleted scenes on the Series One: Part One DVD release.

- The Weevil's head – a radio-controlled animatronic appliance worn by actor Paul Kasey, who had previously portrayed creatures such as Autons and Cybermen in *Doctor Who* – was designed to resemble 'a deformed ape', according the Neill Gorton of Millennium FX, who realised the creature. The idea was that it should look not too far removed from the 'real world', to fit in with the overall style of *Torchwood*.

- During the 8 June 2006 location recording of the scene of Jack standing atop the Altolusso building in Cardiff – for which John Barrowman was doubled by a stuntman – local traffic wardens and police became concerned that someone was attempting to commit suicide.

- Three contemporary music tracks feature in this episode: 'Spitting Games', a 2003 single by Snow Patrol (heard when Owen seduces the young woman in the bar); 'We are the Pipettes', a 2006 album track by the Pipettes (playing in the pub where Gwen gets injured trying to break up a fight); and 'She Moves in Her Own Way', a 2006 single by the Kooks (paying in the Jubilee Pizza outlet).

- Amongst the central Cardiff locations featured in this episode are the multi-storey NCP car park in Tredegar Street (the opening sequence); the Cornwall pub (where Gwen gets hurt breaking up a fight); Mumbai Bay takeaway near the Millennium Centre (the pizza takeaway); an area near Mermaid Quay (the entrance to Ianto's tourist information office); Buffalo Bar in Windsor Place (the bar where Jack and Gwen talk); a bar called Icon on Charles Street (the bar where Owen uses the sex spray); parts of St Mary's Street (the street along which Gwen runs after she witnesses the resurrection of John Tucker, and also later after Jack reveals that he has drugged her); the Altolusso apartment building (Jack's high vantage point); and the Roald Dahl Plass (where the invisible lift exits from the Hub).

- The sequence of Jack telling Gwen about Torchwood over a drink was originally recorded in a different pub. It was reshot to make it more edgy and dramatic. The original version is included as a deleted scene amongst the extras on the Series One: Part One DVD release.

PRODUCTION QUOTES

- '[The scenes shot over three days with a rain machine look] wonderful on the screen, but we all had to wear really attractive wetsuits underneath our clothes. You couldn't bend your arms or legs and it was absolutely freezing – but I'd do it all again tomorrow.' Actress Eve Myles, This is South Wales website, 22 October 2006

- '[The description of the Hub] was fairly detailed in the script. In the first episode, Russell wrote fairly specific ideas about the sense and the feel of the set. Ed Thomas and his design team never put anything into a set that doesn't have a reason to be there. So they always have to justify everything there, but they will. You can literally walk around that set with Ed Thomas and his team and point at anything and go, "Why is that there?", and they'll know.' Producer Richard Stokes, *SFX* Issue 150, December 2006.

- 'Russell gave us an open book on the Hub. He said it needed to do this and that, and have these characteristics, and so we set about designing it on the back of *Doctor Who* last year. I think it was 5 December 2005 when we started the design process, and by the time the first script was coming up, we were ready to rock and roll with a locked-off design … We've come up with a backstory for the waterfall. What there is on location is a sort of antenna inside that sculpture that is continually tracking for alien presence, and the water coming down is actually a cooling agent that prevents the entire mast overheating.' Production Designer Edward Thomas, *Starburst* Special 79, February 2007.

- 'The Hub was one of the main things they wanted in their budget. You have shows like *Spooks* and *Waking the Dead*, and they have their offices as the main set, and *Torchwood* has its Hub. But the set is only on two storeys and we have to make it four storeys, so when the camera gets pointed up, we have to fill in the gap. Ed initially wanted to make it three storeys, but at one of the first meetings, they said: "Could you extend the set for us?" … They wanted to keep it more real. *Raiders of the Lost Ark* was mentioned as a reference point for making the Hub … We took the detailed plans and spent 20 weeks making a 3-D set.' Visual Effects Producer Will Cohen, *Starburst* Special 79, February 2007.

- 'Working in hi-def doesn't really make a lot of difference to us in terms of how we do our work. We always work to a high level of detail with the creatures we build and prosthetics we do. What it does mean is that elements you could previously consider as "background" now need to be as detailed as we make our hero pieces. So the only person that needs to be concerned about that is the production accountant.' Creature effects designer Neill Gorton, *Starburst* Issue 344, December 2006.

OOPS!

- Contrary to what Captain Jack implies, the invisible lift leading down to the Hub is not (quite) in the same place that the TARDIS materialised in the *Doctor Who* episode 'Boom Town'.

- A poster advertising a *Doctor Who* exhibition in Cardiff can be seen briefly in the background of one shot.

- The police state that the two earlier murder victims were female, but in the opening scene, Jack refers to one of the people on whom the team have previously tested the resurrection glove as 'he'. (This could mean, however, that it is not only the murder victims that they have previously used for these purposes.)

PRESS REACTION

- 'It's slick, scary, funny and expensive looking, but it's also very much an establishing story.' Mark Braxton, *Radio Times*, 21-27 October 2006.

- 'New *Who* has made sci-fi socially acceptable but I can see this making it positively hip – I'm certain it's gonna be a hit …They've done a great job of making Cardiff look glamorous, a bit like LA in *Angel* … While it's grown-up it's not too grim or gritty – Russell T Davies's cheeky sense of humour is still very much present … The first episode neatly does everything a pilot needs to in terms of introductions, which is all you can really expect, but there are a couple of great twists, too, which I didn't see coming.' Ian Berriman, *SFX* magazine website, 17 October 2006.

- 'If *Buffy* [*the Vampire Slayer*] was a kids show that appealed to adults, then *Torchwood* comes over like an adult show that will appeal to kids. Let's hope they are allowed to stay up to watch it. Despite a lull in the middle, there is plenty of fun to be had in the opening episode, scripted by executive producer Russell T Davies, and a few memorable lines.' John Plunkett, Guardian Unlimited website, 19 October 2006.

- 'The first episode is an economical, by the numbers introduction to the team and the character of WPC Gwen Cooper … Eve Myles as Gwen is the solid, down to earth character needed to anchor Torchwood to the real world, and her turn is a nice counterpoint to the more fanciful Harkness. John Barrowman is clearly having a ball, running around with a gun and a grin, and his presence means you never quite take things seriously, which is a big help with a big, silly sci-fi series. Does *Torchwood* have what it takes to go the distance? It's certainly bold, the cast are very pretty and the dialogue has a zippy archness to it. Whether that will become grating after a few episodes remains to be seen, but on the basis of the first pair, if you like your sci-fi drama a bit punchier than the whimsical *Doctor Who*, touch wood, you should find a lot to enjoy in the adventures of *Torchwood*.' Mark Wright, *The Stage* magazine website, 19 October 2006.

- 'This was a show where appearances mattered above all else, yet first impressions proved sorely wanting. Glamorous-looking rain doesn't work for this country. It's fine for America, but in the UK, rain has to look dirty and desolate or else it just – ahem – doesn't wash. Watching our ostensible heroes processing through a rainbow of twinkling droplets, only to then see a Welsh forensics expert cussing effusively, was like being pulled not merely between varying moods but different continents. Here, as throughout the episode, were perfectly formed and beautifully [shot] individual pieces of drama never quite managing to resolve into a jigsaw of coherently-ordered entertainment. And as proceedings continued, vignettes of emotion and fragments of speech that felt like they could function perfectly well in isolation just made no impact arranged in sequence.' Ian Jones, Off the Telly website, 23 October 2006.

- 'Those hoping for a dour British take on *The X-Files,* or maybe even the slick, labyrinthine plotting of a Kudos show[61], might be a little disappointed at the more kitsch, retro approach of this opener. In terms of plotting and visual style, it feels like it owes more to the '60s world of *The Avengers* and *Mission Impossible* than *Spooks*. And while there are nods to adult entertainment (gore, swearing, a couple of sexual references) it still clearly exists very much in the slightly bonkers universe of New *Who*.' Dave Golder, *SFX* Issue 150, December 2006.

FAN COMMENT

- 'I've just been to the Manchester [preview] screening … and I honestly can't believe what I've seen. *Torchwood* is possibly the best show ever …The chemistry onscreen between all the [leads] is perfect. Of particular note is Burn Gorman, who's perfect as Owen. His character is so unbelievably cool, but also rather geeky, that your heart breaks when, in a bar, his offer of sex is turned down by a woman. It means that he has to resort to desperate measures – and you'll never look at a spray in the same way ever again! I went away from this screening completely in love with not only Owen, but every single other character as well. Gwen is interesting enough to warrant her heavy amount of screen time, and her emotional journey is one hundred percent believable. Likewise for Indira Varma's Suzie … Her character travels a very real emotional journey in "Everything Changes". This is her story as much as Gwen's.' Anthony Garnon, Torchwood.TV website, 18 October 2006

- 'The word that mostly springs to mind is "derivative". The whole idea of group of strange people investigating even stranger goings on looks a lot like *Angel*. The secret hideaway secreted behind a normal-looking building is all very *The Man From UNCLE*. The

61 Kudos is the production company responsible for such series as *Spooks* and *Hustle*.

Torchwood HQ looks a bit like an untidier version of the Batcave (with a holding cell that is taken directly from *Silence of the Lambs*). The lift that takes you up to the Millennium Centre is like something out of *Thunderbirds*. Oh, and since Captain Jack was brought back to life by Rose Tyler in *Doctor Who* last year, he seems to have mutated into Captain Scarlet.'
Dave Cross, Davblog, 23 October 2006

ANALYSIS

In 'Everything Changes', Russell T Davies takes a tried-and-trusted approach to the task of introducing viewers to the basic set-up of a new series: he establishes an audience-identification figure, the ordinary policewoman Gwen Cooper, and then takes her through the process of meeting the other regular characters for the first time and getting drawn into their extraordinary world. This is essentially the same approach that the original *Doctor Who* production team took in the parent series' very first episode back in 1963, when they had the down-to-earth schoolteachers Ian Chesterton and Barbara Wright stumble upon the out-of-this-world secret of their pupil Susan and her strange grandfather, the Doctor. It is also the same approach that Davies himself adopted in 'Rose', the first new *Doctor Who* episode in 2005, when the audience-identification character was the bored shop girl Rose Tyler. In one respect, Davies pulls off the trick even more effectively the second time around; whereas Rose's initial meeting with the Doctor comes about purely by chance when she gets caught up in events in the basement of Henrik's department store, Gwen's first sighting of the Torchwood team results entirely plausibly from her role as a beat copper called to a murder scene in which they, for reasons of their own, are also taking an interest. Where 'Everything Changes' rather falls down, though, is in moving the story forward to the next stage. In 'Rose', there is a clear, albeit slightly contrived, reason for the two lead characters to run into each other for a second time: Rose has taken a Nestene-animated plastic arm from a store mannequin back to her home, and the Doctor tracks the controlling signal there. In 'Everything Changes', on the other hand, where the logical thing to do would surely have been to have had Gwen track Captain Jack down through police enquiries – which she does indeed initiate – their second meeting is actually a complete coincidence, when she is taken to hospital to get a minor injury treated and he and his team just happen to be there at the same time.

There is another disconcerting awkwardness in the plotting a little later on. Why, after Gwen has infiltrated the Hub, does Jack go to the trouble of telling her about Torchwood, allowing her to observe the Weevil – for a considerable length of time, apparently, as a wall clock subsequently shows that almost an hour has passed since she arrived – and introducing her to his team? In interviews in *Torchwood Declassified*: 'Bad Day at the Office', John Barrowman comments that Gwen's inquisitiveness leads Jack to think that she could become a part of Torchwood, and Eve Myles says, 'He's doing it because he's testing her'. This explanation does not really stand up to scrutiny, however, as at the time when Jack gives Gwen her guided tour of the Hub, he is unaware that he will shortly be having a 'vacancy' on his team and apparently has no intention of allowing her to retain her memories of what she has seen, as he subsequently gives her an amnesia-inducing drug. Perhaps the answer lies instead in another point to which Myles alludes in the same interview: 'There's an instant connection with Gwen and Jack, from the first moment that Jack sees her spying over onto the dead body.' The connection may even be formed a little earlier than that: there is an intriguing moment when, just after he and his team arrive at the crime scene, Jack clearly notices Gwen watching from a distance and pauses for a moment. Does he effectively develop a fascination for her right then, on first sight? If so, perhaps he simply feels compelled to take her into his confidence when she tracks him down to the Hub, in which case his subsequent drugging of her in the bar could be interpreted a reluctant act on his part – or maybe even a further, final test, to see if she is sufficiently resourceful to circumvent the effects of the drug. Although he is content to dismiss her with a casual 'Nice knowing you, Gwen Cooper', there does seem to be more than a hint of regret in his voice.

Another, more troubling issue is raised by Jack's spiking of Gwen's drink, and even more so by Owen's use of an alien spray to seduce a young woman, Linda, in another bar. These scenes, coming in quick succession, inevitably bring to the viewer's mind the scourge of 'date rape' drugs. While Jack's drugging of Gwen obviously has no sexual motive, Owen's use of the spray certainly does. Is Owen, in fact, a rapist? It seems clear that the alien spray makes him not simply more attractive – like a sort of super-effective aftershave lotion – but literally irresistible, so that Linda is acting contrary to her own free will when she kisses him and determines to take him home and have sex with him. The same is also clearly true of her boyfriend, Colin, when Owen uses the spray to affect him in the street outside. To be fair, it is not certain that Owen actually follows through on his predatory intentions. When he hails a taxi at the end of the scene, it could just be with a view to packing Linda and Colin off home, rather than joining them for a threesome. The action isn't played that way, though, and to the extent that Owen shows any concern, it is only over the discovery that Linda has a boyfriend, not over the morality of what he is doing. And as Owen knows of the spray's properties in advance, it seems likely that this is not the first time he has used it. It is difficult to believe that Davies and his colleagues on the production team did not consider the full implications of this, and yet the sequence seems to be intended as an amusing one. If so, then it backfires badly, as the viewer's reaction is more one of discomfort or even distaste.

This highlights another problem with 'Everything Changes': that aside from Jack, with whom most viewers will be familiar already from *Doctor Who*, Gwen is really the only immediately likeable character in it. Gwen's boyfriend Rhys seems a bit of a drip; Ianto features too briefly to make much of an impression; Toshiko also stays mainly in the background, although she is the first to start sniggering over the joke that the team play at Gwen's expense when she first enters the Hub; Owen comes across as a cynical big-head and potential rapist; and Suzie turns out to be a work-obsessed murderer.

The lack of audience familiarity with Suzie in fact somewhat undercuts the impact of the end-of-episode revelation of her criminal activities, which – although admittedly a neat twist that the viewer doesn't see coming – is less shocking than it might be, simply because the character has had barely a couple of minutes' screen time prior to this point. As other reviewers have observed, it would perhaps have been better had Suzie's demise been deferred for, say, two or three episodes. The business with the alien resurrection glove and the knife, and the police's efforts to catch the serial killer, could then have been kept going as a subplot in the background throughout these early episodes, leading to a more satisfying payoff at the end. Davies would, of course, have had to have come up with some different crisis to form the main, self-contained plot of 'Everything Changes'; but this might also have worked to its advantage, as Gwen could have got caught up in the crisis on infiltrating the Hub and become part of the Torchwood team effectively as a *fait accompli*. This would have avoided the need to have Jack drug her – which impacts negatively on his likeability as a character – and then to have her gradually regain her memory, which results in the only lull in the otherwise excellent pacing of the episode. The addition of an ongoing subplot would also, arguably, have benefited the next few episodes, as the 'mission of the week' approach does tend to become a little formulaic, and is also inconsistent with the viewer's experience of real-life organisations, which typically have to juggle several problems at once. Although it is admittedly neater to have Gwen effectively stepping into Suzie's shoes at the end of 'Everything Changes', this is not really a case of her 'filling a vacancy', as Jack implies, as Suzie's specialist area was the investigation of alien hardware, whereas Gwen's skills lie elsewhere – meaning that the team actually still has a vacancy for someone capable of fulfilling Suzie's former role.

All this speculation is perhaps rather pointless, however, as this was not the route that Davies chose to take. And there is no denying that the climactic scene where Suzie confronts Gwen beside the water tower fountain and shoots Jack in the head, only to see him rise to his feet again, is incredibly powerful. Indira Varma and Eve Myles both give fine, compelling performances here, delivering Davies's excellent dialogue with utter conviction; and the apparent death and resurrection of Jack leave the viewer absolutely astounded.

Indeed, as with most of his *Doctor Who* episodes, it is in his stunning set-pieces and his superbly-crafted dialogue, rather than in his plot construction, that Davies really excels here. 'Everything Changes' has more breathtaking stand-out sequences packed into its 50 minutes than many run-of-the-mill dramas can manage in an entire season.

The opening scene, where Gwen witnesses the Torchwood team fruitlessly quizzing the briefly-resurrected murder victim, is a excellent case in point. A captivating juxtaposition of the bleakly mundane and the darkly strange, it immediately sets the tone for the series as a whole and serves as an irresistible hook to draw the viewer into the action. Just who are these mysterious, sexy strangers who can commandeer a cordoned-off crime scene with complete impunity and work the apparent miracle of bringing a dead man back to life?

Possibly even better is the sequence in the hospital corridor, where Gwen has her first encounter with the Weevil – a very well-realised monster that would not have seemed at all out of place in *Buffy the Vampire Slayer*'s Sunnydale. This is an object lesson in the creation of effective suspense. Gwen's ambivalent reaction to the creature – logic telling her that it must be a man fooling about in a mask, but instinct cautioning her that there is something strange going on here and she ought to hold back – is just brilliantly played by Myles. And then the hospital porter, lacking Gwen's perceptiveness, saunters in and goes straight up to the creature, and – as the viewer at home silently, or perhaps not so silently, urges him to be careful – pays the ultimate price. This is really a pivotal scene – as executive producer Julie Gardner puts it in the 'Jack's Back' episode of *Torchwood Declassified*: 'It's the bridge from [Gwen's] normal life into her extraordinary life' – and it could not have been better done.

The scene where Jack takes Gwen down to the Hub's basement and gives her the chance to see the Weevil again, in the cold light of its cell, is another highlight – and a clever homage to *The Silence of the Lambs*. Again it is superbly acted by Myles, showing all the emotions flowing through Gwen as she comes to accept the reality of the Weevil and its alien nature, and yet is able to cope with it and keep her cool when many lesser mortals would no doubt have lost it. This is another key scene for the character. As Myles comments in 'Bad Day at the Office': 'If Gwen had gone down [to the cells] and screamed and fainted, she'd never be in Torchwood.'

Then there is the aforementioned exchange between Jack and Gwen in the bar – another minor classic. Davies's dialogue fairly sparkles here, and again the delivery by the two leads is spot on, as Jack speaks matter-of-factly of alien invasion attempts, Torchwood branches dotted around the UK and the spacio-temporal rift through Cardiff, and Gwen tries to take it all in before facing the horrifying realisation that she has been drugged.

I strongly suspect that, if *Torchwood* has a reasonable life-span as a series, these fantastic scenes will one day take on something of an iconic quality.

Also extremely effective is the way the episode establishes emphatically and from the outset the series' signature visual style – which is very distinctive, particularly for a UK-originated production. The opening sequence must again be highlighted here: the rain-lashed, concrete-clad alley; the blue flashing lights of the police cars; the victim's body, lying in a pool of blood and picked out by a circle of small spotlights; the black Torchwood SUV speeding onto the scene; the fluorescent yellow safety jackets of the police officers and functional white coveralls of the forensics unit contrasting with the cool, dark street attire of Captain Jack and his team. All these things combine to create a riveting – and highly memorable – impression of a dark, gritty, exciting environment, reinforced by some brilliant camerawork and direction. Similar stylistic touches run throughout the episode; and the other realistic urban settings used – the deserted car park, the police station, the hospital, the pizza place, the bars, the streets – form a backdrop to the action that seems mundane and familiar, but at the same time edgy and unsettling.

Then there are the sequences showing the rather more 'glamorous' side of Cardiff, with numerous striking shots of the sleek, modern architecture of the Roald Dahl Plass and panoramic aerial views of various city landmarks. Particularly breathtaking is the shot of Jack stood fearlessly atop the Altolusso building, surveying the vista before him. This is another key moment in the episode, and while it could be read as a simple metaphor for Jack watching over Cardiff – and by extension the Earth, at the start of the century when 'everything changes' – or perhaps keeping vigil for the return of the Doctor, it also foreshadows the later revelation that he is now incapable of dying.

What must life be like for someone who is immortal? Does it become so devoid of threat that it is only through such apparently reckless acts as surmounting tall buildings that one is able to experience any thrill of danger at all? Producer Richard Stokes has described Jack as having a 'haunted' quality following his resurrection by 'goddess Rose' in the *Doctor Who* episode 'The Parting of the Ways', and Julie Gardner comments in 'Jack's Back': 'How does it affect a character if they can't die? Is that a great, glorious, exciting, wonderful thing, or is it a terrible curse as well, and the loneliness of that, and what does it mean?' Once again, it is in the episode's crucial opening sequence that this question is first touched upon, as Jack presses the murder victim to reveal what he saw when he was dead, and the answer he receives is a bleak 'Nothin''. This immediately leads the viewer to wonder what Jack himself saw in the minutes before he was resurrected, and introduces a theme that runs throughout the episode, and will indeed recur throughout the series: that of the finality – or otherwise – of death.

The alien resurrection glove is, of course, central to this. Suzie believes that if she can perfect her operation of the device so that it works to order, and permanently, it would offer, as she puts it: 'Resurrection on demand for the whole world.' She asks, as if trying to convince herself: 'Isn't that good? Isn't it, though?' What the viewer sees of Jack's experience of immortality suggests that the answer to that question is, at best, far from clear-cut.

The idea of making Jack incapable of dying was a shrewd one on Davies's part – notwithstanding that it created a rather unfortunate parallel with another fictional captain who could not be killed, namely Gerry Anderson's 1960s puppet creation Captain Scarlet. Bringing Jack down to Earth and placing him in charge of Torchwood Three – thereby burdening him with leadership responsibilities and the need to concern himself with such workaday matters as budgets and rules of procedure – could have effectively neutered the character; and it must be said that he has indeed lost a little of the reckless, devil-may-care bravado and rampant libido that he had in his introductory *Doctor Who* appearances. But those broader initial traits would arguably not have been sustainable in a character now required to step up from a supporting role to take centre stage throughout an entire series. What was needed was a new, rather deeper take on Jack, and Davies's notion of giving him the decidedly mixed blessing of immortality – a sort of twisted version of the Doctor's ability to regenerate in *Doctor Who* – has imbued him with just the right degree of additional complexity and mystery. As director Brian Kelly comments in 'Jack's Back': 'The thing about Captain Jack in episode one is we learn a lot about him, but we also learn there's a lot more to find out about him.'

John Barrowman's performance as this slightly darker, more enigmatic, even angrier version of Jack is excellent throughout, and firmly establishes him as a commanding presence at the heart of the series. Just as good if not better, though, is the contribution made by Eve Myles, whose depiction of the 'girl next door' policewoman who stumbles upon – as the *Torchwood* official website puts it – 'a dark, paranoid world she never imagined existed' is simply captivating. 'Everything Changes' is really Gwen's episode, told from her perspective and establishing the Torchwood team through her eyes, and it is the prospect of finding out what further experiences lie in store for her that provides perhaps the greatest incentive for the viewer to stick with the series and see what happens next.

In the final analysis, the many plus points of 'Everything Changes' – the strong introduction of Gwen and reintroduction of Jack, the fine performances by the cast, the adept setting-up of the excellent central premise of the Torchwood team and their Hub, the effective establishment of the series' distinctive dramatic and visual style and, most especially, the brilliant set pieces and dialogue – easily outweigh its minus points – chiefly the plotting problems and the misfire scene of Owen in the bar – and overall it has to be judged an undoubted success.

1.02 – DAY ONE

WRITER: Chris Chibnall
DIRECTOR: Brian Kelly

DEBUT TRANSMISSION DETAILS

BBC Three	BBC Two
Date: 22 October 2006.	Date: 25 October 2006.
Scheduled time: 9.50 pm.	Scheduled time: 9.50 pm.
Actual time: 9.52 pm.	Actual time: 9.54 pm.

Duration: 47' 23" (Complete episode duration: 47' 46")[62]

ADDITIONAL CREDITED CAST

Adrian Christopher+ (Private Moriarty), Ross O'Hennessy+ (Sgt Johnson), Sara Lloyd Gregory+ (Carys[63]), Ceri Mears+ (Banksy), Justin McDonald+ (Matt), Tom Price (PC Andy), Brendan Charleson+ (Ivan Fletcher), Rob Storr+ (Gavin), Lloyd Everitt+ (Mikey), Alex Parry+ (Eddie Gwynne), Felicity Rhys+ (Bethan), Naomi Martell+ (Receptionist), David Longden+ (Mr Warton)

PLOT: A meteor-like alien vessel crash-lands on the outskirts of Cardiff, and when Torchwood arrive on the scene, Gwen accidentally lets loose the gaseous creature inside. Arriving in the city centre, the creature possesses the body of a young woman, Carys, and proceeds to seek out sex with as many men as possible, feeding off their orgasmic energy – and destroying them in the process. As Carys weakens, the creature prepares to make Gwen its new host, but Jack traps it inside a forcefield and, unable to survive for long in Earth's atmosphere, it dies.

QUOTE, UNQUOTE

- Gwen: 'He just …'
  Jack: 'Came and went.'

- Gwen: 'I'm not being rude or anything, but … Well, maybe I am, but … How do you switch off from all this stuff? What do you do to relax?'
  Owen: 'I torture people in happy relationships.'

- Gwen: 'Come on then. Where are you from, and why are you trying to invade the Earth? Because you can forget about enslaving us.'
  Carys: 'Who said anything about enslaving?'
  Gwen: 'Well, that's what you lot do … aliens … isn't it?'
  Carys: 'No. I just want the energy. The climax. I live off that energy.'

62 On this episode's debut transmission, in a double bill with 'Everything Changes', the normal opening sequence with Jack's voiceover was omitted and the closing credits were expanded to cover both episodes (with some omissions). 'Day One' had its first (non-HD) transmission in its 'standard' form at 10.30 pm on BBC Three on 27 October 2006.

63 Surname given as 'Fletcher' in the episode.

- Gwen: 'Right, sorry, just to recap, you've travelled here to feed off orgasmic energy.'
  Carys: 'There's nothing else out there like it. You taste so good. You're the best hit there is.'

- Gwen: 'First contact with an alien, not quite what I expected.'

DOCTOR WHO REFERENCES

- The Doctor's severed hand features strongly in this episode as the possessed Carys escapes from the Hub by threatening Jack that she will break its glass container. Jack says: 'Put it down! That's worthless to anyone but me!' Carys does eventually break the container, but Jack is evidently able to rescue the hand and transfer it to a new one.

ALIEN TECH

- The Torchwood team have an alien stone-tablet-like device that can generate a 'portable cell' around a person or object – although its power runs down and lasts for only about an hour. It is used by Owen to catch the escaping Carys, and later by Jack to trap the gas creature.

- Jack uses a tracking device, which could be alien in origin, to detect traces of the entity's presence outside the nightclub.

CONTINUITY POINTS

- The Torchwood SUV contains sophisticated monitoring equipment and computers capable of accessing the police database.

- Gwen learns that, apart from her, none of the Torchwood team members has a partner; their time and energy is fully taken up with their work. (Ianto, however, is not involved in this conversation ...)

'BLOOD AND SNOGGING'

- Carys, possessed by the alien gas creature, has sex with and thereby kills at least seven men, who are reduced to piles of ash.

- In a brief flashback, a nightclub bouncer is implied to be masturbating while he watches via a CCTV monitor as Carys has sex with her first victim – later named as Matt Stevens – in the ladies' toilet.

- Gwen, under the influence of powerful pheromones emitted by the possessed Carys, has a passionate kissing session with her in a cell in the Hub.

- Owen, having also presumably been overcome by the possessed Carys's pheromones, is left naked and handcuffed by her when she escapes from her cell.

- Jack's sexuality is discussed by his team members while he is out of the room. Owen thinks that he is gay, but Toshiko comments that he will 'shag anything if it's gorgeous enough.'

- Owen uses a lab rat to demonstrate the physical changes that Carys is undergoing, causing it to explode.

- Jack kisses Carys in order to imbue her with additional vital energy.

- Gwen kisses Jack in gratitude when he saves her from being possessed by the alien creature.

- Gwen kisses Rhys at their flat.

PRODUCTION NOTES

- Made with 'Everything Changes' as part of Block 1 of production. Much of this episode was actually shot at the beginning of the block, in part to allow the cast and crew time to establish relationships and a good working pattern before recording the bulk of the key introductory episode.

- This episode had the working title 'New Girl'.

- For their kissing scene, Eve Myles imagined that Sara Lloyd Gregory was Johnny Depp, while Sara Lloyd Gregory imagined that Eve Myles was Brad Pitt.

- The scene where Gwen is daydreaming about her exciting life with Jack and his team while Rhys talks about more mundane matters, until he suddenly realises that she is not listening and asks 'Am I boring you?', directly mirrors a scene in the episode 'Crossroads' in the first series of the hit US drama series *Six Feet Under* (HBO, 2001-2005).

- Amongst the central Cardiff locations featured in this episode are the Hollywood Bowl bowling alley in the Red Dragon Centre (where Gwen and Rhys have fun at the start of the episode); the Ask pizza restaurant in the Mill Lane café quarter (where Gwen and Rhys are eating when the meteor passes overhead); the Wyndham Arcade (which Gwen and Rhys run down after leaving the restaurant); City Barbers in Charles Street (as the nightclub front exterior); Minski's Show Bar on Cathedral Walk (as the nightclub interior and rear exterior); Brook Street in the Riverside area of Cardiff (for the establishing shot of Carys's house); Caroline Street, the Hayes and Mermaid Quay (all of which Carys passes as she observes the sexual imagery around her); and the Ultralase laser eye correction surgery in Windsor Place (where the fictional fertility clinic is situated).

- Goldfrapp's 2005 single 'Ooh La La' is used on the soundtrack during the scene where the possessed Carys walks through Cardiff observing all the sexual imagery around her. Also heard in the episode, in the nightclub scene, is 'Saturday Night' by the Kaiser Chiefs.

- Gareth David-Lloyd and Sara Gregory reportedly dated after meeting during the recording of this episode.

PRODUCTION QUOTES

- 'Really the idea behind the episode was "Your first day from hell" – extending the metaphor of breaking the photocopier on your first day at work.' Co-producer Chris Chibnall, *Torchwood Declassified*: 'Bad Day at the Office'.

- 'When [you're] launching a new, adult science-fiction drama, it's kind of inevitable that you're going to do the sex monster! Right from the start, actually, there will be something that [gets] down and dirty. That's Chris Chibnall; that's what he came up with: a sex-gas orgasm-eating monster! How can you not watch that?' Executive Producer Russell T Davies, *Torchwood Declassified*: 'Bad Day at the Office'.

- '[The sex gas] was very tough to do. The actual thing you see is all CG, with some interactive lighting. The options in the past have been to use cloud tanks or some kind of smoke machine to create a similar effect, and it's still hard to do that in CG, but I was determined we were going to do this well. Most of the time whey you see CG smoke it is particles, because it's easier to do, but that looks very flat. We really wanted something that felt solid and alive as well … We spent a lot of time getting that look.' Visual Effects Supervisor Dave Houghton, *Starburst* Special 79, February 2007.

OOPS!

- At the end of the episode, the gas creature is unable to withstand more than a few seconds' exposure to Earth's atmosphere. At the beginning, however, it survives what must be a much longer journey from the meteor crash-landing site to the centre of Cardiff before finding a human host. (This may however be explained by the fact that, as Toshiko observes, the creature is 'pretty weak' by the time Jack traps it in the force field.)

PRESS REACTION

- 'There is an advantage for queer viewers in having a bisexual character whose sexuality is explored – but also in having a queer character who *isn't* seen purely in terms of his sexuality. Captain Jack is a man with a complex, mysterious past, and a demanding, volatile present involving a hugely responsible job. He is a man who would be interesting no matter what his sexuality. In terms of queer representation, that could be *Torchwood*'s biggest breakthrough yet.' Locksley Hall, AfterElton website, 24 October 2006.

- 'You know, the purpose of ageing is to learn finally what you really are, underneath all the lies and denial and hope. And in the ageing I've done [between] Saturday, when I previewed the first episode of *Torchwood*, and now, when I've seen the second episode, I think I have finally caught sight of my real self. Despite all my previous, self-deceiving faux-concerns over *Torchwood*'s long-term dramatic viability, I must now admit that I am a simple woman. I think I really can sustain interest in a series, purely on the basis that Captain Jack Harkness is sexually charismatic, and runs around in period military outfits, flirting. It is enough. It is more than enough. Indeed, it is the point – *Torchwood* is purposefully post-watershed.' Caitlin Moran, *The Times*, 23 October 2006.

- '*Scooby-Doo* (more than, say, *The X-Files* or *Buffy*) is probably the show most analogous to *Torchwood*, in that both series revolve around a fresh-faced team of meddling kids tackling an ever-shifting carnival of monsters in a world of childlike simplicity. The Torchwood gang even have their own version of the Mystery Machine, although theirs is a spectacularly ugly SUV with two daft strips of throbbing LED lights either side of the windscreen whose sole purpose is to make the entire vehicle look outrageously silly … The inside's not much better – LCD screens embedded in every available flat surface, each urgently displaying a wibbly-wobbly screensaver ... It must be like driving around in a flagship branch of PC World.' Charlie Brooker, the *Guardian*, 28 October 2006.

- '[Episode Two] concerned itself with a renegade alien in gas form that had invaded the body of a poor girl who had been dumped by her boyfriend and was now obliged to shag everyone in sight for their orgasmic energy, causing mayhem in a public toilet and turning innocent sperm donors at Cardiff's world-class fertility clinic into piles of dust. It wasn't clever but it was funny, fast-moving and indecent. Children will love it.' Phil Hogan, Guardian Unlimited website, 29 October 2006.

- 'A lot of people in television say that comedy is the most difficult thing to get right, but I'd say it was science-fiction. And the most difficult thing in science-fiction is to stop it becoming comedy. In *Torchwood*, we viewers must believe that a cloud of alien gas might one evening roll up to a Cardiff nightclub and take over the body of a young woman in an attempt to harness the energy of the human orgasm. And we must do that without laughing. Well, only at the right moments. To the great credit of Russell T Davies, we somehow manage it.' Roland White, *The Sunday Times*, 29 October 2006.

- 'While we Earthlings dawdle around with iPods, our cosmic cousins have gismos capable of bringing the dead back to life. You can probably already get them in Tokyo. But there's no need to breathe life into *Torchwood*. It was a compelling idea to make a *Doctor Who* spin-off for adults only. And this X-certificate science-fiction sizzler certainly delivers the grown-up goods – plenty of sex, girl-on-girl action, extreme violence and a filthy script full of four-letter words. No wonder its double episode curtain-raiser pulled in massive audiences on both BBC Three and BBC Two, instantly establishing *Torchwood* as a success story.' Kevin O'Sullivan, *Sunday Mirror*, 29 October 2006.

- 'It was a few minutes into the second episode when my nine-year-old started to shriek and squirm. "Oh no, how gross, I can't look!" he squealed as he hid behind a cushion. The scene showed a woman having sex with a man in the toilets of a nightclub and was very realistic – you almost forgot she was possessed by an alien. I had a brief mental debate about sending both boys to bed (too much aggravation) or turning the TV off (I was enjoying it too much) then settled on having a frank discussion about sex at the end of the programme. What had disturbed my son most was the portrayal of sex. "They didn't tell us about all that shaking and shouting in sex education lessons," he said.' Janette Owen, *Guardian*, 7 November 2006.

FAN COMMENT

- 'There are a few open-ended mysteries at the moment, but one major concern I have is that they may just be making this up as they go along, rather than gradually revealing information that they've already planned out. More specifically, I'm not sure if they've really thought about their basic premise … For instance, is this still the same organisation that Queen Victoria founded, or are they a splinter group? If there are only five of them, and they claim to be a global power that outranks the UN, i.e. they have no particular allegiance to Britain, why do the army and the police just step aside to let them through? I think you can do some interesting stories with that premise (Warren Ellis did something similar with *Stormwatch* and *The Authority*), but I don't think that *Torchwood* is going down that path.' John C Kirk, LiveJournal blog, 23 October 2006.

- 'The sex scene is a little over the top, but why not, there has been nothing like this show ever. That poor actor, gets the call from his agent, "A scene in the new *Doctor Who* spin-off, fantastic! It's a sex scene, okay. I get vaporised at the end, r ... ight, thanks muchly!" It's clever writing, very clever. Gwen still thinks this life will allow her other life to co-exist; maybe it will. The rest of the team become a little more real and likable as it's revealed how unlucky in love they are, and [they are seen] gossiping about Jack when he goes to the toilet. A toilet, in a science-fiction story.' Rob Tizzard, Torchwood Guide website, 24 October 2006.

- 'Nice plot, very "modern" and one where we see just what contribution Gwen is going to make to the team. It does make you wonder how they got anything done without her though. Already characters are beginning to form; Harper is coming across like a sex-starved schoolboy, Tosh is probably the most likeable of the main team, though light years away from her encounter with "Space Pig" in "Aliens of London", Ianto is a bit of a mystery and the Captain himself seems almost, but not quite, the same as when we last saw him staring down the barrel of a Dalek gun. Still I suppose being resurrected can change a guy.' Kevin Millyard, *Celestial Toyroom* Issue 344, December 2006.

ANALYSIS

Stories about powerful or possessed women who use their sexual wiles to ensnare and destroy men have been told for centuries. Such 'energy sapping' female creatures – sometimes depicted as snake-women or other hybrids – are to be found in the myths of Ancient Greece, Asia and Africa; and similar ideas underlie Biblical stories such as those of Adam and Eve and Samson and Delilah. In European medieval legend, the succubus was a demon that took on female form to seduce men in their dreams and steal their potency or even their lives. Coming further up to date, predatory women have also featured frequently in popular culture. In the film noir movies of the 1940s and 1950s – a significant source of thematic and stylistic inspiration for *Torchwood* – the *femme fatale* was a recurring character type; a self-assured and calculating woman who would typically use her sexual allure to exploit a hapless male sap and lead him to his ruin. In more recent decades, the concept of the possessed woman somehow threatening men through sex has been a popular motif with the makers of telefantasy series, possibly inspired in part by fears over the spread of AIDS and other sexually transmitted diseases. Stories of this type have featured in, for example, *Lois & Clark: The New Adventures of Superman* ('Pheromone My Lovely', ABC, 1993), *The Outer Limits* ('Caught in the Act', Showtime, 1995), *Stargate SG-1* ('Hathor', MGM, 1997), *Angel* ('Lonely Hearts', the WB, 1999), *Farscape* ('What Was Lost', Jim Henson Company, 2002) and *Smallville* ('Heat', the WB, 2002).

It is not particularly surprising, then, to find *Torchwood* also mining this rich vein of inspiration, and the plot of 'Day One' is by no means novel – in fact, it bears particularly close similarities to those of the aforementioned episodes of *The Outer Limits* (in which a co-ed – played by a pre-*Charmed* Alyssa Milano – is taken over by a strange power that gives her a voracious sexual appetite and causes the men she seduces to be absorbed into her body), *Stargate SG-1* (in which the victims succumb to a pink gas that enters them through the mouth) and *Angel* (in which a demon possesses the bodies of young people, picked up in singles bars, after having sex with them, leaving its victims as husks). One can only assume that writer Chris Chibnall is being a little disingenuous when, in the 'Bad Day at the Office' episode of *Torchwood Declassified*, he states: 'I genuinely have no idea where [the idea] came from.' In the same programme, Russell T Davies even refers to 'the sex monster' as a standard story device. Many telefantasy fans have, indeed, criticised 'Day One' as being derivative and predictable. This will no doubt have been less of an issue, however, for the great majority of the six-million-plus viewers who saw the episode during the week of its debut transmission; and *Torchwood*'s treatment of the idea is sufficiently stylish and witty to entertain even those who are familiar with the numerous earlier examples of its use. There is a lot of dark humour to relish here in the way that the possessed Carys's conquests literally explode at the point of orgasm, leaving only a small pile of dusty residue in their wake. This is reinforced by Jack's cheeky observation that the victim in the nightclub just 'came and went', and by the brief flashback sequence in which the bouncer is seen masturbating over a CCTV image of said victim having sex with Carys in the ladies' toilet.

A potential problem with this type of story is that, if done badly, it can seem to some degree misogynistic. One is sometimes uncomfortably reminded of the fact that a fear of female sexuality lies at the root of much of the terrible repression that women have suffered over the centuries in many different cultures. Thankfully, 'Day One' largely avoids the trap of demonising Carys, portraying her instead as just as much a victim of the 'alien sex gas' as the men she is forced to destroy. The only really troubling scene in this regard is the one in which she appears to make a conscious decision to kill her sometime boyfriend. On one reading, this element of choice – she tells him 'You could have saved yourself' – suggests that the induced craving for sex is not completely overwhelming, and that she could resist it if only she were to summon up sufficient willpower. Some fans have even opined that her failure to do so makes her effectively a murderer. A more sympathetic interpretation, however, would be that she is utterly incapable of resisting the urge to have sex, and it is only in her choice of partner that she can exercise a degree of control – so perhaps she can be forgiven for seeking out someone who has wronged her in the past, rather than simply a random stranger.[64]

Another point that warrants at least a raised eyebrow occurs a little earlier when, after kissing Gwen in the cell in the Hub, the possessed Carys suddenly pushes her away and says, 'It's no good. It's got to be a man'. This is doubtless simply a contrivance on Chibnall's part, to explain how Gwen manages to escape from the situation with her life; but, coming just moments after the controlling entity has explained that its mission on Earth is to feed off human orgasmic energy, it does carry the rather unfortunate implication that women's orgasms are somehow inferior to men's. Perhaps, though, a preferable rationalisation lies in an assumption on the entity's part that it can achieve satisfaction far more quickly with a man, as demonstrated by the lamentable lack of staying power of the first victim.

One does get the discomfiting suspicion, though, that – as with the arguable 'date rape' incident involving Owen in 'Everything Changes' – these issues have not been as fully thought through as they might have been in a series aimed explicitly at adult viewers. On the other hand, and assuming it is not simply coincidental, the fact that the entity uses essentially the same method to ensnare its victims in 'Day One' as Owen used to seduce the woman and her boyfriend in 'Everything Changes', and that Owen effectively gets 'a taste of his own medicine' when he is left naked, handcuffed and embarrassed in the cell, suggests there may be some clever and subtle character development at work here.

64 A rather more negative impression of Carys would have been given, however, had another recorded scene not been cut before transmission. In this, she seeks out a boy named Mikey and kills him by having sex with him in a car – simply because, when she was eight years old, he was the first boy she ever kissed, and he then upset her by kissing someone else an hour later. This is included amongst the deleted scenes compilation on the series' first DVD release.

Certainly there is a more thoughtful subtext underlying the superficially obvious narrative. One of the episode's best scenes – and the one that Davies cites in 'Bad Day at the Office' as his favourite – has the possessed Carys making her way through the streets of central Cardiff and seeing erotic imagery all around her in adverts, shop signs and even the behaviour of passers-by; a telling comment on the sexualised nature of the world we live in at the beginning of the 21st Century. Carys's craving for sex can also be seen as a metaphor for all types of addiction in modern society, including drug and alcohol addiction – as perhaps alluded to by the nightclub setting. And, as noted on the BBC's Torchwood Institute System Interface website, even the seemingly fanciful idea of an alien being feeding off orgasmic energy is not without some intellectual foundation. In 1940, the Austrian-American psychoanalyst Wilhelm Reich (1897-1957), a one-time friend of Sigmund Freud, posited the existence of a form of energy, 'orgone', that permeates the universe and all living matter and is, or so he believed, responsible for human emotions and sexuality. Although these theories are now generally dismissed by the scientific establishment, they do still have some adherents, and – as again observed on the Torchwood Institute System Interface – resonate with much older ideas such as the 'life energy' ch'i in Chinese philosophy and practices such as tantric sex. (Rather more frivolously, the same website also describes an alien race called the Doovari, who apparently 'power their starships on the sex energy of their incredibly potent crew'!)

Like 'Everything Changes', though, 'Day One' is above all else an episode revolving around Gwen and her gradual integration into the Torchwood team. It is not entirely certain if the 'day one' referred to in the title is supposed to be literally the very next day after the events seen at the conclusion of the previous episode, or simply the first day on which Gwen is required to report for duty at Torchwood, but clearly only a short time has elapsed. This unfortunately poses something of a credibility problem, as – like Gwen's tracking down of Jack in 'Everything Changes' – it requires the viewer to accept a highly implausible coincidence: in this case, the coincidence that on the very first day that Gwen starts her new job as a Torchwood operative, a meteor-like spaceship just happens to crash-land on the outskirts of Cardiff and cause Jack's team to swing into action. It seems strange that, having established the presence of the spacio-temporal rift as a very plausible reason for other-worldly phenomena to be centred around Cardiff, those responsible for the series have effectively cast this aside in the very next episode and had an alien visitation occurring just outside the city for no good reason at all – unless, of course, the implication is that the residents of Cardiff have the best orgasms to be found anywhere on Earth …?

This slightly jarring lead-in to the story is quickly forgotten, however, as the main action kicks in and the Torchwood team arrive at the site of the meteor's arrival – only to find that the regular army have got there ahead of them. The inclusion of this sequence with the army is somewhat curious, given that it adds absolutely nothing of substance to the story and must presumably have placed quite a strain on the episode's budget, involving a number of additional cast members and extras, plus vehicles and equipment, in an inherently expensive night shoot on location. One can only speculate that it was intended purely for effect – to give the production a slicker, more cinematic look – or else perhaps to demonstrate (although this could surely have been achieved just as easily, and much more cheaply, through dialogue alone) that Torchwood's authority trumps the army's, just as it did the police's in 'Everything Changes'. There is, though, one other noteworthy aspect of the scene, which is that Jack and his team do not appear to show any identification or other form of documentation to establish their credentials. The most straightforward reading of this would be that it either happens off-camera or is unnecessary because the army officer has encountered them before and already knows who they are – which would be consistent with his initial disbelief of Gwen's claim that she is part of the team – but a more intriguing alternative would be that Jack takes control of the situation by exercising some sort of mental influence over the soldiers. There is one particular shot in which he casts what seems to be a very significant look at the officer, who then simply allows the Torchwood team to get on and do, as Jack puts it, 'the real work.' Whether or not this was intentional on the production team's part, however, must remain a moot point, as it is not something that is followed up in later episodes.

At any rate, the Torchwood team do gain access to the crash-landing site, where Gwen penetrates the meteor with a tool and releases the gas – a neat sexual metaphor presaging the events to come. This is a key moment in the episode, as it sets up the theme of Gwen having, as she later puts it, 'The worst first day ever.' This is then carried through into the subsequent scene in the Hub, where the viewer gains a good insight into the main team members' respective characters from the way in which each of them reacts to what has happened. While Owen is sarcastically critical of the 'new girl', Toshiko tells him to 'give her a break', and Jack simply says, 'We all make mistakes; get over it.' Gwen seems to take this latter advice to heart, as Eve Myles observes in 'Bad Day at the Office': 'She's made a mistake; she doesn't run out crying about it, she doesn't think "Oh god, I give up." She apologises – she realises that it's her fault – and she gets on with it, and she goes on the hunt. She comes in, she deals with the families, she deals with the profiling, she deals with researching people's backgrounds. You know, she brings all that into it; it's a new kind of aspect, it's a new way of working, that she brings in.'

In reality, of course, anyone who made a careless mistake at work that indirectly led to the deaths of at least seven innocent people would probably be wracked with guilt for many years to come, and possibly even prosecuted for negligence. It would, however, be wrong to criticise *Torchwood* for taking some dramatic licence here, as it is a standard and accepted approach in genre TV series. If that were not the case, every police or medical drama there is would have to devote much of its time to depicting its regular characters undergoing counselling or psychiatric treatment – which, although more realistic, would be considerably less entertaining.

Even allowing for dramatic licence, though, it does strike the viewer as distinctly odd that none of the Torchwood team seems at all affected by, or even mentions, the very recent death of their colleague Suzie. This contrasts poorly with the handling of similar issues in some other telefantasy series – a good case in point being the fall-out from Toby Wren's demise in the '70s eco-drama *Doomwatch*.[65] It is in occasional lapses such as this that – in these early episodes, at least – *Torchwood* falls a little short of Davies's stated aim of having the fantastical exploits of Captain Jack and his team grounded in the real world.

Another key scene in the episode, and one that will doubtless be remembered – and replayed repeatedly – for years to come, is that of the aforementioned kissing incident between Gwen and Carys in the cell. Some critics have argued that this serves no purpose other than pure titillation – although opinions have differed as to whether that is a good thing or a bad thing. In truth, though, it is a lot cleverer than that. It actually prompts the viewer to question his or her response to the presentation of such sexual imagery on TV by raising the uncomfortable possibility that it is not too far removed from that of Gwen's colleagues, who are placed in the position of voyeurs

65 See Chapter Ten.

excitedly watching the girl-on-girl action via a monitor, or indeed that of the nightclub bouncer, masturbating as he enjoys a 'sex scene' displayed on his CCTV screen. It thus ties in well with the underlying themes of the episode as discussed above, and neatly foreshadows the sequence of Carys being affected by the erotic imagery she sees all around her in Cardiff.

The kissing scene also serves an important character development purpose by bringing home to Gwen the realisation that the rules by which she normally lives – including the sexual ones – are liable to break down in her new working environment of the Hub. This is reinforced by the very nice touch of her then receiving a call on her mobile phone from her amusingly domesticated boyfriend Rhys – who wants to know how her new job is going, and innocently asks 'Is it exciting, though? Have you had loads of excitement?' – illustrating perfectly the marked contrast between her new life and her old.

It is clear though that, when not under the influence of the alien-generated pheromones, Gwen finds herself far more attracted to Jack than she does to Carys. This is neatly conveyed in the brilliantly written and acted scene in the boardroom where the rest of the team discuss Jack in his absence. When Owen states that Jack is gay, Gwen's snap response is 'No he's not. Really, do you think?' Then, when Owen says 'Period military is not the dress code of a straight man', she retorts 'I think it suits him.' All in all, a dead giveaway as to her feelings toward her new boss.

It has been suggested by some fans that the relatively high sexual content of this episode is essentially gratuitous, as it would have worked just as well if the alien creature had been addicted to, say, human blood rather than orgasmic energy. It could then have been presented as a vampire story rather than a succubus one, with the denouement occurring in a blood bank rather than a fertility clinic, and could even perhaps have been made suitable for a younger audience. Vampire stories are fine, of course, but there have been even more of these in telefantasy than there have succubus stories – probably at least ten of the former for every one of the latter – and the simple fact of the matter is that the sexual content of 'Day One' is *not* gratuitous: as discussed above, it prompts the viewer to consider some interesting questions about the use of sexual imagery in advertising and the media in modern society, and helps to advance the characterisation of the regulars. No-one would claim that its treatment of the subject is particularly deep or serious, but the aim here is still first and foremost to present an entertaining science-fiction story, not a worthy social commentary. The whole point of *Torchwood* being a post-watershed show is that it has the opportunity to feature story material that would be unsuitable for a family audience; and if that opportunity is there, why should it not be taken?

In production terms, 'Day One' is difficult to fault. Brian Kelly's direction, both of this episode and of 'Everything Changes', is excellent throughout; the CGI and other effects work is highly effective; and the whole thing looks suitably slick and classy. *Torchwood* obviously does not enjoy as high a budget as *Doctor Who*, but the way it is set up – with a small group of regular cast members, a single, and highly impressive, main standing set in the Hub, and a dedicated production base within easy reach of a good variety of different settings and environments for location recording – means that it is able to take advantage of economies of scale and make the best possible use of its resources, getting as much of the money as possible up on screen. The extensive night shooting is unusual for a British production, and makes an important contribution to the overall look of the episode, in line with the dark, ominous tone for which the series is aiming.

It has sometimes been said that if a programme's incidental music is noticed by the viewer, then it has failed, as its function should be to counterpoint the action subtly and unobtrusively.

Judged by that criterion, Murray Gold's music would be deemed to have failed more often than not, as it is frequently ostentatious and attention-grabbing, so that it can scarcely be ignored by the viewer. Some critics have complained that it can even occasionally drown out the characters' dialogue. What Gold does, though, is to approach his work as if he were composing a film score rather than incidental music for a TV programme, and this has the welcome effect of giving the whole thing a much more cinematic and large-scale feel than would otherwise be the case. In line with this filmic approach, Gold is also not averse to incorporating pieces of contemporary pop and rock music into his soundtracks. This is demonstrated to particularly good effect in 'Day One' – for which, as will generally be the case on *Torchwood*, Gold collaborates with arranger Ben Foster, conductor of the BBC National Orchestra of Wales – with the excellent use of Goldfrapp's 'Ooh La La' to accompany Carys's flight thought the sex-charged streets of Cardiff. In truth, it is difficult to imagine *Torchwood* – or indeed the new *Doctor Who* – without Gold's contribution, as, while not to everyone's taste, it constitutes an integral part of the signature style and overall impact of the production.

In summary, then, 'Day One' is a highly enjoyable episode, and one with more substance than a lot of fan critics have given it credit for, building on the success of 'Everything Changes' and completing a strong start for *Torchwood*.

1.03 – GHOST MACHINE

WRITER: Helen Raynor
DIRECTOR: Colin Teague

DEBUT TRANSMISSION DETAILS

BBC Three	BBC Two
Date: 29 October 2006.	Date: 1 November 2006.
Scheduled time: 10.00 pm.	Scheduled time: 9.00 pm.
Actual time: 10.00 pm.	Actual time: 9.02 pm.

Duration: 48' 25"

ADDITIONAL CREDITED CAST

Gareth Thomas (Ed Morgan), Ben McKay (Bernie[66]), Llinos Daniel (Eleri), John Normington (Tom Flanagan[67]), Emily Evans (Lizzie Lewis), Christopher Elson (Young Ed Morgan), Christopher Greene (Young Tom Flanagan), Julie Gibbs (Bernie's Mum), Ian Kay (Snooker Player), Ryan Conway (Kid in Arcade), Kathryn Howard (Woman in Shop)

PLOT: Torchwood pursue a fleeing hoodie, Bernie Harris, and Gwen retrieves from him an alien object: a machine that allows the user to view ghost-like images of emotion-charged incidents from the past. The machine later causes Owen to experience a harrowing vision of an old unsolved crime – the rape and murder of a young woman, Lizzie Lewis, in 1963 – and he seeks out the perpetrator, the now-elderly Ed Morgan. The team then recover the second half of the machine, which affords visions of possible futures, and this leads Gwen to believe that Owen may be going to kill Bernie with a knife. In the event, however, Morgan kills himself by walking onto the knife in her hands.

QUOTE, UNQUOTE

- Gwen: 'When do you get to go home? You seem to live here. You don't, do you?'
  Jack: 'Gotta be ready. The 21st Century is when it all changes … and I hate the commute.'
  Gwen: 'Where do you sleep?'
  Jack: 'I don't.'
  Gwen: 'Doesn't it get lonely at night?'

- Ed Morgan: 'I used to see it in people's faces when they looked at me. They knew. I tried to hide, but they *knew*.'

- Jack: 'Bernie said he saw himself dead in that street. You saw Owen with the knife.'
  Gwen: 'But I was holding it. My hands were covered in blood.'
  Jack: 'That was one future. One of many possible futures. Whatever you saw, what Bernie saw, might not happen.'

66 Real name given in the episode as 'Sean Harris'.

67 Full name given in the episode as 'Tom Erasmus Flanagan'.

- Jack: 'The city will be awake soon. All those people. All that energy.'
  Gwen: 'All those ghosts.'
  Jack: 'We're surrounded by them. We can't see them. We can't touch them. But, they're there all right. A million shadows of human emotion. We've just got to learn to live with them.'

DOCTOR WHO REFERENCES

- Amongst the fake ID cards that Owen carries is one for UNIT – the United Nations Intelligence Taskforce – as introduced in the 1968 *Doctor Who* story 'The Invasion' and most recently featured in 'The Christmas Invasion'.

- Graffiti seen on the side of a rubbish bin incorporates the letter 'P' in a circle – the symbol of the Preachers in the Series Two *Doctor Who* story 'Rise of the Cybermen'/'The Age of Steel'.

ALIEN TECH

- The 'ghost machine' of the episode's title has come to Cardiff via the rift, along with some alien coins and rock. It is in two halves: one is used to view 'shadows of human emotion' from the past, the other to view similar images from the future. It is a quantum transducer that makes use of nanotechnology, and is retained by Torchwood under lock and key at the end of the episode.

CONTINUITY POINTS

- Torchwood are able to track alien technology, apparently by the energy it emits, on their equipment in the Hub. They also have direct access to the images from CCTV cameras around the city.

'BLOOD AND SNOGGING'

- Lizzie Lewis is raped and murdered by Ed Morgan in 1963, although this is not explicitly depicted on screen.

- Gwen kisses Rhys when they make up after an argument, telling him he is 'gorgeous'.

- Gwen sees a vision of her future self with a knife in her blood-soaked hands. It later transpires that Ed Morgan commits suicide by impaling himself on the knife.

PRODUCTION NOTES

- Made with 'Greeks Bearing Gifts' as part of Block 2 of production.

- As scripted, the opening chase sequence was to have featured Captain Jack running with Gwen and Owen after the fleeing Bernie Harris. However, John Barrowman twisted his ankle on the Hub set shortly before the sequence was due to be recorded and was unable to run for about ten days, so it had to be rewritten to have Jack join the chase in the Torchwood SUV.

- Location scenes for this episode were recorded on the bank of the River Taff (where the Torchwood team eat pasties); in Cardiff's main shopping area, including Queen Street and the Hayes (where the first chase takes place); at Cardiff Central Station; and in various places in the Splott and Butetown areas.

- Director Colin Teague used lots of titled camera angles in the scene leading up to Ed Morgan's death in order to convey an impression of what the character was feeling.

- The 2001 single 'Sing' by Travis is heard in the background in the pub where Torchwood question Bernie Harris, and the 2004 single 'Can't Stand Me Now' by the Libertines is heard in the later scene with Toshiko and Owen in a different pub.

PRODUCTION QUOTES

- 'In the script, the ghost machine was described as mobile-phone-shaped; a nice symmetry to it, something that would fit in the pocket. So it had to look cool. Because it's alien, you can let yourself go a bit mad.' Concept artist Peter McKinstry, *Torchwood* official website, 30 October 2006.

- 'It just sums up how *Torchwood* works. It's like, there's an alien device, but it's not a laser beam, it's not going to destroy the world, it just taps into humans and it taps into memories.' Executive Producer Russell T Davies, *Torchwood Declassified*: 'Living History', 30 October 2006.

- 'The Cardiff setting for me is an absolute gift, because I live here. I can walk around town and think "Wow, that's a brilliant bridge," or "That's actually a fantastic landmark," or "Wouldn't it be amazing to have a scene up there?"' Writer Helen Raynor, *Torchwood Declassified*: 'Living History', 30 October 2006.

- 'Obviously there are things I'd do differently if I was doing it again, but it does achieve one thing. I can't stand when you're watching a drama and you can see something coming five minutes away. It has to keep delivering something new and keep taking you to another level. For example, it's obvious that one of the team is going to see themselves in a past or future moment. That's the kind of thing you do with a story like that. But it's making sure when you get to that moment that it's actually something quite unexpected and freaky.' Writer Helen Raynor, *Starburst* Issue 344, December 2006.

- 'Owen essentially wants to make the old man suffer, in return for having raped and killed this girl Lizzie Lewis. What he actually does is push an unstable man over the edge, with terrible consequences.' Writer Helen Raynor, *Torchwood* Series One: Part One DVD set extra, December 2006.

- 'These transformations [between time zones] were a double imaging thing we did in editing. We tried some stuff through the HD camera, and it didn't quite work, and then we were going to do stop-frame 360 [degree] camera moves. Then we just thought, "Why don't we just lay it over – double the image?" It gave us the weird effect of taking us somewhere. We shot some extra stuff on the night of the rape sequence or the boy in the tunnel and then made it grainy and a bit like super-8. We put that into the sequence as well, which gave it a spooky effect, which a lot of people quite liked.' Director Colin Teague, *Starburst* Issue 346, February 2007.

PRESS REACTION

- '*Torchwood* is Hollywoodblockbuster-slick, fast-paced and tabloid-scary and, despite pitting its cast of characters against weird forces from the outer reaches of the cosmos, it's more concerned with journeys in inner space: the human heart and psyche. For instance, last night's episode was, in part, about getting the balance right between relationships in the home and the workplace. Sassy space-copette Gwen Cooper hasn't had her troubles to seek on that score. Things haven't been easy at home for Gwen since she signed up for the Torchwood Institute and ceased plodding a regular police beat. Her lumpy-faced, wittering, live-in boyfriend is pretty dull fare compared to her all-action, multi-coloured, multidimensional job – and especially compared to the enigmatic Cap'n Jack. Why, when Jack isn't turning poor Gwen's head by narrowing his eyes and making hurt-sounding pronouncements about humanity's slim long-term chances of survival – chicks love that – he's giving her up-close-and-personal lessons in firing a handgun down at the target-range. Hands-on? More like hands-all-over and cheek-to-cheek into the bargain, the cheeky sex-monkey.' David Belcher, the *Herald*, 2 November 2006.

- '*Ghost Machine* is deceptive; at first it could be a fairly average episode, but the central idea, of a device that converts quantum energy into images and emotions, is a great one. And the script shoots off in unforeseen directions that never stop twisting, slipping through shades of light and dark, while Teague's direction is very visual and energised.' David Richardson, *Starburst* Issue 344, December 2006.

FAN COMMENT

- 'We get to see more of the dark, brooding Jack, to which I hope we get some more answers soon. This is not the same Captain Jack we knew in *Doctor Who*. Something has changed him. Something is under his skin. Yet, he always shows a soft spot for Gwen. And, just how is Gwen's relationship with Rhys going to turn out? She obviously loves him, but does she love him enough? Hiding the alien device right behind his back seems to be a metaphor of how their life is going to be now. Can they survive?' Tobias Rogers, Torchwood Guide website, 1 November 2006.

- 'Myles does more of her stern "I've got a boyfriend" act when we can clearly see her brittle charade crumbling in front of Jack's "Sexual Harassment and Gun Training for Dummies". The scene has absolutely nothing to do with "Ghost Machine" but has everything to do with the story arc of Gwen in Torchwood, detailing the future of Gwen's relationship with Jack and the certainty that she will be using weapons. The scene switches between clumsy cliché and steamy sensuality, but has all the dubious morality of *Straw Dogs*' rape scene. Think about the scene again but with Owen doing the training and you might see it in a different light.' Steve Preston, Kasterborous website, 8 November 2006.

- 'What did Torchwood even accomplish this time around? They prevented the potential murder of a feckless dolt whom the whole estate would have been glad to see the back of anyway; helped to hasten the perpetrator's departure by a probable hour or so, given that he was already on the suicide watch list twice over; and they consigned the first of no doubt many magic-wand devices to the bin with only the vaguest non-answers to its origin, purpose or who the hell even found it in the first place. In short, sod all. So they solved a 40-

year-old murder case. Big deal; after they disappear into the shadows again, who's left to know, care or be believed? There's no consequence, and therefore no point. There are episodes of *Lost* more conclusive than this.' David Sanders, Behind the Sofa website, 3 November 2006.

- 'Helen Raynor's script is a decent SF twist on a traditional haunting narrative, and there are some very nice contemporary urban touches, including a couple of wonderfully unglamorous chase sequences between Torchwood and their hoodie quarry. By concentrating on the stronger members of the regular cast, particularly Burn Gorman's compellingly dodgy Owen, the episode gets good character mileage from the concept, with the scene where Owen witnesses the build-up to a decades old crime particularly well executed.' Mark Clapham, Shiny Shelf website, 9 November 2006.

- 'What Gwen sees through her involvement with Torchwood is more scary and unpleasant and less awe-inspiring than what Rose saw through her involvement with the Doctor. (And … this isn't just me: Suzie had a frantic speech … in "Everything Changes" about how all the stuff that came through the rift seemed to be garbage, as if Earth was a sewer.) So when she goes home to Rhys and gets a funny look in her eyes, it's not because she's seen wonders he can't possibly comprehend: it's because she feels herself being drawn into a dark and nasty world and isn't sure that she fits in the daylight. The Doctor may be a "lonely god", above mundane people and their lives, but Torchwood is underground, beneath them: secret not because ordinary people are too closed-minded to understand the wonder of what they see, but because any time somebody comes close to sniffing them out, Jack drugs their drinks.' 'puritybrown', LiveJournal blog, 13 November 2006.

ANALYSIS

Ghosts have featured quite frequently over the years in TV science-fiction, which has generally eschewed the traditional belief that they are the spirits of the dead and instead rationalised them in a variety of different ways. In *Doctor Who* they have been described as, amongst other things, elusive time travellers ('Day of the Daleks'), gas-dwelling alien creatures ('The Unquiet Dead') and Cybermen crossing over from another universe ('Army of Ghosts'/'Doomsday'). Celebrated scriptwriter Nigel Kneale, best known for his *Quatermass …* serials, offered up two notable ideas in his plays: in *The Road* (BBC, 1963) the apparitions witnessed by the 18th Century protagonists were pre-echoes of a 20th Century nuclear holocaust, while in *The Stone Tape* (BBC One, 1972) the ghosts were recordings of past traumatic events captured within the stonework of an old house. These explanations are not mutually exclusive, of course, and 'Ghost Machine' presents another intriguing variation on the theme: that ghosts are 'shadows of human emotion' around us all the time, and that all one needs in order to be able to see them is a suitable 'playback' device – the machine of the episode's title.

This is an imaginative and compelling story premise from writer Helen Raynor, and becomes even more so when Torchwood learn that there is a second half to the machine, which allows the user to see 'shadows' of future events as well as past ones – or at least of *possible* future events, as it is implied that these are not immutable. Bernie Harris does not die as he foresaw himself doing, and – if that is insufficiently conclusive, given that he could arguably have been seeing a little further ahead in time – the words that Gwen speaks after Ed Morgan dies at the end of the episode are not quite the same as those she envisioned herself saying. This ties in well with the idea of the machine being a 'quantum transducer' – something that, as Toshiko explains, converts and amplifies quantum energy, turning human emotions into visual images – given that, as all physics students will know, the 'many worlds' interpretation of quantum mechanics posits that history can be split into an infinite number of different 'branches' encompassing every possible outcome; a concept probably more familiar to science-fiction fans from parallel-universe-type stories. Viewed against this scientific background, it is quite credible that the machine should be able to 'tap into' such quantum possibilities.

In storytelling terms, the machine is very well used throughout, both as a catalyst to advance the plot and as a device to facilitate some further character development of the regulars. Two scenes in particular really stand out here. The first is the one in which Owen, through the operation of the machine, witnesses – or perhaps 'experiences' is a better description – the attack by the young Ed Morgan on the ill-fated Lizzie Lewis. This could perhaps be seen as the concluding incident in a short 'education of Owen' story arc, in which he starts out as a potential rapist himself in 'Everything Changes', is left naked and humiliated when something akin to a 'date rape' drug is used on him in 'Day One', and finally emerges a changed man after he vicariously experiences the true terror and helplessness felt by a rape victim in 'Ghost Machine'. The second particularly noteworthy scene is the one in which Gwen, having taken the machine back to her home, 'relives' the happy times she has had there with Rhys. This comes in the wake of them having had an argument over the phone about the antisocial hours Gwen is keeping in her new job, and serves the dual purpose of making the viewer feel more sympathetic toward Rhys – who up to this point has seemed so dull that it has been hard to understand what Gwen sees in him – and highlighting very nicely the increasing tension that Gwen is experiencing between the attractions of her familiar home life and those of her exciting new life in Torchwood.

And, as in 'Day One', it is clear that one of the main advantages of that new life for Gwen is the opportunity it affords her to work closely with Jack – quite literally so when he takes her down to the Hub's firing range for a training session. This latter sequence, much discussed by fans and likened by some to the famous 'potter's wheel' incident in the 1990 movie *Ghost*, is an amusingly over-the-top piece of action in which Gwen clearly relishes the physical contact with Jack as he presses up against her, coupled with the adrenaline rush – and classic sexual symbolism – of firing the guns, while Jack obviously finds the experience equally enjoyable. There is then a highly charged exchange of dialogue as, on being told by Jack that he doesn't sleep, Gwen asks 'Doesn't it get lonely at night?' before deciding that it is about time she went home … As the viewer has come to expect by this point, John Barrowman and Eve Myles both give excellent performances here, convincingly conveying the growing sexual tension between the two characters.

Another pleasing aspect of the episode is that the grimness of the main story is leavened by some nice moments of humour dotted throughout. A good example of this is the scene where Jack and Toshiko start trying to trace Tom Flanagan using the Hub's sophisticated IT resources and Owen beats them to it by the simple expedient of referring to the Cardiff telephone directory. Another comes when, on their arrival at Flanagan's house, Gwen introduces Owen as a trainee and sends him off to help the man's daughter make tea in the kitchen. And then there is the amusing depiction of Bernie Harris, a young man unable to make the grade even as a petty criminal and referred to in less than flattering terms by all his acquaintances – 'I wouldn't piss on him if he was on fire' – and even his own mother. The character is cast in a more serious light, however, when it is revealed that he has been extorting money from those whose past crimes the machine has shown him, and when Gwen learns that he is living in fear after having a vision of his own apparently imminent death.

Also very well drawn are the contemporary versions of both Tom Flanagan and Ed Morgan. Flanagan makes only a brief appearance, but his account of being evacuated from London as a young boy during the War is touching in its matter-of-factness, and brings home very effectively how traumatic it must have been for many children in that position to be wrenched from their homes and parents, never knowing for sure if they would ever see them again. This is all the more notable for the fact that it seems to have been included purely for the sake of offering an interesting and sympathetic character piece; once it has established the simple fact that this is the same person that Gwen saw as a young boy at the station, it makes no other contribution toward advancing the plot. Morgan plays a rather bigger part in the main action, and is convincingly presented as a somewhat pathetic character who seems deeply troubled by the memory of the crime he committed back in 1963. As Toshiko says at one point, having accessed his medical records, 'He's claustrophobic, paranoid, depressive, got a couple of recorded attempts at suicide; he's barely left his house in years.' The only drawback to this is that it does seem at times as if the script is trying to evoke sympathy for Morgan, which – coming in the wake of the effective rehabilitation of Owen following his highly questionable actions in 'Everything Changes'– leaves the viewer with the slightly uncomfortable feeling that *Torchwood* is making a habit of portraying rapists in a forgiving light. At heart, though, this is a story about having to face the consequences of one's own actions – in Buddhist terms, karma. Just as Harris's use of the machine for nefarious purposes is of little consolation to him when he is presented with a disturbing vision of his own impending demise, so Morgan's past crime haunts him through the years and ultimately leads him to kill himself. Even Owen pays the price for his earlier vengeful and threatening actions toward Morgan when he finds himself having to try to resuscitate the dying man – and is left depressed when his attempts prove to be in vain. 'It's about consequences; it's about changing consequences,' notes Burn Gorman in the 'Living History' episode of *Torchwood Declassified*.

It is not only in its inventiveness, characterisation and dialogue that Raynor's script impresses, but also in its pacing and structure. The opening sequence serves as a good illustration of this, as the viewer is thrown straight into the action with the exciting pursuit of Harris through the streets of central Cardiff, only to be pulled up short, as Gwen is herself, by the eerie sight of the young Flanagan's ghostly image at the station. This clever switching of tempos is repeated to good effect later in the episode too, and the action flows well from beginning to end. The only scene that really jars is the one in the Hub where the characters spout exposition at each other and Toshiko gives a brief tutorial on the principles of transduction that sounds like she is quoting from the *Ladybird Book of Electronics*. This scene is really rather clumsily written, and in such stark contrast to the rest of the script that it is tempting to think that it must have been contributed by one of Raynor's production team colleagues, perhaps in the well-meaning – but misguided – belief that the viewer needed to be spoon-fed some more explanation at this point.[68] Fortunately the action then moves swiftly on

68 Another similar, but even more wordy, exposition scene was recorded, with Jack talking to Owen, Gwen and Toshiko in the Hub's boardroom, comparing the ghost machine to a car's sat-nav device and suggesting that its purpose is to enable ghosts to navigate via 'quantum hotspots'. The transmitted scene discussed above – which gives a completely different explanation of the machine's function – appears to have been substituted in place of this one, which is included amongst the deleted scenes package on the series' first DVD release.

to the aforementioned firing range scene.

As if the opening chase sequence wasn't impressive enough, the episode then presents a second, arguably even better one – this time shot not in central Cardiff but in the rather less glamorous location of Splott. In stark contrast to the slick but generally rather improbable chase sequences typical of US-produced series, this one is amusingly messy and realistic, with Owen chasing Harris through streets, along a graffiti-adorned bridge, across cluttered back gardens, over walls and fences, into a paddling pool and even past a clutch of squawking chickens before finally cornering him by a locked gate.

This episode in fact makes excellent use of its locations throughout, presenting a different and (with no disrespect to the local residents) rather more shabby aspect of Cardiff than any seen previously in the series. As Russell T Davies puts it in 'Living History': 'I was very keen to sort of think that actually Cardiff is real, and you want to show it all. This is down among your sort of *Prime Suspect* areas of Cardiff. It's not all glossy, it is full of real people.' This again illustrates what a great variety of settings are to be found within a relatively small radius of the city centre, making Cardiff an ideal production base for *Torchwood*. Other good examples are the river bank in the shadow of the Millennium Stadium where Gwen, Owen and Toshiko bemoan their lack of success in tracking down Harris; the nearby bridge beneath which Owen has his vision of the murderous attack back in 1963; and the dingy street where the climactic showdown takes place.

Colin Teague's direction here is just as strong as Brian Kelly's was on the first two episodes and, if anything, takes the series into even darker territory. Aiding greatly in this are some excellent performances from the cast, both main and supporting. This is another very strong episode for Eve Myles as Gwen, around whom the action again largely revolves, notwithstanding that Burn Gorman as Owen also has some very good material to get to grips with this time around. The only regulars who have so far had little opportunity to shine in the series are Toshiko and Ianto, although clearly they will take their turns in the spotlight later on. Of the guest cast, Gareth Thomas is particularly impressive as the elderly Morgan. Although well known to telefantasy fans from his starring role as Blake in the *Blake's 7* series of the late 1970s, he has aged to the extent that he is not immediately recognisable. Indeed, some fans apparently failed to realise that it was Thomas in the role until they saw the cast list at the end of the episode. This must also be a tribute to his skills as an actor, as his portrayal of the fearful, tormented Morgan is compelling and never for one moment recalls his celebrated performance as the bold, no-nonsense antihero Blake. John Normington, playing the grown-up Flanagan, is another actor familiar to *Doctor Who* fans, from his guest roles as Morgus in 'The Caves of Androzani' (1984) and as Trevor Sigma in 'The Happiness Patrol' (1988). He turns in a gentle and affecting performance here that is again a world apart from those earlier, more larger-than-life appearances.

As good as 'Everything Changes' and 'Day One' were as introductory episodes to *Torchwood*, 'Ghost Machine' is arguably even better, and one of the highlights of the early part of the series.

1.04 – CYBERWOMAN

WRITER: Chris Chibnall
DIRECTOR: James Strong

Cybermen created by Kit Pedler and Gerry Davis

DEBUT TRANSMISSION DETAILS

BBC Three	BBC Two
Date: 5 November 2006.	Date: 8 November 2006.
Scheduled time: 10.00 pm.	Scheduled time: 9.00 pm.
Actual time: 10.00 pm.	Actual time: 9.01 pm.

Duration: 49' 08"

ADDITIONAL CREDITED CAST

Caroline Chikezie (Lisa[69]), Togo Igawa (Dr Tanizaki), Bethan Walker (Annie)

PLOT: Ianto's girlfriend Lisa was part-converted into a Cyberman in their recent invasion attempt. He has since smuggled her, and the Cyber-conversion equipment that now acts as her life support system, into the Hub's basement store-room, and secretly enlisted the aid of cybernetics expert Dr Tanizaki to try to 'cure' her. She is beyond saving, however, and the lingering influence of the Cybermen almost spells disaster for the whole Torchwood team. The Cyberwoman ultimately transfers her brain into the body of a pizza delivery girl, Annie, who stumbles into the situation, and Captain Jack and his team have no choice but to shoot and kill the innocent victim.

QUOTE, UNQUOTE

- Dr Tanizaki: 'Sometimes, in order to save what we love, we have to risk losing it.'

- Jack: 'Did you know that thing was down there?'
  Ianto: 'I put her there.'
  Jack: 'You hid a Cyberman within Torchwood, and you didn't tell us? What else are you keeping from us?

- Ianto: 'Lisa, please. I brought you here to heal you. So we could be together.'
  Lisa: 'Together. Yes. Transplant my brain into your body. The two of us, together. Fused. We will be one complete person. Isn't that what love is?'
  Ianto: 'No.'
  Lisa: 'Then we .. are not … compatible.'

- Owen: 'You should be dead.'
  Jack: 'I'm the stubborn type.'

69 Surname given as 'Hallett' in dialogue.

- Gwen: 'When she had hold of you, I thought, just for a moment I thought, maybe you could die after all.'
  Jack: 'Wanna know a secret?'
  Gwen: 'Mm.'
  Jack: 'So did I. And just for a second there I felt so *alive*.'

DOCTOR WHO REFERENCES

- The Cyberwoman was left part-converted at the end of events seen in the Series Two *Doctor Who* story 'Army of Ghosts'/'Doomsday', and was rescued by Ianto from Torchwood One – the base at Canary Wharf. The Cyber-conversion equipment seen here is of a type similar to that featured both in 'Army of Ghosts'/'Doomsday' and in the earlier Series Two story 'Rise of the Cybermen'/'The Age of Steel'.

- The Jubilee Pizza delivery service, first referenced in the *Doctor Who* story 'Dalek', makes a further appearance here, having been established in 'Everything Changes' as Torchwood's local takeaway.

ALIEN TECH

- The Cyberwoman's artificial parts must have been made using materials from the standard *Doctor Who*/*Torchwood* universe, as must the Cyber-conversion equipment, given that they were not pulled back through the void to the parallel world at the end of 'Army of Ghosts'/'Doomsday'. They were however designed on that parallel world, by scientists working under John Lumic's direction, as seen in 'Rise of the Cybermen'/'The Age of Steel'.

- Torchwood have an alien device that Suzie claimed could open any lock in 45 seconds. Toshiko seems not to recognise it immediately, but it appears to be the same device that she used in 'Everything Changes' to scan the pages of a book without opening it. If so, this suggests that it is multi-functional.

- Jack gives Toshiko two rod-like devices with which to restore power to the Hub. It is possible that these are alien in origin, as the technology does not seem to correspond to any known on Earth at present.

CONTINUITY POINTS

- In the *Doctor Who* story 'Rise of the Cybermen'/'The Age of Steel', it was established that the Cybermen created on the parallel Earth consisted of human brains transplanted into robotic bodies. Lisa, however, is different from this. Ianto says: 'It was the end of the Canary Wharf battle. The Cybermen needed soldiers fast. They started upgrading whole bodies instead of transplanting brains, using Earth technology. Lisa was half way through the process when the machinery shut down.' This makes Lisa more similar to the Cybermen of the standard *Doctor Who*/*Torchwood* universe, as first introduced in the *Doctor Who* story 'The Tenth Planet' in 1966, whose human bodies have been modified with artificial replacement parts and augmentations. It also seems that Jack may be familiar with the ways of these 'standard' Cybermen. He tells Ianto: 'These creatures regain a foothold by exploiting human weakness. Then they take a base, rebuild their forces, and before you know it, the Cyber-race is spreading out across the universe, erasing worlds, assimilating populations.'

- It seems that not everyone is aware of the full details of what occurred in and prior to the battle of Canary Wharf. Gwen has to ask Jack what the Cyberwoman is. He tells her she is 'Some form of Cyberman. They're us, upgraded; humans with emotions removed, created on a parallel world and supposedly destroyed on this one.' This ignorance of alien incursions is consistent with what Gwen says in 'Everything Changes' when Jack mentions previous examples, including the attempted invasion by the Cybermen: 'My boyfriend says it's like a sort of terrorism. Like they put drugs in the water supplies. Psychotropic drugs. Causing mass hallucinations and stuff.'

- The Hub's power is supplied by a generator in the basement. If the power is totally shut off, the base goes into 'lockdown', so that anyone inside is trapped there. It normally takes over six hours for the power to come back on line.

- Toshiko states that normally no intruder can enter the Hub without disabling seven separate alarms.

'BLOOD AND SNOGGING'

- Ianto tenderly kisses Lisa.

- Lisa's attempt to convert Dr Tanazaki into a Cyberman goes badly wrong, leaving him dead with metal components embedded in his head and his body mutilated and bloody.

- Owen and Gwen kiss passionately while they are hiding from the Cyberwoman in what appears to be a mortuary body compartment in the Hub's autopsy room.

- Owen impales Lisa in the stomach with a metal autopsy instrument, but she survives.

- Jack sets the Torchwood pterodactyl on Lisa. She survives but is left with multiple cuts oozing blood. Of the pterodactyl, nothing more is seen. It is heard apparently falling from the air to the ground after Annie enters the Hub, leading the viewer to fear the worst for it. Later, however, when Ianto returns to the scene, its screech is heard overhead again, so presumably it too was only injured.

- Lisa transplants her brain into Annie's body, destroying the girl's own brain in the process and giving her a bloody gash across her forehead. Jack, Gwen, Owen and Toshiko then shoot Annie dead. Lisa's lifeless body is left lying in a pool of blood.

PRODUCTION NOTES

- Made with 'They Keep Killing Suzie' as part of Block 3 of production.

- This episode had the working title 'The Trouble with Lisa'.

- The cast and crew gave the pterodactyl the Welsh nickname 'Myfanwy'.

- An instrumental piece entitled 'We're No Here' by Mogwai from the 2006 album *Miami Vice: Original Motion Picture Soundtrack* is used at the beginning of the episode as the

Cyberwoman is revealed. The 2004 single 'Chocolate' by Snow Patrol is heard playing in the bar where Jack, Gwen, Toshiko and Owen enjoy a drink after work.

- Naoko Mori sprained her ankle during this block of recording, but fortunately quickly recovered.
- Burn Gorman's son was born during this block of recording, and this was consequently a particularly tiring time for him.
- A scene cut from the very end of the episode had Toshiko bringing a coffee to Ianto in the tourist information office and trying unsuccessfully to make small talk with him before going through into the Hub, leaving him a lonely figure seated at his computer. This is included amongst the deleted scenes in the extras on the Series One: Part One DVD release.

PRODUCTION QUOTES

- 'James, the director, has chosen to shoot episode four in a very sort of hand-held style, which gives it an edginess, a feeling that you're involved in the action. And we're able to delve into areas, with the music … and the cutting, the editing, [such that] it just feels a lot more edgy … than the standard approach that you would [take] for BBC drama.' Editor Mike Jones, *Torchwood* official website, 6 November 2006.
- 'This was the first episode set pretty much entirely within the Hub, and … the challenge was to [take] … their base – which is what they retreat to, it's their place of security, it's where they have all their security procedures, and where they … escape from the outside world, if you like – [and say] "What if that becomes a place of danger, and a place of peril?" and, quite literally, "What happens when the lights go out?" So it was kind of looking at the set and trying to see it in a completely different light, if you like; and quite literally a different light.' Director James Strong, *Torchwood* official website, 6 November 2006.
- 'Our two main ideas were to maintain the silhouette of the Cybermen by having the handlebars on the head and on the arms and legs. Beyond that, we just tried to make her look sexy. The initial discussions were about her being quite asymmetrical and beat up and horrific looking, but I pitched the idea that she should be sexy looking. I wanted her to be a poster girl.' Creature effects designer Neill Gorton, *Starburst* Issue 344, December 2006.

OOPS!

- If Jack has a device that can open any lock within 45 seconds, why does he not use this to open the Hub's sealed weapons store?

PRESS REACTION

- 'The Cybermen work within the confines of the more fanciful [*Doctor*] *Who*, but put one into *Torchwood*'s reality-tinged world and it just seems incongruous. Which is a great shame, because while Chibnall's script does fire off a number of genre clichés (think *Star Trek: First Contact* in Cardiff), it's also a platform for the actors to do some great work. Gareth David-Lloyd … suddenly becomes a key player and delivers some powerfully wrought scenes, often matched by an intense, fiery Barrowman. And while [director] Strong does his best to create an atmosphere of danger and urgency, there's a real disparity between the *Hellraiser* style of the effects, the dramatic intensity, and the rather flimsy romp that they inhabit.' David Richardson, *Starburst* Issue 344, December 2006

- 'Oh dear. Just as it was all looking so promising, what have we here? [Its] flaws (and there are a few of them) wouldn't be so glaring but for the shockingly inept construction of the episode. In short, this is [a typical] third-episode-of-a-four-part *Doctor Who* in which almost nothing happens except for lots of running up and down dark corridors.' Keith Topping, *TV Zone* Issue 210, December 2006.

FAN COMMENT

- 'The whole idea of the butler having a life was excellent, and his emotional link to Lisa (the Cyberwoman of the title) was a masterstroke. Try as I might, however, I can't quite figure out what this tale was about. I enjoyed it thoroughly, yet looking back, I feel slightly empty. It's nothing to do with the logistics involved in transporting a Cyber-conversion unit from London to Cardiff, but more along the lines of what was happening. What's going on with the pterodactyl – was he or she mortally wounded? Why exactly was Toshiko going upstairs? How long does it take to deliver a pizza in Cardiff?'[70] Christian Cawley, Kasterborous website, 9 November 2006.

- 'For people to interpret the post-"Cyberwoman" Jack/Ianto relationship as Ianto resenting and hating Jack and thinking of him as "the man who killed Lisa" – which comes up again and *again* in fanfic, with no acknowledgement that the others also shot at her and there's no way to know whose shots ultimately killed her – well … it doesn't make sense to me. Because it is crystal clear to me that in that moment, Ianto *understands*. He knows that Jack is right, and that Lisa can't be allowed to live. It's that knowledge that breaks him. Not just grief, not just horror at what Lisa's become, but guilt because he didn't see it earlier, because he was blinded by his own need for her, because he, too, is responsible for the deaths of Tanizaki and the pizza girl, and for Lisa's stunted lingering half-life. When he comes back, he has no reason to hate Jack. He has reason, perhaps, to fear him; to fear that he will follow through on his threat: "Execute her, or I'll execute you both!" But Jack is a forgiving kind of guy … He has no more intention of executing Ianto than Ianto now has of letting Jack "suffer and die". Both Jack's threat and Ianto's were based on Ianto still believing Lisa could be saved, and once he stopped believing that, they both became irrelevant. The final scene shows us Ianto, evidently shaken and fragile, coming back to work, picking up the rubbish; and Jack, looking down on him, nodding at him as if to say "I knew you'd be back."' 'puritybrown', LiveJournal blog, 6 January 2007.

ANALYSIS

Of all the episodes in *Torchwood*'s first series, 'Cyberwoman' is the one with the strongest links to *Doctor Who*, in that it features a famous *Doctor Who* monster – albeit in a rather different form than seen previously – and refers back directly to the events of the parent series' most recently transmitted story, 'Army of Ghosts'/'Doomsday'. In addition, it adopts the 'base under siege' model that has been used frequently, and highly effectively, in *Doctor Who* over the years, in stories such as 'The Moonbase' (1967), 'Fury from the Deep' (1968), 'The Ark in Space'

70 Although a lengthy interval elapses between Ianto ordering the pizza and Annie bringing it into the Hub, he actually asks for it to be delivered at the 'usual time' that night, not straight away, so – contrary to what some critics have suggested – this is not a plot problem.

(1975) and, more recently, 'Bad Wolf'/'The Parting of the Ways' (2005). One corollary of this is that it is also the only episode to be set almost entirely within the Hub, with only a small amount of material shot on location. Due to a combination of these factors, it seems a somewhat atypical entry in the series, almost as if it doesn't quite fit the established format. Much of the appeal of *Torchwood* lies in the way that it places the otherworldly problems faced by Captain Jack and his team against the very real backdrop of contemporary Cardiff. That simply doesn't happen in 'Cyberwoman'. Instead, a fantastical story is played out within an essentially artificial environment. This does admittedly give the viewer an excellent opportunity to see more of the highly impressive standing set created by production designer Ed Thomas and his team; but in story terms, the Hub is so far removed from the real world that it could just as easily be a spaceship interior or a colony dome on an alien planet.

Some fans have indeed questioned the episode's believability more generally. It has for instance been suggested that it is not credible that Ianto could have got Lisa and the Cyber-conversion equipment from London to Cardiff and hidden them away in the Hub without anyone noticing. This, however, overlooks the fact that the country would no doubt have been in utter turmoil in the aftermath of the Cybermen's invasion attempt. There is also nothing in the episode to indicate exactly how long Ianto has been keeping Lisa in the Hub's store-room. It is possible that he has only recently smuggled her down there – while the rest of the team were away on a mission, perhaps, and under cover of darkness or using the invisible lift – having previously had her concealed somewhere else, such as in his own home. Certainly his nervous and furtive manner at the start of 'Cyberwoman' is very different from the calm and collected demeanour he has displayed hitherto. Perhaps he has only just been forced to move Lisa into the Hub, to make use of its power supply or to give Dr Tanizaki access to the sort of facilities he needs in order to attempt a cure. This of course is all pure speculation; there are other possible explanations too. But the question is, does the viewer really need to have such things spelt out in detail? Is it not enough, for the purposes of the story, just to know and accept that Ianto has somehow managed to smuggle the part-converted Lisa into the Hub's store-room, and that the other team members have been so wrapped up in their own lives and concerns that they have simply failed to register what has been going on almost beneath their noses?

Further negative comment has focused on the implausibility of the actual design of the Cyberwoman. It does admittedly seem odd that the production team should have decided to make her not only threatening and powerful but also – in the words of Russell T Davies in the 'Girl Trouble' episode of *Torchwood Declassified* – 'as sexy as possible', complete with Cyber-bra and high-heeled boots. It almost makes one wonder why they did not go the whole hog and retitle the episode 'Cyberbabe'. It is also a poor reflection on Ianto's character to suggest – as creature effects designer Neill Gorton does, citing Davies, in an interview on the *Torchwood* official website – that it is Lisa's sexiness that makes the ostensibly meek Torchwood operative 'put so much on the line to try and rescue his girlfriend, or what's left of her'; the obvious implication being that he would not have felt such continued love and devotion for her if she was no longer attractive. On the other hand, there is nothing in the episode itself to suggest that Ianto is so shallow; and this would certainly not be the first time that the makers of a science-fiction production have sacrificed a little technical authenticity for the sake of creating a memorable and iconic image. 'There's a very long history of sexy, pneumatic, hydraulic women, strangely, in science-fiction,' notes Davies in 'Girl Trouble', 'and we actually wanted to tap into that and give a Cyberman version of that, which is just irresistible.'

It could be argued that the Cyberwoman's lineage can be traced right back to the beautiful robot that is given the form of the woman Maria in *Metropolis*, director Fritz Lang's silent cinema classic released in 1927, only six years after the term 'robot' was first coined by Karel Capek in his play *Rossum's Universal Robots*. The Cyberwoman in fact bears an almost uncanny likeness to the 'machine human' in Lang's film, albeit that the latter is initially wholly artificial and so has no human skin visible; and in character terms, both become the object of a lover's devotion (although in *Metropolis*, this is only when the young man Freder believes the robot to be the real Maria) but ultimately cause death and destruction. The big difference is that, whereas the robot in *Metropolis* is actually designed by its maker to resemble a beautiful woman, there is no apparent reason, in plot terms, for the Cyberwoman to look sexy. It would seem from the evidence of the – albeit failed – conversion of Dr Tanizaki that the face is normally one of the first parts of the body to receive artificial implants; and certainly all the Cybermen seen previously in the new *Doctor Who* have had a completely uniform appearance, which has not included such features as high-heeled boots. Perhaps, though, Lisa's distinctive appearance is accounted for in part by the fact that, as explained by Jack, the final stages of the Battle of Canary Wharf saw the Cybermen departing from their usual conversion process by adapting human bodies rather than using completely artificial ones. It is possible, too, that Lisa might have looked more like a standard Cyberman had the curtailment of the process not forestalled the placing of further layers of armour on her body.

Doubts have also been expressed as to how exactly Lisa manages to transplant her brain into the body of the pizza delivery girl Annie, particularly when her own lifeless body is subsequently found lying on the ground with the head – as far as can be seen – essentially intact. One possibility is that Lisa placed Annie in the Cyber-conversion unit and then stood beside it while the machine removed her brain from the rear and performed the operation. It may also be significant that Lisa's body is found lying in almost exactly the same position as was Dr Tanizaki's; perhaps this is where the machine dumps its 'waste'? Again, though, the question has to be asked, is the episode's failure to provide a specific explanation really so problematic? Mary Shelley did not, after all, give any detailed scientific description as to how Dr Frankenstein animated his monster in *Frankenstein; or, The Modern Prometheus* – to which novel, and its cinematic adaptations, 'Cyberwoman' clearly owes another debt of inspiration, as highlighted visually by the stitched-up gash across Annie's forehead after the brain transplant. The real significance of Frankenstein's monster lay not in the process by which it was created but in what it represented, both to the other characters in the story and in allegorical terms to the reader.

It might perhaps be considered absurd to liken 'Cyberwoman' to such masterworks as *Metropolis* and *Frankenstein*; but the salient point here is that pedantic nitpicking over the technical correctness of a story can easily obscure what is really important about it. And what is really important about 'Cyberwoman' is not the mechanics of the Cyberwoman's conversion, or the engineering principles underlying its design, or the method by which its brain transplant is achieved. What is important is the dramatic conflict that the creature's presence in the Hub precipitates, and in particular the changes it brings about in how the regular characters view and relate to each other.

This is, to a large extent, Ianto's episode. Previously in the series, everything that has been seen of this character has tended to suggest that he is diffident, obliging, conscientious and devoted to Jack and the other members of the Torchwood team. Russell T Davies puts it very well in 'Girl Trouble': 'He's like the Admirable Crichton[71]; he's the perfect butler ... He's got a

71 This is a reference to the title character of J M Barrie's 1902 comedy play *The Admirable Crichton*, of which there were subsequently a number of movie adaptations, most notably a 1957 production directed by Lewis Gilbert and starring Kenneth More as Crichton.

great sense of humour, but is very passive … He doesn't push himself forward to the front of a scene, he's been faithful, he's does his job, they can rely on him, everyone takes him for granted.' In 'Cyberwoman', though, it quickly becomes apparent that this outwardly quiet, unassuming, efficient man is actually a far more complex character than anyone has ever had cause to suspect. 'He's the janitor,' notes John Barrowman, also in 'Girl Trouble'. 'That's what everyone looks at him [as]; the guy who's the janitor. And it turns out that this guy, who everybody thought was one way, has got a very dark secret.'

This 'dark secret' is, of course, Lisa, and his almost obsessive devotion to her, which has caused him to conceal her within the Hub. It is however clear that, to start with, he does not believe her to pose any threat. He is absolutely horrified when he discovers that Dr Tanizaki has been killed, and warns Lisa not to go near the other Torchwood team members. 'You didn't mean to do this,' he says. 'Something's happened to your mind. Just some kind of side effect of this whole process. It's post-traumatic.' He insists: 'This can't happen again, Lisa. If you harm anyone else, I'll …' However, he falls silent when Lisa replies, 'Yes? What will you do?'

From this point on, events effectively spiral out of Ianto's control, and he ends up knowingly endangering the lives of all his colleagues – even at one point threatening to shoot anyone who stands in his way. But how much allegiance does he actually feel, or even owe, toward those colleagues? 'I clear up your shit,' he tells Jack. 'No questions asked, and that's the way you like it. When did you last ask me anything about my life?' Jack does not dispute this, and it seems that Ianto has indeed been taken very much for granted up until now. He certainly has no doubt where his loyalty lies: 'My loyalty is to her. She worked for Torchwood. She was caught up in battle. I owe it to Lisa – we owe it to her – to find a cure.' Even when Jack insists that there is no cure, and that Cyber-conversion cannot be reversed, he clings desperately to the hope that Lisa might be the exception to the rule.

'Ianto's main focus [is] the fact that he [is] in love,' observes Gareth David-Lloyd in an interview on the *Torchwood* official website. 'He would do anything for this girl that's had this horrible semi-Cyber-conversion happen to her, and he uses Torchwood to help, because that's his only option.' Even after Lisa has taken over Annie's body, Ianto finds that he still can't bring himself to shoot her.

A scene that has given rise to some controversy is the one where Owen kisses Gwen while they are hiding from the Cyberwoman, pressed up against each other inside a freezer compartment in the autopsy room. Is this another example of Owen forcing his sexual attentions on a potentially unwilling partner? While it could be viewed that way, arguably a less strained interpretation is that the two characters have been feeling a gradual build up of sexual tension – of which their verbal sparring over the previous three episodes has really all been part and parcel – and that Owen, fearing imminent death at the hands of the Cyberwoman, kisses Gwen on impulse, believing that she will be receptive to this. As it turns out, she is indeed receptive, and responds with some enthusiasm. 'You didn't exactly struggle, did you?' he later notes. Some fan commentators have expressed surprise that an intelligent woman like Gwen could be attracted to a man displaying such obvious jack-the-lad tendencies as Owen, but one can only suppose that these critics have led rather sheltered lives. Common sense does not always prevail in matters of emotion – particularly when people are embroiled in life-or-death struggles. As Burn Gorman is quoted as saying in a BBC press release of 24 October 2006: 'In Owen's job, every day could be his last. It's like a wartime mentality. And you know what happened in the war! People didn't know if they'd still be here the next day. So if you've got the opportunity to get it on with someone, you're going to do it. Owen takes those chances.'

Is it really believable that two characters who think they are on the point of being killed would suddenly become consumed by thoughts of sex, even to the extent that – as Gwen subsequently observes – Owen has a 'hard on'? Possibly not. But is the kiss totally gratuitous, as some have argued? No, because the relationship between Owen and Gwen is an important thread running throughout the rest of the series, and this is a key moment in its development.

In fact, the scene is all the more interesting for being intercut with one where Jack kisses the unconscious Ianto. Jack's motivation here is left tantalisingly unclear. One possibility is that he is overcome by emotion at the sight of his stricken colleague. The kiss seems almost as passionate as that between Owen and Gwen, suggesting a greater depth of feeling than has previously been apparent. An alternative possibility, however, is that Jack is simply attempting to revive the unconscious man. While his actions do not correspond to the conventional 'kiss of life' resuscitation technique, he could be transferring life-force to Ianto in the same way as he did to Carys in 'Day One'. Ianto's body does not glow in the way that Carys's did in that earlier episode, but he does regain consciousness almost immediately. Whatever view one takes of it, the incident remains an intriguing one, particularly given the 'power of love' theme of the episode.

The overwhelming power of Ianto's love for Lisa is demonstrated once again when, having been taken by force up to the Roald Dahl Plass while the Cyberwoman is under attack from the Torchwood pterodactyl, he punches Jack in the face, knocking him to the ground, and tells him: 'You could have saved her! You're worse than anything locked up down there! One day, I'll have the chance to save you, and I'll watch you suffer and die.' This leads on to a confrontation in the tourist information office at the Hub's front entrance, where Jack holds Ianto at gunpoint and gives him an ultimatum: 'You wanna go back in there, you go in to finish the job. If she's still alive, you execute her … You brought this down on us. You hid her. You hid yourself from us. Now it's time for you to stand as part of the team … The girl you loved has gone. Your loyalty is to us now.' If *Torchwood* were a more conventional drama, this is probably the point at which the misguided traitor would accept the truth of what his leader is telling him, realise the error of his ways and resolve to 'do the right thing'. The viewer is actually somewhat taken aback when, far from reacting in that way, Ianto remains stubbornly defiant, replying: 'You can't order me to do that … I won't do it. You can't make me. You like to think you're a hero, but you're the biggest monster of all.'

This latter comment is tantalisingly ambiguous. Does it refer simply to what Jack has just done, or to something else in his past, to which only Ianto is privy? It also makes one wonder exactly how long Ianto has been working at Torchwood Three. On the reasonable assumption that he could not have kept Lisa hidden for a lengthy period of time, even if he initially put her somewhere other than in the Hub's store-room, the destruction of Torchwood One – to which they were both originally assigned, as confirmed by documents on the Torchwood Institute System Interface website – must have occurred only a few months earlier at most. This could well mean that, Gwen aside, Ianto is the most recent addition to Torchwood Three's staff. If so, then one might expect him to know less about Jack than the other team members, not more. On the other hand, however, he could have discovered things about Jack from the Torchwood archives, possibly even while he was still at Torchwood One, as record-keeping seems to be one of the functions he undertakes.

Perhaps the only thing it is safe to conclude is that there will surely be further developments to come in the relationship between Ianto and Jack, given that Ianto is allowed to continue working in the Hub at the conclusion of the action. It is here that the believability of the episode, and of the series more generally, does take something of a knock. The Torchwood

Institute may well be short staffed, having lost a lot of people in the Battle of Canary Wharf, and Ianto may well have acted out of love rather than malice, but nevertheless it just doesn't ring true that he is allowed to keep his job when he has threatened to watch Jack 'suffer and die' at some point in the future and when his treacherous actions have already resulted in the deaths of two innocent people – which will now presumably have to be covered up – and could have had equally fatal consequences for his colleagues, and perhaps even for the whole world. Just what does one have to do in order to get fired from Torchwood? This lapse in credibility – a far more serious one than those discussed earlier, because it relates not to points of plotting or design but to the characters and their motivations – recalls the lack of any discernible aftermath to Suzie's demise in 'Everything Changes' and highlights an undoubted weakness in these early episodes of *Torchwood*. It would have made far more sense, in dramatic terms, if Ianto had been killed off at the end of 'Cyberwoman'. With Suzie already gone, however, *Torchwood* could obviously not afford to lose another, more bona fide regular so early in its run.

The episode's closing scene, where Ianto is seen stoically returning to work as though nothing has happened, is somewhat redeemed by an excellent exchange of dialogue between Gwen and Jack that points up the growing closeness between them. Reflecting on Ianto's devotion to Lisa, Gwen asks, 'So, have you ever loved anyone that much?' Jack's only reply is to cast her an enigmatic glance. Gwen then goes on to admit the fear she felt, during the attack by the Cyberwoman, that Jack might be able to die after all. This is an extremely clever piece of writing, as the viewer is left in no doubt that the significance lies not so much in what is being said but in what is left unspoken.

Having done an excellent job on *Doctor Who*'s most recent 'base under siege' story, 'The Impossible Planet'/'The Satan Pit', James Strong was an ideal choice to direct the similarly confined and claustrophobic 'Cyberwoman', and he handles it extremely well. Thrown into near-darkness, the Hub becomes an unfamiliar and treacherous environment, and the tension builds to fever pitch as the Torchwood team find themselves trapped inside with the deadly threat of the Cyberwoman. The scene where Owen and Gwen first approach the store-room, each with a torch in one hand and a gun in the other, effectively pays homage to *The X-Files*, and the episode certainly delivers its fair share of scares. The cast all give great performances, and particular kudos must go to David-Lloyd for his bravura portrayal of the emotion-wracked Ianto. The effects work is also superb throughout, particularly in the aforementioned struggle between the Cyberwoman and the pterodactyl, which is one of the series' most jaw-dropping and memorable sequences, almost like something out of a classic Japanese monster movie in the *Godzilla* vein – although much more convincingly realised. Again this has been slated by some as an absurdity, but perhaps these critics simply don't 'get' *Torchwood*. It is in scenes such as this that 'Cyberwoman' takes on something approaching a 'grand guignol' quality, and one almost wishes that it could have been pushed even further in that direction – with more copious quantities of blood pouring from Lisa's wounds, perhaps, or a more graphic depiction of the after-effects of the brain transplant, leaving Annie resembling the famous image of the gore-drenched Carrie from the climax of Brian de Palma's classic 1976 horror movie of the same name. But maybe there is a limit to how far a *Doctor Who* spin-off can go, even in a post-watershed slot.

With its winning combination of high intensity emotion, edge-of-the-seat thrills and 'popcorn movie' outrageousness, 'Cyberwoman' gives the viewer something really quite unique. Atypical though it may be of the series as a whole, it stands as an excellent episode, marred only slightly by the perhaps unavoidable pressing of the 'reset button' at the end.

1.05 – SMALL WORLDS

WRITER: Peter J Hammond
DIRECTOR: Alice Troughton

DEBUT TRANSMISSION DETAILS

BBC Three	BBC Two
Date: 12 November 2006.	Date: 15 November 2006.
Scheduled time: 10.00 pm.	Scheduled time: 9.00 pm.
Actual time: 10.00 pm.	Actual time: 9.03 pm.

Duration: 46' 45"

ADDITIONAL CREDITED CAST[72]

Eve Pearce (Estelle Cole), Lara Phillipart+ (Jasmine[73]), Adrienne O'Sullivan+ (Lynn), William Travis+ (Roy), Roger Barclay+ (Goodson[74]), Heledd Baskerville+ (Kate), Ffion Wilkins+ (WPC), Nathan Sussex+ (Custody Sergeant), Paul Jones+ (Man in Street), Sophie Davies+, Victoria Gourlay+ (Bullies)

PLOT: Fairies – ancient elemental forces living alongside but only occasionally glimpsed by humanity – are watching over their 'Chosen One', the young girl Jasmine, and attempting to lure her away with them. Torchwood become involved when Jack's elderly friend Estelle Cole – who first knew him during the Second World War, when they were lovers – sees the fairies gathering in Roundstone Wood and inadvertently incurs their displeasure. Estelle is killed by the fairies, and Jack ultimately decides to let Jasmine go to join them, which is what she wants to do, thus saving the rest of humanity from their wrath.

QUOTE, UNQUOTE

- Gwen: 'Are we talking alien?'
  Jack: 'Worse.'
  Gwen: 'How come?'
  Jack: 'Because they're part of us, part of our world, yet we know nothing about them. So we pretend to know what they look like. We see them as happy. We imagine they have tiny little wings and are bathed in moonlight.'
  Gwen: 'But they're not?'
  Jack: 'No. Think dangerous. Think something you can only half see, like a glimpse, like something out of the corner of your eye, with a touch of myth, a touch of the spirit world, a touch of reality, all jumbled together. Old moments and memories that are frozen in amongst it, like debris spinning around a ringed planet, tossing, turning, whirling, backwards and forwards through time. If that's them, we have to find them, before all hell breaks loose.'

---

72 The fairy voices were supplied, uncredited, by Lara Phillipart.

73 Surname given as 'Pearce' in the dialogue of the episode.

74 First name given as 'Mark' in the dialogue of the episode.

- Jack: 'That's the way these creatures like to do things. They play games, they torment and they kill.
  Gwen: 'Why?'
  Jack: 'As a punishment, or a warning to others. They protect their own: the Chosen Ones. Somehow children and the spirit world, they go together.'

- Jack: 'All these so-called fairies were children once, from different moments in time, going back millennia. Part of the lost lands.'
  Gwen: 'Lost lands? What?'
  Jack: 'The lands that belonged to them.'

DOCTOR WHO REFERENCES

- Jack theorises that the fairies are 'part Mara', noting that the word 'nightmare' derives from the name of these creatures and that they can steal the breath away from their victims. This appears to be a reference to the Mara of Scandinavian/Germanic legend. In *Doctor Who*, the Mara are elemental creatures from the planet Deva Loka that can take the form of a snake, as featured in the stories 'Kinda' and 'Snakedance'. The Mara of those stories were inspired by the Buddhist demon of the same name.

- Jack's comment 'I am so sorry' to Jasmine's mother, after he lets Jasmine go to the fairies, echoes a phrase used by the Doctor on a number of occasions during Series Two of *Doctor Who*.

ALIEN TECH

- Even the Hub's monitoring equipment cannot detect the fairies' presence; as Jack explains, they 'come in under the radar'. They may, however, be tracked indirectly through the unnatural weather patterns they cause. Jack also appears to use his wrist device as a scanner in Roundstone Wood.

'BLOOD AND SNOGGING'

- The fairies attack a paedophile, Goodson, who is threatening Jasmine, giving him a bloody nose. They later kill the man, and also Jack's friend Estelle and Jasmine's stepfather Roy. Goodson and Roy are choked by having their throats filled with rose petals. This is also the method that the fairies used to kill 15 troops under Jack's command in Lahore, India, in 1909, after their truck accidentally ran over a young girl – a Chosen One – in the wake of a drinking spree.

PRODUCTION NOTES

- Made with 'Out of Time' as part of Block 4 of production.

- The market through which Goodson staggers while being attacked by the fairies – a scene shot on 10 August 2006 – is Cardiff Market in the Hayes, leading on to St Mary's Street. The police station to which he is subsequently taken – in a sequence recorded ten days later – is a genuine police station in Clifton Road, Splott. The school scenes were shot at Radyr Primary School in the leafy Radyr suburb of Cardiff. Estelle gives her lecture in the Paget Rooms, an historic theatre on Victoria Road, Penarth. The location of Estelle's house is identified on a monitor screen in the Torchwood SUV as being in Plymouth Road, Penarth, which was the actual location used for recording. Jasmine's house is in or near 'Old Forest

Road'. This is a fictional name, not corresponding to any real road in the Cardiff area; but these scenes are also believed to have been shot in Penarth.

- In the CGI shot of the fairy attacking Goodson in the police cell, the fairy's face is largely obscured by shadow, unlike in the 'Next Time' sequence at the end of the previous episode.

- Three contemporary music tracks are heard during the party scene at the climax of the episode: 'Born to be a Dancer' from the 2005 album *Employment* by the Kaiser Chiefs, 'Better Do Better' from the 2005 album *Stars of CCTV* by Hard-Fi and 'Ooh La' from the 2006 album *Inside In/Inside Out* by the Kooks. The hymn 'Lord of the Dance' is also featured in the episode, in the scenes of the fairy attack at Jasmine's school.

- The episode ends with a fairy voice reciting an extract from the poem 'The Stolen Child' by W B Yeats (1865-1939):

> Come away, O human child!
> To the waters and the wild
> With a faery, hand in hand,
> For the world's more full of weeping that you can understand.

PRODUCTION QUOTES

- 'It's a very great chance in this story to discover more about Jack's past, which is still a mysterious past, where we see that actually his timelessness is a literal thing: we find him in Lahore in [1909].' Executive Producer Russell T Davies, *Torchwood* Declassified: 'Away with the Fairies', 13 November 2006.

- 'We wanted a world that was very rooted, very kind of, you know, normal: mum and step-dad.' Executive producer Julie Gardner, *Torchwood* Declassified: 'Away with the Fairies', 13 November 2006.

- 'There's a lot of imagery, especially in the British and Irish history of folk stories about fairies, so we very much drew on that as a basis. Peter [Hammond] had put a lovely description in about them looking like a medieval woodcut, so that was also another sort of starting point on the images of devils and gargoyles that you get in … pre-Christian mythology … So we wanted a … kind of traditional look … that then we could somehow … make … a little bit more horrific.' Director Alice Troughton, *Torchwood* official website, 13 November 2006.

- 'We really wanted to make [the fairies] Puck-ish and give them that playful element even though they're malevolent. So they're jumping and skipping around when they are attacking people rather than just using brute force.' Visual Effects Supervisor Dave Houghton, *Starburst* Special 79, February 2007.

OOPS!

- Contrary to what Owen suggests, Harry Houdini did not share Arthur Conan Doyle's belief that the Cottingley Fairies photographs were genuine.

PRESS REACTION

- 'P J Hammond finally arrives with a beautiful story about lost innocence on several levels … What we've got here is a properly constructed script. A story with a beginning, a middle and an (admittedly somewhat ambiguous but conceptually-fascinating) end … I like the delve into fairy-lore, too, and the little side-route plot about a child molester thankfully didn't outstay its welcome, as well as providing the episode with its most iconic moment (the [rose] petals).' Keith Topping, *TV Zone* Issue 210, December 2006.

- 'Last week, *Torchwood* was all about some fairies who killed a paedophile by stuffing rose petals in his mouth – an episode clearly written by Stevie Nicks, after a joint, under a pseudonym. I love *Torchwood* – and I haven't even seen Captain Jack's beautiful naked back yet. Imagine what will happen when I see Captain Jack's beautiful naked back! I'll pay my next 15 TV licences early, and then faint, probably.' Caitlin Moran, *The Times*, 27 November 2006.

FAN COMMENT

- 'After a fitful start, at five episodes in it's great to see *Torchwood* at last firing on all cylinders with this deliciously dark tale from the mind of Peter J Hammond (yes, he of *Sapphire & Steel* fame), a tale of mischievous fairies and their dangerous powers to manipulate, control, coerce, terrify and kill those who threaten their beloved Chosen One, a small child destined to join their ranks in eternity. The story opens with a terrific scene in a wooded glade at night, at its centre a tiny stone circle where seemingly beautiful creatures play amongst the branches, observed by an elderly lady, who having sought them out, is here to take photographic evidence. The tone of the scene is so wonderfully reminiscent of *Doctor Who*'s gothic peak ("The Daemons", "Image of the Fendahl" and "The Stones of Blood" immediately springing to mind) that any sense of guardedness you have from previous episodes' failings is immediately put aside to enjoy what surely must be *Torchwood*'s first classic.' Steve Preston, Kasterborous website, 2 December 2006.

ANALYSIS

Just as 'Cyberwoman', with its 'base under siege' scenario, tells a type of story that has been seen on numerous occasions in *Doctor Who*, so too does 'Small Worlds'. The type of story in this instance is one in which a popular myth, legend or fable is given a science-fiction 'explanation'. Notable examples in *Doctor Who* include 'The Abominable Snowmen' (1967), in which the Yeti glimpsed from time to time by Himalayan explorers turn out to be fur-covered robots controlled by a disembodied intelligence (although, at the very end, a 'real' Yeti is seen too); 'The Daemons' (1971), in which the traditional image of the Devil as a cloven-hoofed horned beast is found to be derived from the appearance of the powerful race of Daemons; and 'Terror of the Zygons' (1975), in which the Loch Ness Monster is revealed to be a cyborg brought to Earth by the alien Zygons. In 'Small Worlds', it is the turn of fairies to be given a similar treatment, although here the explanation offered by Jack – that they are 'something from the dawn of time … part of our world, yet we know nothing about them … with a touch of myth, a touch of the spirit world, a touch of reality, all jumbled together' – is rather more mystical, and recalls the 'evil from the dawn of time' that the seventh Doctor encountered in the form of the Haemovores in 'The Curse of Fenric' (1989); a concept later expanded upon in a number of the original *Doctor Who* novels.

Fairy-like beings can be found in the myths and folklore of many different cultures dating back hundreds if not thousands of years. They are nowadays generally thought of as beautiful little creatures, female in form, with delicate, gauze-like wings and gossamer dresses; but this has not always been the case. Prior to the Victorian era, they were often seen in a much more sinister light, as mischief-making or even malicious spirits posing a distinct threat to the unwary. Many fairy legends involve them abducting babies and young children. So when writer Peter J Hammond says, in the 'Away with the Fairies' episode of *Torchwood Declassified*, that the creatures in his story are 'not your everyday fairies; they are evil', and that he 'wanted to take away the idea of bluebell hats and mushrooms', he is really talking about stripping away modern preconceptions and getting back to a more traditional view. As Russell T Davies adds: 'Fairies aren't just those storybook, Victorian, sweet creatures. It's a dark [premise]; it's ancient creatures, in woodlands, existing under different rules.'

The episode actually seems to imply that the fairies can take on two different forms: an ugly, malevolent one, and a beautiful, gentle one as first seen by Estelle – the latter of which does fit the modern stereotype. This does not come across too clearly on screen, however, and the scripting seems generally rather confused in relation to the creatures' powers and motivations. For instance, there seems to be an implication that the fairies are unable to attack Estelle or Jasmine's mother in their own homes, when the doors are shut against them, and yet they obviously have no difficulty entering Gwen's flat uninvited. Then again, why should they even want to wreck Gwen's flat, or later kill Estelle, given that neither of the two women is threatening Jasmine or in any way impeding their attempts to lure the girl away? Perhaps they want to dissuade Jack from interfering and, knowing that he cannot be killed himself, are attacking his friends instead, thereby giving him warnings of increasing severity – which would also explain the rose petal he finds in the Hub early on in the episode. If so, however, it is by no means apparent; and it turns out that Jack is powerless to stop them in any case.

Also rather odd, to say the least, is the suggestion at the end of the episode that Jasmine is one of the fairies pictured in the famous Cottingley Fairies glass-plate photographs. Anyone who cares to take the trouble could fairly easily track down a copy of the photograph in question – which is actually one of the retouched versions produced for the *Strand* magazine in the 1920s and not one of the much murkier originals – and see that Jasmine is *not* one of the fairies depicted. It could perhaps have been Hammond's intention to suggest here that Jasmine becomes 'timeless' after she is taken away, and that the photograph then changes as a result. This, though, overlooks the fact that the Cottingley Fairies photographs – of which there were five in total, all taken by young cousins Frances Griffiths and Elsie Wright at Cottingley in Yorkshire between 1917 and 1920 – have been conclusively shown to be fakes. Even the two girls themselves changed their stories several times subsequently, and in the end – as Gwen rightly notes – effectively admitted that they had practised a deception. This seriously undermines the credibility of the episode, and takes it into the realms of fantasy.

Matters are not helped in this regard by the fact that – as touched on above – the explanation put forward for the fairies owes rather more to magic than to science, contrary to Davies's oft-stated preference; and in 'Away with the Fairies', the executive producer cheerfully concedes that this episode delves into 'magic and the supernatural'. It has to be said that for some viewers, and some science-fiction fans in particular, this sort of thing is simply a turn-off. Moreover, the fact that the fairies manifest in this particular location seems to have nothing at all to do with the existence of the spacio-temporal rift, so for the second time in only five episodes the emergence of a danger in close proximity to Cardiff is a complete coincidence. The superficial reason for the fairies' presence is their interest in Jasmine, but no explanation is ever given as to how Jasmine came to have Chosen One status; is it something that was innate in her at birth, or something that they have recently conferred upon her? This is not the only coincidence in the story, either, as it is soon revealed that Jack's friend – and, it later transpires, one-time love – Estelle just happens to be interested in fairies, and just happens to live conveniently close by. Then, again by complete coincidence, Jack turns out to have encountered the fairies before, in Lahore, India, in 1909.

Most of these problems could have been ironed out with a little rewriting, and it seems that the script would have benefited greatly from going through one or two more drafts before entering production. How much more satisfactory it would have been, for instance, if Jack's initial encounter with the fairies had occurred not in Lahore in 1909 but in London in the 1940s when he first met Estelle. The flashback could then have shown the two of them together as a young couple and helped to establish their relationship, and also have given Estelle a reason to be interested in the fairies. She could then perhaps have run into Jack again by chance while visiting Cardiff on a lecture tour or to investigate reports of the fairies in Roundstone Wood, and Jack could have decided on the spur of the moment to claim that he was the son of the man she once knew. The fairies themselves could have been explained as creatures that gather around spacio-temporal anomalies. No doubt there are other ways in which the various plot contrivances could have been avoided; and the fact that they were left unaddressed is both surprising and disappointing.

The relationship between Jack and Estelle is actually the most interesting aspect of 'Small Worlds'. The pain and loneliness that Jack feels as his friend ages and dies while he remains unaffected by the ravages of time show that immortality can be the same 'curse' for him as it is for the Doctor, as explored in the Series Two *Doctor Who* episodes 'School Reunion' and 'The Girl in the Fireplace'. The scene in which Jack holds Estelle's lifeless body in his arms, admitting to Gwen the truth of their past love as tears run down his face, is undeniably a very moving one, and also serves to strengthen the bond between the two regulars. That said, it is a great pity that Estelle's death is not held back until much later in the episode, as it closes off this story strand prematurely, leaving the viewer feeling that it has not been developed to anything like its full potential – as if Madame de Pompadour had been killed off half-way through 'The Girl in the Fireplace' and the story had then focused simply on the Doctor's attempts to destroy the Clockwork Men. Again it seems that a little more effort invested in the scripting could have brought considerable dividends here.

The underselling of this aspect of the story is all the more irksome for the fact that there is a certain amount of padding in evidence elsewhere. The material involving the paedophile Goodson who stalks Jessica in his car and the later sequence of the bullies getting their comeuppance at the school are both quite effectively done, but nevertheless serve exactly the same purpose: to demonstrate that the fairies are watching over Jasmine and will ruthlessly protect her against anyone who tries to harm her. Either of them could have been dropped altogether without the slightest detriment to the plot. On balance, the paedophile incident would probably have been the wisest omission, as the referencing of this very real evil in such a fantasy-orientated episode does sit a little uncomfortably.

It is puzzling that there should be so many weaknesses in the plotting and structure of this episode, given that Hammond is a highly experienced writer and certainly no stranger to telefantasy, having created and handled most of the scripting on the cult classic *Sapphire & Steel*. That series, produced by ATV between 1979 and 1982[75], involved two mysterious

75 An audio CD spin-off series has since been released by Big Finish Productions.

interdimensional 'operatives' – played by Joanna Lumley and David McCallum – whose function was to rectify time anomalies. 'Small Worlds' is actually somewhat reminiscent of *Sapphire & Steel* in a number of respects. Like the latter's title characters, Jack is seen to have been active in a number of different periods of history, and the fairies are described as a timeless, elemental force that has existed side-by-side with humanity, largely without its knowledge. A number of specific plot points in 'Small Worlds' also recall similar elements in the earlier series. The snapshot of Jack and Estelle together in the 1940s, for instance, brings to mind the collection of photographs paradoxically mixing contemporary and past events in the fourth *Sapphire & Steel* story, generally referred to as 'The Man Without a Face'; and, most notably, Jack's decision to let Jasmine go with the fairies at the end of the episode is akin to Steel's agreement to let the Darkness take the final few years of the character George Tulley's life at the conclusion of the second *Sapphire & Steel* story, commonly known as 'The Railway Station'.[76] Perhaps the problem is that the *Sapphire & Steel* style of storytelling, which is essentially fantasy-orientated and favours explanations rooted in the mystical or even the supernatural, does not fit well within the gritty, realistic, science-fiction-based world of *Torchwood* – despite 'Small Worlds' paying what is perhaps the series' most obvious homage to *The X-Files*, with Jack and Gwen initially fulfilling the Mulder and Scully roles of 'believer' and 'sceptic', complete with underlying sexual tension, as they attend Estelle's lecture on the fairies.

Certainly the episode is atypical in being played out largely in bright sunshine in relatively pleasant, leafy suburban surroundings. Jack's aforementioned capitulation in allowing Jasmine to join the fairies also makes for a strangely unsatisfying resolution. While it could be argued that this merely reflects the adult nature of *Torchwood*, in that its writers are able to present stories without clear-cut 'happy endings', it has the unfortunate effect of showing Jack in a decidedly impotent, unheroic light, and somewhat tarnishes the character. Discussing this point in 'Away with the Fairies', Hammond says: 'Jack is protecting the world. Had the girl pleaded not to go with the fairies, it would have been a different story altogether. Then he would have [had] to have fought to keep her, but because she wanted to go – she preferred to be with them, where she rightfully belonged – then it seemed to me to be okay, and Jack could let her go, but with misgivings and a great deal of sorrow.' This argument is a hollow one, however, as children cannot be relied upon to make sensible decisions about their own lives and futures; besides which, the way the story is set up, even if Jasmine *was* unwilling to go with the fairies, Jack would still presumably be powerless to intervene.

Are the fairies playing mind games with Jack when they tell him that, if Jasmine joins them, 'she lives forever'? This assertion seems almost calculated to touch a nerve with him, given his ambivalent feelings about, and understandable preoccupation with, his own immortality – which is by this point emerging as a key theme of the entire series. Whatever his reasons for letting Jasmine go without a fight, there is no doubting the disgust with which Gwen, Toshiko and Owen view his actions – even though they themselves had no other options to suggest. As Julie Gardner puts it in 'Away with the Fairies', 'At the end, ... we reinforce ... what it's like, the price of being the leader. And sometimes that is making the unpopular decisions, it is making the hard decisions.'

Having incurred Ianto's resentment in 'Cyberwoman', Jack now seems to have alienated the rest of his small team. Whether or not this will have any longer-term repercussions will become apparent only in later episodes, although it seems likely that there will be at least a

76 The *Sapphire & Steel* stories were untitled on screen.

temporary cooling off of his relationship with Gwen. As far as his current standing with Ianto is concerned, some light is shed on this by a telling exchange of dialogue just a few minutes into the episode, when Jack tells Ianto 'You shouldn't be here' and Ianto replies 'Neither should you'. While on a superficial level the two men are simply acknowledging each other's presence in the Hub late at night, their remarks seem to have a deeper meaning as well – particularly given that, as Jack has a bed in the Hub, his being there at that hour is surely not unexpected.[77] They may well be reflecting on the fact that – notwithstanding Jack's immortality, of which Ianto may or may not be aware – they are both fortunate to have survived the events of 'Cyberwoman', or perhaps in Ianto's case that he is fortunate to have kept his job in Torchwood. Jack then places his hand on Ianto's shoulder in a curiously intimate gesture, recalling the way he revived the younger man with a kiss in the preceding episode, and the pair exchange what seems to be a significant look. Is Jack simply attempting to reassure Ianto with a gesture of reconciliation, or is this a further suggestion that there may be more complex feelings between the two than have so far surfaced?

In production terms, the episode is well directed by Alice Troughton and boasts some good performances from all the cast, including notably Lara Phillipart – described by Troughton in 'Away With the Fairies' as 'a genuine find as a child actress' – in the demanding role of the seven-year-old Jasmine. The sequence of Goodson stumbling through the market and spewing blood-red rose petals from his mouth, then being arrested by the WPC and taken in a state of terror to the police station, is particularly well handled, and very memorable. The only less than fully satisfactory aspect of the episode's on-screen realisation is that the fairies never look like anything other than CGI creations. The evidence of recent telefantasy productions in general would seem to suggest that there is a danger of CGI becoming to the 2000s what CSO[78] was to the 1970s – a convenient means of achieving effects that would be much more difficult, if not impossible, to accomplish by more conventional means, but one that starts to become overused and has an unfortunate tendency to pull the viewer out of the reality of the drama by inadvertently highlighting its artificiality. Perhaps, though, the fact that CGI work is relatively expensive will prevent this becoming too great a problem on the modestly-budgeted *Torchwood*.

'Small Worlds' has in general been a very well-received episode amongst fans. This is rather surprising however as, all things considered, it is actually one of the weaker entries in *Torchwood*'s first series.

77 In 'Ghost Machine', Jack implies in a conversation with Gwen that he actually lives in the Hub. Some doubt is later cast on this, however, by a Torchwood Institute System Interface record of an instant messaging exchange between Ianto and Gwen, during the events of 'Random Shoes', in which Jack is said to have 'gone home'. This would seem to suggest that Jack has a home elsewhere, although it is possible that it may mean simply that he has retired to his quarters.

78 Colour separation overlay (CSO), also known as chromakey or green- or blue-screen, is an electronic effect by way of which certain areas of a video image that are in a key colour – generally green, blue or yellow – can be replaced with the equivalent areas of a different image.

1.06 – COUNTRYCIDE

WRITER: Chris Chibnall
DIRECTOR: Andy Goddard

DEBUT TRANSMISSION DETAILS

BBC Three	BBC Two
Date: 19 November 2006.	Date: 22 November 2006.
Scheduled time: 10.00 pm.	Scheduled time: 9.00 pm.
Actual time: 10.00 pm.	Actual time: 9.02 pm.

Duration: 46' 51"

ADDITIONAL CREDITED CAST

Owen Teale (Evan Sherman), Maxine Evans (Helen Sherman), Calum Callaghan (Kieran), Rhys ap Trefor (Huw), Emily Bowker (Ellie[79]), Robert Barton (Martin)

PLOT: The Torchwood team investigate a series of mysterious disappearances in the Brecon Beacons and find themselves under threat from a group of cannibals in an isolated community. More horrifying still, the cannibals are not, as they first assumed, monsters deposited there by the spacio-temporal rift, but ordinary – albeit twisted – human beings. Jack is able to rescue his trapped colleagues, and the police are called in to arrest the cannibal community.

QUOTE, UNQUOTE

- Gwen: 'Do you miss being a doctor?'
  Owen: 'Excuse me; I still am a doctor. I just don't deal with patients any more, that's all. It's ideal. That was the bit I always hated.'

- Gwen: 'The whole village was involved.'
  Evan: 'Every generation. Our tradition. Once a decade, target those travelling through; those most likely to disappear.'
  Gwen: 'And butcher them. What sort of people are you, that you wake up in the morning and think, "This is what I'm gonna do"? Why do you do it? Come on, make me understand.'
  Evan: 'Why do you care?'
  Gwen: 'I have seen things you would never believe, and this is the only thing I can't understand.'

- Gwen: 'I had a good job before this. I thought in a year or two perhaps a baby – I know Rhys would be a good dad – and I could try for desk sergeant, and … well it was all slotting into place. And then I met you lot. All these things. All these things, they're changing me, changing how I see the world, and I can't share them with anyone.'
  Owen: 'You can now.'

79 Surname given in the dialogue of the episode as 'Johnson'.

DOCTOR WHO REFERENCES

- None.

ALIEN TECH

- None.

CONTINUITY POINTS

- There have been a total of 17 unexplained disappearances of people passing through the area of the Brecon Beacons around which this Torchwood investigation centres. It is uncertain whether or not the spacio-temporal rift spreads out this far: Jack says 'We don't know that much about it to be certain, and it's increasing in activity all the time.'

- Jack says that the human race is the only one in the universe that goes camping.

'BLOOD AND SNOGGING'

- This episode features copious amounts of blood and gore, as the Torchwood team discover the cannibal community's victims – or what is left of them …

- Owen and Gwen have an erotically-charged clinch against a tree, but stop just short of actually kissing.

- Gwen sustains a shotgun wound to her side, leaving her bleeding heavily and with a number of bullets embedded in her flesh – although luckily these are lodged near the surface, and Owen is able to remove them with a pair of tweezers.

- The cannibal leader, Evan Sherman, kisses his wife Helen as they relish the prospect of fresh 'meat'.

- Ianto head butts Evan, giving him a bloody nose, and gets punched in the face and hit with a rifle butt in return.

PRODUCTION NOTES

- Made with 'Combat' as part of Block 5 of production.

- 'Monster', a 2006 single and album track by The Automatic, is heard during the pre-titles sequence at the beginning of the episode.

- There was some behind-the-scenes debate about the presentation of the action sequence of Jack rescuing the rest of the team at the end of the episode. One option was to have him moving calmly and stealthily, picking off the cannibalistic villagers precisely with his shotgun; the other was to have him bursting in and blasting away angrily, with a guttural roar. The latter was the approach that director Andy Goddard and star John Barrowman decided to take when recording the sequence, but it later transpired that executive producers Russell T Davies and Julie Gardner favoured the alternative. A compromise was therefore worked out in editing, which involved the cutting of some of Jack's dialogue – 'What's the matter with you people? It's not enough that a whole cosmos of chaos is gonna descend upon you in the next few centuries. The thing you most have to fear is yourselves' – and parts of the action being played out in slow motion, giving it something of an 'operatic' quality.[80]

- The hotel where the cast and crew stayed while shooting on location in the Brecon Beacons national park was reputedly haunted, and a number of the team members were spooked by it. Eve Myles even stayed in John Barrowman's room overnight.

PRODUCTION QUOTES

- 'I read a lot about the subject [of cannibalistic murders], and what I was struggling to understand was, "How, as a human being, do you get to that place?", and so that scene [between Gwen and Evan at the end] was very much asking that question. And it was a very unsettling script to write.' Writer Chris Chibnall, *Torchwood* official website, 20 November 2006.

- 'Shooting the forest scene with Owen Teale, who is just one of the most amazing actors, was actually horrific. I can't even imagine being in that kind of situation: the absolute desperation and terror.' Actress Naoko Mori, Torchwood official website, 20 November 2006.

- 'This is a blood and gore story, but we never luxuriate in it.' Executive Producer Russell T Davies, *Torchwood Declassified*: 'The Country Club', 20 November 2006.

- '[Toshiko is] a very practical person, she loves problem-solving. With "Countrycide", I think it really shook her, because it was so horrific. What can you do? Run! I think I'm fairly fit, but it was freezing, it was so cold. I'd sprained my ankle really badly about a month before that, when we were filming Ianto's big episode. I tore a ligament, my tendon in my right ankle. So I was like "Oh my god, I have to run!" But it was all right.' Actress Naoko Mori, *Eclipse Magazine*, January 2007.

- 'I think "Countrycide" works because you're moving Gwen's character on and building to her affair with Owen. That's about her being shot in the stomach, seeing how brilliant he is as a doctor, nearly dying on him and, having seen humanity at its worst, not being able to go back to talk to her boyfriend, so needing to find someone else ... Also, the other pivotal character there is Ianto; it's the first time you see him out of the Hub, the first time you see him have a real individual opinion about Torchwood, which is, who protects them?' Executive Producer Julie Gardner, *Dreamwatch* Issue 150, March 2007.

PRESS REACTION

- 'I can't help thinking there's something inappropriate about a *Doctor Who* spin-off where one character asks another, "When was the last time you came so hard, you forgot where you were?" It's further proof that Davies just couldn't decide what sort of show *Torchwood* was meant to be. Funnily enough, when one of the team goes missing, the name they call out – "Tosh! Tosh! Tosh!" – is exactly the word I would use to describe it.' Jim Shelley, *Daily Mirror*, 21 November 2006.

---

80 Goddard's original cut of the scene is due to be included in the deleted scenes package on the Series One: Part Two DVD set.

- 'This is the series we were originally promised: dark, daring and convincingly adult, while testing the perceived boundaries of what is acceptable on TV ... This is all about mood, tapping into our primal fears of dark country lanes and deserted woods, and it's deeply unnerving while punctuated by leap-out-of-your seat moments.' David Richardson, *Starburst* Issue 345, January 2007.

FAN COMMENT

- 'Gwen tries desperately to assemble Knowns, going so far as to compartmentalise the deaths – "So they've killed 17, good" – as long as it stays on the other side of the wall. (As long as she doesn't look at the gunshot wound, she's okay.) She's being presented with a world where people – not aliens, not monsters, not Weevils – are capable of horror. She's not buying. If that's true, then it's the kind of world that she could fuck Owen and nobody would care. Leading up to the "It made me happy" line ... we see Gwen in full-on anger/denial mode, screaming that she wants answers. But the answer she gets is that people just do things, sometimes. "It made me happy" to eat human flesh. That's the moment she gives in: to Owen, to Torchwood, to the fact that she's got the Torchwood Look no matter how she denies it. She can call it "sharing secrets" or being part of Torchwood or whatever she wants, but the fact is that when the guy said that, her world broke open permanently. No rules, no authority, no good, no evil. Just things that happen. As a cop, she's used to rules like that. As a person, she's never had to develop a moral system of her own accord: just the common terms of what's right and what's wrong.' Jacob Clifton, Television Without Pity website, 24 November 2006.

- 'The plot twist at the end of the show was *the* most incredible example of irony I have witnessed on television. The simple assumption that the team, and indeed the audience, had made about the attackers being alien was thwarted in such shocking fashion that even when it was clear the show was winding up, I was still waiting for the aliens to reveal themselves. Surely, tentacles were going to come out of Evan's mouth at any moment while he was being interrogated! Surely, these were creatures with technology like the Slitheen and they were aliens in human skin suits! No, these horrible monsters were *human*; the collective shudder of the audience will undoubtedly still be reverberating in future episodes, as we have been poignantly warned that even humans aren't alien to inhumanity.' Ceres D'Aleo, Torchwood Guide website, November 2006.

ANALYSIS

Interviewed in the *Torchwood Declassified* mini-documentary 'The Country Club', Russell T Davies recalls the initial point from which 'Countrycide' developed: 'Right at the start of the series, when we planned it, I was always sitting there going "*The Hills Have Eyes*; we must do *The Hills Have Eyes*".' This notorious Wes Craven horror film from 1977, an even more brutal remake of which was released in the spring of 2006 at around the time that 'Countryside' was going into production, involves a family being stalked and killed by a group of cannibalistic savages after their car breaks down in a cordoned-off desert location. It is one of many movies owing a debt of inspiration to Tobe Hooper's 1974 opus *The Texas Chain Saw Massacre*, itself the subject of a remake in 2003, in which a group of five young people visit a remote old house in rural Texas and are terrorised by a chainsaw-wielding maniac and his family of grave-robbing cannibals. This gives a good indication of the type of story that Chris Chibnall was aiming to tell in 'Countrycide'.

As he puts it in 'The Country Club': 'I really wanted to write something that was very scary, and put [the Torchwood team] in real danger, real personal danger.'

While it never approaches the extremes of its horror film antecedents, 'Countrycide' is certainly the goriest, and scariest, episode of *Torchwood* to date. The spine-tingling teaser – in which a lone woman driver in a remote location at night is tricked into leaving her car to investigate what appears to be a body in the road and is then ambushed and attacked by a barely-glimpsed assailant – brilliantly establishes the tone of the piece, and gives the viewer a chilling taste of what is to come.

This is followed, immediately after the opening titles, by what could just be the best-written-and-directed five-minutes' worth of character interplay in the entire first series of *Torchwood*, as Jack and his team arrive on the scene in their SUV, pause at a roadside fast-food van for a burger and then start to set up camp, only to be distracted by the discovery of a mutilated corpse in the woods and have the SUV stolen from under their noses, with their tents wrecked in the process. The dialogue between the five regulars fairly sparkles throughout this entire sequence. Owen's comments about the countryside being 'dirty and unhygienic' with a 'disgusting' smell of grass, and his subsequent horror at the idea of camping in the open, neatly encapsulate the outlook of a typical 'townie'; and the disconcerted reaction of the others when Toshiko mentions, just as they are biting into their burgers, that a friend of hers once contracted hepatitis from just such a source, is a humorous moment to savour. A more telling exchange occurs when Toshiko jokingly offers to help Owen erect his tent – 'Need a hand getting it up, Owen?'– and appears crestfallen when he responds with the sharp put-down 'If I did, I wouldn't ask you.' The clear implication of this – that Toshiko has a crush on Owen, which he is either oblivious to or has no interest in indulging – is immediately reinforced when Gwen initiates a 'Who was the last person you snogged?' round-robin and Toshiko admits that in her case it was Owen, the previous Christmas Eve (obviously some months ago), when she had some mistletoe. This 'bit of fun' backfires even more badly when Owen divulges to all and sundry that the last person he kissed was Gwen herself – a revelation that clearly surprises Jack and arouses jealousy in Toshiko – and when Ianto glumly states that in his case it was Lisa. These references back to the events of 'Cyberwoman' are very welcome, showing some good character continuity that was rather lacking previously in the series. They are followed up straight away when Owen and Gwen go off alone into the woods, ostensibly to look for firewood, and argue over their earlier encounter. They end up in a clinch against a tree, with Owen challenging Gwen: 'When was the last time you screwed all night? When was the last time you came so hard and so long you forgot where you are? Doesn't happen with [Rhys], does it? You're too familiar. Whereas you and me, we're not cosy at all. We'd be *amazing*, and that scares the shit out of you.' It is clearly only their sudden realisation that they are being watched by someone lurking in the trees that forestalls them from kissing passionately again. Like the 'Cyberwoman' incident itself, this has been criticised by some on the basis that Gwen's obvious arousal in the face of such sexual aggression from Owen is distasteful and/or implausible. One thing *Torchwood* certainly isn't, however, is 'politically correct.' John Barrowman neatly sums up the situation between Owen and Gwen when he says in 'The Country Club': 'They get to that point where they're like two kettles that are ready to just … steam off, and they're in that heated moment, and boom, it happens.'

These opening minutes of action provide, all told, something of a masterclass in the effective illumination and development of character through well-crafted dialogue. While it might perhaps be unrealistic to expect this sort of standard to be maintained throughout, there are some further excellent character moments later on as well. A good example comes in the scene where Ianto and Toshiko find themselves locked up together in a basement cell. Ianto's fearfulness and vulnerability again come to the fore here, whereas Toshiko shows an unexpected degree of courage and resourcefulness, giving the viewer a good insight into why she was considered well-suited to become a Torchwood member in the first place:

> Ianto: 'You're used to this, aren't you? That facial expression, you all share, when things get a bit out of control. Like you enjoy it. Like you get a high from the danger.'
> Toshiko: 'You want me to apologise for that?'
> Ianto: 'Don't you ever wonder how long you can survive before you go mad, or get killed, or lose a loved one?'
> Toshiko: 'It's worth the risk! To protect people!'
> Ianto: 'Then who protects us?'

Again, this is simply fantastic dialogue from Chibnall, and superbly delivered by both Gareth David-Lloyd and Naoko Mori.

The character who goes through undoubtedly the most gruelling emotional journey in 'Countrycide', though, is Gwen. The mangled corpses that she and the others discover in the eerily deserted houses of the isolated community are doubtless more appalling than anything she has ever witnessed before as a lowly WPC, and she is terrified by the experience, fearfully protesting: 'I should be at home, having dinner with Rhys. What am I doing here with you? Don't you ever get scared, Jack?' She is thus seen to be more akin to Ianto than to Toshiko in terms of her horror threshold, recalling just how recent an addition she is to the Torchwood team. Her trepidation is quickly seen to be completely justified, too, as she falls victim to a sudden shotgun blast that leaves her lying bleeding on the ground. Her distress and shock are palpable here, and there follows another superbly-written character interaction scene as her wounds are tended to by Owen and it becomes apparent that there is a growing feeling of trust and closeness between the pair. This is something that Jack himself clearly notes, as he casts a significant glance in their direction when Owen insists on supporting Gwen en route to the village pub, The Tap House, where they have decided to make a base. Does this perhaps foreshadow some rivalry between Jack and Owen for Gwen's affections? Or will Jack be content to step back now and let things take their course between the other two, content perhaps to maintain a purely platonic relationship with Gwen? Certainly this presents some intriguing possibilities for further development in the episodes to come.

Even more horrifying to Gwen than being wounded is the later discovery that – in a surprising twist – it is not aliens or monsters who have been carrying out the cannibalistic killings but the villagers themselves. Desperate to understand why they have committed these terrible crimes, she insists on being given time to question the head man, Evan Sherman; but the only answer he can give her is: ''Cause it made me happy.'

This is an absolutely key scene that deepens, if not completes, Gwen's assimilation into the world of Torchwood. As producer Richard Stokes puts it in 'The Country Club': 'Suddenly to be confronted by something that is human but that horrifying, is just appalling, and horribly ugly, and that's what Gwen reacts to.'

'Actually,' adds Davies, 'the whole thing is designed to push Gwen towards Owen. Even though she can't stand him half the time, … she's leading this extraordinary life and cannot go home and say what's going on; and actually, in those circumstances, that's when you start to have the affair at work.'

The culmination of all these events comes in the episode's final scene, where Gwen reflects on her situation in what is obviously a post-coital moment at Owen's flat. She is now effectively leading two distinct lives: her cosy domestic life with Rhys; and, kept separate and hidden from him, her exciting working life with Owen and her other Torchwood colleagues.

To some science-fiction fans, the discovery that there were no aliens or monsters behind this particular spate of killings in the Brecon Beacons may perhaps have been disappointing. It was always intended, though, that *Torchwood* would involve both alien *and* human crime – indeed this was made clear in the BBC's very first press release about the series, issued on 17 October 2005 – and the variation helps to keep the series fresh and interesting. This actually mirrors rather cleverly the approach taken in the early *Doctor Who* series of the mid-1960s, where science-fiction stories – typically involving alien monsters – would be alternated with historical ones – pitting the Doctor and his companions against purely human adversaries. It was often the historical stories that were the more mature and dramatically effective of the two types; and arguably the same can be said of 'Countrycide' by comparison with the earlier *Torchwood* episodes. Certainly it suits this story's dramatic purposes far better to have the Torchwood team, and Gwen in particular, encountering a decidedly human evil rather than an alien one. As Davies succinctly puts it in 'The Country Club': 'This is our little peek into the dark corners of the human soul.'

'Countrycide' is the first *Torchwood* episode to have no scenes whatsoever set within the Hub (apart from in the 'Next Time' preview of 'Greeks Bearing Gifts' at the end), and it is much the better for it, not only because it makes it all the more scary to have the team taken out of their 'comfort zone' and into unfamiliar territory – deprived of their usual sophisticated technology and gadgetry and having to rely on their wits – but also because to have had the action cutting back periodically to such an inherently artificial environment would have jarred the viewer out of the stark realism of the location-shot material. While it might perhaps have been more logical, in operational terms, for Jack to have left one of his team – presumably Ianto – behind to 'man the fort', in case any other crises developed elsewhere, it is fortunate for the sake of the drama that he elected not do so – and that there was no attempted alien invasion of Newport at this particular time!

It is the unremitting stark realism that makes 'Countrycide' so chilling. The action is utterly compelling, with a gradual escalation of tension as the team split up to explore and Toshiko and Ianto get captured and locked in the cellar, where they find a fridge full of body parts, while Jack, Owen and the wounded Gwen barricade themselves with the petrified young man Kieran in the pub – creating a temporary 'base under siege' scenario far more terrifying than that seen in 'Cyberwoman'. Andy Goddard's direction, while it at times relies, perhaps inevitably, on some tried-and-trusted horror film techniques to create the shocks and scares, is superb throughout, supported by excellent camerawork and lighting – most of the interior scenes are played out in semi-darkness, giving them a suitably unsettling quality – and benefiting from some highly impressive work from Neill Gorton and his Millennium Effects colleagues on the corpse and body part props and blood and gore effects, which are all disturbingly convincing.

The regulars all turn in excellent performances once again; and, of the guest cast, Owen Teale is particularly good as the repulsive Evan, investing him with a creepy relish in scenes such as where he menaces Toshiko with a baseball bat, running his tongue around his lips as he comments on the need for meat to be 'tenderised', and later has a cat-and-mouse chase with her through the darkened woods.

It is, in fact, difficult to fault this episode in any way, and it is certainly one of the best of the debut series; perhaps the first bona fide *Torchwood* classic.

1.07 – GREEKS BEARING GIFTS

WRITER: Toby Whithouse[81]
DIRECTOR: Colin Teague

DEBUT TRANSMISSION DETAILS

BBC Three	BBC Two
Date: 26 November 2006.	Date: 29 November 2006.
Scheduled time: 10.00 pm.	Scheduled time: 9.00 pm
Actual time: 10.01 pm.	Actual time: 9.00 pm.

Duration: 49' 37"

ADDITIONAL CREDITED CAST[82]

Daniela Denby-Ashe (Mary), Tom Robertson (Soldier), Ravin J Gantra (Neil), Eiry Thomas (Carol), Shaheen Jafargholi (Danny), Paul Kasey (Weevil)

PLOT: Toshiko meets a young woman named Mary who gives her a pendant that enables the wearer to read people's minds. They begin a relationship, but it transpires that Mary is really an alien criminal who was exiled to Earth in 1812 and has since killed many people, ripping out their hearts for her to feed on. She is just using Toshiko in order to gain access to the Hub, where the Torchwood team have taken the transporter device that brought her to Earth in the first place. She now plans to return to her home planet, but Jack has pre-programmed the transporter to deposit her in the heart of the sun.

QUOTE, UNQUOTE

- Toshiko: 'I've never seen anything like it. It's incredible.'
  Mary: 'It's more than incredible. With this you can read people's minds. It levels the pitch between man and god.'

- Toshiko: 'What you're thinking now, that's pretty graphic.'
  Mary: 'That wasn't my thought.'
  Toshiko: 'What?'
  Mary: 'I wasn't thinking anything. That wasn't my thought. Must have been yours.'
  Toshiko: 'That one! There! That's yours.'
  Mary: 'Yeah. That was mine.'
  Toshiko: 'I, um … I certainly seem to be enjoying myself.'
  Mary: 'You would. You will.'

- Mary: 'The freedom you have; when I first got here, I found it almost obscene. My world was savage, enforced worship in temples the size of cities, execution squads roaming the streets. Dissent of any kind meant death, or transportation, to what they call a feral outpost.'

81 Miscredited as 'Toby Whitehouse' in *Radio Times*.

82 The passers-by whose thoughts Toshiko 'overhears' are all uncredited. The one reciting lines from the movie *Goldfinger* was played by Jazz Dhiman.

- Mary: 'You'll examine me. Assess whether or not I'm useful, whether I'm a danger, and then lock me in a cell. You're not interested in understanding alien cultures. It's just as well you haven't got the technology to reach other planets yet. Yours is a culture of invasion. Do you really think I'm going to walk, hands raised in surrender, into that?'

- Toshiko: 'Why couldn't I read your mind?'
  Jack: 'I don't know; though I could feel you scrabbling around in there.'
  Toshiko: 'But I got nothing. It was like you were … I don't know … dead.'

DOCTOR WHO REFERENCES

- Toshiko is said to be working, at Jack's request, on a 'list' for UNIT.

- Owen tells Gwen that there are copies of a statement on her desk from a (presumably deranged) man named Michael Hamilton: 'He's still seeing Cybermen outside his mother's house.'

ALIEN TECH

- The alien pendant that Mary presents to Toshiko gives her the ability to 'hear' the thoughts of people around her. Mary's race use such devices to communicate with each other telepathically. It is destroyed at the end of the episode when Toshiko crushes it under her boot.

- The Torchwood team dig up an alien device that Jack later reveals to be a two-man interplanetary transporter.

'BLOOD AND SNOGGING'

- The human Mary in 1812 is a prostitute, seen leading a soldier into the woods presumably to have sex with him. He hits her, and she scratches his face, leaving bloody marks.

- Toshiko is seduced by Mary, kisses her passionately and (unseen on screen) has sex with her at least once. She is later seen to kiss her again, in a café.

- Gwen and Owen have had sex for a second time (following on from their liaison at the end of 'Countrycide') in Owen's car earlier that morning. They are full of lustful thoughts for each other. They share a private joke about something being 'a bit of a mouthful'.

- It is confirmed that Toshiko has a crush on Owen, but she says that nothing has ever happened between them, and nothing ever will now that – through the use of the pendant – she has found out what he really thinks of her. However, she is obviously delighted when Owen later tells her, after she gives him a cup of coffee, 'You are gorgeous.'

- Many of the people whose thoughts Toshiko 'overhears' are preoccupied with sexual matters.

PRODUCTION NOTES

- Made with 'Ghost Machine' as part of Block 2 of production.

- In the first draft of Toby Whithouse's script, the character taken over by the alien was a man. Russell T Davies suggested changing this to a woman, to give an added twist to the sex scenes involving Toshiko without actually making it a 'gay story'.

- The line 'Six cigarettes today, and all of them post-coital' – one of the thoughts 'overheard' by Toshiko when she tries out the pendant in the Queen Street shopping precinct – pays homage to a similar line in Helen Fielding's *Bridget Jones's Diary*, in the 2001 film adaptation of which writer Toby Whithouse had an acting role as Alastair.

- The bar in which Toshiko first meets Mary is the Fat Cat Bar in Greyfriars Road. She is later seen to use the pendant not only in Queen Street but also on the walkway by the Millennium Stadium. The café where she and Mary kiss is the Fortes Café on Barry Island. The building on top of which Jack is seen standing toward the end of the episode is Cardiff City Hall, near the clock tower.

- The episode contains allusions to: Quincy (the lead character of the US series *Quincy ME* (NBC, 1976-1983)); actress Amanda Burton (in reference to her role as a pathologist in the BBC series *Silent Witness*); M C Hammer (whose catchphrase 'It's Hammer time' is 'overheard' by Toshiko amongst the thoughts of a barman in the Fat Cat Bar); Philoctetes (in Greek legend, an archer in the army sent to capture Troy, who was left by his comrades in exile for a decade on the island of Lemnos); the famous 'chest burster' sequence involving actor John Hurt in the movie *Alien* (20th Century Fox, 1979)[83]; the James Bond movie *Goldfinger*, some dialogue from which is running through the head of one of the passers-by in Queen Street; and Samuel Taylor Coleridge's poem 'Kubla Khan', the opening lines of which are quoted by Mary when she enters the Hub. The episode's title is itself an allusion to the proverb 'Beware of Greeks bearing gifts', which derives from the story of the Trojan War.

- In the scene where Toshiko and Mary meet in the bar, three tracks are heard faintly in the background: 'Spitting Games' by Snow Patrol (previously featured in 'Everything Changes'), 'Sing' by Travis (previously featured in 'Ghost Machine') and the 2006 album track 'Drag' by Placebo. Later, in the café scene, the 2005 single 'Suddenly I See' by K T Tunstall is playing in the background.

PRODUCTION QUOTES

- 'Without making it political or dull, this is going to be a very bisexual programme. I want to knock down the barriers so we can't define which of the characters is gay. We need to start mixing things up, rather than thinking, "This is a gay character and he'll only ever go off with men."' Executive Producer Russell T Davies, *Gay Times*, October 2006.

- 'I think Tosh, [of all] the team, is the most guarded and private person, and she's not particularly good at expressing herself at the best of times. She can be frank and honest, but she's quite shy, because she's a private person. So for her, ['Greeks Bearing Gifts'] probably turned her world upside down. It was a big learning curve for her – I think she's learnt that it's okay to feel these things and show emotions. Mary was like a really good friend, an ally, someone she can talk to, and if anything, the sexual thing came as an afterthought. She

83 For further details, see the book *Beautiful Monsters:The Unofficial and Unauthorised Guide to the Alien and Predator Films* by David McIntee (Telos Publishing, 2005).

didn't even realise it was happening. We were made to feel very safe [recording the kissing scene. Colin Teague is] a real actor's director, and very open and communicative. We had a good couple of days of rehearsal beforehand, because we wanted to make sure we pitched it right. That it didn't just become, "Oh, a girl's kissing a girl". Because I think a lot of it is a deeper thing.' Actress Naoko Mori, *Eclipse Magazine*, January 2007.

- 'It would have been nice to have gone a bit further [with the sexual relationship between Toshiko and Mary]. Mine was one of the first episodes to go – we were in the second block – and there had been some teething problems. The shoot was delayed a bit, so Naoko didn't get the time with Daniela. That's not to say the relationship wasn't there – when they met it was great – but it meant we let the audience fill in the gaps. I wouldn't have objected to going a step further, but I was really pleased with how that turned out. You understood that she has fallen for this girl, hangs on her every word, and it all ends in tears.' Director Colin Teague, *Starburst* Issue 346, February 2007.

- 'I'd recently been to Monterrey aquarium and I'd taken video footage of squids and jellyfish and things. One of our guys looked at these jellyfish with their electrical charges circulating around their bodies. We wanted something that was slightly beautiful, but also had that underwater element, even though it was above water. After we'd decided what we wanted, we had a little Mill design competition, and some of our 3-D guys sat down and did some sketches. A guy called Alan Burnett drew this beautiful picture of this thing in the woods, which is pretty much the model that we built.' Visual Effects Supervisor Dave Houghton, *Starburst* Special 79, February 2007.

OOPS!

- In the scene between Toshiko and Mary in the bar, Naoko Mori mistakenly delivers the line 'How many of you are there?' as 'How many of there are you?'

PRESS REACTION

- 'There's quality here: nice effects, pacy action and fluid photography. But somehow it doesn't gel. Does *Torchwood* want to be *The X-Files* or *Hollyoaks: After Hours*? Seven episodes in, it's still hard to tell.' Mark Braxton, *Radio Times*, 25 November-1 December 2006.

- 'What would you hear if your iPod could pick up the thoughts of that bloke sitting next to you on the bus? Of if you could eavesdrop into what your colleagues were really talking about round the water cooler? Tapping into the idea that knowledge is power, *Torchwood* made a techie dream come true by introducing into the proceedings an alien pendant able to unlock our innermost thoughts ... But this twist on *What Women Want* brought team geek Tosh rather more than she bargained for. Much more than just a *Doctor Who* spin-off, *Torchwood* works because it mixes sci-fi with human vulnerability and a random approach to plotting that means you're never sure who they're going to bump off next. They've missed a trick by having obviously gay medic Owen cop off with PC Gwen – what about cool Captain Jack? – but *Torchwood* delights in keeping us guessing.' Keith Watson, *Metro*, 27 November 2006.

FAN COMMENT

- 'Then there's the disturbing depiction of a lesbian woman as a predatory mind-rapist who uses her telepathic mojo as a means of getting into another woman's knickers – if this weren't so inherently offensive it would be funny; but then it is so it isn't. Mind rape leading to physical rape? Maybe I'm taking this all a bit too seriously, but I'm getting a bit sick and tired of dramas in general – and *Torchwood* in particular – portraying [non-heterosexual women] as pseudo-men acting purely on their libidos. Recast Mary's part with a male in the role tonight and you'd hardly have to change a single line, from the post-coital swagger as she ridicules Tosh's shame and self-disgust to the manipulative manner which got her there in the first place. Fourteen years on from gays and lesbians picketing *Basic Instinct*'s less than complimentary take on same-sex relationships, and it seems we haven't made that much progress after all.' Sean Alexander, Behind the Sofa website, 27 November 2006.

- 'You might not like it, and you especially might not fancy it where sci-fi is concerned – but *Torchwood* seems to thrive on the notion that adult audiences fancy a bit of girl-on-girl action in order to reel in the numbers for a show which would otherwise probably only attract nerdy types with unkempt facial hair and poor personal hygiene. Oh, sure, it certainly gets your attention in the trailers, but it often seems an unnecessary [element] … but for once, the steamy action formed a genuine part of the central plot (which probably owed more to M Night Shyamalan's *Unbreakable* than anything else).' Martin Conaghan, TV Squad website, 28 November 2006.

- 'Even [Daniela Denby-Ashe's] presence wasn't enough to cover up a barely perceptible main course of wafer thin adult drama served on a bed of tepid lesbo action. And as for an alien artefact that allows you to experience the pointless thoughts of other people, all you need to simulate that is … a feed from the blogsphere mixed with a quick spin through the short wave dial in the dead of night.' Damon Querry, Behind the Sofa website, 2 December 2006.

- 'Naoko Mori finally gets a story to herself, and the two-dimensional computer whiz Toshiko Sato becomes more rounded as a result. *Torchwood* often chooses to divide its stories between the hyper-reality of the Hub (with its alien tech) and the normal everyday life of its characters. It's a balancing act the show usually struggles with, as the difference between these two "worlds" [is] so pronounced they just clash. This is probably why you never saw Mulder and Scully in the supermarket or walking the dog. Amazingly, "Greeks Bearing Gifts" successfully mixes the two worlds, presenting us with a believable social life for Tosh that doesn't jar with the exaggerated SF of Torchwood. A lot of this success is down to Mori and the performance of Daniela Denby-Ashe as Mary, who is superb as the episode's *femme fatale*. As a bonus, Denby-Ashe and Mori share genuine chemistry that helps immensely.' Dan Owen, Blogcritics.org website, 3 December 2006.

ANALYSIS

Scriptwriter Toby Whithouse's excellent 'School Reunion' having been one of the highlights of Series Two of *Doctor Who*, fans had high hopes for his contribution to *Torchwood*; and 'Greeks Bearing Gifts' largely lives up to those expectations. While not, perhaps, one of the stand-out episodes of the series, it is by no means one of the weakest either. It has an intriguing premise, centring around the telepathy-inducing alien pendant, and exploits this well to deliver an entertaining, and in some respects quite thought-provoking, tale.

The basic plot is similar to that of 'Cyberwoman', in that it focuses on a Torchwood member who has not previously had an opportunity to take centre-stage and who ends up placing the rest of the team in danger after being betrayed by a lover under an alien influence. The regular who comes to the fore in this instance is Toshiko, and 'Greeks Bearing Gifts' is essentially a character study of her. Maintaining the improved continuity in this regard seen in 'Countrycide', it picks up and confirms that episode's suggestion of her having a crush on Owen – she has on her fridge door a snapshot of the two of them together, and keeps beside her bed a card he gave her on her birthday in July (clearly some time ago) – but no real love life. This also recalls the scene back in 'Day One' where Gwen asked her new colleagues if they had partners, and Toshiko replied, slightly defensively, 'Don't have time with this job'. She is, it now transpires, painfully lonely and desperate for affection; and it is here that her vulnerability lies – a fact that Mary fully recognises and exploits.

Even allowing for this vulnerability, though, the readiness with which Toshiko gives Mary information about Torchwood when they first meet in the bar is difficult to credit. 'I could be fired, just for telling you that,' she admits, and – although the viewer rather doubts this, given that Ianto was guilty of far worse in 'Cyberwoman' and still kept his job – it does suggest a naivety on her part that is at odds with, and somewhat undermines, the impression of resilience and determination conveyed by her actions in 'Countrycide'. It would perhaps have been preferable had the script indicated here that Mary was exercising a degree of telepathic influence over Toshiko rather than simply relying on her craving for company – although, having said that, the implication that Toshiko has an almost irresistible urge to talk to someone about her work ties in well with the idea established at the end of 'Countrycide' that Gwen feels such a need to share her experiences in Torchwood that it effectively drives her to begin her affair with Owen.

As a number of critics have observed, 'Greeks Bearing Gifts' appears to draw a certain amount of inspiration from the *Buffy the Vampire Slayer* episode 'Earshot'. In the latter, Buffy also gains telepathic abilities; starts to become alienated from her friends as a result; finds herself unable to read the thoughts of an immortal character (Angel), although he is aware that she is trying to do so; uncovers a sexual relationship (between her mother and Giles) of which she was previously unaware; retreats to her bed as she becomes gradually overwhelmed by what she is experiencing; and learns of a murder plot that she is then able to foil. This, though, was by no means the first telefantasy programme to feature a plot involving a character who gains the power to read minds – another notable example, to which 'Earshot' itself bore some similarities, was the episode 'A Penny for Your Thoughts' from the second season of the classic US series *The Twilight Zone* way back in 1961 – and it would be fair to say that, as with the use of the 'sex monster' device in 'Day One', *Torchwood* is simply presenting its own distinctive take on a fairly common science-fiction story type.

The 'inner voice' dialogue that Whithouse gives to Gwen, Owen and Ianto is nicely-crafted and appropriate to their current situations. Gwen and Owen, still in the early throes of their affair, are naturally preoccupied with thoughts of sex, to the extent that they are scarcely able to concentrate on their work; and Ianto, who on the surface would seem to have reverted to the calm, efficient, unflappable factotum of the series' earliest episodes, is inwardly still consumed with grief and hurt following the loss of Lisa in 'Cyberwoman'. Even in their outward behaviour, Gwen and Owen are patently having a whale of a time together. Gwen in particular is acting like a dizzy schoolgirl in love; but there is something slightly false, almost manic, in her high-spirited banter, such as in the scene where she teases Owen over his initial mistaken assessment of the characteristics and cause of death of the decayed corpse found at the building site at the beginning of the episode; and – in a particularly clever piece of writing – her 'inner voice' reveals that she is actually feeling a good deal of uncertainty and even insecurity over her relationship with Owen. She wonders if, having had sex for the second time that morning, they now have an 'arrangement', and feels hurt when, later on, he avoids looking at her – not realising that the real reason for this is that he is trying to contain his lustful feelings!

One can only have a great deal of sympathy for Toshiko as she picks up her colleagues' rather unflattering perceptions of her; although, once again, it does suggest a certain naivety, and possibly a lack of self-awareness, on her part that she is *quite* so surprised and hurt to find that they view her as up-tight, work-fixated and geeky. Owen has, after all, already told her to her face: 'Sometimes I think even that stick up your arse has got a stick up its arse.' And she could have been forgiven for feeling that Gwen and Owen were 'bastard little kids' even before she could read their minds, given their earlier juvenile behaviour when they accidentally disconnected her computer while larking about with a football.

It is, at any rate, easy to see why Toshiko feels isolated from her colleagues and drawn to Mary – who is very well portrayed by Daniela Denby-Ashe, probably best known previously for her semi-regular role as Sarah Hills in *EastEnders* (1996-99). The scene in her flat where they first kiss, after exchanging thoughts that are – as Toshiko puts it – not exactly pure, is wonderful, and carries a genuine erotic charge. After they have made love, though, Toshiko seems almost ashamed of it. Does she perhaps feel that the influence of the pendant has caused her to act in a way that she would not otherwise have chosen to do? If so, there might be a parallel to be drawn here between Mary's use of the pendant and Owen's deployment of the pheromone spray in 'Everything Changes'. Judging from her later actions, however, it seems likely that Toshiko is simply having misgivings of a rather more mundane kind after jumping into bed with a near-stranger – and, it appears, the first woman she has ever had sex with – on a lust-fuelled impulse.

It is at this point that Mary persuades her that, in order to appreciate the pendant's benefits, she needs to try it out 'somewhere public, somewhere crowded'. This leads on to a very well-written-and-realised sequence in which Toshiko 'overhears' the thoughts of various passers-by in a busy pedestrian precinct – including those of a man intent on murdering his ex-wife and son with a shotgun. Her prevention of this crime by knocking the man unconscious with a golf club has an amusing follow-up when, in what appears to be an in-joke incorporated by Whithouse for the benefit of the fans, Mary tells Toshiko: 'They should make an action figure of you.'

Toshiko now seems more comfortable to be carrying on a relationship with Mary, even kissing her in public in a café – albeit rather bashfully. Jack has already started to notice her state of distraction, however, and – in another well-written and amusing scene – he reveals that he has found out about her recent heroics from a police officer, and questions her as to why she did not tell him herself: 'So, you secretly fight crime, is that it, Tosh?' The same scene ends with Toshiko realising that she is unable to read Jack's thoughts – and Jack apparently realising that she has been trying to do so.

Mary's revelation of her true alien form to Toshiko is excellently done. The alien itself is very well realised by the Mill: this is the type of creature effect for which CGI is ideally suited, because – unlike the fairies that attack Jasmine's stepfather Roy in 'Small Worlds' – it is intended to have an ethereal, insubstantial quality, and this is precisely what is achieved. Speaking in an interview on the *Torchwood* official website, visual effects supervisor Barney

Curnow describes the thinking that went into the design: 'The first photos that we got were mainly kind of underwater things; they were kind of little jellyfish and microscopic organisms and those little fish that have see-through bodies you can see the bones and the veins coming through. So, although it wasn't … necessarily an underwater kind of creature that we wanted, it was something that had those kind of light qualities, because it's a creature of light, basically. So we wanted some kind of sense of translucency; … we wanted to be able to … diffract the backgrounds slightly through parts of the creature … but also have it very kind of floaty and elegant.' The end result is a highly impressive; and it was pleasing to see the same creature – or, presumably, another, less-criminally-inclined member of the same race – being given a cameo appearance in *The Sarah Jane Adventures*: 'Invasion of the Bane', allowing younger viewers an opportunity to appreciate it (while also, no doubt, saving the production team the expense of creating a new monster specifically for that sequence!)

The historical sequences in the wood in 1812 – including the excellent pre-titles teaser – make for a good contrast to the series' standard contemporary urban setting, and are more integral to the plot than the shorter, sepia-toned flashbacks to 1909 in 'Small Worlds', in that they fill in the crucial back-story of how the alien came to possess Mary's body. Again it has to be noted that the fact that the alien arrives in close proximity to Cardiff appears to be a complete coincidence, rather than a consequence of the presence of the spacio-temporal rift; but having the event set almost 200 years in the past somehow makes this more acceptable, as it seems reasonable to suppose that (in the *Doctor Who/Torchwood* universe, at least!) there would have been at least one or two alien visitations around the Cardiff area within such a long period of time.

If the episode has a weakness, it is in its denouement. It is not too implausible that Toshiko should think that none of her colleagues will be present in the Hub when she takes Mary there, on the assumption that – as would seem to be suggested by the following scene between her and Jack in the Roald Dahl Plass – it is after dark when she does so, and later than the time they would normally have gone home (leaving aside the slight uncertainty as to whether or not Jack actually has any other home than the Hub). Nor is it too difficult to accept that Mary should have the ability to flit about at great speed – even though she has not previously demonstrated this – when she moves almost instantaneously to seize Toshiko and hold a knife to her throat, setting up a very tense and well-worked stand-off situation. Less believable, though, is Jack's sudden revelation that the device dug up at the building site is a two-person transporter. If he knew this all along, why was he so secretive about it earlier on? And if he didn't know, how has he deduced it, even to the extent of working out how to program the device with sufficient precision to deposit the alien in the heart of the sun? This all seems a bit too convenient, and provides an overly pat and abrupt resolution to this particular 'problem of the week'. It also suggests that Jack has a rather ruthless streak, as he seems to feel no qualms about acting as judge and executioner to Mary, killing her without compunction rather than, for instance, imprisoning her in a cell within the Hub as she earlier anticipated that he might do. This contrasts with his treatment of the cannibals at the end of 'Countrycide', when he clearly shoots to disable rather than kill, and could even be taken to suggest that he values alien life less highly than human life – a point that will be returned to later in the series in 'Combat', when Toshiko questions his mistreatment of a Weevil. Certainly it confirms Mary's cynical comment to Toshiko: 'If I go in that place, I won't come out again'.

The aforementioned closing scene between Toshiko and Jack beside the water tower fountain is, though, a very good one, and very well played by both Naoko Mori and John

Barrowman. Reflecting on her experiences with the pendant, Toshiko says: 'It changes how you see people. How can I live with that? … I don't mean about Gwen and Ianto and Owen, I mean the whole world.' This echoes the distraught feelings she expressed a little earlier, while lying prone on her bed with tears streaming down her face, as Mary looked on dispassionately from a nearby chair, legs crossed and cigarette poised between her fingers in a classic *femme fatale* pose: 'I can't stand it any more. The weight of it, the depravity, the fear, it fills me up. It's in my mouth, in my hair, in my eyes, like I'm drowning in ink. And even when I don't have the pendant on, it's not like there's nothing. I can't forget the things I've seen, the things I've heard … It's like a curse; something the gods send to drive someone mad. I had hope I'd see something; some little, random act of kindness to make me think we were safe, that there's some essential good in us. But there isn't. It's like one of the Weevils. Look inside, and there's just this great, yawning scream.'

Again it is tempting to suggest that Toshiko is being overly sensitive here as – aside from the murderous intentions of the man with the shotgun – none of the random thoughts she picked up earlier while out in public would seem to have been so cynical or shocking as to have justified quite the degree of distress she shows. Perhaps, though, the 'curse' of the pendant lies not so much in the specific thoughts that the wearer picks up as in the overall impact it has on his or her perceptions of the human psyche.

Ending with a montage of night-time aerial shots of Cardiff, effectively making the point that life goes on as normal in the city for its thousands of ordinary inhabitants, all with their own private thoughts and feelings, 'Greeks Bearing Gifts' gives the viewer plenty to think about as well, and makes for a very enjoyable and satisfying episode.

1.08 – THEY KEEP KILLING SUZIE

WRITER: Paul Tomalin and Daniel McCulloch
DIRECTOR: James Strong

DEBUT TRANSMISSION DETAILS

BBC Three	BBC Two
Date: 3 December 2006.	Date: 6 December 2006.
Scheduled time: 10.00 pm.	Scheduled time: 9.00 pm.
Actual time: 10.00 pm.	Actual time: 9.00 pm.

Duration: 52' 43"

ADDITIONAL CREDITED CAST

Yasmin Bannerman (Swanson[84]), Daniel Llewelyn-Williams (Alex Arwyn[85]), Gary Pillai (Mark Brisco[86]), Shend[87] (Max[88]), Badi Uzzaman (Suzie's father)

PLOT: Investigating a spate of bloody killings, the Torchwood team deduce that these are in some way related to their deceased colleague Suzie. Using the alien resurrection glove and knife on which Suzie had been working, they are able to revive her. This, though, turns out to be all part of a devious plan by Suzie to ensure her survival and escape. With the aid of the Cardiff police force, Jack and his team are able to thwart this plan. Gwen's 'life force' has been draining into Suzie, making her seemingly invulnerable to Jack's gunshots, but she is eventually killed when, on Jack's instructions, Toshiko destroys the resurrection glove, breaking the 'circuit'.

QUOTE, UNQUOTE

- Suzie: 'Can I see my father?'
  Jack: 'No.'
  Gwen: 'You wiped your records. We had no trace of him.'
  Suzie: 'So he doesn't even know I'm dead?'
  Gwen: 'Well, you're not anymore.'
  Suzie: 'This is sick.'
  Jack: 'You started it.'

- Suzie: 'That's the glove, Gwen. Gets inside your mind.'
  Gwen: 'Yeah, all right, Suzie, stop creeping me out.'

---

84 First name given in dialogue as 'Cathy'. Her police rank is Detective.

85 Surname misspelt 'Arwen' in *Radio Times*. Arwyn is described in dialogue as '28, single, estate agent'.

86 The victims at the murder scene examined by Torchwood in the opening pre-titles sequence are named in the episode as Mark and Sara Briscoe, both 33 years old, married, a surveyor and an education worker respectively. Sara however is a non-speaking part, so while Mark is listed in the closing credits, she is not. 'Briscoe' is assumed to be correct spelling of their surname, as it is shown on a computer screen in the Hub during the course of the action, although 'Brisco' is how it appears in the closing credits.

87 Credited as 'The Shend' in *Radio Times*.

88 Surname given in dialogue as 'Tresillian'.

- Suzie: 'Do you believe in heaven?'
  Gwen: 'I don't know.'
  Suzie: 'Yes you do. What do you believe?'
  Gwen: 'It's stupid, but I always sort of think, like, you know, white light and all that. And I think of my gran, like she'd be there, waiting for me, the smell of carbolic.'
  Suzie: 'Your faith never left primary school.'
  Gwen: 'So, what's up then?'
  Suzie: 'Nothing, just nothing.'
  Gwen: 'But … but if there's nothing, what's the point of it all?'
  Suzie: 'This is. Driving through the dark. All this stupid, tiny stuff. We're just animals, howling in the night, because it's better than silence. I used to think about Torchwood, all those aliens coming to Earth: what the hell for? But it's just instinct. They come here 'cause there's life, that's all. Moths around a flame. Creatures clinging together in the cold.'

- Ianto: 'I'll put a lock on the door, just in case she goes walking again.'
  Jack: 'Nah. No chance of that. The resurrection days are over, thank god.'
  Ianto: 'Oh, I wouldn't be too sure. That's the thing about gloves, sir. They come in pairs.'

DOCTOR WHO REFERENCES

- Some fans have speculated that the Wolf Bar's name is a subtle reference to the 'Bad Wolf' story arc of *Doctor Who*'s 2005 series.

ALIEN TECH

- The alien resurrection glove and knife first seen in 'Everything Changes' are central to the plot of this episode – and are nicknamed the 'risen mitten' and the 'life knife' respectively by Ianto. Owen states that they are both made of the same metal. The glove is said to have fallen through the rift about 40 years ago and lain at the bottom of Cardiff Bay until Torchwood dredged it up. Jack speculates that it was not lost but deliberately discarded by whoever made it.

- This episode provides the first clear indication that, as implied in documents on the Torchwood Institute System Interface website, the Hub's computer system is of alien origin with an organic infrastructure. When Toshiko goes to type in a code and Jack points out that the keyboards aren't working because the power has been cut off, she replies: 'But the membrane underneath might just recognise the code.' This indeed proves to be the case. No current computer system on Earth would respond in such a way.

CONTINUITY POINTS

- The drug retcon is referred to as compound 'B67' in a forensic report on a sample of the murderer's hair.

- When Torchwood staff members die, their corpses are kept forever in cold storage lockers in the Hub, and all their possessions are retained in storage – in Suzie's case, in a lock-up garage.

- Suzie wiped all her computer records when she went on the run from Torchwood at the end of 'Everything Changes', to the extent that it has not even been possible for the rest of the team to trace her father.

- An on-screen graphic in the Hub reveals that the hospital where Suzie's father is being treated is called the Greenleaves Hospital in Armiston, near Woolbridge and Pendomer and close to the B465 and B198 roads. This is a fictional location: while Woolbridge and Pendomer are real places in Dorset and Somerset respectively (although not so large as to merit mention on a map in preference to other, more major towns), there is no such place as Armiston, and the B465 road is actually in Middlesex, while the B198 is in Cambridgeshire – suggesting that the UK of the *Doctor Who/Torchwood* universe has a different road numbering system from ours. From its position in relation to Woolbridge and Pendomer on the on-screen graphic, Armiston would appear to be in either Dorset or possibly Wiltshire. On the other hand, when one of Detective Swanson's police colleagues checks the Torchwood SUV's route on a map, he appears to be looking toward the west of Wales. The quay where Jack and Owen catch up with the fleeing Suzie and Gwen is the similarly fictional location of Hedley Quay at Hedley Point, said by Toshiko to be reached via the B587 road.[89] From here, 'some sort of ferry goes out to the islands'; it is unclear, though, which islands these are. In 'our' universe, the B587 road is actually in Leicestershire. It takes Jack and Owen approximately two hours to catch up with Suzie and Gwen, driving at well over the speed limit in the Torchwood SUV, so it is just possible that Hedley Point could be somewhere on the Bristol Channel in Somerset, perhaps near Weston-Super-Mare, but more likely that it is on the west coast of Wales.

'BLOOD AND SNOGGING'

- Mark and Sara Briscoe, the murder victims in the pre-titles sequence, are found lying on their bed covered in blood, with 'Torchwood' written in blood on the wall behind them.

- Suzie, when revived, has an entry wound under her chin and a large, bloody exit wound at the back of her head from where she shot herself at the end of 'Everything Changes.' These gradually heal during the course of the episode.

- Jack mentions a former boyfriend who was one of a pair of twin acrobats.

- Gwen starts to bleed from the back of her head as Suzie's wound 'transfers' to her.

- Suzie kisses the unconscious Gwen as she leaves her behind on the quay.

- Suzie is shot repeatedly by Jack, leaving her coat and the surrounding ground covered with blood.

- At the end of the episode, Gwen gives Jack what seems to be a highly significant look, suggesting that there has been at least a strengthening of the bond between them, no doubt due in part to Jack's willingness to kill Suzie in order to save her. This impression is reinforced by the use of a love song, Lamb's 'Gorecki', on the soundtrack.

- Ianto points out to Jack that there's 'quite a list' of things that can be done with a stopwatch. Jack then decides to send the other team members home early, and asks Ianto to join him in his office in ten minutes' time. The implication appears to be that they are planning to

89 In a deleted scene – due to be included amongst the extras on the Series One: Part Two DVD set – Detective Swanson also tells Jack that Gwen's car has been spotted on the B587 road.

indulge in some unspecified sexual practices involving use of the stopwatch.

PRODUCTION NOTES

- Made with 'Cyberwoman' as part of Block 3 of production.
- The series' standard opening sequence is extended on this occasion with a number of clips from 'Everything Changes', to remind viewers about Suzie and about the storyline involving the resurrection glove.
- Although Russell T Davies always had in mind the possibility that Suzie could be brought back through the use of the resurrection glove, he initially had no plans to develop such a story. When the idea emerged in discussions and writers Paul Tomalin and Dan McCulloch delivered their script, the episode had to be rushed into production. This was because Indira Varma was about to go to the USA to work on the series *3 lbs*, and had only a limited period of availability to reprise her *Torchwood* role.
- The title of this episode recalls that of 'They Keep Killing Steed' from the final season of *The Avengers* (ABC, 1961-1969).
- The 2002 album track 'Red is the New Black' by Funeral for a Friend is the record playing in the Wolf Bar, where the Torchwood team arrest Max. The song playing on the radio in Gwen's car is 'Soley, Soley', a 1971 single by the Scottish band Middle of the Road. After Suzie is finally killed, Manchester-based duo Lamb's 1997 single and album track 'Gorecki' (based on composer Henryk Gorecki's Symphony No. 3 Opus 36) is used on the soundtrack.
- The first stanza of the Emily Dickinson (1830-1886) poem 'Because I Could Not Stop for Death' – sometimes referred to as 'The Chariot', and probably composed around 1863 – is the 'key' that Max is programmed to recite to cause the Hub to go into lockdown. Dickinson is now generally acclaimed as one of the great American poets, but was unrecognised during her lifetime – of the 1,789 poems she is known to have written, only ten were published before her death, anonymously and probably without her knowledge. Her life and work are the subject of much debate and even controversy amongst scholars, owing in part to the fact that when the poems eventually saw print in the years following her death, they were initially subject to heavy editing, and in some cases there is a lack of consensus as to which are the 'definitive' versions.
- When Suzie says to Jack, 'Captain, my captain', as she lies bleeding on the quay, she is slightly misquoting the title and opening line of 'O Captain! My Captain!' by famous American poet – and contemporary of Emily Dickinson – Walt Whitman (1819-1892).
- Actress Yasmin Bannerman, seen here as Detective Swanson, appeared in the Series One *Doctor Who* episode 'The End of the World' as tree-person Jabe.

PRODUCTION QUOTES

- 'In a way, you kind of want Suzie to get away with it, because she's such a brilliant character, and Indira gives her such a humanity, and such an emotional resonance.' Director James Strong, *Torchwood Declassified*: 'Beyond the Grave', 4 December 2006.

- 'Dan McCulloch and Paul Tomalin … were very much focused on writing a thriller; … quite a heavy genre piece, that would have a ticking clock, more and more corpses, Torchwood involved with the police. And very quickly, in conversation with Russell, it became clear that the most exciting way, and the freshest way, to investigate and dramatise that type of terrain was with Suzie; you know, how wonderful to bring Indira Varma back … not just for the thrills and spills of that story, but to look at what it does psychologically to the team, and particularly to Gwen.' Executive Producer Julie Gardner, *Torchwood* official website, 4 December 2006.

- 'I love it; I absolutely love it. It not something *Torchwood* can do all the time, because I think we would be the most miserable series on Earth if we were this dark all the time; but, oh, I'm so proud of it. I think it's my favourite episode'. Executive Producer Russell T Davies, *Torchwood Declassified*: 'Beyond the Grave', 4 December 2006.

OOPS!

- In the scene where Jack and the team deduce Suzie's plan, the line 'He doesn't see her for three months …' – the 'he' referring to the character Max – is mistakenly delivered by Naoko Mori as 'She doesn't see her for three months …'

- The ISBN number quoted in this episode – 0-19860-058-5 – is actually for the hardback book *The Oxford Dictionary of Quotations* and not, as stated, for the paperback book *The Complete Poems* by Emily Dickinson. The correct ISBN of the latter book is 0-57110-864-4. (Could *The Oxford Dictionary of Quotations* possibly have been the book used by Suzie in an early draft of the script?)

PRESS REACTION

- 'Having stand-alone episodes works well for *Doctor Who*, but adults like a bit of complexity, subtext and story arc. The return of Suzie, an undead woman walking and forced to face the mess she created, brings an extra resonance, and in turn there are hints of things to come. "Something out there in the dark, and it's moving."' David Richardson, *Starburst* Issue 345, January 2007.

FAN COMMENT

- This, for me, was the episode which reached a level of comfort and total rightness – which was odd, because the events in it were, on the whole, quite disquieting … It was in the middle of the scene where the entire police station was gathered around the speaker phone to hear Captain Jack explain, once more, that entirely owing to their own incompetence most of the Torchwood team had managed to get themselves locked into their own Hub and they were reliant on the despised regulars to help them to get out of it (and *weren't* the regulars savouring the moment!) when it suddenly hit me. That scene was – give or take 30 years added/subtracted to the average age of the participants, and a joke or so – straight out of *Dad's Army*. Cast the ARP warden as the police chief, and Captain Mainwaring as Captain Jack, and, well – there you are … Torchwood Three aren't in the least "the best of the best of the best." They've been chosen for their particular task not because they've gone through a selection process tougher than anyone of flesh and blood could be expected to survive, but on the immortally British principle of "Are you free Tuesday?" … They are the laughable remnants of a once formidable force. No-one could possibly take them seriously. To do so is to be whistling in the dark: "Who do you think you are kidding Mr Alien, If you think that Torchwood's done?" 'crepe_suzettes', LiveJournal blog, 4 December 2006

- 'Suzie's escape from the Torchwood base is well staged – the empathy Gwen is feeling for Suzie is clearly linked to the life force energy drain that is occurring, vampire-like, from her body, and therefore it's quite believable that she might want to help Suzie see her father before he dies of terminal cancer in a hospital. The plot grows ever more complex as the base goes into lockdown, and the reality of what is happening dawns on the team. Suzie has set them up. Her revival via the glove was planned by herself, as was the lockdown, triggered by Max, the patsy killer who recites poetry (like a coded instruction) to bring about the scenario. It's about this point the production swerves from good, to bad, to awful. Jack phones the police to help them escape from the locked down base, and the department must have a lot of spare time on its hands, as the detective sergeant seems quite happy to spend the evening reading poetry down a telephone line to help them out. Added to this is the daft leap of faith to try the ISBN book number as a release code, which, I'm sorry, is just too much to take. They're busy looking for coded poetry to open the lock, and for Toshiko to suddenly think of this without some kind of hint [is] jarring.' Steve Preston, Kasterborous website, 13 December 2006.

ANALYSIS

What exactly is Suzie's plan here? Certain aspects of it are quite clear. She has conditioned the man Max so that, in the event of her death, he will start killing people and writing the word 'Torchwood' on the walls in their blood. Jack and his team are then bound to be called in, are bound to find the drug retcon in trace evidence left by the killer at the scene, and are bound to make the connection to her. She reasons that they will then use the alien resurrection glove on her in the hope of establishing the killer's identity. So far, so good. But to the best of Suzie's knowledge – or so the viewer has been previously led to think – those on whom the glove is used are restored to life for a meagre two minutes at most. Has she really done all this just to gain an extra couple of minutes of life, in less than ideal circumstances? It seems unlikely. Perhaps, though, she assumed, or at least hoped, that by the time she died, she would have found a way of making the glove work better – she spoke at the end of 'Everything Changes' of its potential to resurrect permanently – or that someone else might come along after her who could do so. Alternatively, perhaps she had discovered a lot more about the glove and about how it works than she admitted to her colleagues; she appears to be aware, even before it happens, that Gwen's 'life force' is going to be drained into her. When Gwen says, 'Bit more colour in your cheeks,' she replies, with irony, 'It's all thanks to you.'

At any rate, it does certainly appear that she believed she might be restored to life permanently, as she has also conditioned Max to recite the section of an Emily Dickinson poem that will cause the Hub to go into lockdown, in order to effect her escape. How, though, does she know that he will do this at exactly the right time to allow her to get away but prevent the others from following? Is she able to trigger him in some way, not seen on screen, before she leaves the Hub? Maybe so. The really big question, though, is why she shot herself at the end of 'Everything Changes'. Was this just a part of her escape plan, as Jack seems to think? Or did she actually intend to commit suicide? The former explanation seems unlikely, as it would mean that she was willing to risk her life on the – surely tenuous – hope that the others would indeed use the resurrection glove on her, that they would succeed where she had failed in making its effect permanent, and that she would then stand a better chance of getting away than she had in the first place. This would undoubtedly be the craziest escape plan in history. The latter explanation is also implausible, though, as the lengths to which Suzie has gone in setting up her plan would appear to indicate that her life is very precious to her indeed, and that she is not the sort of person who would kill herself simply in order to avoid being brought to justice for the murders she has carried out. When Jack asks her why she is allowing Gwen to die to save herself, she replies, 'Because life is all, Jack. You should know. I'd do anything to stay; anything.' If she really did intend to commit suicide at the end of 'Everything Changes', it would be a terrible irony that her previously-conceived plan then succeeded and she was brought back to life. On balance, as hard as it is to accept, the former explanation seems the better of the two.

Then, too, there is the business about Suzie's cancer-stricken father. Gwen's initial assumption is that the reason why Suzie became so obsessed with the resurrection glove in the first place was that she saw it as having the potential to revive the old man after he died. This is clearly not the case, however, as when Suzie is finally reunited with her father, it turns out that all she really wants to do is kill him. But why is it so important to her to have him dead that she is willing to delay her escape in order to go to the hospital and arrange it herself? He is, after all, dying anyway. And if it is that important, why did she not finish him off long before the events of 'Everything Changes'? Is her apparently newfound determination to do so a consequence of her now having seen the dark nothingness that awaits after death? She says that killing 'the bastard' was 'worth coming back for', but surely that cannot have been one of the actual aims of her plan?

This is all rather mystifying. If, though, one can suspend one's disbelief of Suzie's plan – and that is, admittedly, a big 'if', given that it is so central to the story; although it must be said that the full extent of its implausibility does not really become apparent on first viewing, only when thinking about it later on – then in other respects this is a really outstanding episode. To bring back Suzie was an inspired idea; and in retrospect it seems amazing that it was not firmly planned from the outset, particularly given that her involvement in the plot of 'Everything Changes' centred around a device capable of resurrecting the dead. Indira Varma gets more screen time in her second episode than in her first, and delivers a fantastic performance. It is also good to see, at last, the reactions of the other team members to having lost – and then regained – their former colleague. The lack of any such follow-up in 'Day One' was a notable flaw; and although Russell T Davies seeks to explain this in *Torchwood Declassified*: 'Beyond the Grave' by saying 'we just [wanted] to get on with setting up a new series there', that's a rather weak argument. There should at least have been some lingering sense of shock displayed by Jack, Owen and Toshiko over Suzie's death; although their apparent failure to mourn her passing is now made at least a bit more understandable by the revelation that none of them actually knew her very well – despite the fact that, as she clearly intimates to Gwen, she and Owen at one point shared a sexual relationship.

Owen tries to avoid the resurrected Suzie, admitting 'You frighten the shit out of me', while Toshiko can barely bring herself to look at the woman. Of all the Torchwood team, it is Gwen who shows the most sympathy toward her predecessor. There is an interesting dynamic between the two women, as Davies observes in 'Beyond the Grave': '[Gwen] has replaced [Suzie]. She is the new girl, [and] actually this woman shot herself in front of her. It's not Gwen's fault, but you would think it was your fault; that's human nature, ... to think "Oh, it's all my fault. I set all that in motion."' Gwen must, in short, feel a degree of guilt over having 'stepped into the shoes' of the woman whose death her investigation precipitated. She also, though, blames Jack for having taken insufficient account of the impact that working with the resurrection glove was likely to have on Suzie. And when Suzie tells her, 'You got my job, almost like you planned it,' she retorts, 'Except I didn't. And I'm sorry, but I've got my own function at Torchwood, and I'm a lot more than just a replacement.' Her reaction to Suzie is, nevertheless, an emotional one; and it is this that the resurrected woman relies on and exploits in order to effect her escape from the Hub.

Two running themes established in earlier episodes are developed further here. First, there is another indication of the near-compulsion that the Torchwood team members feel to discuss their uniquely challenging work with others – the root cause of Gwen beginning her affair with Owen in 'Countrycide' and of Toshiko becoming embroiled with Mary in 'Greeks Bearing Gifts'. When asked why she drugged Max with the amnesia-inducing pill on a weekly basis over a two year period, Suzie explains: 'I wanted someone to talk to, about this place. It was driving me mad.' Secondly, and more significantly, the key *Torchwood* theme of the nature of life and, more particularly, of death is really central to the narrative of this episode. There is clearly some sort of 'life force' that passes from the user of the resurrection glove to the dead person, bringing about the latter's revival – on a permanent basis if the 'life knife' is plunged into the victim to complete the 'circuit' and if the user is sufficiently adept, albeit at the eventual cost of his or her own life. The precise nature of this 'life force' is left unclear, but when it passes from the user of the glove to the victim of the knife, it seems to cause them to 'swap places', in the sense that the former takes on, and ultimately dies from, the injuries of the latter – as becomes apparent when Gwen starts bleeding from the back of the head and Suzie, whose own wound is revealed to have almost healed, memorably tells her: 'You're getting shot in the head, slowly; and believe me, it hurts.' But how can it be possible for a woman who has been dead for three months, presumably with no brain activity at all, suddenly to return to life, with her personality and memories seemingly unaffected? Does this not suggest that the 'essence' of a person must somehow endure beyond death, independent of the physical body and its processes?

In raising this question of the existence, or otherwise, of life after death, *Torchwood* ventures into some very deep religious and philosophical territory, in a way that *Doctor Who* probably never could (although it came close in 'The Impossible Planet'/'The Satan Pit', and closer still in some of the original novels). This is admirable, and really delivers on the promise of a thought-provoking adult series. The most important scene in this regard is the one between Gwen and Suzie in the former's car as they drive from the Hub to the hospital where Suzie's father is being treated. It is here that Gwen asks what must surely be the most essential question that anyone could put to a person who has been resurrected: 'When you're dead … I mean, when you die … what happens?' Suzie's response, 'Nothing, just nothing … Darkness', echoes what the murder victim John Tucker said in the opening scene of 'Everything Changes'. This is not as straightforward an answer as it might at first appear, however, as it indicates not only that there is 'nothing' after death, but also that the dead person is actually *aware* of that nothingness. This seems to confirm that there is indeed some 'essence' of a person that survives beyond death, and moreover remains conscious, albeit only of eternal nothingness. Reinforcing this idea, when Gwen asks, 'And you're all alone? There's no-one else?', Suzie replies, 'I didn't say that … Why do you think I'm so desperate to come back? There's something out there, in the dark, and it's moving.' This is undoubtedly the most terrifying concept that *Torchwood* has so far presented, and is expanded upon in the scene on Hedley Quay toward the end of the episode, when Suzie tells Jack, in what turn out to be her final words: 'Do you want to know a secret? There's something moving in the dark, and it's coming, Jack Harkness, it's coming for *you*.'

In Davies's eyes, the scene in the car is absolutely crucial to the episode, as he explains in 'Beyond the Grave': 'You … start some episodes … with images. You just think, you know, there's the plot, and there's the story, and there's the characters, but sometimes you're driven by images, and this [episode] was always those two women, in that car, at night. And that was a big set up, actually. It's more complicated than you'd think, [recording] two women in a car at night. But it's the one thing I would never let go from the script. I said, "You can cut [other things], but that is the heart of the story." It's not about the glove, it's not about Suzie coming back [to] life, it's about two women driving through the night, talking about the fact that there is no afterlife.'

Suzie appears for a time to have become effectively immortal as a consequence of her resurrection. This creates an intriguing parallel between her and Jack, as Gwen notes earlier on, when talking to the latter in his office: 'What if she never dies? Have you thought of that? Like, undying forever, just you and her?' Jack responds: 'I wouldn't wish that on her. I'd sooner kill her right now.' This reinforces the suggestions in earlier episodes that Jack views his immortality as more of a curse than a blessing. It also, though, raises the question of whether or not it is actually possible for Suzie to die. Jack certainly seems to think that it is, as he replies 'Oh yeah!' when Gwen expresses doubt about this; although her question is ambiguously phrased, and could in fact relate to whether or not he could bring himself to kill his former team member, rather than whether or not she could actually be killed. In the climactic confrontation on the quay, it is only Jack's sudden realisation that the resurrection glove needs to be destroyed, in order to break the 'circuit', that enables him to kill her.

A related issue is what exactly happens to Gwen in the latter scene. Her reaction when the resurrection glove is destroyed seems very similar to that of the murder victims when they were earlier revived using the device. Is she in fact brought back from the dead herself here? This may well be the case, as Owen, a trained doctor, is unable to detect any signs of life when he first examines her. Given that Suzie's injuries are being transferred to Gwen, it may not help that Jack is pumping bullets into his former colleague; although possibly it is only those injuries that led to Suzie's original death that are subject to this process of transference.

The glove itself is a fascinating conception, and one that certainly merited being explored further after its introduction in 'Everything Changes'. As producer Richard Stokes comments in 'Beyond the Grave': '[It has] always been a very powerful, iconic object and image for the whole series.' There are again suggestions here that the glove exerts some sort of influence over its user, causing him or her to become fixated with it. The team now learn that, for some time prior to her death, Suzie was involved with an organisation, Pilgrim, described by Toshiko as: 'A religious support group, more like a debating society: "The meaning of life", "Does God exist?", all that sort of stuff.' The implication seems to be that it was the glove, or at least her work at Torchwood more generally, that sparked Suzie's interest in these profound issues concerning life and death. 'Is it Suzie that's evil,' muses Gareth David-Lloyd in 'Beyond the Grave', 'or is it the glove that's made her evil?' Gwen seems at first to succumb to the glove's allure, almost hysterically demanding that she be allowed to attempt a second revival of the murder victim Alex Arwyn, even though Jack insists that the device works only once on each victim. 'It's the glove,' says Jack, after Gwen revives Suzie. 'I told you, they get hooked!' And Suzie herself later comments that the device 'gets inside your mind.' An alternative possibility, though, is that the reason why users of the glove tend to become seduced by it is that it gives them, albeit temporarily, the god-like power to bestow life – surely the ultimate high; or, as John Barrowman puts it in 'Beyond the Grave', 'It's an adrenaline rush, and it's a turn-on.'

Another theme that gets by no means its first *Torchwood* airing here is that of betrayal. Suzie initially betrayed her colleagues way back in 'Everything Changes', of course, when she went on her 'murder spree' and – unbeknown to them and the viewer – set her plan in motion. Ianto then betrayed the others in 'Cyberwoman' by secretly bringing an alien threat into the Hub, and Toshiko did essentially the same in 'Greeks Bearing Gifts'. Gwen has meanwhile betrayed Rhys by beginning her love affair with Owen; and now she too betrays the rest of the Torchwood team, as Eve Myles notes in 'Beyond the Grave': 'I think it's a huge betrayal that Gwen takes Suzie out of the Hub, and takes her to see her father, and they go on that kind of road trip together.' Gwen in turn is betrayed by Suzie, as director James Strong observes: 'The whole plan of Suzie … relies upon the fact that Gwen will react to Suzie in an emotional way … That's the kind of twist in the tale, that's the deceit, that's the … ultimate betrayal, in a way: she using Gwen's goodness and Gwen's heart as a weapon against her.' While betrayal is of course a stock plot ingredient of most dramatic stories, it has by this point recurred sufficiently frequently in *Torchwood* for it now to be considered a further key motif of the series.

Paul Tomalin and Daniel McCulloch are reportedly a relatively new and inexperienced writing team, but that certainly isn't apparent from their work here, which is of a very high standard indeed. The only really serious lapse – again, if one can overlook the implausibility of Suzie's plan – comes in the scene where Toshiko suddenly, and without any clue to prompt her, realises that it is the ISBN number of the Emily Dickinson book, rather than the words of one of the poems within it, that is the key to reversing the lockdown of the Hub. The fact that there is – and has for many years been – only a single edition of that book in print in the UK makes this slightly less unbelievable than it might otherwise have been, since it means that the copy bought by Detective Swanson's team is almost bound to have the same ISBN number as Suzie's (leaving aside the fact that the number quoted is actually for a different book altogether – a rather clumsy error, albeit one that only those who bothered to check will have spotted), but it still tests the viewer's credulity just a little too far, particularly when coupled with the rather strange idea that Toshiko's keyboard can recognise the code even though the computer's power is off. In a similar vein, although perhaps not quite so incredible, is the sudden deductive leap that Jack makes on the quay, when he realises that the way to kill Suzie and thereby save Gwen is to destroy the resurrection glove. Rather curious, too, is the closing exchange of dialogue between Ianto and Jack about stopwatches. This is clearly intended to have some sort of sexual connotation but, beyond that, will surely have left the vast majority of viewers completely bemused. The latter scene is quickly redeemed, however, by the excellent line – inserted into the script by Davies – about gloves coming in pairs, neatly setting up the possibility of a further resurrection-glove-themed episode in a later *Torchwood* series.

Returning to the question of the Hub's lockdown, it is rather unfortunate that no explanation is given as to why this cannot be reversed in exactly the same way as it was in 'Cyberwoman', much more quickly and easily than through recourse to the Emily Dickinson book – always assuming that the use of the phrase 'total lockdown', as opposed to just 'lockdown', is not supposed to constitute an explanation in itself. Tomalin and McCulloch can hardly be criticised for this, however, given that they had no involvement with 'Cyberwoman'. It is the sort of point that ought really to have been picked up by script editor Brian Minchin; or perhaps, failing that, by James Strong, given that he was responsible for making both 'Cyberwoman' and 'They Keep Killing Suzie' together in the same production block and must surely have noticed the plot discrepancy between them.

It seems almost churlish, though, to attach any blame to Strong, as his handling of the episode is excellent throughout. In terms of style and presentation, 'They Keep Killing Suzie' is very much in the mould of a thriller, with crisp dialogue, a fast pace and plenty of twists and turns, and the director's approach is well suited to this. He invests the action with a genuine slickness and sense of urgency; and key scenes such as the night-time discussion between Gwen and Suzie in the car and the climactic confrontation on the quay have a truly cinematic quality to them, giving the episode a classy, high-budget look. His direction of the cast is also superb, and brings out some great performances from all concerned.

All in all, a strong, compelling episode, with many memorable scenes and, again, plenty of food for thought.

1.09 – RANDOM SHOES

WRITER: Jacquetta May[90]
DIRECTOR: James Erskine

DEBUT TRANSMISSION DETAILS

BBC Three	BBC Two
Date: 10 December 2006.	Date: 13 December 2006.
Scheduled time: 10.00 pm.	Scheduled time: 9.00 pm.
Actual time: 10.00 pm.	Actual time: 9.02 pm.

Duration: 49' 14"

ADDITIONAL CREDITED CAST[91]
Paul Chequer (Eugene[92]), Luke Bromley (Young Eugene), Nicola Duffett (Bronwen Jones), Roger Ashton-Griffiths (Mr Garrett), Steven Meo (Josh), Celyn Jones (Gary), Robyn Isaac (Linda), Gareth Potter (Shaun Jones), Joshua Hughes (Terry Jones), Amy Starling (Waitress), Leroy Liburd (Café Owner), Ryan Chappell (Pete)

PLOT: Eugene Jones – a fan of the Torchwood team – is killed in a hit-and-run road accident but returns as an invisible ghost and subtly prompts Gwen as she investigates the circumstances of his death. It transpires that he died while fleeing from two supposed friends who were attempting to steal from him an alien eye that he was given in his childhood by a teacher. He swallowed the eye in order to keep it from them, and it is this that has enabled him to relive and gradually recall the events leading up to his demise. Eugene regains corporeal form just in time to save Gwen herself from being run down by a car, and then shoots off into the heavens.

QUOTE, UNQUOTE

- Eugene: 'Life can be such a let-down, can't it? All those years, I believed my dad had gone to America because I was a failure, and here he was all along, doing his important, secret work in Filey Road, Cardiff! When I found him, I couldn't even bear to say hello. I'd spent my life believing in stupid stories, fantasies. I've wasted my life. Once I'd seen him there, everything I'd dreamed about was like rubbish. It was just a crock of shit. Including the eye. So why not sell it? Along with the woodworm treatment and loft insulation and all the other crap floating around the world. Linda was welcome to the money.'

- Eugene: 'By rights, I should be well pissed off. My mates had cheated on me and I didn't get to meet any aliens. But I realised that when I swallowed the eye at the Happy Cook, I was given a chance, to look back on my life and see it for what it really was.'

90 Credited in *Radio Times* to Jacquetta May and Russell T Davies jointly.

91 A scene featuring Eugene's boss, Craig Telford, was recorded but edited out before transmission. As this was his only scene, the actor who played Craig was uncredited, and his identity is unknown at the time of writing. This scene is due to be included in the deleted scenes package on the Series One: Part Two DVD set.

92 Surname given as 'Jones' in the dialogue of the episode.

- Eugene: 'The average life is full of near misses and absolute hits, of great love and small disasters. It's made up of banana milkshakes, loft insulation and random shoes. It's dead ordinary and truly, truly amazing. What you've got to realise is, it's all here, now, so breathe deep and swallow it whole, because, take it from me, life just whizzes by, and then, all of a sudden, it's …'

DOCTOR WHO REFERENCES

- Young Eugene has what appears to be a home-made model of the Doctor's robot dog K-9 on a shelf in his bedroom, near his telescope.

- Jack and Toshiko are seen examining the bolt gun previously featured in the Series Two *Doctor Who* story 'The Impossible Planet'/'The Satan Pit'. The latter involves an expeditionary team from the 'Torchwood Archive' but is set centuries in the future on a far-flung planet, so it is difficult to understand how the same piece of equipment – or perhaps two identical items – could be present in both places.

ALIEN TECH

- The alien eye was found by Eugene's childhood science teacher Mr Garrett when it fell from the sky into a bunker on the golf course where he was playing a round. Jack guesses that it is a sought-after Dogon Sixth Eye. 'It's one in the back,' he says. 'Let's you see behind you, where you've been. It kind of puts things in perspective. It's useful, fun, slightly terrifying; that's why they were in demand.' A report by Owen on the Torchwood Institute System Interface website says of the Dogon, in part: 'They seem to have shown up on Earth a few times and then a couple of years ago one of their ships crashed into the Humber. The crew of 20 were "investigated" by Doctor Rajesh Singh[93] in Torchwood One – before he got distracted by bigger and better things ... These Eyes pop up all over the internet and throughout history. Samuel Pepys even mentions one in the unedited version of his diary … There are various reports of Eyes just falling from the sky and a whole bunch of them appeared on eBay after the destruction of Torchwood One. And for some reason they're very popular in Belgium.'

- Eugene's collection may include some other genuine alien artefacts, alongside some fakes. He refers to a group of coins as 'pre-gorgon Pilurian currency', although Gwen thinks that they may be Roman.

- Eugene recognises what seems to be an alien head preserved in a jar in the Hub, but is mystified by the Doctor's severed hand in the adjacent container.

CONTINUITY POINTS

- The Torchwood team realised that Eugene was following some of their investigations but apparently considered him too innocuous to warrant the use of their amnesia-inducing drug – a supposition confirmed in a report by Owen on the Torchwood Institute System Interface website.

---

93 A character seen working for Torchwood in London in the *Doctor Who* story 'Army of Ghosts'/'Doomsday'.

- Do Gwen's empathic qualities extend to having low-level psychic abilities? This would seem to be implied by the fact that she alone is able to sense the presence of the ghostly Eugene. More grist to the mill, perhaps, for those who believe that Gwen may have some connection with the young medium Gwyneth (also played by Eve Myles) in the *Doctor Who* episode 'The Unquiet Dead' – although Russell T Davies has denied that there is any such link between the two characters.

- Passmore Telesales, the company where Eugene worked, is engaged in telephone selling of a range of products and services, including kitchens, home insurance and barbeque sets.

- Eugene and his friend Gary were due to attend a lecture on 'Black Holes and the Uncertainty Principle' at the North Wales Astronomy Society Convention, held at Aberystwyth University's (fictional) Science and Natural History Museum.

'BLOOD AND SNOGGING'

- Eugene's bloody corpse is found lying in a roadside ditch at the start of the episode.

- Owen suggests to Gwen that she should carry out the autopsy on Eugene's body, presumably as a kind of training exercise. She is about to plunge a scalpel into his chest when Ianto brings the news that the driver who ran Eugene down has confessed to the crime.

- The video store employee Josh tries some corny, and unsuccessful, chat-up lines on Gwen.

- Gwen and Owen frequently argue with and snipe at each other during the course of this episode, suggesting that their affair is on the rocks.

- The invisible Eugene stands right in front of Gwen and blows her hair as she looks out of her hotel room window, then lies down next to her on the bed when she retires for the night.

- Gwen kisses Eugene after he saves her life at the end of the episode.

PRODUCTION NOTES

- Made as a single-episode Block 6 of production, 'double banked' with other recordings; hence the limited availability of the regular cast to feature in the action and the increased responsibility placed on Sophie Fante, meriting her joint producer credit.

- This episode had the working title 'Invisible Eugene', which was changed so close to transmission that it was listed incorrectly in *Radio Times*.

- Jacquetta May's script was reportedly reworked extensively by Russell T Davies. May is the only writer named on screen, but *Radio Times* gave a joint credit to her and Davies.

- David Bowie's classic 1972 single 'Starman' is the track heard playing over the scene where Young Eugene looks out of his bedroom window as his father drives off in his car. 'Hope There's Someone', a 2005 single by Antony and the Johnsons, accompanies the sequence where the ghostly Eugene contemplates his own dead body in the Hub's morgue and then observes his grieving mother through the window of their house. At Eugene's funeral, his father sings the Irish song folk song 'Danny Boy', the lyrics of which were composed by English solicitor Frederick Weatherly in 1910 and set to the tune of the traditional 'Londonderry Air' in 1913.

- Cardiff locations used for this episode included the offices of the Black Horse finance company in St William House, Tresillian Terrace (for the interiors of Passmore Telesales – scenes shot on 8 October 2006, just a few days after some action for *The Sarah Jane Adventures*: 'Invasion of the Bane' had been recorded on another floor of the same building); Ramon's Breakfast Bar on Salisbury Road, Cathays Park (the café where the invisible Eugene sees Gwen have breakfast – a sequence recorded on 18 October 2006); Spanish restaurant La Tasca in the Brewery Quarter (where Gwen meets Linda for lunch); the National Museum building in Cathays (doubling for the University of Aberystwyth's Science and Natural History Museum – material recorded on 2 October 2006); and the road outside Ramon's Breakfast Bar (for the shot of Eugene letting go of Gwen's hands and starting to rise into the sky at the end of the episode – recorded on 19 October 2006 – although the exteriors of Eugene's family home were done elsewhere). The garage where Eugene's father works is said in the episode to be Filey Garage in Filey Road, but this is a fictional location. It is implied that the fictional Happy Cook restaurant is on the A48 road.

- The television programme that Owen is seen watching in the Hub is an episode of *A for Andromeda*, a famous seven-part BBC science-fiction serial from 1961, the surviving material from which had just been released on DVD by 2 Entertain, along with its sequel *The Andromeda Breakthrough*, at the time when 'Random Shoes' was in production. Owen admits that this was one of Eugene's DVDs, on loan from a video store, which he 'borrowed'.

- The name, logo and décor of the roadside Happy Cook restaurant seen toward the end of the episode strongly recall those of the real-life Happy Eater chain. This operated in the UK – mostly in the South East of England – from 1973 to 1997, after which its then-owners, Granada, converted the restaurants to Little Chef and Burger King outlets.

PRODUCTION QUOTES

- 'What the writer wanted to do was … have this sense that life is very short, that life whizzes by, that we all spend every day worrying about our day-to-day problems, and actually it's only once you reach death – or beyond it, in this case – [that] you look back and think, "My god, I was here for such a short space of time."' Producer Richard Stokes, *Torchwood* official website, 11 December 2006.

- 'We just loved the idea of an ordinary guy who is tempted by Torchwood. You know, Torchwood is the most magical, glamorous world, and he wants a part of it.' Executive Producer Julie Gardner, *Torchwood Declassified*: 'Dead Man Walking', 11 December 2006.

- 'The challenge in "Invisible Eugene" was to shoot it without making Eugene invisible, so that the audience could see him all the time, and there were only one or two moments when actually we show that he is invisible to the characters on screen. So actually I think it was probably quite a tough one for the actors.' Producer Richard Stokes, *Torchwood Declassified*:

'Dead Man Walking', 11 December 2006.

OOPS!

- Eugene states at the end of the episode that it was a Saturday morning when he died. Gwen spends some time investigating his death – presumably a few days, since it seems to be a weekday when she visits Passmore Telesales, and Eugene's colleagues have had time to buy a condolences card to sign for his mother – and is then told by Jack that she can have 'the weekend' to finish doing so. Then, in the climactic scene in the Happy Cook restaurant, Josh says that he and Gary were previously there 'last week'. This suggests that Gwen's investigation concludes seven or perhaps eight days after the Saturday when Eugene died. However, between being given the weekend deadline by Jack and visiting the Happy Cook, Gwen encounters Gary at the University of Aberystwyth's Science and Natural History Museum attending an event that, according to the flier, is due to take place on a Thursday; and she is away from Cardiff for one night. (One possible explanation for this apparent inconsistency is that it is actually, say, the Wednesday of the week after Eugene's accident when Jack gives Gwen the deadline; but then 'You've got the weekend' would be an odd way to express it, as opposed to, say, 'You've got until next Monday'. Alternatively, perhaps Gwen's visit to the Museum in Aberystwyth comes not on the actual day of the event but, say, the Saturday beforehand; the Museum's posters for the event could be advertising it as a 'forthcoming attraction'. If so, however, it is strange that Gary should be there too, unless the convention during which the event occurs lasts for several days and he is attending the whole thing.)

- Why does Eugene not have a Welsh accent, unlike everyone else in his family? (Could he possibly have been adopted by the Jones family as a young boy, having been born in England?)

- On its debut airing, this episode initially had a CBBC digital onscreen graphic (DOG) mistakenly superimposed in the top left-hand corner of the screen in place of the normal BBC Three one. This was removed after just over six minutes, and the rest of the episode was then DOG-free.

PRESS REACTION

- 'It's nicely acted, occasionally very funny and asks some very awkward questions about the audience's collective prejudices. But, we've been here before and it's never as good second time around.' Keith Topping, *TV Zone* Issue 211, February 2007.

FAN COMMENT

- 'It's about the little people, specifically a happy-go-lucky guy who actually considered himself a bit of a failure, something I found disturbingly easy to relate to. But strange circumstances complete the gaps in his life before he finally moves on. He was well thought of by his friends, his dad was just like him deep down and the girl he admired from afar could have loved him. I so wanted him to live at the end and almost thought he would. Clever trick.' Rob Tizzard, Torchwood Guide website, 14 December 2006.

- 'Wasn't it great … that despite being played straighter than "Love & Monsters", "Random

Shoes" has far more laugh-out-loud-funny moments? I mean, how intrinsically hilarious is the idea of selling an alien artefact on eBay, followed by the bittersweet topping of succeeding, only to be thwarted again by your own mates? I practically pissed myself at how Eugene was able to place [a] name on everything he saw in the base except the Doctor's hand – the one thing that we were able to recognise. "Oh wow. A hand. In … a jar." Owen's "Disney moment" cynicism for once provoked a grin instead of making me want to smash him in the face. Eugene fainting at his own autopsy? Very obvious. Been done. Still funny. Good job too how they cut it short without drawing your attention to the fact, since if Owen had been arsed [to do] it properly, the eye would have been found in no time at all.' David Sanders, Behind the Sofa website, 16 December 2006.

- 'Called "Random Shoes", this episode could just as easily have been titled "Random Plot". A hit-and-run accident victim … finds that his consciousness persists and he's able to follow the Torchwood team as they investigate his death. It sounded good in theory but the idea of a ghostly entity wandering around as an invisible observer – possibly due to an alien artefact – has been done many times before in sci-fi, especially in *Stargate [SG-1]*, which at least usually does [it] with more wit. Eugene emerges as someone with a long-term interest in the Torchwood operation and he harbours an unrequited love for Gwen Cooper … He also serves as a narrator for the episode. Not only is this dramatically weak, but the concept resembles "Love & Monsters", the mid-2006 episode of *Doctor Who* [that] ranks in many viewers' minds as one of the worst stories of Russell T Davies's "reimagined" *Doctor Who* series. Why the producers decided to do it all over again for this companion series is a mystery far deeper than anything that the patchy *Torchwood* has managed to put on screen.' Uncredited reviewer, HDTV UK website, 12 December 2006.

- '"Random Shoes" was a series-stealer, on a parallel with the classic *X-Files* episode featuring the late Peter Boyle, "Clyde Bruckman's Final Repose". I can honestly say I almost had a tear in my eye towards the end; certainly, my wife was snivelling in the corner, rubbing her eyes and producing a heart-warming smile at this decidedly down-to-earth story of a young lad who simply needed some direction in life.' Martin Conaghan, TV Squad website, 14 December 2006.

- 'Not a bad premise, but seems to be a mishmash of [*Star*] *Trek* [and] *Quantum Leap* with a dash of *Touched By An Angel* at the end. In place of a real plot, some sci-fi geekboy gets himself killed under the wheels of something big and highly visible, but due to the alien eyeball he ingested earlier (as you do in the Home Counties and Wales, it seems) his spirit hangs around and stalks Gwen trying to do something I frankly didn't bother to pay attention to.' Dale Who, Doctor Who Online website, 19 December 2006.

ANALYSIS

It seems a fair assumption that the great majority of regular *Torchwood* viewers will also be regular *Doctor Who* viewers. As such, they cannot have failed to spot the similarities between 'Random Shoes' and the Russell T Davies-scripted *Doctor Who* episode 'Love & Monsters' transmitted just six months earlier – similarities that have indeed been commented upon, mostly unfavourably, by just about every fan and genre press reviewer. The main parallels are that in each case a guest character takes centre stage, narrating events in the first person and introducing the viewer to his life and social circle with frequent use of flashbacks, while the regulars play a much lesser role than usual; and the guest character in question is a rather geeky young man with other-worldly interests who develops a particular attachment to one of the main team. 'Random Shoes' even features a character called Linda, in apparent homage to the self-styled LINDA group of 'Love & Monsters'.

There are two problems here: the first is that these similarities in approach and story content make 'Random Shoes' seem derivative and unoriginal; the second, and more serious, is that while it is an enjoyable, if somewhat below-par, *Torchwood* episode when judged purely on its own merits, it is not as good as 'Love & Monsters' and pales by comparison. Partly because of these factors, this is probably the low point of *Torchwood*'s first series.

'Love & Monsters' can be seen an affectionate homage to fandom – both fandom in general and *Doctor Who* fandom in particular. Its central character, Elton Pope (played by Marc Warren), is presented as a sweet, unassuming man with an infectious enthusiasm, a love of music and a happy coterie of like-minded friends, belying the common misconception of the science-fiction fan as an obsessional, socially-inadequate nerd; and the overall tone of the piece is warm and life-affirming. In 'Random Shoes', by contrast, the central character, Eugene Jones (Paul Chequer), is far less appealing, and does lean rather more toward the derogatory stereotype of a fixated loser with a bad haircut and a tendency to spout arcane trivia. In the 'Dead Man Walking' episode of *Torchwood Declassified*, Russell T Davies comments: 'What I like about [*Torchwood*] is that a lot of the staff, and I include myself, are geeks. So there was no way that we would write a geek as an idiot, as anally-retentive, as thick.' Unfortunately, the way Eugene is depicted on screen doesn't really bear this out. His only significant interest appears to be in UFOs and his rather sad little collection of purportedly-alien artefacts (which actually includes at least one fake, identified by Owen as being made out of Rice Krispies); he has no girlfriend and lives at home with his mother, who has managed to fool him for almost 15 years about his father's whereabouts and status; his performance in his dead-end telesales job is so poor that his boss is implied to be keeping him on only out of sympathy; and his supposed friends Gary and Josh have played a cruel deception on him, tried to rip him off and ultimately driven him to his death. His jacket even looks suspiciously like an anorak. This is all really rather depressing.

Where 'Random Shoes' does depart significantly from the template of 'Love & Monsters' is in the fact that Eugene Jones, unlike Elton Pope, is dead, and is thus effectively narrating his story from beyond the grave – although he maintains a spectral presence throughout, albeit invisible to the other characters until the end, and is seen alive (including as a young boy) in a number of the flashback sequences. This evokes memories of the classic Frank Capra movie *It's a Wonderful Life* (RKO Radio Pictures, 1946), in which the main character, George Bailey (James Stewart), is dissuaded from committing suicide when his guardian angel, Clarence (Henry Travers), shows him how much poorer the lives of his friends and family would have been if he had never been born. Another obvious cinematic influence is the Jerry Zucker-directed romantic comedy *Ghost* (Paramount Pictures, 1990), in which the ghostly Sam Wheat (Patrick Swayze) investigates the circumstances that led to his own death and finally becomes tangible just in time to exchange a kiss with his girlfriend Molly Jensen (Demi Moore) before ascending to the afterlife. Even in this respect, though, 'Random Shoes' is less than fully successful, mainly because it fails to make the most of the opportunity to explore the impact of Eugene's death on his friends and family and instead spends time developing a completely unbelievable 'love story' between Eugene and Gwen.

The idea that Gwen might suddenly develop some sort of affection for Eugene is patently absurd – and, more than that, frankly rather demeaning to her character. Not only is she already in a long-term relationship with Rhys and also carrying on an affair with Owen, which must surely leave little room for any further romantic entanglements, but Eugene – good-hearted and well-meaning though he may be – is clearly not the sort of person who would hold any attraction for her even if he was still alive, let alone now that he is dead. There seems to be some suggestion – voiced by Owen at one point – that her keenness to investigate his death stems in part from a feeling of guilt over the fact that she dismissed him so casually when, in life, he tried to ingratiate himself with her and the rest of the Torchwood team. That is fair enough. So too is the idea that Eugene might believe himself to be in love with Gwen. Where the whole thing falls down is in the implication that Gwen to some extent reciprocates Eugene's feelings.

The scene where the invisible Eugene is seen lying beside Gwen in her hotel room bed is actually more creepy than romantic. If Gwen really did sense the presence of this ghostly stalker – and probable peeping tom, given that, although not shown on screen, he has presumably watched her undress before she retired for the night – surely her immediate reaction would be to run out screaming, not to stay curled up next to him. Similarly, while one can accept that Gwen would feel grateful toward Eugene when – in a neat reversal of his own fate – he saves her from being run down by a car at the end of the episode, and that she would be happy to have her belief in his continued existence vindicated, for her to actually kiss him – not just with affection on the cheek, but full on the lips – feels forced and out of character. With no disrespect to Paul Chequer, he is no Patrick Swayze; and this whole romantic subplot seems completely misjudged.

Far more successful is the depiction of Gwen's dogged investigation into Eugene's death, which allows her to use the skills she acquired in the police force to great effect in breaking the bad news to Eugene's mother; finding clues; making deductions; and questioning witnesses. There are a number of excellent scenes here, including the one where Gwen has lunch with Eugene's colleague Linda, who recounts his attempt to sell the alien eye in an eBay auction with the remarkably generous aim of financing her desired trip to Australia. 'He was just trying to look after me,' explains Linda. 'He said, "Don't sit here and waste your life waiting for something that may never happen."' This is significant, because it clearly indicates that, having waited expectantly since he was a young boy for the alien to return for its eye, Eugene recently became disillusioned and effectively gave up on his dream – although he still believed the eye to be genuine, and it seems that someone else did too, as the bidding in the auction eventually ended at an incredible £15,005.50. The reason for Eugene's disillusionment, as Gwen learns from his younger brother, was his discovery that, far from having an important job in a big American corporation as his mother had always maintained, his father actually worked as a night cashier at a local garage in Cardiff.

This leads on to another very effective sequence in which Gwen, following up a lead from a flier found in Eugene's bedroom, encounters Gary at the University of Aberystwyth's Science and Natural History Museum and learns that Eugene's dream was rekindled when he concluded that it must be the alien who was bidding for the eye, on the basis that no-one else would consider it worth that much – although, as Gary now sheepishly admits, the real reason the bidding went so high was that he had artificially inflated it using three or four false online identities.

Gwen finally gets to the bottom of the mystery when she runs into Gary and Josh again after another clue amongst Eugene's possessions leads her to a Happy Cook restaurant on a road not far from where he died. It transpires that, having revealed themselves to Eugene as the true winners of his auction, Gary and Josh tried to persuade him to part with the eye for a mere £34, secretly planning to resell it to a genuine bidder – one C Blackstaff, described by Josh as 'a collector of alien ephemera and Nazi memorabilia, also Beanie Babies; a teeny bit cuckoo, but endearingly rich' – for the £15,000 he had been willing to pay. Catching on to their intentions, Eugene swallowed the eye in order to keep it from them, and then fled outside – where, after running across a field and onto another road, he met with his accident.

The only slight disappointment here is that the photographs of the titular 'random shoes' on Eugene's mobile phone turn out to be just that – random. The suggestion seems to be that, rather than being left intentionally as a clue, they were taken simply by accident when Eugene attempted to call for a taxi to collect him. This, though, is no more than a minor quibble, particularly given that the restaurant sequence as a whole is so well-conceived and – like the rest of the action throughout – so well-directed and acted, and that it brings Gwen's investigation to such a neat and satisfying conclusion.

Sadly, however, the episode then falters rather at the end. It would actually have been far better had it closed on the very moving scene of Eugene's estranged father singing 'Danny Boy' at his funeral, with perhaps an additional shot of the ghostly image of Eugene slowly fading away as his body was cremated and the alien eye left amongst the ashes. As it is, it carries on for another five minutes or so beyond that; and – even leaving aside the misfire of the kiss between Eugene and Gwen – this subsequent material feels tacked on and unnecessary. It also serves to create considerable confusion. Why exactly does Eugene's ghostly presence persist when the alien eye is no longer within his body? How is he able to regain corporeal form, just at the point when it allows him to bundle Gwen out of the path of the oncoming car? What really happens at the very end, when he is apparently drawn up into the sky in a halo of light? Has he been brought back to life and – in a final realisation of his long-cherished dream – been whisked off to join the Dogon? Or is he, in fact, a spirit ascending to some kind of heaven? While there is certainly something to be said for an adult-orientated drama series refraining from spoon-feeding explanations to its viewers, there are just too many important loose ends left hanging here.

The closing monologue, in which Eugene reflects on the random and fleeting nature of life and urges the viewer to 'breathe deep and swallow it whole', to some extent echoes the 'life is all' thread of Suzie's comments in the memorable car scene in 'They Keep Killing Suzie', but nevertheless comes across as a last-ditch – and only partially successful – attempt to overlay some sort of deeper meaning on the preceding events. This is one of the aspects in which 'Random Shoes' most obviously fails to match up to the standard set by 'Love & Monsters'.

The uncertainty over what happens to Eugene at the end also serves to highlight the unfortunate fact that the whole premise of 'Random Shoes' seems to be completely at odds with the usual *Torchwood* doctrine – established in 'Everything Changes' and reinforced in 'They Keep Killing Suzie' – that there is no afterlife, save perhaps for an eternal dark nothingness. Does the alien eye somehow bestow an afterlife on Eugene, or possibly even lead to him being gradually resurrected in the manner of Suzie? Or is his post-death manifestation just the product of some sort of time distortion? As the episode ends, the viewer is left to make up his or her own mind on all these points, which seems hardly satisfactory.

Still, at least the script resists the temptation to have anyone tell Eugene that he needs to 'get a life'.

1.10 – OUT OF TIME

WRITER: Catherine Tregenna
DIRECTOR: Alice Troughton

DEBUT TRANSMISSION DETAILS

BBC Three	BBC Two
Date: 17 December 2006.	Date: 20 December 2006.
Scheduled time: 10.00 pm.	Scheduled time: 9.00 pm.
Actual time: 10.00 pm.	Actual time: 9.02 pm.

Duration: 49' 41"

ADDITIONAL CREDITED CAST

Louise Delamere (Diane[94]), Mark Lewis Jones (John Ellis), Olivia Hallinan (Emma[95]), Sam Beazley[96] (Alan Ellis), Marion Fenner[+] (Nurse), Janine Carrington (Alesha), Rhea Bailey (Jade), Andrew MacBean[+] (Flying Instructor), Ciaran Dowd[+] (Barman)

PLOT: A small plane from 1953 carrying pilot Diane Holmes and her passengers Emma Louise Cowell and John Ellis flies through the rift and lands in modern-day Cardiff. The Torchwood team take charge of the three newcomers and try to help them come to terms with life in the early 21st Century. While Emma is able to adapt, and leaves to take up a job in London, John commits suicide and Diane takes off again in her plane, hoping to make it back through the rift.

QUOTE, UNQUOTE

- Jack: 'John's witnessing the end of his world, the end of his line, and we can't help. There's no puzzle to solve, no enemy to fight; just three lost people, who've somehow become our responsibility.'

- Gwen: 'Sex is nothing to be ashamed of. And as for you, well, your first time should be with someone special.'
  Emma: 'Do you wish you'd waited for Rhys? He's your special someone, isn't he?'
  Gwen: 'Yes, yes, I suppose.'
  Emma: 'I bet sex with him is better than with the others.'
  Gwen: 'Well …'
  Emma: 'Well, I will wait for Mr Right, I think. I'm really not the kind of girl who sleeps around. I'm going to brush my teeth. Thanks, for the chat.'
  Gwen: 'Not a problem.'

- Gwen: 'It's like two separate worlds. There's Torchwood, then there's real life.'
  Emma: 'That's why you've got to let me go.'

---

94 Surname given in dialogue as 'Holmes'.

95 Full name given in dialouge as 'Emma Louise Cowell'.

96 Surname misspelt 'Beezely' in closing credits but spelt correctly in *Radio Times*.

- Jack: 'You don't get reunited, John. It just goes black.'
  John: 'How do you know?'
  Jack: 'I died once.'
  John: 'Who are you?'
  Jack: 'A man, like you, out of his time, alone and scared.'
  John: 'How do you cope?'
  Jack: 'It's just bearable. It has to be. I don't have a choice.'

DOCTOR WHO REFERENCES

- None.

ALIEN TECH

- None.

CONTINUITY POINTS

- The Torchwood team seem to have a procedure already in place for taking the three newcomers' details, putting them up in a hostel, providing them with false identities and backgrounds and helping them to start new lives, suggesting that this may not be the first time that ordinary people from other time periods have fallen through the rift and ended up in their care. It is however said to be a 'one in a zillion' chance that Diane, John and Emma have arrived in this place and time; and there is now no way that they can get back to their point of origin.

- According to history, Diane's plane, the 'Sky Gypsy', was believed lost at sea after taking off from 1953, with all three occupants presumed dead.

- Diane achieved the feat of flying from England to Australia in only four days in 1952.

- The coach on which Emma leaves for London is operated by (the fictional) CitySwift line.

'BLOOD AND SNOGGING'

- Owen quickly falls in love with Diane and they have sex on at least two occasions at his flat, are seen to kiss numerous times and dance together in the light of a full moon – the heat of their passion obviously keeping them warm in the cold December air, given that Diane in particular is wearing only a flimsy dress, at least until Owen drapes his jacket over her shoulders.

- Emma is shocked to see Rhys walking naked around Gwen's flat, before Rhys realises that she is there.

- Gwen kisses Rhys at the nightclub, and says that this is a reward for putting up with her – to which Rhys replies, 'I deserve a lot more for doing that'.

- Emma has 'a kiss and a cuddle' with a stranger at the nightclub. Gwen intervenes, telling her: 'He was after a lot more than that.'

- Gwen tries to explain to Emma how attitudes to sex in the early 21st Century differ from those in 1953. She shows her a copy of a teenage girls' magazine, *Miss B*, which includes an article rather curiously entitled '10 Steam It Sex Moves To Drive Him Wild'; Emma finds this 'disgusting'.

PRODUCTION NOTES

- Made with 'Small Worlds' as part of Block 4 of production.

- Diane's plane, the 'Sky Gypsy', is a de Havilland DH.89 Dragon Rapide. She says that its name derives from the fact that it has 'de Havilland Gypsy Six' engines – which is a correct historical detail.

- The scenes of the (fictional) QM supermarket to which Ianto takes the three visitors from the 1950s were shot at the Asda store in Cardiff Bay. The Chinese restaurant where Owen and Diane have dinner is the Pearl of the Orient on Mermaid Quay, Cardiff. John is dropped off from Ianto's car at the Millennium Stadium. Owen's flat overlooks Cardiff Bay. Gwen sees Emma off to London at the Cardiff Bus Station – a scene shot on 20 August 2006. John gives his address in 1953 as '14 Park Place, Grangetown', but this is a fictional location: while there is indeed a Park Place in Cardiff, it is north of the city centre, some way from the Grangetown area.

- Beethoven's classical composition 'Moonlight Sonata' is heard, initially on a station on John's radio, in the sequence of the newcomers settling into the hostel. The soundtrack also features: the 2004 album track and 2005 single 'Trouble' by Ray LaMontagne, which is playing at Owen's flat when he and Diane first arrive there; 'I See You Baby', a 1999 single by Groove Armada, heard at the start of the nightclub scene; and Tony Bennett's 1962-recorded classic 'The Good Life', to which Owen and Diane dance in the moonlight. The latter track was a last-minute replacement for 'Fly Me to the Moon', which was included on preview copies of the episode sent out to the press but had to be dropped shortly before transmission for rights reasons. The song sung by Emma is 'Just Blew in From the Windy City' from the movie *Calamity Jane*.

PRODUCTION QUOTES

- 'It was what they called the *Play for Today* of the series, a very character-driven concept, and it was a great way for me to ease myself in … Having done all the aliens, fairies and all that, this was about dealing with three human beings from a different time. It allowed me to explore the characters of the Torchwood team. Their first instinct was to say, "At least it wasn't a spaceship full of aliens". As Jack says, "That might have been easier," because, ultimately, these human lives touch the team in devastatingly emotional ways. It just shows the wonderful scope for something like *Torchwood*.' Writer Catherine Tregenna, interviewed in *Starburst* Issue 345, January 2007.

- 'As most writers do, you aim for the stars and chuck in five special effects and hope you get two. Toward the end of the run, production funds are inevitably running a bit low, but I got my plane! I did write a scene with a flying lesson in the air, with a Cessna 150, looping the loop, which eventually became a chat in an office. Practically, I couldn't justify the narrative

– I couldn't say, "Yes, we absolutely need that scene."' Writer Catherine Tregenna, interviewed in *Starburst* Issue 345, January 2007.

OOPS!

- Emma says that she and her friend have seen *Calamity Jane* five times, but the movie was not released in the UK until 1954. (Perhaps they have recently been in the USA, where it came out in November 1953? Or could its UK release have been some time earlier in the *Doctor Who*/*Torchwood* universe than in ours?)

- Diane states that aviator Amelia Earhart disappeared in 1932; in fact, it was in 1937.

PRESS REACTION

- 'At last, *Torchwood* manages to fulfil its great on-paper potential and combine form and substance to produce an episode tinged with genius ... There's a real and genuine sense of strangeness to the episode's key themes of repression, guilt and resistance to change. With its pointed comments on equality, sexual politics, the horrors of ageing and loss, "Out of Time" avoids the more complex narrative structures of earlier episodes and, in its linear progression, rewards audience patience with a story with both heart and soul.' Keith Topping, *TV Zone* Issue 211, February 2007.

FAN COMMENT

- 'Man, Jack would totally suck as a grief counsellor. "My wife is dead and I want to kill myself!" "Really? ... Okay. I'll be sure and hold your hand while you die!" This is more grist to the mill of those who believe in Suicidal Jack, which would not have included me until this episode ... Is it just me, or does Jack have a tendency to project his mortality issues? Like, he didn't try that hard with John because he secretly wants to die himself? It's a theory ...' 'puritybrown', LiveJournal blog, 18 December 2006.

- 'I really loved the concept behind *Torchwood* this week. The episode was slow-paced and not what you'd call action-packed, but of all the episodes they've had so far ... this one seemed to really fit in with the concept of the show best of all. They took the basic concept of the rift and made use of it in a simple yet elegant way ... No thrills or spills to the episode, just three ordinary people stranded in time and struggling to adjust, and becoming the responsibility of Team Torchwood by default. Although not much happened, overall, I enjoyed the slower pace, seeing how the three very different time-lost strandees coped in their new environment, although I regretted that the amount of screen-time given to these guest characters meant we didn't get to see so much of Team Torchwood, who are the people I actually want to get to know better. Toshiko was barely there, and Ianto didn't fare much better, although he had that very amusing scene with the strandees at the supermarket. I'm a sucker for deadpan humour.' 'Llywela', BuffyWorld Forum, 20 December 2006.

- 'Lipstick, powder and paint. A gorgeous wine-red dress, a dash of scarlet lipstick. In one sense this episode is all dressed up, more finery than substance – and by that I mean that at its heart, "Out of Time" is a tale of people pulled from time and place – a theme which is overtly central to this show and this 'verse – yet the 1953 side of this story isn't, as I read it, really about one being "out of time" (about a clash of culture, behaviour and the anomie of alienation) as much as speaking to connections, relationships [and] the lack of them especially at Christmas. The festive period is barely mentioned directly, but it is not at all irrelevant … This is a Christmas of dysfunction. The flipside of Hallmark and mistletoe. [The situation with] Rhys, Gwen and Emma – as the long-lost-cousin-who-isn't – is a brilliant illumination of how so many of us feel and have felt, around imposing, intruding, never-going-home-again family. And John's story, the inverse of a son's tragedy with an aged parent, becomes a parent's tragedy – yet it's a universal one about loss, age and infirmity. Read from out of the corner of a viewer's eye, Jack's support of John can even be seen as the nightmare of crisis/Christmas-line. And yes, I admit I might be reaching there – just a tad. But this episode *is* all about disconnection, far more so than connection; about how we, in our consumerist society, get hammered and hook up with ease, yet can find ourselves little more than strangers in the night with lovers.' 'Boji', LiveJournal blog, 18 December 2006.

ANALYSIS

One of the most remarkable aspects of *Torchwood*'s first series is how incredibly varied its stories are, in terms both of style and of content. While this has the downside that it can sometimes seem as if the producers couldn't quite make up their minds exactly what sort of series they wanted to be, it also has the considerable upside that it keeps things fresh, interesting and surprising and can occasionally lead to the viewer's expectations being completely confounded by an episode that is very different from any that have gone before. This is certainly the case with 'Out of Time', which – save for the fact that its three main guest characters have been displaced in time – is more straight drama than science-fiction, and turns out to be one of the stand-out episodes of the series.

It has to be conceded that the central premise of the story is not entirely original. Way back in 1960, the first season of Rod Serling's seminal US series *The Twilight Zone* presented an episode, 'The Last Flight' by Richard Matheson, in which a pilot – in this case a military one – lands his plane at an unfamiliar airfield, only to find that he has travelled forward in time from 1917 to the present day, where he is astonished to see such modern inventions as jet aircraft. The pilot eventually returns to his plane and takes off again in the hope of reversing his journey and getting back to his own time. Episodes in which groups of 20th Century characters are revived after many years in cryogenic suspension, and then face the prospect of coming to terms with all the changes that have taken place in the interim, have also featured in two of the *Star Trek* series: 'The Neutral Zone' in *Star Trek: The Next Generation* and 'The 37s' in *Star Trek: Voyager*. In the latter of these, two of the revived humans are famous aviator Amelia Earhart and her co-pilot Fred Noonan, whose disappearance from 1937 is revealed to be the result of alien intervention. The title of Catherine Tregenna's debut *Torchwood* contribution also recalls that of science-fiction author Larry Niven's 1976 novel *A World Out of Time*, in which a man from 1970 is revived in 2190 – although in other respects this is a very different type of story.

Where 'Out of Time' wins out over all these earlier variations on the theme, however, is in its depiction of how the three time-displaced characters – Emma Louise Cowell, John Ellis and their pilot Diane Holmes – cope with the challenge of adjusting to what are routine aspects of everyday life in the viewer's own time. This allows not only for some humorous confusions to arise over certain specific developments – such as Diane's puzzlement at the 'Smoking Kills' warning on a packet of cigarettes and Emma's unfamiliarity with teabags, which she rips open in order to tip the contents into a teapot – but also for some well-observed and often wry social commentary on the changes in lifestyle and attitudes that have occurred in the UK over the past 50 years or so. An excellent example of this comes when Ianto takes the three newcomers to a supermarket and makes an apologetic comment about the advent of the 'consumer society', only to find that from their perspective of post-wartime privation it is – as John puts it – 'bloody fantastic', with Diane obviously considering the ready availability of bananas a greater cause for excitement than the innovation of the automatic door-opening mechanism.

This early sequence also points up for the first time that one of the most significant cultural changes to have occurred over the past half-century is the liberalisation in attitudes toward sex, as John is shocked to find on open display a magazine with a picture of a scantily-clad celebrity on the cover. This aspect of the story is explored principally through the character of Emma, who is clearly taken aback to discover that Gwen and Rhys are living together as an unmarried couple, and whose naïve behaviour at a nightclub leads on to the funniest scene of the episode – if not of the entire series – as Gwen attempts, not wholly successfully, to set her straight on modern-day sexual mores. In Diane's case, though, there is rather less adjustment to do in this regard, as she is clearly a sexually liberated and experienced young woman already – making her something of a pioneer in this regard as well as in the field of aviation. When Owen expresses some surprise about this after they make love for the first time at his flat, commenting 'I always thought the '50s were uptight and sexually repressed,' she amusedly replies, 'You didn't invent it, you know.'

As the episode progresses, each of the 1950s characters is effectively paired up with one of the Torchwood team: Emma with Gwen, Diane with Owen and John with Jack. Gwen displays something of a maternal streak here, taking the orphaned Emma under her wing and trying to shield her from the harsher realities of contemporary life – something that Emma clearly finds much more acceptable than John's earlier attempt at taking a paternal stance with her. When Emma secures a job in London (presumably thanks in large part to the false identity that Torchwood have given her, bearing in mind that she would have no legitimate employment history or references), the anxiety that Gwen shows is certainly very much akin to that of the typical mother, or perhaps older sister, when the young daughter of the family leaves home to start work in the 'big city'. This is carried through to the scene at the bus station near the end of the episode, where Gwen waves Emma off on her journey to London, having bought her a return ticket 'just in case', warned her not to talk to any strangers and asked her to phone as soon as she arrives. Rhys, meanwhile, has discovered that Emma is not, as Gwen claimed, her aunt's step-daughter, but a stranger she has met through her mysterious job. 'What worries me,' he fumes, 'is how easy it seems to be for you to lie to me, Gwen.' He doesn't know the half of it, of course, and it seems odds-on that there will be further trouble in store for their relationship …

Jack, for his part, forms a bond of respect and friendship with John, responding sympathetically when he objects to taking on a new name (a point that will come to have rather greater significance when viewed from the perspective of the series' penultimate episode, 'Captain Jack Harkness') and later sharing a drink and having a 'man to man' conversation with him in a local pub. He clearly regards him as a kindred spirit, in that they are both exiles from another time and place who have ended up stranded in 21st Century Cardiff. John's story turns out to be a particularly tragic one, though, as he learns that not only is his wife dead and his former home vacant and boarded up, but his now-elderly son, Alan, is living in a nursing home and suffering from senile dementia. An especially poignant sequence has him showing Alan photographs of the two of them together in the 1950s and trying desperately, but to no avail, to explain who he is. Unlike the teenager Emma, John is unable to adjust and make a fresh start in life in this new century. When Jack tells him, 'You're still young, you can get work, make friends, start a family,' he replies, 'I did all that, Jack, years ago, when I was meant to.' This comes in the lead-up to what is arguably the series' most controversial scene, and certainly one of its darkest, in which the invulnerable Jack sits with John to comfort him as he kills himself by inhaling poisonous exhaust fumes in Ianto's car. Although some have criticised this as effectively an endorsement of (assisted) suicide, a better interpretation would be that it is simply a demonstration of Jack's empathy and compassion. There is, after all, no doubt that if John is prevented from killing himself on this occasion, it will be only a matter of time – and a short time at that – before he makes another, successful, attempt, alone and without solace.

The real heart of 'Out of Time', though, is the relationship between Owen and Diane. The scenes of the two of them together at the airfield and enjoying themselves out and about in Cardiff are wonderfully romantic, and none more so than when they dance together on a moonlit rooftop to the strains of Tony Bennett's classic 'The Good Life', Diane looking absolutely radiant in the classy red evening dress that Owen has bought for her. Rather less successful, sadly, is the presentation of the more intimate moments between them. Russell T Davies has spoken with some pride in interviews about that fact that, unlike most adult-orientated series, *Torchwood* has so far avoided the inclusion of any female nudity.[97] While that is no doubt a laudable policy where the nudity in question would be gratuitous, here it actually works to the episode's detriment, as it means that director Alice Troughton has to resort to the clumsy and deeply unrealistic cliché of having the couple keep themselves carefully swathed in sheets or otherwise covered up while making love. Even allowing for this, the sex scenes between Owen and Diane are disappointingly stilted and passionless, with a notable lack of real chemistry between Burn Gorman and superb guest star Louise Delamere – previously best known for her regular role as Lia Costoya in the Channel 4 series *No Angels*. Gorman in particular looks rather ill-at-ease with the whole business; although, to be fair, this could perhaps be an intentional reflection of the awkwardness Owen is feeling at being drawn into a much deeper emotional relationship than he has experienced with any of his previous, more casual lovers – or, as he describes them, 'fuck buddies', amongst whom he clearly categorises Gwen, given that he tells Diane, with apparent sincerity, that he has no girlfriend. As Owen confesses, the intensity of his love for Diane actually scares him.

'I think that in this episode we see Owen's true feelings,' notes Gorman in the 'Time Flies' episode of *Torchwood Declassified*. 'We see his vulnerability, we see his history; and ultimately it's [a] human being talking to another human being with their souls absolutely bared … I think that Owen doesn't give a lot away – he's not somebody who wears his heart on his sleeve – and so for him to break down at all is a massive thing.'

'Once [he's] sort of lost his act, or his guile in a way,' comments Tregenna in the same programme, 'it [is] what's there, and it's a frightened boy, really.' This is a shrewd observation, and one that is borne out in the scene at the end of the episode when Diane, having the maturity to realise that she cannot give up her life of excitement in the skies for any man, gently brushes aside Owen's objections and pleas and takes off again in her beloved plane, 'Sky Gypsy', leaving him a forlorn and lonely figure abandoned at the end of the runway.

Diane has effectively reached the same conclusion as John – that is, that she is unable to

97 This is not, strictly speaking, correct, as 'Greeks Bearing Gifts' features black-and-white stills of the naked torsos of a couple of women – supposedly images of murder victims – displayed on Owen's monitor screen in the Hub.

adapt to life in the 21st Century – but, unlike him, has remained undaunted and taken a risky gamble on getting back through the rift and being transported 'somewhere new'. In response to Owen's warning that they don't know how the rift works and she could end up anywhere, she simply says: 'That's the beauty of it.' Whether or not she actually succeeds in re-entering the rift is left a slightly moot point at the end of the episode; although the fact that the screen goes completely white and a rift-type sound effect is heard as the plane disappears from view suggests that she does, and that her courage will be rewarded with many further adventures in other times and places.

Through the characters of Emma, John and Diane, Tregenna thus neatly illustrates the three distinct options open to those who find themselves unexpectedly cut off from their familiar everyday lives: adapting to their new circumstances; giving in to despair; or taking a gamble and moving on elsewhere. In doing so, she ensures that 'Out of Time', like all good drama, carries a serious message that is applicable well beyond its immediate context, and that the viewer may one day find relevant to his or her own situation.

In production terms, the episode was clearly a relatively undemanding one, with very few visual effects requirements, no alien creatures to be realised and no big action set-pieces to be staged. However, the costume and make-up departments do their usual excellent job in giving each of the three new arrivals a fitting and authentic 1950s look, and the whole thing has the classiness and polish that the viewer has by this point come to recognise as a hallmark of *Torchwood*, with excellent guest stars in Louise Delamere, Mark Lewis Jones and Olivia Hallinan and some fine direction from Troughton, who seems to relish handling such a character-driven story as this.

Recalling the episode's origins in 'Time Flies', Davies notes: 'A big decision that we made at the start of "Out of Time", which was such a good decision in the end, was not to have a big monster or enemy.' Elaborating, producer Richard Stokes explains: 'Russell just happened to say he wanted to … see a love story: "Wouldn't it be great if we started a show with an image of a plane from the 1950s just flying through the clouds, and they land, and Torchwood are there, and they have to look after them and integrate them into modern society."' From this relatively simple starting point, the writer and production team have come up with a story that is beautifully crafted and highly effective. While it may disappoint those science-fiction fans who are unable to appreciate a good drama unless it involves spaceships, high-intensity action or hordes of alien monsters, most viewers will surely recognise this as a genuine treat, and a shining example of the series at its very best.

1.11 – COMBAT

WRITER: Noel Clarke
DIRECTOR: Andy Goddard

DEBUT TRANSMISSION DETAILS

BBC Three	BBC Two
Date: 24 December 2006.	Date: 27 December 2006.
Scheduled time: 9.30 pm.	Scheduled time: 10.00 pm.
Actual time: 9.30 pm.	Actual time: 10.02 pm.

Duration: 47' 50"

ADDITIONAL CREDITED CAST[98, 99]
Alex Hassell (Mark Lynch), Paul Kasey (Weevil)[100], Alexandra Dunn (Barmaid), Matthew Raymond (Boyfriend[101]), David Gyasi (Hospital Patient)

PLOT: Someone is kidnapping Weevils off the streets of Cardiff. Going undercover, Owen makes contact with estate agent Mark Lynch, who turns out to be behind a secret club in which angry, disenfranchised young men try to prove themselves by taking on Weevils in unarmed combat in a cage in an abandoned warehouse. The depressed Torchwood operative walks a dark path that ultimately leads him to attempt suicide by entering the cage himself. Jack and the rest of the team arrive just in time to save him and put an end to the club.

QUOTE, UNQUOTE

- Toshiko: 'Just so I know where we stand. We would never deliberately put a human being through that. But Weevils are fair game, is that right?'
  Jack: 'We need to follow them.'

- Lynch: 'You're not even living here yet, and you've got people coming after you.'
  Owen: 'Yeah, well, some people need teaching a lesson.'
  Lynch: 'I'm not criticising. You're not the only pissed off bloke out there. That's what the world does to us. Fancy a beer?'
  Owen: 'Yeah, why not.'
  Lynch: 'You work yourself stupid, get a house, a car, a plasma screen, and you end up with a workforce; people there specifically to look after your every whim. You're officially successful, but what does it bring? Nothing. Success is no worth, other than itself. Seriously, I could live without all this. It doesn't define me.'

98 Other than Lynch, the fight club members are uncredited. One was played by Jazz Dhiman, who also had an uncredited part in 'Greeks Bearing Gifts'.

99 An additional artiste was credited in *Radio Times* but not on screen: Angharad Williams (Woman). It is possible that she appeared in a scene deleted from the final edit of the episode, as no such character seems to feature in the action.

100 Paul Kasey played all the principal Weevils. Stuntman Jason Hujan also played a Weevil, but was not credited on screen or in *Radio Times*.

101 Named as 'Tommy' in dialogue.

Owen: 'Yeah. Nice to have it, though, you know.'
Lynch: 'Ask yourself: what is the point of your life?'

- Gwen: 'I need to tell you something.'
  Rhys: 'What sort of thing?'
  Gwen: 'I've been sleeping – I've been having sex – with someone else, from work. His name's Owen. I mean, he's a bit of a tosser, actually, and it's all gonna stop, but –'
  Rhys: 'Shut up!'
  Gwen: 'I'm sorry. I'm really sorry.'
  Rhys: 'You wouldn't do that.'
  Gwen: 'But I have.'
  Rhys: 'Then why are you telling me?'
  Gwen: 'Because I'm ashamed, and I'm angry, and I want – I need – I need you to forgive me. And because I've drugged you.'

DOCTOR WHO REFERENCES

- The search engine that Mark Lynch uses on his computer is at www.search-wise.net. This was created specifically for general use in TV and film productions, and was seen in the *Doctor Who* episode 'Rose'.

- Gwen again buys two takeaway pizzas from Jubilee Pizza.

ALIEN TECH

- Owen, while working undercover, uses a – presumably alien – scanning device to extract information from the hard drive of Mark Lynch's computer and transmit it back to the Hub. It looks similar to, but not quite the same as, the one used by Toshiko to scan a book in 'Everything Changes' and to unlock the Hub's main exit door in 'Cyberwoman'.

CONTINUITY POINTS

- The Torchwood team use an 'anti-Weevil spray' to subdue the creatures, but this is starting to lose its effect, suggesting that they are mutating or evolving.

- Owen adopts an undercover guise as the head of Harper's Eels, a company exporting jellied eels. This cover story has presumably been prepared some time in advance, for use as and when required, as it is supported by a website that includes information, photographs and even a promotional video featuring Owen, along with a freephone number that connects to the Hub, where it is answered by Toshiko using the name 'Jenny Harper' – although when Lynch asks Owen if he has any family to relocate to Cardiff along with his business he replies, 'Just me. It's better that way.'

'BLOOD AND SNOGGING'

- Jack gets into a fight with a Weevil at the start of the episode, leaving him with bloody scratch marks across his chest.

- Ianto reports that there has been a surge of unusual injuries reported at the hospital's A&E unit – presumably the result of Weevil attacks.

- The dead body of a web publishing software salesman, Dan Hodges, is found by Jack and Toshiko in an empty warehouse, lying in a pool of his own blood. The body is later examined by Owen and found to have extensive injuries, and a fatal Weevil bite to the neck.

- The unnamed hospital patient visited by Jack and Ianto has visible wounds to the face and is recovering from a ten hour operation to repair the damage after his heart was almost torn from his rib cage in an (unseen) Weevil attack at the fight club.

- Owen is involved in two bar fights, the second and more violent of which leaves him with a cut lip.

- A Weevil is kept chained up and used as a living punch-bag at Lynch's house, and has bloody cut marks on its head.

- Owen receives multiple bloody injuries when he is attacked by the Weevil in the cage. He is saved when Jack shoots the Weevil in one arm.

- Mark Lynch dies at the claws and teeth of the Weevil when he too enters the cage.

PRODUCTION NOTES

- Made with 'Countrycide' as part of Block 5 of production.

- The series' standard opening sequence is extended on this occasion with a number of clips from 'Out of Time', to remind viewers about Owen's recent relationship with Diane.

- The name of the fictional estate agency Lynch-Frost appears to be a homage to David Lynch and Mark Frost, who created and, through their Lynch/Frost company, produced the cult American series *Twin Peaks* (ABC, 1990-1991). The preoccupation of *Twin Peaks*' agent Dale Cooper with 'damn fine coffee' has been to some extent echoed in *Torchwood,* with coffee featuring regularly as the team's drink of choice, and the making and/or exchanging of cups of it being accorded some significance in character interactions in episodes such as 'Cyberwoman' and 'Greeks Bearing Gifts'.

- Jack calls one of the Weevils 'Janet'. This refers back to a scene recorded for 'Greeks Bearing Gifts' but deleted before transmission. In this, Jack shows Toshiko the same Weevil in the Hub's cells and explains that, when it was found, it was burying one of its children, which could have been either learned behaviour or evidence that the Weevils have the capacity for sentiment.[102]

- The barmaid with whom Owen has a conversation – before her boyfriend intervenes – mentions movie star Greta Garbo (1905-1990), in reference to her famous phrase 'I want to be alone' from the film *Grand Hotel* (MGM, 1932).

- Jack's comment 'The Weevil has landed' is a reference to astronaut Neil Armstrong's famous 'The Eagle has landed', reporting the touchdown of the Eagle Lunar Module on the moon's surface on 20 July 1969.

102 This scene is due to be included in the deleted scenes package on the Series One: Part Two DVD set.

- Hot Chip's 2006 single 'Over and Over' is playing in the bar where Owen fights the barmaid's boyfriend. 'Be There', a 1999 single by Unkle featuring Ian Brown, is the song heard in the bar where Owen and Lynch have their later fight with the same man and his friends. Muse's 'Assassin', a track from their 2006 album 'Black Holes and Revelations', is heard as Owen and Lynch enter the fight club warehouse. Dan Hodges has the infamous 'Crazy Frog' ring-tone from Jamba! on his mobile phone.

PRODUCTION QUOTES

- 'The Weevils have been a real high point for me. I love that kind of real old school character that is a blend of animatronic mask and performer. It works so well and is so flexible in allowing a performer to really do his stuff. Paul Kasey is such a good performer and it's always fun seeing what added dimension he can bring to the character once our bit is done.' Creature effects designer Neill Gorton, *Starburst* Issue 344, December 2006.

- 'The Christmas Eve episode is the darkest piece of television in the world! I can't believe that we're showing it on Christmas Eve. Oh my god, it's the pits of hell!' Executive Producer Russell T Davies, interviewed in *Doctor Who Magazine* Issue 378, 31 January 2007.

- 'I was really trying to capture the darkness of people. I wanted to put one of the Torchwood team in real danger – mental, emotional and physical. For a moment, the viewers would think, "Fuck, Owen might actually die, or go mad here!" That was my big thing. He had to be in real danger, not Will Riker-type danger, where you know that he'll be fine.[103] That's scarier than any monster.' Writer Noel Clarke, interviewed in *Doctor Who Magazine* Issue 378, 31 January 2007.

- 'It'd be so like humans to find something like a Weevil, and have a blatant disregard and disrespect for that which is different, and end up torturing and fighting them, just for kicks – a mix of adrenaline junkies looking for a new rush, and people who need to get out their pent-up anger, or put meaning in their routine, faithless little lives. Next, they'll be blaming Weevils for taking their jobs and their women! After Weevils, it'll be something else, until there's no-one else left to blame, and nothing left to live for.' Writer Noel Clarke, interviewed in *Doctor Who Magazine* Issue 378, 31 January 2007.

PRESS REACTION

- 'The narrative builds efficiently, there's a tantalising tease for the season finale, but "Combat" never really flies. For me, the problem is that it's not particularly original, as we're watching *Fight Club* with Weevils. Even the wealthy gang members' rationalisation ("Ordinary blokes trying to find meaning in a world that doesn't have any") is straight out of Chuck Palahniuk. I've read the book, seen the movie – I didn't need the *Torchwood* episode too.' David Richardson, *Starburst* Issue 346, February 2007.

FAN COMMENT

- '*Torchwood* has in its first season been a run through the darker edged side of human emotion. From love to loss to displacement, and now we are shown one of the more deadly and uncontrollable parts of the human condition … anger. This episode starts out well, with a great

103 Riker was second-in-command on the star ship 'Enterprise' in *Star Trek: The Next Generation.*

Weevil scene with Jack, as he becomes more and more the focus and the motivator for the series' plots. It also has a great James Bond turn later on for Owen Harper, as he infiltrates the group that is kidnapping Weevils off the streets. Sadly what started off as a really impressive script from Noel Clarke turns into a shallow and blatant rip-off of one of my all time favourite films … *Fight Club*.' Thomas William Spychalski, Kasterborous website, 31 December 2006.

- 'If Gwen could talk to her boyfriend about Torchwood, she might be able to find a balance between her work and her home life. But she can't. And Torchwood is changing her. Or perhaps even magnifying the faults that she already has. But just as the Weevils are mutating, so the employees of Torchwood are being changed by their environment. Gwen just wants to be forgiven – to the point where she merely wants to hear the words, without changing anything about how she actually lives. The fact she gave Rhys the amnesia drug will be controversial – but it's an extension of how much the job is changing her. Not only on an emotional level, but simply because she has access to these kinds of drugs. From the first episode, there has been an underlying theme of the Torchwood employees using the things they find to their own benefit. Humans are weak and easily tempted. One thing that struck me about this episode in particular is the difference between Gwen and Rose in *Doctor Who*. They were originally both human women who were our eyes and ears into the worlds of Torchwood and the Doctor respectively. But while Rose disappeared with the Doctor, Gwen is still stuck in Cardiff; Rose didn't have to find a balance between her adventures with the Doctor and her family – they were separate things – while Gwen is forced to find a balance – and it's increasingly difficult.' 'crossoverman', LiveJournal blog, 26 December 2006.

- 'My theory on the theme of *Torchwood* is given yet more confirmation. At this stage I am absolutely certain that they're doing it on purpose and it is not just me making shit up and over-intellectualising as usual. Because, seriously, this was *all about* staring into the abyss and having the abyss stare back; and not just that, but Owen's willingness to go into the cage and let the Weevil maul him had come pretty much entirely out of his being left first by Diane and then by Gwen, and then spending time alone in bars, not answering his phone, not showing up for work – i.e. a lack of connection to other people. In the end he forges a connection with the Weevils, which may *just* be enough to keep him from falling in. But probably not.' 'puritybrown', LiveJournal blog, 27 December 2006.

ANALYSIS

Just as 'Countrycide' paid homage to *The Hills Have Eyes* and its ilk, so 'Combat' obviously draws a great deal of inspiration from the cult David Fincher-directed movie *Fight Club* (20th Century Fox, 1999) based on the novel of the same title by Chuck Palahniuk (Hyperion Books, 1996) – so obviously, in fact, that its accompanying *Torchwood Declassified* mini-documentary is even called 'Weevil Fight Club'. In the movie, two 'angry young man' characters, the nameless narrator (Edward Norton) and Tyler Durden (Brad Pitt), who eventually turn out to be two aspects of a single individual with a split personality, set up an underground boxing club as an antidote to what they see as the beleaguered state of masculinity in the face of rampant commercialism in contemporary American society. In 'Combat', Owen is effectively placed in the position of the narrator, and guest character Mark Lynch – superbly portrayed by Alex Hassell – takes on the darker Tyler Durden role. While they are not, in this case, literally two sides of the same individual, they nevertheless have a great deal in common, and a similar relationship to that of their movie counterparts. 'They meet each other practically as cop and criminal,' notes Russell T Davies in

'Weevil Fight Club', 'but what's interesting is how similar they are, how angry they both are, how attracted to the same darkness they both are; and they are just gravitating closer and closer and closer.' The main themes of 'Combat' also strongly recall those of *Fight Club*, as is perhaps most evident in the brilliantly-scripted scene where Lynch tells Owen that the members of the club are: 'Same as us: ordinary blokes just trying to find meaning in a world that doesn't haven't any … We're the dispossessed now, Owen. All the certainties our fathers had are gone. We're a generation of no faith, in society, in religion or in life. All we can do is reduce ourselves to the basics.'

As producer Richard Stokes observes, also in 'Weevil Fight Club': 'There is something about the sort of alpha-male, testosterone-driven [attitude of] "What is life worth? What is it all about?" that … is just really terrifying; when you think about what they're actually saying, when they're … talking about … "How do you find your thrills in a life that seems to have taken everything from you?"'

'This [episode] touches on contemporary … concerns,' adds director Andy Goddard in an interview on the *Torchwood* official website. 'Themes about belonging, the idea that we all want to belong to something; people all have a need to belong to some family, or some faction or some group. And I think this [episode taps] into that; this idea of … young, disenfranchised men with money to burn. And I think [that in] the times we live in – the magazine culture and the celebrity culture – … there is this sense that people are looking to stake their claim in something. There's something quite vacuous about it. I think that's what makes this episode quite disturbing for me.'

Fight Club is certainly not the episode's only point of reference. Real-life underground fight clubs, often of the bare-knuckle variety, have operated in the UK from the Victorian era right up to the present day, and boxing has been traditionally seen as an outlet for aggressive and disaffected adolescents to prove themselves. The difference, of course, is that all these clubs involve young men fighting each other, not alien Weevils!

Owen's state of mind is absolutely central to 'Combat'. In a welcome departure from the pattern of the early part of the series, when the events of one episode tended not to be followed up on to any significant degree in the next – examples of this being Suzie's death in 'Everything Changes', which was barely acknowledged in 'Day One', and Ianto's gross betrayal of the team in 'Cyberwoman', which seemed to have been almost forgotten about by 'Small Worlds' – here the despair that Owen feels following his recent abandonment by Diane at the end 'Out of Time' is a crucial factor driving the narrative. The early scenes of the episode thus show him drinking alone in a bar, ignoring mobile phone calls from work and getting involved in a fight with the barmaid's boyfriend (after which he tells her 'You really ought to upgrade your boyfriend' – an interesting choice of phrase, bearing in mind the fate of Ianto's girlfriend Lisa in 'Cyberwoman'). 'He's out in a bar,' comments Burn Gorman in 'Weevil Fight Club', 'just drowning his sorrows, and there's a lot of anger. He's a lost boy, and rejected, and losing his relationships, and also not liking himself very much, I think. You know, a lot of self-hatred.' It is, indeed, not only his relationship with Diane that Owen loses, but also his affair with Gwen, as they agree to call it off when, having learned from Toshiko about his 'thing' with the other woman, she asks him 'Why are we still doing this, me and you?' and he bitterly replies 'Fine. Let's not. I was getting bored of your fuck tricks anyway.' 'You can be such a wanker sometimes, Owen, do you know that?' retorts an upset Gwen as she drives off in the Torchwood SUV, leaving him at the roadside – just as Diane flew off in her plane, leaving him on the runway. 'I do, as a matter of fact,' he says.

It is Owen's bleak state of mind that renders him vulnerable to being drawn into Lynch's world when, in the wake of another, even more vicious bar fight – which is cleverly juxtaposed with the violent kidnapping of a Weevil by the fight club – he is invited back to the man's home for a drink and, on breaking into a padlocked room, discovers the Weevil that is being kept chained up there. There is a fascinating dynamic to these scenes, and the viewer becomes increasingly uncertain as to whether

Owen will remain loyal to Torchwood or be won over by Lynch's promises of 'so much more, if you know where to look.' As Goddard observes in 'Weevil Fight Club,' this is the first time in the series that Owen has been seen in the context of another male figure of a similar age – other than his colleagues Ianto and Jack – and the encounter is an absorbing one. 'Something's coming, out there, in the darkness,' says Lynch, in an ominous echo of Suzie's warning to Jack at the end of 'They Keep Killing Suzie.' It is almost as if Owen is being subtly seduced by Lynch, and some of the exchanges between the two have a decidedly homoerotic undercurrent – particularly when, a little later on, they talk at the fight club warehouse as, all around them, groups of sweaty, excited young men brawl with each other in dimly-lit rooms as a 'warm up' for the main event. As Davies notes, again in 'Weevil Fight Club': 'You've got this face-punching, bloody-broken-nose, broken-tooth extravaganza that is hard and hostile and brutal and urban and vicious, and to see Owen entering into that world, becoming part of it, and actually wanting to be part of it, shows what a dark path he's walking down.'

This culminates in the astonishingly dark climactic scene where Owen – in an action later emulated by Lynch, reinforcing the similarity between the two men – goes willingly into the cage with the Weevil, clearly intending to end it all. 'I didn't want saving,' he tells Jack later, in the hospital. 'For a few seconds in that cage, I felt totally at peace, and then you blunder in. Do you always know best, Jack? Is that what you believe?' The fact that Jack did save him makes for an interesting contrast with his acceptance of John's decision to commit suicide in 'Out of Time' – and indeed his failure to step in and rescue Lynch here, although this is perhaps a less clear-cut parallel, as it could be seen as just a case of rough justice. Why does he treat Owen differently from John? Is it because he sees a distinction between their respective situations – Owen's death-wish arising from his hopefully-temporary state of depression and self-pity and not, as in John's case, a reasoned conclusion that there is nothing left for him to live for – or simply, and more selfishly, because he needs Owen to continue working at Torchwood? Or does he simply not realise that Owen has entered the cage by choice, rather than – as would probably be the logical thing for him to assume when he first arrives on the scene – under duress?

This is not the only question that is left tantalisingly open, either, as the action ends with an intriguing scene in which Owen snarls at two Weevils in the cells at the Hub, and they respond by cowering away from him. Has being bitten by a Weevil in the cage had some sort of lasting effect on Owen, or even – in the manner of a vampire or werewolf bite – made him part-Weevil? Or is this simply a demonstration of the empathy he has with the Weevils, as alluded to earlier in the episode? Questioned about this in 'Weevil Fight Club,' Richard Stokes simply says, 'I think we'll have to wait and see.'

It is not only Owen who benefits from some excellent characterisation in this episode, but also Gwen. Her relationship with Rhys really hits rock bottom here. The tension between the two separate aspects of her life is illustrated in absolutely stark terms at the beginning of the episode, when she is obviously bored and thinking about work while she shares a meal with Rhys at a table outside a French restaurant, and is then whisked away by the passing Jack to help him catch a Weevil – ignoring Rhys's frustrated demand that she 'Sit the fuck down!' When she subsequently calls Rhys to apologise, he declines to pick up the phone and then deletes her message from the answering machine. The following morning, when she eventually returns home, he is on his way out, wearing what she describes as his 'pulling top,' to join his friend Dav's all-day stag-do celebration of staying single: 'A few beers, see what transpires; strip club; that sort of thing.' Events take an incredibly dark turn when she later confesses to Rhys about her now-ended affair with Owen, but only in the hope of getting him to say that he forgives her – which, as it turns out, he fails to do – as she has added a dose of Torchwood's amnesia-inducing drug to his drink to ensure that he forgets all about it. This is a truly shocking scene, because it demonstrates the extent to which Gwen has changed since she first joined Torchwood. Jack seems to be growing concerned about this himself, as he reminds her 'You promised to keep hold of your life' and, after their initial Weevil hunt, repeatedly instructs her to go home and take time off. Perhaps he senses that her valuable role as the 'heart' of his team is becoming compromised as she gets sucked further and further into Torchwood's murky world. This story strand leads up to a really heart-rending scene where, perhaps in a subconscious attempt to recall her initial innocence, Gwen effectively re-enacts her original entry into the Hub in 'Everything Changes', arriving in the base carrying two takeaway pizza boxes from Jubilee Pizza. This time, though, she finds the place deserted, and she sits eating the pizza alone, sobbing fitfully as she reflects on her situation and perhaps her loss of moral compass.

Although obviously not regulars in quite the same sense as Owen and Gwen, the Weevils have by this point become established as *Torchwood*'s signature monster race, and they get their biggest slice of the action yet in 'Combat'. 'What I liked about this episode [was that] there's a kind of *King Kong* element; there's a kind of sympathy for the Weevil,' notes Andy Goddard in 'Weevil Fight Club', while John Barrowman theorises that the creatures' viciousness in earlier episodes could have been due in part to the way they had been treated by the fight club, which has apparently been going on for some time. In production terms, they are a really superb piece of design and effects work, and Paul Kasey, as the lead Weevil actor – consolidating his position as resident 'monster man' on the *Doctor Who*/*Torchwood* team, having previously portrayed Autons, Slitheen and Cybermen amongst others in *Doctor Who* – does a great job in bringing them to life and expressively conveying their thoughts and feelings through body movement alone, his own features being completely encased in prosthetics.

Goddard seems to have been earmarked as the director to be assigned the grimmest and most disturbing *Torchwood* episodes. As on 'Countrycide', he acquits himself brilliantly here, imparting a spine-tingling intensity to the action set-pieces – the best of these being the ones where fight club members enter the cage to take on the Weevil while a baying crowd goads them on from the balcony above – and handling the quieter, but no less intense character-focused scenes with equal assurance. He also draws superb performances from all the cast. Burn Gorman and Eve Myles, as the regulars upon whom most of the attention is focused, take full opportunity to shine. Gorman's performance in particular is a real *tour de force*, and possibly his best of the entire series so far.

But where 'Combat' excels more than in any other respect is in its scripting. Noel Clarke, best known to fans for playing the part of Rose's erstwhile boyfriend Mickey Smith in *Doctor Who*, proves here that he is just as good a writer as he is an actor, if not even better. His script is not only thematically strong and dramatically compelling but also impresses with its first-rate characterisation, consistently sharp dialogue and powerful action sequences. It also has some pleasing elements of dark humour – most notably in Owen's rather fitting undercover guise as the head of company exporting jellied eels! One of the best things about it, though, is its faultless structure. The action flows seamlessly from scene to scene, and every move the characters make seems well-motivated and believable, never contrived simply in order to serve some particular plot purpose. In short, the guiding hand of the writer remains completely invisible to the viewer, who is never given cause to question the reality of what is being presented and can remain utterly immersed in the story. This is a rarely-achieved hallmark of great writing, which makes 'Combat' probably *Torchwood*'s best-scripted episode to date; and one can only hope that Clarke is invited back to contribute to the second series as well.

Dark and disquieting, urban and gritty, sexy and thrilling, 'Combat' really sums up what *Torchwood* is all about. It is an outstanding episode – and an outstanding piece of television drama, full stop.

1.12 – CAPTAIN JACK HARKNESS

WRITER: Catherine Tregenna[104]
DIRECTOR: Ashley Way

DEBUT TRANSMISSION DETAILS

BBC Three	BBC Two
Date: 1 January 2007.	Date: 3 January 2007.
Scheduled time: 9.30 pm.	Scheduled time: 9.00 pm.
Actual time: 9.30 pm.	Actual time: 8.59 pm.

Duration: 46' 58" (Complete episode duration: 48' 11")[105]

ADDITIONAL CREDITED CAST

Matt Rippy (The Captain), Murray Melvin (Bilis[106]), Elen Rhys (Nancy), Nadine Beaton (Audrey), Gavin Brocker (George), Peter Sandys-Clark (Tim), Ciaran Joyce (Smiler), Melissa Moore[+] (Singer)

PLOT: Investigating reports of ghostly music emanating from an empty building, formerly the Ritz dancehall, Jack and Toshiko find themselves transported back in time to a 'Kiss the Boys Goodbye' dance for servicemen and their wives and girlfriends at the height of the wartime Blitz. There, Jack is disconcerted to meet the real American officer whose name he adopted – particularly as he realises that the man is due to die in action the following day. As a gentle romance develops between the two Jacks, the sinister Bilis Manger, apparently the caretaker of the dancehall, schemes to ensure that, back in modern-day Cardiff, the other Torchwood members are forced to open the rift in order to save their colleagues from being trapped in the past. Bilis's plan apparently succeeds, and Jack and Toshiko return to the 21st Century, sadly leaving the original Jack to his heroic fate.

QUOTE, UNQUOTE

- Ianto: 'You have to let Diane go, like I did with Lisa.'
  Owen: 'Don't compare yourself to me. You're just a tea boy.'
  Ianto: 'I'm much more than that. Jack needs me.'
  Owen: 'In your dreams, Ianto. Your sad wet-dreams when you're his part-time shag, maybe. That rift took my lover, and the Captain, so if I die trying to beat it, then it will all be in the line of duty.'

- Jack (Torchwood): 'I went to war when I was a boy. I was with my best friend. We got caught crossing the border over enemy lines. They tortured him, not me, because he was weaker,

104 Credited as 'Cath Tregenna' in *Radio Times*.

105 On this episode's debut transmission, in a double bill with 'End of Days', the 'Next Time …' teaser and closing credits were removed. Its first transmission in its 'standard' form, complete with this material, was at 9.00 pm on BBC Three on 4 January 2007.

106 Surname given in the episode as 'Manger'.

but they made me watch him die. Then they let me go.'
Jack (original): 'Who were "they"?'
Jack (Torchwood): 'The worst possible creatures you can imagine. I persuaded him to join up. I said it would be an adventure. He hadn't lived.'
Jack (original): 'Have any of us?'

- Jack (Torchwood): 'I thought you'd gone. This could be your last chance.'
  Jack (original): 'That's why I came back.'
  Jack (Torchwood): 'I might have to leave before the night is over.'
  Jack (original): 'Well, make the most of now.'

DOCTOR WHO REFERENCES

- In the modern-day scenes, a number of 'Vote Saxon' fliers can be seen pasted on the exterior wall and door of the Ritz. These allude to a running storyline in Series Three of *Doctor Who*, which was also foreshadowed in a newspaper headline in the Series Two episode 'Love & Monsters' and in an order relayed by a tank commander in the Christmas special 'The Runaway Bride'. Graffiti seen inside the building incorporates the phrase 'Bad Wolf' – a reference to the running storyline of Series One of *Doctor Who* that culminated in Jack being brought back from the dead – and the letter 'P' in a circle – the symbol of the Preachers in the Series Two story 'Rise of the Cybermen'/'The Age of Steel', as seen also in 'Ghost Machine'.

- Jack again refers to his resurrection, as seen in *Doctor Who*'s 'The Parting of the Ways': 'Someone saved my life, brought me back from death, and ever since then, it's been like they're keeping me for something, and I don't know what it is.'

- The rift manipulator device, built into the base of the water tower fountain, bears certain similarities to the central column of the TARDIS control console.

ALIEN TECH

- It seems likely that the rift manipulator is of alien origin, or at least of alien design.

- Owen opens Bilis's safe using what appears to be the same device that Toshiko used to scan the pages of a book in 'Everything Changes' and to open the Hub's main exit door in 'Cyberwoman'.

- When searching through Jack's safe to find the rift manipulator blueprints, Owen comes across the 'life knife' (from 'Everything Changes' and 'They Keep Killing Suzie') and the 'ghost machine' (from 'Ghost Machine').

CONTINUITY POINTS

- At the start of the episode, Toshiko is preparing to attend a party for her grandfather's eighty-eighth birthday – which explains why she is fortunately wearing a dress that does not look too out-of-place in 1941. She is also heard having a phone conversation with someone in Japanese, indicating that she is bilingual. Later, she comments that she never goes anywhere without her laptop computer.

- Owen states that the date when Diane flew back through the rift in 'Out of Time' was 24 December.

- Jack introduces himself as 'Captain James Harper' when he meets his namesake in 1941.

- It appears that Jack feels some sort of affinity with his namesake even before meeting him, having clearly researched his life and war record. He has a small model of a P-51 Mustang fighter plane on his desk in the Hub, and the implication seems to be that this is the type of plane that the original Jack flew (although this may well have been when he was still in his native America, as the model has American markings and the RAF did not buy in and start using these planes in Britain until 1942).

- The password for the safe in Jack's office in the Hub is 'Rhea Silva' – in myth, the name of the mother of Romulus and Remus, the twins who founded the city of Rome.

'BLOOD AND SNOGGING'

- Toshiko deliberately cuts her hand on the sharp rim of a tin so as to be able to write a message in her own blood.

- Airmen are seen kissing their sweethearts at the Ritz.

- The original Captain Jack kisses his friend Nancy goodbye, and she tells him that she loves him.

- Ianto shoots Owen in the shoulder in an unsuccessful attempt to prevent him from activating the rift manipulator. Owen is later seen tending to his own wound, which by this point is covered with a blood-soaked bandage.

- The two Captain Jacks dance together and kiss passionately.

PRODUCTION NOTES

- Made with 'End of Days' as part of Block 7 of production.

- The series' standard opening sequence is extended on this occasion with a number of clips from 'Out of Time' and 'Combat', to remind viewers about Owen's recent relationship with Diane and his dark state of mind following her departure.

- Costume designer Ray Holman found it a time-consuming task to track down original 1940s clothes that were sufficiently well-preserved to withstand the scrutiny of HD television.

- Three authentic period songs are heard in this episode, all performed by credited singer Melissa Moore: 'My Melancholy Baby' (when George dances with Toshiko), 'The White Cliffs of Dover' (during the air raid) and 'A Nightingale Sang in Berkeley Square' (when the two Jacks dance together). 'A Nightingale Sang in Berkeley Square' contains the lyric 'There were angels dining at the Ritz', which is changed in the episode to 'There were angels dancing at the Ritz' – a line then quoted by Jack at the end of the episode as he recalls his dance with the other Jack.

- The Ritz interior scenes were recorded on location at the Baltica (formerly the Toad and before that the Westgate Hotel) in Commercial Road, Newport over a period of around five days in the second week of October 2006. The exterior shots were recorded at the Old Town Hall in the High Street, Merthyr Tydfil.

PRODUCTION QUOTES

- 'I was the person who said [as] the starting point …, "Who is the one man that Captain Jack is going to fall in love with?", and that's himself! It's a Captain Jack Harkness; which I think is a great gag.' Executive Producer Russell T Davies, *Torchwood Declassified*: 'Blast from the Past', 2 January 2007.

- 'The beauty of having Toshiko there is that she knows Pearl Harbour is coming, so there's that lovely back reference. I researched it in some detail, but there's a timelessness about boys going to war, like we know now with Iraq. So, as well as getting all the period detail, you want to bring the humanity out of it.' Writer Catherine Tregenna interviewed in *Starburst* Issue 345, January 2007.

- 'I had to write [this] one quite quickly and it was a really good exercise. We were up against time and I was getting notes directly from Russell. When you're at the end of it, you do feel like bleating, "Oh, come on, I made this up from scratch! Give me a break!" But then you realise, "Oh no, he is so right. That was a terrible scene!" Writer Catherine Tregenna interviewed in *Starburst* Issue 345, January 2007.

- 'The look and feel for this episode [were of] a 1940s romantic drama. I think the design team and Ashley, who directed it, and all the actors – I mean, once you sort of got everybody wearing those 1940s dresses, and the hair, and the make-up and the uniforms – … everyone who walked into that set when they were doing the 1940s stuff just … took a step back and a gasp. It just looks beautiful.' Producer Richard Stokes, *Torchwood Declassified*: 'Blast from the Past', 2 January 2007.

- 'It was very important that the [1941] environment was very rich, very colourful, very plush and just very romantic, with the chandeliers and the velvets and the flags, and just the sense that everybody was actually having a good time.' Supervising Art Director Keith Dunne, *Torchwood Declassified*: 'Blast from the Past', 2 January 2007.

OOPS!

- When Gwen reads Toshiko's blood-written equation to Ianto over the phone, she gets it wrong, beginning 'Cos sin squared …' when it should be 'Integral sin squared …' Fortunately, Ianto seems to know what she means, as he types the correct symbol on his screen in the Hub!

PRESS REACTION

- '*Torchwood*'s finest 50 minutes so far conspires to subvert the somewhat clichéd ideas at its core ("trapped in time") and go, instead, for a wonderfully human story of loss, courage and ambience. The pre-publicity for "Captain Jack Harkness" promised a plethora of revelation, and, indeed, that's what we ultimately get, although not, perhaps, in quite the way that most viewers would have expected it … Touchingly played and brilliantly executed, again, *Torchwood* is at its best when it's dealing with people and emotions rather than concepts, no matter how bold and ambitious they may be.' Keith Topping, *TV Zone* Issue 212, March 2007.

- '"Captain Jack Harkness" is an intriguing and atmospheric start to the two-part finale, with Jack and Toshiko sucked into an eerie World War II dance hall, lorded over by a mysterious time-hopping gentleman (whose background is, annoyingly, never properly explained in "End of Days"). This is an example of *Torchwood* as a contemporary *Sapphire & Steel* – which it echoes when it's good.' Brigid Cherry, *Dreamwatch* Issue 150, March 2007.

FAN COMMENT

- 'It's a good episode, indicative of the upward swing in quality that has characterised the second half of *Torchwood*'s first series. Looking back through the last few episodes, especially in the case of Owen, there's a clear setting up of events leading to the series finale – a kind of cause-and-effect that looks like it might pay off quite nicely. This is also a very brave episode. [It] not only addresses the idea of a Japanese woman in 1940s UK and deals with it realistically, it also acknowledges the repressed homosexuality of the era. Now, *Torchwood* has never been a show to shy away from homosexuality, and it certainly hasn't been afraid to imply (controversially) that every single person is really, deep down, bisexual. But I honestly can't remember the last time a graphic man-on-man make-out session was shown in a sci-fi show.' 'Luke', Cult Fiction website, 9 January 2007.

- 'Far more so than in "Out Of Time", the culture and attitude clash between different times is central to "Captain Jack Harkness"'s drama, and Catherine Treganna writes it with aplomb. It makes such perfect sense that our Jack would assume the identity of a man so similar to himself, and he's put further and further through the wringer as he tries to persuade his real-world counterpart to do the right thing, without alerting him to his ultimate fate and thereby possibly changing history – though you can tell he's sorely tempted to. And finally, when sympathy turns to affection and then genuine love, and it all boils over into that poignant slow dance in soft focus, it's absolutely wince-making to watch because you *know* it's all going to crash down in flames for both of them the moment our Jack returns to the present day, an era he's so much less comfortable in. The Blinovich Limitation Effect has taken two aspirins and retired to bed with a migraine.' David Sanders, Behind the Sofa website, 5 January 2007.

- 'Ianto says to Owen in one scene, "You only knew Diane for a week," comparing Owen's love for Diane to his own love [for] Lisa, to which Owen replies "And it wasn't enough." Love transcending time is an important theme in this episode. When … in the next scene the real Captain Jack tells Nancy "It's been a good few weeks" before she whispers into his ear "I love you," it is an echo of exactly what is happening between the real and the fake Captain Jack. The real Jack clearly falls in love at first sight with the fake [one] and is at both love's and time's mercy … It is … knowing that it [could] be the last time that he will ever see the fake Captain Jack … that makes it such a final night for him. To the real Captain Jack, the fake one suggesting to him that he has to seize the day (*carpe diem*) is a cruel twist. His own longing for reciprocation is probably what prompts him to answer "Maybe I should" when the [fake] Jack tells him to go to Nancy, although he had already settled the conflict of choosing between being nice to Nancy and being responsible to her. Love cannot be controlled; but actions can be suppressed. When he turns back to look for the Captain James

Harper he knows, to eventually share a moment with him, he finally takes the advice given to him and stops suppressing his feelings.' 'IamSooty', LiveJournal blog, 9 January 2007.

ANALYSIS

'Captain Jack Harkness' breaks new ground for *Torchwood*, in that it is the first episode to entail members of the regular team passing through the rift and finding themselves in a different era, with no apparent way of getting back home – a sort of reversal of the situation in 'Out of Time', writer Catherine Tregenna's previous contribution to the series, in which they played host to three time-displaced characters who wound up in contemporary Cardiff. It is also the first episode to be so closely linked to the following one that it can almost be considered the opening half of a two-part story; an impression reinforced on its debut transmission by the fact that it was presented in a continuous double-bill with the concluding episode, 'End of Days'.

The time travellers in this instance are Jack and Toshiko, and the year to which they are transported is 1941. This is the year in which Jack was living when first seen by viewers in the *Doctor Who* story 'The Empty Child'/'The Doctor Dances'; a fact that becomes crucial when, apparently by chance, he encounters the *original* Captain Jack Harkness: the American serviceman whose identity he adopted while pursuing his previous line of work as a con-artist in this time period. It eventually transpires that this meeting is not in fact a chance one, but has been set up by the mysterious, but seemingly malevolent, Bilis Manger as part of a devious plan to get the Torchwood team to use a rift manipulator device within the base of the water tower fountain in the Hub in order to open the rift.

Bilis is a great character – arguably the best new villain to have been introduced either in *Torchwood* or the new *Doctor Who* to date – and superbly well-played by veteran British actor Murray Melvin, who started out with Joan Littlewood's Theatre Workshop company at the Theatre Royal, Stratford East, while still a student in the 1940s and went on to have a very distinguished stage and film career, perhaps most notably originating the role of Geoffrey in the play *A Taste of Honey* and its 1961 film adaptation, for the latter of which he won Best Actor award at the following year's Cannes Film Festival. At the risk of seeming rude, it has to be said that Melvin has an extraordinarily sinister countenance, with an intriguing hint of the oriental about the eyes; and he portrays Bilis with an effete creepiness that is highly unsettling.

There are two interconnected aspects to Bilis's plan. The first is to give Owen, Gwen and Ianto a powerful incentive to open the rift, by leading them to believe that this offers their only hope of getting Jack and Toshiko back from 1941. The second is to ensure that they have the equations they need in order to achieve this, and also the missing component they require in order to make the rift manipulator work, but to do so in such a way that they think they are discovering these through their own endeavours and not – as is actually the case – being handed them on a plate by him. This involves him getting them to carry out a sort of stage-managed 'treasure hunt' for clues that he has subtly manoeuvred Toshiko into leaving for them in the past, and that he has presumably kept secure – or perhaps even transferred to the 21st Century himself – when they might otherwise have got lost or destroyed over the years. All this is very carefully worked out by Tregenna, and a very clever piece of writing. It does perhaps seem rather over-optimistic on Toshiko's part to suppose that the places where she conceals her messages will remain undisturbed for over 60 years, and that her colleagues will then think to look for them there. The only real illogicality, though, arises when Bilis deliberately scratches out the last few numbers in Toshiko's final message, written in her own blood. It is hard to understand why he should do this, as it would seem to run counter to the overall objective of his plan. Were it not for the fact that Owen is able to gain access to the rift manipulator blueprints in Jack's safe – surely not something that Bilis could have counted on – the lack of these final few numbers would apparently present an insurmountable obstacle. What does it matter to Bilis whether the opening of the rift is achieved by way of a complete set of equations, or by way of a partial set of equations and the use of the rift manipulator to 'improvise' the remainder? Surely all that matters, from his point of view, is that the rift is opened?

Even though Owen does get the blueprints, Bilis still comes close to failing, as Ianto realises how he has been deceiving them. It is only Owen's desperate hope that opening the rift will enable him to be reunited with his lost love Diane that blinds him to the truth and drives him on to activate the rift manipulator, despite Ianto shooting him in the shoulder to try to prevent this. So the rift is opened, Bilis's fiendish plan succeeds and … nothing happens, except that Jack and Toshiko are brought back from 1941, vindicating what has previously seemed to be a misguided belief on Owen's part. No death, no destruction, no adverse consequence of any kind ensues, and it appears that Ianto's fears have been completely unfounded. This is a major shortcoming of 'Captain Jack Harkness': if viewed as a stand-alone episode, it gives the impression that the only thing Bilis has accomplished is to extricate Jack and Toshiko from the trap that he lured them into in the first place; and in this respect the ending is a huge anti-climax. It is only when considered from the perspective of what comes later in 'End of Days' that Bilis's actions start to make more sense; although, even then, it remains unclear why he could not have used the opening of the rift in 'Captain Jack Harkness' to achieve his ultimate goal, and is still left unexplained why he scratched out those last few numbers on Toshiko's message. The 'Next Time …' trailer for 'End of Days' (not included on the original double-bill transmission) does at least tip the viewer off that Bilis will be returning, and that things are not as neatly tied up as they seem, but nevertheless, as a self-contained story of Torchwood engaged in a battle of wits with Bilis, 'Captain Jack Harkness' doesn't really work.

Fortunately, this is not all that the episode has to offer: there is also the love story between the two Captain Jacks. Again, though, this is less than fully satisfying, because it fails to address the issue of what life was really like for gay servicemen back in 1941. Not only does this leave a potentially rich vein of dramatic potential completely untapped, it also undermines the effectiveness of the climactic scene in which the two Captain Jacks dance together and share a passionate – and brilliantly acted – kiss as the others in the dancehall look on. The viewer's most likely response to this latter scene is not to get caught up in the emotion of it, as was obviously intended, but to question its truthfulness. Even today, many gay men would doubtless baulk at kissing so openly in public – other, of course, than in a gay club or bar – for fear of the negative reaction it might provoke, so to suggest that the original Captain Jack could even contemplate acting in such a way back in 1941, when attitudes toward sexuality were generally far less liberal, and indeed homosexuality was still criminalised in the UK, arguably places a serious strain on the episode's credibility.

This is a point that has been much debated amongst fans. While some have asserted that, surprising though it may seem, homosexual liaisons were tacitly accepted in the armed forces during the Second World War, others have argued that any real-life officer who acted in the way that the original Captain Jack does here would probably have been beaten up by his peers and, at the very least, severely reprimanded by his senior officers. Judging from historical accounts, the truth probably lies somewhere between these two extremes. While it is undoubtedly the case that gay men and women found the armed forces more accepting of them during the Second World War than at other times either before or since, simply because the services needed all the able-bodied recruits they could get, it is also fair to say that the public flaunting of same-sex relationships was not tolerated, and that any display of affection as open as that depicted in 'Captain Jack Harkness' would have elicited shock and outrage, even if the officers involved were both American, and thus – according to the popular perception of the time – naturally inclined to act in a more decadent and immoral manner than their British counterparts.

Against this background, the original Captain Jack's decision to 'come out' to the assembled throng – which is effectively what he does, although the concept would not even have been recognised in 1941 – is perhaps best viewed as the courageous act of a man who, having had brought home to him the fact that he lives in the shadow of death, is no longer prepared to go on hiding his true nature simply in order to conform with social expectations. The fact remains, however, that none of these issues is explored in the episode itself, and consequently this crucial scene is deprived of any real context. Again, the viewer is left with the dissatisfied feeling that only part of the story has been told. This has to be considered a great pity; particularly as the actual romance is very well developed and portrayed, and at times extremely moving, notwithstanding the somewhat cheesy concluding shot of the original Captain Jack saluting. The only real downside to it is that – following on from Toshiko becoming infatuated with Mary after just a single meeting in 'Greeks Bearing Gifts' and Owen falling for Diane at the drop of a scarf in 'Out of Time' – it does tend to reinforce the impression that Torchwood members have a strange propensity to fall in love virtually instantaneously, which can perhaps be excused to some extent on the grounds of dramatic license, but nevertheless works against the regulars coming across as realistic and believable people.

A big question left unanswered at the end of the episode is how the opening of the rift impacts on the original Captain Jack and the others present in the dancehall. Do they witness the two Torchwood members disappearing in a blaze of white light, as the viewer does, or are they left in a state of confusion, or perhaps under the impression that the two strangers have simply walked out of the hall? The latter possibility seems the most likely, given that the contemporary newspaper reports displayed on the monitor screens in the Hub, and reproduced in part on the Torchwood Institute System Interface website, apparently make no mention of any supernatural event having occurred at the dance. The fact that Torchwood's Captain Jack and Toshiko are both clearly pictured in these reports also rules out the possibility that the opening of the rift simply restored history to its original course and erased their involvement in 1941 – which would have been a great shame, as it would have rendered the whole love story effectively pointless.

Will the original Captain Jack really be physically attacked for what he has done, as some have suggested? It seems highly improbable. Not only is he a respected war hero, but he also appears to be the most senior officer present at the dance. The worst consequence he is likely to face is being cold-shouldered by some of his men and their sweethearts, or having people gossip about him behind his back. Will anyone report his behaviour to a higher authority? Quite possibly. But any consideration of this by his commanding officers will be pre-empted by his death in action the following day.

Where 'Captain Jack Harkness' succeeds best is in its superb realisation of the 1941 scenes. The BBC has a long track-record of excellence in the presentation of period dramas in general, and of those set during the Second World War in particular, and that standard is well maintained here. The dancehall set-dressings, props, make-up and costumes are all superb, and it is no surprise to learn that the latter are made up mostly of genuine 1940s clothes. It is also good to see Torchwood's Captain Jack back in the era in which he made his debut in 'The Empty Child'/'The Doctor Dances'; he seems, for some reason, to fit in particularly well here, as Toshiko quickly notices. From the way it has been treated in past TV dramas, one could almost be forgiven for thinking that the Blitz was something that affected only London, so it is very welcome to have a reminder here that other cities were attacked as well – Cardiff's docks making it a prime target for the Nazi bombers.

Ashley Way's direction is excellent throughout, and there are some highly atmospheric sequences, not only in the 1941 parts of the story but also in the modern-day parts, such as where Gwen explores the eerily deserted Ritz. Particular kudos is due also to John Barrowman and Matt Rippy for their outstanding performances as the two Captain Jacks. The casting of Rippy was an inspired move, as he has just the right degree of physical and vocal similarity to Barrowman to establish a convincing resonance between their two characters. 'Matt completely rose to the occasion and did a superb job,' comments Barrowman in the 'Blast from the Past' episode of *Torchwood Declassified*, 'and it was great, because I watched him and I tried to see what things I would bring into Jack from him.' It is good, too, to see Naoko Mori being given a bigger slice of the action this time around, after a run of episodes in which she has been somewhat underused – the worst offender being 'Random Shoes', in which she had only three lines. In fact, after 'Greeks Bearing Gifts', this is probably her second most prominent appearance of the series, and she does a great job in portraying Toshiko's fears over how she will fare if she remains trapped in this environment of growing hostility toward the Japanese – a type of prejudice that the episode does accurately depict – and her desperate yet resourceful attempts to leave messages that will survive the passage of time and be picked up by her colleagues over 60 years in the future. Burn Gorman and Gareth David Lloyd also turn in performances well up to their usual high standards, particularly in their scenes together in the Hub, where their heated disagreement over whether or not to proceed with opening the rift eventually erupts into violent conflict.

Ultimately, though, its failure to deliver a satisfactory pay-off to Bilis's machinations, coupled with its disappointing lack of insight into the issue of wartime attitudes toward gay servicemen, means that – particularly if viewed as a self-contained story, rather than as the first half of a two-parter – 'Captain Jack Harkness' must be counted one of the series' weaker entries.

1.13 – END OF DAYS

WRITER: Chris Chibnall
DIRECTOR: Ashley Way

DEBUT TRANSMISSION DETAILS

BBC Three	BBC Two
Date: 1 January 2007.	Date: 3 January 2007.
Scheduled time: 10.20 pm.	Scheduled time: 9.50 pm.
Actual time: 10.17 pm.	Actual time: 9.46 pm.

Duration: 46' 18" (Complete episode duration: 46' 42")[107]

ADDITIONAL CREDITED CAST

Murray Melvin (Bilis[108]), Tom Price+ (PC Andy), Caroline Chikezie+ (Lisa), Louise Delamere+ (Diane), Matthew Gravelle+[109] (Doctor), Noriko Aida+ (Toshiko's Mother), Russell Jones[110] (Policeman), Jamie Belton+ (Roman Soldier), Carrie Gracie+ (Newsreader), Paul Kasey+[111] (Weevil), Rhian Wyn Jones+[112] (Religious Woman)

PLOT: The rift is splintering as a result of Owen opening it to retrieve Jack and Toshiko from 1941. This is causing an outbreak of strange phenomena, including people from numerous past times appearing in the present day. The sinister Bilis Manger, by giving the Torchwood members visions of their lost loved ones, seeks to tempt them into opening the rift again in order to put things right. Jack is ultimately betrayed by his team, who proceed to open the rift. Although the splintering is indeed repaired, this enables Bilis to achieve his ultimate goal: the release of the demonic, life-devouring beast Abaddon from imprisonment beneath the rift. Abaddon is eventually destroyed when it tries to absorb Jack's life-force and is overwhelmed by it. Jack seems to be dead, but eventually revives at a kiss from Gwen. He then disappears from the Hub after a strange wheezing, groaning noise is heard.

QUOTE, UNQUOTE

- Gwen: 'Did you have to pick on him in public like that?'
  Jack: 'All of our actions have consequences.'
  Gwen: 'And all your staff have feelings, Jack. Even Owen!'
  Jack: 'Well, you would know.'

- Doctor: 'We've waited for you. You've got to stop this. You've got to do something'

107 On this episode's debut transmission, in a double bill with 'Captain Jack Harkness', the normal opening sequence with Jack's voiceover was omitted and the closing credits were expanded to cover both episodes (with some omissions and additions). 'End of Days' had its first transmission in its 'standard' form at 9.00 pm on BBC Three on 5 January 2007.

108 Surname given in the episode as 'Manger'.

109 Credited on debut transmission double-bill compilation but not on 'standard' single-episode version.

110 Credited on 'standard' single episode version but not on debut transmission double-bill compilation.

111 Credited on debut transmission double-bill compilation but not on 'standard' single-episode version.

112 Credited on debut transmission double-bill compilation but not on 'standard' single-episode version.

Owen: 'No, you've got to do something. People are dropping through time and they are gonna bring every disease in history through your doors, so you'd better be ready!'
Toshiko: 'Owen!'
Owen: 'You scared enough yet? 'Cause fuck knows I am!'

- Gwen: 'How can you be in two time zones at once?'
  Bilis: 'I can step across eras, like you'd walk into another room. At first it was the most incredible gift. Now I know the reality, it's a curse.'
  Gwen: 'Why?'
  Bilis: 'I can see the whole of history, but I don't belong anywhere within it.'

- Bilis: 'From out of the darkness he is come.'
  Gwen: 'What is he talking about?'
  Bilis: 'Son of the great Beast, cast out before time, chained in rock and imprisoned beneath the rift.'
  Gwen: 'What?'
  Bilis: 'All hail Abaddon, the Great Devourer, come to feast on life. The whole world shall lie beneath his shadow.'

DOCTOR WHO REFERENCES

- The spaceships shown hovering over the Taj Mahal in a TV news report look the same as the Jathaa Sun Glider seen inside Torchwood Tower in the *Doctor Who* story 'Army of Ghosts'/'Doomsday'.

- Jack again refers to UNIT.

- Jack's speculation that the Weevils are 'time sensitive' may be an allusion to Telos Publishing's *Time Hunter* novellas, a *Doctor Who* spin-off range in which one of the two main characters, Honoré Lechasseur, is a time sensitive. The plot of 'End of Days' bears some notable similarities to that of *Time Hunter: The Tunnel at the End of the Light*, written by Stefan Petrucha and published in 2004, and the Weevils resemble the subterranean creatures featured in that story. However, the concept of time sensitives has also cropped up elsewhere in *Doctor Who*, most notably in the 1980 story 'Warriors' Gate'.

- Abaddon was first mentioned by the Ood in the *Doctor Who* story 'The Impossible Planet'/'The Satan Pit' as a name used in some cultures for that story's monster, the Beast. Here, Bilis says that Abaddon is the 'son of the Beast' and that – in common with that creature – it comes from 'before time'.

- As in 'Everything Changes', Jack mentions his desire to see 'the right kind of Doctor'.

- The Doctor's severed hand, as seen in previous episodes such as 'Everything Changes' and 'Random Shoes', reacts to the approach of the TARDIS at the end of the episode, causing the preservative fluid in the jar around it to bubble.

- A TARDIS materialisation sound is heard at the end of the story, just before Jack disappears. This is presumably from the Doctor's TARDIS, as he is said in the then-current background to that show to be the last of the Time Lords.

ALIEN TECH

- The stun-gun used by Gwen on Rhys may possibly be of alien origin.

- When Bilis 'time jumps' away from the Hub after killing Rhys, he appears to use a small device held in his left hand. Previously, though, when he vanished in his shop, his hands were both empty.

CONTINUITY POINTS

- The Hub has nine levels of cells (corresponding to the 105-step staircase mentioned in a wall-notice seen several times during the series), and apparently an unspecified number of other, unused levels below these.

- Owen believes that within 24 hours of his (later reversed) dismissal from Torchwood, Jack will somehow slip him a retcon amnesia drug that will wipe all his memories of the organisation. This would seem to refer to a variant, or perhaps larger dose, of the drug featured in previous episodes, which has been used to remove only the most recent of the subject's memories.

- Owen appears to recognise Rhys when he first sees his blood-soaked body lying in the Hub's mortuary. If so, this would mean that he has met or at least seen Rhys before, either in an incident not shown in the televised episodes or perhaps in photographs.

'BLOOD AND SNOGGING'

- Gwen kisses Rhys in bed. He then gets up, and his naked rear is seen as he walks across the room.

- The bodies of plague victims are seen at Cardiff Hospital, with characteristic lesions on their skin. Owen identifies the plague as bubonic, although in fact it is more likely to be pneumonic in view of how rapidly others at the Hospital succumb to the infection.

- Bilis shows Gwen a vision in which Rhys lies dead in their flat, with blood all around him.

- Bilis stabs Rhys twice in the midriff in the corridor outside the cells in the Hub, killing him. Rhys's blood-soaked body is then taken to the Hub's mortuary, and Gwen also gets his blood smeared on her face, hands and clothes.

- Owen shoots Jack in the head and chest, but his wounds subsequently heal, leaving only a couple of small, blood-rimmed bullet holes in his shirt.

- Numerous Cardiff residents are killed when Abaddon's shadow passes over them, but their deaths are bloodless. There is no reason to believe that these deaths are reversed when Abaddon is destroyed. A report by Owen on the Torchwood Institute System Interface website indicates that they are subsequently blamed on a 'short-lived airborne infection escaping from … Cardiff Hospital'. According to the same report, the plague victims are not restored to life either, although 'the corpses have all helpfully vanished back through the rift', presumably owing to the plague bacteria themselves having been displaced from their period of origin.

- Gwen kisses Rhys when she finds him alive back at their flat, the opening of the rift having reversed his death at Bilis's hands and left him with no memory of it.

- Gwen revives the seemingly-dead Jack with a kiss.

- Jack kisses Ianto on the lips after he revives at the end of the story, lending support to the suggestion in earlier episodes that they are lovers, and he also kisses the sobbing Owen paternally on the top of his head.

PRODUCTION NOTES

- Made with 'Captain Jack Harkness' as part of Block 7 of production.

- In the single-episode version of 'End of Days,' the series' standard opening sequence is extended with a number of clips from 'Captain Jack Harkness,' to remind the viewer of the events involving Bilis and the opening of the rift. (The sequence was omitted altogether from the debut transmission double-bill compilation version.) Brief clips from 'Cyberwoman' and 'Out of Time' are seen later in the episode, accompanying Ianto's vision of Lisa and Owen's vision of Diane respectively.

- This episode at one point had the working title 'Apocalypse', but reverted to its original title, 'End of Days', shortly before transmission.

- Real-life BBC News 24 newsreader Carrie Gracie makes a cameo appearance as herself in this episode, reporting a number of strange occurrences caused by the splintering of the rift – specifically, UFOs hovering over the Taj Mahal in India and a shoot-out taking place in London after the sudden appearance of people in 'historic dress' – including, as seen in the accompanying pictures, troops from the era of the English Civil War. Although not mentioned in dialogue, a news-crawl at the bottom of the screen refers to three other similar events: 'Beatles on the roof of Abbey Road studios. Fears of guillotine appearance in Paris. Samurai warrior on the rampage in Tokyo subway system.'

- *The X-Files* (Fox, 1993-2002) is alluded to when PC Andy calls Jack and Gwen 'Mulder and Scully'. When Owen calls one of the hospital doctors 'House', this could be a reference to the title character of *House MD* (Fox, 2004-) – although, on the other hand, it could mean simply that the doctor holds the post of House Surgeon. The shot where Ianto, believing Jack to be dead, holds his coat up to his face and smells it, appears to be a homage to a similar scene at the end of the cowboy movie *Brokeback Mountain* (Focus Features, 2006).

- The first two drafts of the script had Gwen taking Rhys to a hotel to protect him from being killed in their flat, rather than stunning him and taking him to the Hub as in the transmitted version. He subsequently went back to the flat because he had forgotten to pack any underpants, and this led to him dying in exactly the way that Gwen had foreseen in the vision shown to her by Bilis.

- For the scene where the Hub is shaken by an earthquake as the rift opens, the required impression was achieved by having some windows blown out; a collapsing girder; falling and sparking cables; and 'drop boxes' of polystyrene rubble and dust opened out of camera shot. These effects took about three hours to set up, and were designed so as not to damage the actual set – or injure the cast.

- The Stone Roses' 1995 single 'Begging You' is heard in the bar where Owen is drinking when he sees his vision of Diane.

- The police station scenes were recorded at a real police station in Clifton Road, Splott, as previously featured in 'Small Worlds'. As a joke, the crew briefly locked director Ashley Way in one of the station's Victorian-era cells. Bilis's shop, A Stitch in Time, is in the same arcade in central Cardiff as is seen in the chase sequence at the start of 'Ghost Machine'. The scene where the team confront Bilis just before Abaddon makes its first appearance was shot at the side of the offices of the *Western Mail and Echo* newspaper in Havelock Street, Cardiff.

PRODUCTION QUOTES

- 'I think the original vision of the finale was always simply the time rift opening and something striding over Cardiff. Doesn't every drama start with that: "Something striding over Cardiff; that's where we must end!"' Executive Producer Russell T Davies, *Torchwood Declassified*: 'To the End', 2 January 2007.

- 'It wasn't conceived as a two-part [story], but there are elements in Episode 12 [that] obviously flow through into Episode 13 … The state of mind of all the characters – particular Owen – is kind of … the feed-through from the end of Episode 12 into Episode 13.' Producer Richard Stokes, *Torchwood Declassified*: 'To the End', 2 January 2007.

- 'In the outline for the episode … Rhys died at the end ... And … when I was writing the first draft, literally when I was writing the scenes, I thought, "I have never wanted to kill a character less than Rhys," because I absolutely love him, and he's the most generous, human, warm character … Then, after I'd submitted the first draft, I had a little e-mail from Russell, which just pinged up, saying, "This is fantastic. Just one thing: I don't think we should kill Rhys," and I was like, "Hooray! Thank you!"' Writer Chris Chibnall, *Torchwood* official website, 2 January 2007.

PRESS REACTION

- 'I'm disappointed to have to write this, but "End of Days" is a disappointment. A case of a production biting off slightly more than it can chew in an effort to produce something spectacular. The story is too scattergun, too piecemeal to effectively work ([although] there are great moments – Owen in the hospital faced with an outbreak of plague, for example). There is, simply, too much going on in such a short space of time for this to work as [the] cap on what has been, after all, a mostly successful season.' Keith Topping, *TV Zone* Issue 212, March 2007.

- 'There are so many gaps and dangling plot threads as to be downright annoying, and a muddled post-climax sequence.' Brigid Cherry, *Dreamwatch* Issue 150, March 2007.

FAN COMMENT

- 'Although it devolves into an exercise in sustained hysteria, the final episode is heir to the myriad unresolved tensions and neuroses that the characters have exhibited over the course of the season. It's perhaps inevitable, and even part of the point, that these should take over the episode and turn a crisis into the ultimate personal showdown. The cathartic nature of the story for the characters (albeit at the expense of most of the population of Cardiff) is highlighted in the closing scenes as [they] sob and hug and make up with their resurrected boss in a series of touching moments of forgiveness. What's lacking is any sense that this forgiveness is earned. None of the characters' flaws have been examined in any depth. No special insights or resolutions have been reached. No-one has learned from their selfish mistakes. On the contrary, in this episode they blunder into their biggest atrocity yet, and their hugs appear to be nothing more than relief that everything has turned out for the best. Forgiveness feels particularly unearned for Owen, who is only fortunate that Jack turns out to be immortal so that he can have his moment of catharsis by shooting his boss in the head and still get a big hug afterwards. The rest of us should be so lucky.' Iain Clark, Strange Horizons website, 11 January 2007.

- 'Right, this has got to stop. Not content with paying homage to various genre shows through *Torchwood*'s run, Chris Chibnall has now found an excuse to reference *Godzilla* – and, judging by the quality of the script and the dodgy CG work on ol' Abaddon, it's the 1998 Hollywood remake. For God's sake, man, try writing without referencing your DVD collection! All joking aside, this was a real disappointment. Chibnall has presented us with a season climax centred around a big bad that, as well as being a really unconvincing giant CG monster, hasn't been mentioned once throughout the entire season … To put this in context, this would be like removing all mention of Bad Wolf and the Heart of the TARDIS from *Doctor Who* but still ending with "The Parting of the Ways" and expecting viewers to swallow it. Moreover, there are far too many moments throughout the episode that are clearly supposed to up the emotional ante but, having been dropped in out of the blue like the whole Abaddon thing, just feel disjointed and wrong. So, all of a sudden Jack gets nasty with his colleagues, Owen is fired only to return about ten minutes later (hardly tension-building) and Ianto is suddenly Jack's on-off lover.' Chris Patmore, Sci-Fi-London website, January 2007.

- 'Bland. Just bland. After 12 episodes of increasing tension, excitement and surprise, I found the finale excruciatingly predictable (oh look, those visions were just tricks), twee (thank God everyone came back to life at the end, eh, just like real life – and don't even get me started on Gwen's kiss of life), embarrassing (Barrowman screaming at the shadow) and, worst of all, reliant on the parent series for a good cliff-hanger ending. *Torchwood* has come into its own so well these last three months, dragging Jack back into the world of TARDISes, Daleks and Cybermen for the last few seconds seemed like ... well, like a cheat. Much better for them to have left him dead over the season break (although that would [have been] one more *Buffy* rip-off), or at least have him disappear without the TARDIS sound effect … As it is, we're just left feeling that we've spent the last 12 weeks watching "Mission to the Unknown"[113], and now we're going to find out how Jack's experiences will affect the far more important world of the Doctor.' Arthur Penn, Torchwood Guide website, January 2007.

- 'I did once think that *Torchwood* was a great show but it's ruined itself with all these unnecessary references to coffee. I'm a lifelong tea drinker and it's an established fact that 90% of all people in Britain are tea drinkers too. Yet, throughout *Torchwood* there have been constant references to coffee drinking. I understand that there are people out there that drink coffee and I'm not coffee-phobic. In fact I once used to work next to a coffee-drinker and I never once complained about the smell. So you see I'm not a beverage-bigot. But the

113 'Mission to the Unknown' was a single-episode 1965 *Doctor Who* story that did not feature the Doctor but acted as a lead-in to the 12-part story 'The Daleks' Master Plan'.

regular references to coffee drinking have now got out of hand. In the finale there were numerous references to coffee. From Owen's comment about crying into their lattes through to the very final scene where Jack asked where the others were with the coffees. The references were unending. And then to make it worse, Ianto, Owen and Tosh walked in actually holding cups of coffee. I mean, if a kid stumbled across this show, how could you explain it to them?' 'DdWho', Outpost Gallifrey Forum, 7 January 2007.

ANALYSIS

Early on in 'End of Days', Ianto reads a passage from the Bible – specifically, from the King James Version of the Old Testament's Book of Daniel 12:8-9 (although he mistakenly says that it is 12:10) – referring to the 'time of the end'. He then goes on to quote a more arcane (fictional) text mentioning 'Abaddon, the Great Devourer, who will lead the world into shadow'. This is also, in effect, an allusion to the Bible, and in particular to the New Testament's Book of Revelation 9:7-11, which is believed to have been the first place where the name Abaddon – derived from the Hebrew word for 'destruction' – was attached to a demonic 'angel of the abyss' rather than, as in the Old Testament's Book of Job 26:6 and Book of Proverbs 15:11, a hellish place or 'realm of the dead'. Subsequently the name entered into more widespread use in demonology – as chief of the demons of 'the seventh hierarchy' – and even in Satanism – as one of the 'infernal names' – but it is clearly its use in the Book of Revelation that writer Chris Chibnall has in mind in 'End of Days', which also at one point had the working title 'Apocalypse'. The Book of Revelation, otherwise known as the Apocalypse and generally regarded as having been heavily influenced by the Book of Daniel, describes two visions, the second of which is of the end of the world, involving Satan's rebellion at Armageddon, God's ultimate defeat of Satan, and the establishment of a 'new Jerusalem'. This has clear parallels in 'End of Days', in which the world is likewise threatened with destruction, Jack takes on and defeats Abaddon, and peace is restored.

Continuing the religious theme, 'End of Days' can also be seen as a sort of *Torchwood* retelling of the Biblical story of Easter. The betrayal of Jack by his team members mirrors the betrayal of Jesus by his disciples – Owen's repeated questioning of Jack's identity and leadership in particular recalling Peter's repeated denial of knowing Jesus. Then, after Jack sacrifices himself to save the world, with his arms outstretched in an obvious crucifixion pose, Gwen's insistence that she will 'sit with him' is an unmistakable allusion to the Jewish practice of 'sitting shiva' with a deceased loved one, as Mary Magdalene effectively does with Jesus in the Biblical tale. The parallels continue as Jack's body is kept for a number of days (presumably three) in its 'tomb' (the Hub) with a 'boulder' (the big circular door) rolled over the entrance. Jack is then resurrected, appears before his 'disciples' – telling Owen that he forgives him and accepts him back into the fold, just as Jesus does Peter in the final chapter of the Gospel of John – and finally 'ascends to heaven' in the TARDIS.

Jack is thus explicitly identified in this episode as a Christ-like figure – and the Doctor, by analogy, as his 'father in heaven' – and it will be interesting to see if this angle is pursued further in subsequent episodes of *Torchwood*, or indeed of *Doctor Who*. Some fans have even indulged in speculation that Jack may ultimately be revealed to be the Doctor's son (and perhaps the father of the Doctor's granddaughter Susan – a character introduced in the first ever episode of *Doctor Who* in 1963 and eventually written out at the end of 1964), although others have expressed considerable scepticism that the production team would go down that road.

This religious subtext certainly adds an interesting extra dimension to 'End of Days', but doesn't really compensate for the fact that the ending is completely predictable and lacking in suspense. Even leaving aside the well-publicised fact that Jack is due to return in the third series of *Doctor*

Who and that there is then to be a second series of *Torchwood*, which makes it obvious that the lead character will not be killed off, it has already been very well established that Jack cannot die – a point that is, indeed, re-emphasised a little earlier in the episode, when he recovers after being shot in the head and chest by Owen. This renders his sudden resurrection completely unsurprising to the viewer, if not to Gwen and the other Torchwood regulars, who seem to have conveniently forgotten his invulnerability. In fact, 'resurrection' is probably the wrong word to use here, as in this instance, unlike in *Doctor Who*'s 'The Parting of the Ways', he presumably never actually dies as such, but is simply left in a deeply comatose state following Abaddon's attack.

In terms of its visual representation, Abaddon has dog-like facial features but otherwise draws on generic religious iconography of goat-horned, cloven-hoofed demons. It thus resembles the Beast in the Series Two *Doctor Who* adventure 'The Impossible Planet'/'The Satan Pit' and, going rather further back, the Destroyer – which is actually one of the alternative names for Abaddon in demonology – in the 1989 story 'Battlefield' and Azal – based on Azazel, a fallen angel in the Book of Enoch – in the 1971 story 'The Daemons'. In plot terms, too, the fact that Abaddon is initially trapped below the rift in Cardiff clearly recalls the idea of the Beast being trapped in a pit at the heart of the Impossible Planet, of the Destroyer being bound in chains and of Azal being entombed in miniaturised form in its spaceship. The function of Bilis Manger here is thus somewhat akin to that of the Ood in 'The Impossible Planet'/'The Satan Pit', of the witch Morgaine in 'Battlefield' and of the Doctor's arch-enemy the Master in 'The Daemons', in that they each contrive to release their respective demon, generally at its own instigation, invoking it by way of occult (or pseudo occult) incantations.

Another likely influence on 'End of Days' is *Buffy the Vampire Slayer*, and in particular episodes such as the first season finale 'Prophecy Girl' – which has a character seeing apocalyptic visions and, at its climax, that series' own Master releasing a huge monster from the Hellmouth – and the seventh season's 'Conversations with Dead People' – which involves the villain tempting the regulars with visions of dead loved ones.[114] The series *Hex* (Sky One, 2004-2005) also has apocalyptic themes running throughout, drawn in part from religious texts such as the Book of Enoch, and its final episode tells an 'end of days' story. Similarly, in the cinema, the 1999 Arnold Schwarzenegger horror/action film *End of Days* concludes with a Satanic beast bursting free from below ground and menacing a city – in this case, New York rather than Cardiff.

Bilis's ingenious method of earning a living – bringing period clocks through time to sell in an antiques shop in the present day – appears to be directly inspired by the identical trade practiced by Edward Waterfield in the 1967 *Doctor Who* story 'The Evil of the Daleks', although a similar idea has also featured in the BBC sitcom *Goodnight Sweetheart* (1993-1999). Although already implied in 'Captain Jack Harkness', it is made explicit here that Bilis has the ability to move between different time periods seemingly at will. How exactly he achieves this is not revealed – although one possible explanation is that this 'most incredible gift', as he says it was to start with, was conferred upon him by Abaddon – but it has the effect of making him an even more intriguing villain. Having said that, his plan in 'End of Days' – to subtly manipulate the members of the Torchwood team into using the equipment within the Hub in order to open the rift – is unfortunately exactly the same as his plan in 'Captain Jack Harkness', leaving the viewer with an uncomfortable feeling of *déjà vu*. Bearing in mind that the plan succeeds on both occasions, it also begs the question why he could not simply release Abaddon the first time the rift is opened, rather than put himself to the trouble of going

114 *Buffy the Vampire Slayer*'s penultimate episode in 2003 also bears the title 'End of Days', but shares no significant plot points with the *Torchwood* episode.

through the whole thing again. It is almost as if the production team couldn't quite make up their minds whether they wanted 'Captain Jack Harkness' and 'End of Days' to make up a single, fully-integrated story or to stand as two separate, self-contained ones, and ended up with a rather awkward compromise that falls between the two stools.

There seem also to be some inconsistencies between the two episodes. Whereas in 'Captain Jack Harkness' it appears that the rift can be opened only by entering a complete set of Toshiko's equations into the Hub's computer, or else by entering a near-complete set and then using the rift manipulator to fill in the rest, in 'End of Days' it turns out that the same thing can be achieved by way of an established procedure, referred to by Ianto as 'Emergency Protocol One', which involves entering a set of commands into the computer, then a password – 'Rhea Silva', conveniently identical to the one that gave access to Jack's safe in 'Captain Jack Harkness' – and finally the retina prints of all five team members. (Presumably this was updated when Suzie was killed and Gwen came on board, but it still seems a rather dangerous assumption on the part of whoever designed the procedure that everyone would be present if and when an emergency arose that necessitated the opening of the rift!)

One way of making sense of all this would be to assume that what is seen at the end of 'Captain Jack Harkness' is only a partial opening of the rift, and that Bilis's scratching out of the final few numbers in Toshiko's message is designed to ensure that this goes wrong and causes the rift to splinter, so that Torchwood will then be forced to try to rectify matters by proceeding with a full opening – something that can be achieved only with a complete set of their retina prints – sufficient for him to be able to release Abaddon. This, though, would be very much a case of the viewer supplying a rationalisation that is at best only hinted at in the episodes themselves.

The way that Bilis goes about manipulating the Torchwood team members in 'End of Days' is at least different from the approach he takes in 'Captain Jack Harkness', relying this time on exploiting their feelings toward lost loved ones – although in Owen's case this again comes down to taking advantage of the depression he has felt since Diane left him at the end of 'Out of Time'. It is not entirely clear how Bilis manages to create the visions that Owen, Ianto and Toshiko see, but these nevertheless provide the opportunity for a couple of nice cameo appearances by Louise Delamere as Diane and Caroline Chikezie as a somewhat woodenly-acted pre-cybernisation Lisa, which – along with the return of Gwen's former colleague PC Andy from 'Everything Changes' and 'Day One' – have the added benefit of imparting a greater sense of coherence to the series as a whole. Viewed in this light, it is actually rather surprising that Toshiko's vision is of her dead mother and not of her lover Mary from 'Greeks Bearing Gifts' – leading one to wonder if perhaps Daniela Denby-Ashe was not available to reprise her role. Also arguably something of a missed opportunity is the failure to write in another vignette for Suzie – who could perhaps have appeared either to Gwen or to Jack, neither of whom would have been likely to fall for the trick – although actress Indira Varma's limited availability might again have posed a problem, unless arrangements could have been made to shoot this at the same time as her scenes for 'They Keep Killing Suzie'.

A notable aspect of Bilis's scheme is that it seems he is actually telling the truth when he insists that opening the rift will repair the splintering it has undergone, thereby not only 'undoing' Rhys's murder but also, presumably, returning all the alien spacecraft and time-displaced individuals – Roman soldiers, plague victims *et al* – to their proper times and places. Owen still doesn't get Diane back, though, and of course Bilis isn't telling the *whole* truth, as he conceals his ulterior motive of releasing Abaddon. The downside of this is that the sudden revelation that Bilis is a follower of Abaddon comes completely of the blue for the viewer as well; it would have been better if this had been trailed in some way – perhaps through a couple of shots of him secretly worshipping at an occult altar in the back room of his antiques shop, or something of that sort – so as to convey an early inkling of the dire consequences that would flow from Torchwood falling for his deception, raising the stakes and racking up still further the tension of the conflict between Jack and his team.

No explicit explanation is provided as to why Abaddon is ultimately destroyed – a crucial aspect of the story – or why the rift closes again at the same time, although it is probably safe to assume that the creature simply 'overdoses' on the seemingly-inexhaustible supply of life-energy drawn from Jack – similar to the way that the Great One is killed by a surfeit of the power she craves in the 1974 *Doctor Who* story 'Planet of the Spiders', for those with long memories. A point left completely up in the air, though, is what becomes of Bilis after Abaddon's demise. Presumably he escapes to fight another day, leaving open the possibility of him making what would be a very welcome return appearance in *Torchwood*'s second series; but this is pure conjecture, and it seems rather unsatisfactory that such an important question is left unaddressed within the episode itself.

One of the most successful aspects of 'End of Days' is its treatment of Gwen. Her story essentially comes full circle here, her ultimate rejection of Owen and reaffirmation of her love for Rhys effectively symbolising her eschewal of the darker side of Torchwood's world and rediscovery of her moral compass. Indeed, it is only through killing Rhys, and holding out the prospect of this being reversed through the opening of the rift, that Bilis is able to tempt Gwen – possibly a further religious allusion – as director Ashley Way notes in the 'To the End' episode of *Torchwood Declassified*: 'She feels the betrayal of Rhys [through her affair with Owen] as well as his death, and it drives her even more now to do the right thing for Rhys, even [though] now she betrays Jack; and … Gwen's rebellion [is] kind of the last straw; … once that's done, the entire team just breaks.'

Crowning a season of excellent performances, Eve Myles is particularly outstanding in the scenes following the discovery of Rhys's blood-soaked body in the basement of the Hub, portraying Gwen's frenzied reaction with a spine-chilling intensity and conviction. '[Rhys] is the only thing she got that's normal,' observes Myles in 'To the End', 'and then when she finds him dead, she goes insane.'

Even though Gwen does join Owen, Toshiko and Ianto in betraying Jack, it is to her alone that he later turns in order to help get him away from the city centre so that he can confront Abaddon on open ground. Their special bond is thus re-established, and Gwen repays Jack's faith by keeping vigil over his prone form for days after the others have all written him off as dead, ultimately reviving him by way of a kiss. After a joyful reunion for the team, the episode then concludes with what Russell T Davies correctly predicted would be a 'fan-pleasing' final scene, in which a familiar wheezing, groaning sound is heard and Jack is whisked away from the Hub to resume his adventures in *Doctor Who* – leaving Gwen, Owen, Toshiko and Ianto to wonder what has become of him.

All in all, while not the strongest of episodes, 'End of Days' has a fittingly apocalyptic quality to it, a creepy villain in Bilis, an impressively fearsome and fairly-well-realised monster in Abaddon and some great performances from all the cast, and rounds off *Torchwood*'s first season in suitably enjoyable fashion.

SERIES OVERVIEW

As noted in Chapter Six, and discussed in detail in Appendix D, the official ratings and audience reaction data clearly demonstrate that the first series of *Torchwood* was a tremendous success with the general viewing public, fully justifying the considerable faith shown in it by the BBC. However, it was not universally popular. A glance through the 'Press Reaction' and 'Fan Comment' entries in this book will quickly confirm that its critical reception was somewhat mixed. How can this apparent contradiction be accounted for? There are two interrelated explanations.

First, it was always the programme-makers' intention to present a science-fiction-themed series that would have a relatively broad appeal to the adult TV-viewing population in general, not one that would be narrowly targeted at the cult audience of dedicated telefantasy fans. It was thus almost inevitable that a proportion of the latter group would feel alienated and unable to relate to the series. Writing in *The Times* of 21 October 2006 about *Doctor Who* – but it could just as easily have been about *Torchwood* in this regard – Russell T Davies explained: '[The series] attracts a lot of geeks. You can't deny that when you get a mailbag like mine. And what we've done on *Doctor Who* is to take it away from them, which has left a lot of the men screaming and crying. But to get eight million people watching it, which is the whole point, the male, white, middle-class audience that dominated the audience for so long has to put up with no longer being pandered to.' It is thus no surprise to find that some science-fiction fans – particularly, perhaps, those of the kind most predisposed to express their views forcefully and repeatedly on internet forums – have been critical of *Torchwood*; but, at the same time, Davies has again succeeded in his aim of entertaining a large general audience – one clear indication of which is that, as revealed by a detailed analysis of the ratings, the series had a near-equal split between male and female viewers (with women actually outnumbering men on some transmissions); certainly not the traditional profile for a science-fiction audience, at least in the UK.

This cannot be the sole explanation, however, as it is only a very small minority of fans who have expressed dissatisfaction with Davies's version of *Doctor Who* – in fact, a much smaller minority than would appear to warrant his rather provocative comments in *The Times* – whereas there has been a much greater split of fan opinion over *Torchwood*. The second factor has to do with expectations. Most new series take some time to acquire a dedicated following, as viewers come to them fresh and without preconceptions, other perhaps than a general idea of what genre they are in and a few early impressions formed from pre-publicity. In *Torchwood*'s case, by contrast, there was a ready-made fan-base taking a strong interest in the series right from the outset – even, indeed, from the time when it was first announced, months before it reached transmission. This, though, was not a *Torchwood* fan-base as such, but a *Doctor Who* fan-base. It is, in fact, highly questionable to what extent the 'fan comment' or 'fan opinion' reported throughout this book has been that of *Torchwood* fans – that is, people who have been drawn to the series purely on its own merits, having watched and developed an affection for it over a period of time – as opposed to that of *Doctor Who* fans whose interest in it was prompted largely if not wholly by its status as a spin-off. In this sense, *Torchwood*'s association with *Doctor Who* has been as much a curse as a blessing to it, as it has made it the focus of a huge weight of different, and often conflicting, expectations.

Judging from the criticisms that have been expressed, some *Doctor Who* fans expected the spin-off to explore more sophisticated themes than the parent, and perhaps to go further in terms of presenting frightening or horrific scenes, but to continue to steer clear of such taboo territory as sex and swearing; consequently, they felt that the series as transmitted went over the top in its adult approach. 'Far too much X-rated content,' was the opinion of one such fan, name of Winter-Wright, as expressed in a letter printed in Issue 344 of the *Doctor Who* Appreciation Society magazine *Celestial Toyroom*. 'I expected slightly more adult content than *Doctor Who*, but I think they have gone too far. Cannot let my teenage son watch this again!' Some, on the other hand, clearly felt that the new series had not gone far enough, either because they had expected to see more explicit sexual content, nudity or gory violence – having perhaps equated 'adult' with material more likely to be rated 18 than 15 on a DVD release – or because they considered that the sex and violence that *was* depicted was treated in a way that was more adolescent than adult. But, again, it is really no surprise that *Torchwood* failed to win over the entirety of *Doctor Who* fandom, as it was never designed to appeal specifically to that audience.

The promotion of *Torchwood* as 'science-fiction' also created expectations, particularly amongst those who take a rather narrow view of that genre, that it would routinely feature elements such as alien planets, intergalactic spaceships and hordes of unearthly beings – and consequently, despite the fact that no such thing had ever been promised, disappointment was expressed when episodes like 'Countrycide' failed to meet those expectations.

Science-fiction fans are not the only ones, either, who have strong expectations about the type of material that ought or ought not to be presented in such a series, or in TV drama more generally, even when aimed explicitly at adults. There are, for instance, some who find any depiction of sex or use of coarse language inherently unwelcome or even offensive, and others who have a serious problem with the positive representation of gay, lesbian or bisexual characters. These are aversions and prejudices with which *Doctor Who* has rarely if ever had to contend. *Torchwood*'s content, on the other hand, brings it into direct conflict with those who hold such opinions.

Of course, the criticisms that have been made of *Torchwood* have not all been couched in such general terms; many have been more specific. One frequently-aired complaint was put quite succinctly by journalist James Stanley in the *Metro* free newspaper of 29 November 2006: 'Though it was billed as an adult spin-off of *Doctor Who*, *Torchwood* is more like an unruly teenager, giggling because it's allowed to include sex and swearing.' Expressing himself rather more colourfully in the *Guardian* of 16 December 2006, columnist Charlie Brooker wrote: 'The award for the Year's Most Jarring Show goes to the *Doctor Who* spin-off *Torchwood*, which somehow managed to feel like both a multi-coloured children's show and a heaving sex-and-gore bodice-ripper at the same time. The constant clash of mutually-incongruous tones meant watching it felt like stumbling across a hitherto secret episode of *Postman Pat* in which Pat runs down 15 villagers while masturbating at the wheel of his van. Interesting, but possibly aimed at madmen.'

This may be a funny joke, but is it really fair to suggest that the series has childish characters and/or storylines? Consider, first, the five Torchwood regulars. The leader's outward bravado masks the fact that he is a deeply lonely man, displaced in time and haunted both by his mysterious past and by the fact that he is unable to die. The resident medic appears on the surface to be a cocky jack-the-lad of dubious morality, but is at heart an insecure and vulnerable boy whose despair on losing a newfound lover drives him to attempt suicide. The technical expert is a work-fixated geek whose reserved demeanour hides a craving for affection. The administrative officer has maintained a quiet, efficient façade while secretly working to his own agenda behind his colleagues' backs, and is now consumed with grief following the death of his girlfriend. The newest recruit starts out as a balanced, compassionate young woman with a stable relationship but finds herself becoming increasingly corrupted by the dark world she has entered into, embarking on an affair with one of her colleagues and selfishly mistreating her long-term partner. Are these really the sort of characters that one might find in a children's series? Clearly not. What, then, of *Torchwood*'s storylines? The key themes explored to date include the nature of mortality; the existence, or otherwise, of life after death; the compelling need felt by those in challenging jobs such as Torchwood's to have someone with whom they can discuss their experiences; and the idea that love keeps people at its mercy and can potentially lead them to betray their friends and colleagues. Again, nothing particularly childish there.

Arguably the only way this criticism really makes any sort of sense is if one takes the view that there is something *inherently* juvenile or childish about TV science-fiction, and that presenting it in an adult context is thus bound to produce an incongruity. Of all types of genre fiction, in literature as well as in drama, science-fiction has probably been the most disdained and derided over the years. TV as a medium has also been traditionally looked down upon by many critics and commentators as a poor relation to the theatre and the cinema. So, in some people's eyes, TV science-fiction is absolutely the lowest of the low; fit to be treated only as 'kids' stuff'. This is just rank cultural snobbery; but it is nevertheless a very ingrained and pervasive attitude. Just consider the semantics: whereas those who like vintage wine, fine art or good food are typically referred to as 'connoisseurs', 'experts' or 'gourmets' respectively, those who enjoy TV science-fiction (or other supposedly 'low culture' entertainments such as football) are labelled 'fans' – literally, fanatics. Although one might suppose that those who like TV science-fiction themselves would be less inclined to subscribe to such negative views, that is not necessarily the case.

But if one rejects the notion that *Torchwood* is in any way childish, what possible problem can there be with it including sex scenes and swearing? Of course, as noted above, some viewers baulk at such content on principle, even in an adult-orientated series. Others would no doubt assert that it is not a prerequisite for good drama. While there may be some truth in that, it is difficult to think of even a single example of a contemporary post-watershed British drama series that does *not* feature sexual storylines and realistic dialogue. If *Torchwood* were to be produced in such a way, it would arguably appear very old-fashioned, and lose at least a degree of its appeal to the general viewing public.

Are the series' sex scenes gratuitous? No. As discussed in depth in the 'Analysis' sections above, they invariably serve important plot or character development purposes. Sex is, after all, an integral part of everyday adult life, as co-producer Chris Chibnall observes in an interview on the Series One: Part Two DVD set: 'It's part of adult life, so you're not going to ignore it. It's an adult drama; you're going to have some sex in there. The sex between the regular characters and other characters is there to tell us where they are emotionally and what they're going through. And something like Gwen and Owen at the end of Episode Six, "Countrycide", is absolutely about Gwen's horror at what she's seen and her inability to share it with Rhys, and just the changing nature of her world, really.'

What, then, about the swearing? It is, of course, always possible for writers to avoid this in their scripts; but in an otherwise adult-orientated series, to do so is liable seriously to undermine the credibility of the drama. At worst, it can result in dialogue as unrealistic as that of certain American shows such as *CSI: Las Vegas* – in which, as if to compensate for the fact that no profanity is allowed, almost every significant line seems to be delivered with such melodramatic gravitas that it becomes quite laughable. Captain Jack, as *Torchwood*'s non-swearing regular (and quite rightly so, given that he has to work equally well as a character in *Doctor Who*) has in fact had the occasional 'Gil Grissom moment'[115] – an example that springs to mind being his 'No, we have!' line in response to Toshiko's 'Where's the SUV? Has it been stolen?' at the end of the pre-titles teaser in 'Captain Jack Harkness' – and that sort of approach would be very corny if applied across the board in *Torchwood*.

Another, very different complaint made by some fan critics is that *Torchwood* lacks originality. The argument here seems to be that because it has drawn general inspiration from sources such as *Buffy the Vampire Slayer*, *Angel* and *The X-Files*, and because some of its storylines have explored ideas that have previously featured in other series, then it is unacceptably derivative, or even guilty of 'ripping off' those other series. Again, this point seems hard to fathom. Any work of fiction, if analysed closely, will be found to have drawn at least a degree of inspiration from earlier sources, and to bear certain similarities to other stories. These similarities may be either intentional homages or complete coincidences. There are, quite simply, only so many different stories that can be told. To be wholly original, whether in science-fiction or in any other genre, is effectively impossible. Is *Torchwood* any more derivative or unoriginal than other contemporary series? Far from it. To the extent that this criticism is made by *Doctor Who* fans, it is also arguably somewhat hypocritical. *Doctor Who* has frequently been lauded for its reinterpretation of classic science-fiction and horror stories – 'Pyramids of Mars' for its pastiche of *The Mummy* and its ilk, 'The Brain of Morbius' for its retelling of *Frankenstein* and 'The Talons of Weng-Chiang' for its homage to the *Fu Manchu* stories, to cite just three examples from a particularly popular period in the mid-'70s – and it has been said, so often that it is now almost a cliché, that 'the series is at its best when its sources are showing'. Yet when *Torchwood* presents its own take on *The Hills Have Eyes* in 'Countrycide', or on *Fight Club* in 'Combat', this seems to be something that some of these seem fans find objectionable.

Another frequent fan complaint is that *Torchwood* has an uneven tone and lacks a clear identity. It is easy to see what lies behind this. One of *Torchwood*'s most distinctive qualities is that its stories are incredibly varied, both in content and in style. This sets it apart from most other series, which tend to tell the same type of story, in a familiar and unvarying style, week in and week out. Quizzed about this in an interview for *Dreamwatch* Issue 150, dated March 2007, Executive Producer Julie Gardner replied: 'What I love about *Torchwood* is ... that each episode can be so different. That's sometimes difficult on a long-running series. American shows are often very heavily formatted. What I love about *Torchwood* is that you can tell a very dark episode like "Countrycide", very slasher and dark, with cannibals in the countryside, and then go to ["Out of Time"], which is so romantic and emotional, and such a chamber piece about three characters. That's why I like sci-fi as much as I do: in a format like *Torchwood*, you can be that varied, but you've still got the consistency of the characters at its heart.' Of course, not everyone would agree with this. Some people like to be able to tune in to a favourite series knowing exactly the kind of story they are going to get and exactly the sort of style in which it is going to be told. This,

115 Gil Grissom, played by William H Petersen, is the lead character in *CSI: Las Vegas*.

though, is very much a question of personal preference. Surely it is hardly fair to criticise *Torchwood* for failing to be the type of show that it never set out to be in the first place? There are plenty of other series around that provide predictable 'comfort viewing', for those who seek it.

A far more valid criticism is that there has sometimes been inadequate continuity, and particularly character continuity, between episodes; in other words, a major event or character development will occur in one story that is not then followed up on, or even referred to, in the next. A number of instances of this are highlighted in the 'Analysis' sections above, but perhaps the most obvious example is the death of Suzie in 'Everything Changes', which appears to have been completely forgotten about in 'Day One'. It seems clear that the production team set out with no predetermined plan as regards the character development that each of the regulars would undergo during the course of the series, and with no overall story arc in mind, but relied instead on working things out with the writers as they went along. This feeling of aimlessness tends to undermine the credibility of the series and the believability of its characters.

Another legitimate concern is that the writers have so far tended to take a rather formulaic 'problem of the week' – or 'alien artefact of the week' – approach in their scripts, which is over-simplistic and lacks sophistication. In this respect, *Torchwood* compares unfavourably with most contemporary adult series, in which the stories generally feature not only an 'A plot' but also a 'B plot' and sometimes even a 'C plot'. The absence of any running theme – like the 'Bad Wolf' arc in the first series of *Doctor Who* or the 'Torchwood' arc in the second – is also rather disappointing, and compounds the feeling of events being too self-contained and devoid of longer-term ramifications. It would have been far more effective had the coming of Abaddon in 'End of Days' been foreshadowed much earlier on in the series, perhaps even by making Bilis a recurring villain or by suggesting that some of the other crises the Torchwood team had to deal with were prompted by his intervention.

In addition, it is fair to say that the series hasn't really lived up to Russell T Davies's promise to portray characters coping with 'having an extraordinary day job but keeping [their] home life going at the same time', as he put it in his *Wales Today* interview on 18 October 2006. Of the five Torchwood team regulars, it is only Gwen who actually *has* a home life to speak of. Jack, Owen, Toshiko and Ianto are all narrowly focused on their work, notwithstanding that each of them has been given a 'love interest of the week' – the real Captain Jack, Diane, Mary and Lisa respectively – at some point during the first series. The underlying problem here is that, apart from Rhys, the series lacks any regular or semi-regular secondary characters. Not only does this mean that the Torchwood team have no friends or family members with whom they can be seen to interact on an ongoing basis, it also leaves them with no apparent support or back-up in their missions – which begs the question what would happen if several of them happened to be off sick with a bout of the 'flu at the point when a crisis arose. The absurdity of this is unfortunately highlighted in the scene in 'End of Days' where Jack dismisses Owen and says to the others: 'Anyone who agrees with Owen, leave now.' It is just as well that none of them takes him up on this, or Jack could have found himself left with a team of only one or two people to defend the world against alien incursion. Thank goodness, too, that the production office thought better of their original intention to have Rhys killed off, as this would have only exacerbated the problem.

Having said all this, it is noticeable that most of these issues were already starting to be addressed by the end of the first series. Certainly across the last four episodes there is some excellent character continuity for the regulars, which to a large extent actually drives the narrative. There is also an increasing complexity apparent in the stories – 'Captain Jack Harkness', for instance, has two essentially separate plots running in parallel, one involving Bilis Manger's attempts to manipulate the Torchwood team, the other concerning the romance between the two Captain Jacks – and the events of 'Captain Jack Harkness' and 'End of Days' are of course closely linked. Moreover, there is some evidence of attempts being made to trail the coming of Abaddon at least a few episodes in advance, with the ominous comments about 'something out there in the dark ... moving' in 'They Keep Killing Suzie' and 'Combat'. This suggests that the shortcomings identified above may well have been to some extent 'teething problems', doubtless resulting in part from the fact that the series was rushed into production with a much shorter planning period than would normally be allowed – one consequence of which was that the writers of all the early episodes had to work on their scripts more or less simultaneously, generally without the benefit of knowing what would be happening in either the preceding or the following stories. Most fan commentators and genre press critics appear to have felt that the series overall got progressively stronger as it went along, and it would be difficult to disagree with that.

The remaining problems would seem to be ones that could be quite readily addressed in *Torchwood*'s second series, most obviously through the introduction of some further regular or semi-regular characters in support of the core Torchwood team. While there are no doubt budgetary constraints to be borne in mind here, it would be good to see Owen, Toshiko and Ianto in particular acquiring some ongoing outside interests and relationships – not necessarily of the romantic kind – to aid in character development and bring an extra layer of complication to the stories, as well as an added potential for audience identification. It would also be good to see the second series having some sort of overall story arc, or at least showing some evidence of following a preconceived plan.

What is clearly *not* needed, however, is any radical revamp of the series' format or overhaul of the main group of characters – contrary to the opinion of those fans and others, admittedly few in number, who have written at length in internet forum postings, magazine columns and the like about changes that it is 'essential' should be made for the second series 'if *Torchwood* is to succeed'. Things really need to be kept in perspective here: *Torchwood* is already an outstanding success with its target audience – adults amongst the general viewing public – and would no doubt continue to be so even if no changes at all were made to it.

Perhaps, in the final analysis, what the small minority of critics really find disconcerting about *Torchwood* is the same thing that the large majority of viewers find so appealing: it's uniqueness. As John Barrowman astutely puts it in the 'Preview' episode of *Torchwood Declassified*: 'It's ... British television like you've never seen it before.'

APPENDICES

APPENDIX A – TIE-IN MERCHANDISE

Most genre series these days tend to generate a wide variety of unlicensed merchandise, offered for sale to fans through the eBay online auction website and other similar outlets. Such items tend to be produced in small quantities, make illicit use of copyright photographs and logos and have a somewhat 'home made' feel to them. In *Torchwood*'s case, examples that have been spotted to date – often in various different forms from different sellers – include key rings, mugs, CD-clocks, posters, T-shirts, fleeces, iron-on transfers, novelty banknotes, fridge magnets, bookmarks, snow globes, mousemats, calendars, drinks coasters, Christmas cards, ID cards, artwork prints, photographic prints, a PC game and even cross-stitch charts.

Official BBC-licensed *Torchwood* merchandise has so far been far less plentiful – although a couple of big-name manufacturers are currently planning products for announcement during the course of 2007. Captain Jack is already available in action figure form as part of Character Options' range of *Doctor Who* toys; has been pictured on *Doctor Who* stickers, trading cards and other items; and has also featured in three of BBC Books' official *Doctor Who* novels, *The Deviant Strain* by Justin Richards, *The Stealers of Dreams* by Steve Lyons and *Only Human* by Gareth Roberts. As far as *Torchwood*-specific collectables are concerned, there have to date been: four promotional postcards and two promotional posters (some copies of which have a BBC Wales logo and some a BBC Three logo) – plus one *Torchwood Declassified* promotional postcard – of which copies have been supplied free of charge by the production office for publicity purposes and in response to enquiries from members of the public; three commercially-produced posters (two of them featuring images identical to the BBC's promotional posters) from a company called Mysterious World; a double-DVD set containing the series' first five episodes plus an outstanding package of extras including a selection of deleted scenes and a number of new featurettes put together by the *Torchwood Declassified* team, with two more double-DVD sets, each containing a further four episodes plus extras, due to be released after this book goes to print; three original spin-off novels[116], which are also due to be released in talking book form – with John Barrowman, Eve Myles and Burn Gorman reading one each – in April 2007; and a set of four small button badges, with images of Jack, Gwen, a Weevil and the *Torchwood* logo respectively, given away as a 'free gift' with Issue 153 of the genre magazine *SFX*. Rumours abound of two complete-series DVD box-sets to be released toward the end of 2007 – one of them either simply collecting together the six previously-released discs or else re-presenting the episodes with new or additional extras such as commentaries and outtakes, the other making the series available in the new HD-DVD format – but these are unconfirmed at the time of writing.

116 See Appendix B for full details.

APPENDIX B – ORIGINAL NOVELS

11 January 2007 saw the publication of the first three in what is intended to be an ongoing series of original *Torchwood* novels from BBC Books, an imprint of Ebury Publishing, which is a division of Random House Group Ltd. These are thus far the only commercially-available items to have presented new, officially-sanctioned *Torchwood* fiction. Steve Tribe was credited as project editor on all three titles, and Peter Hunt as production controller. Mathew Clayton was also on the editorial team; and *Torchwood* script editor Brian Minchin and assistant script editor Gary Russell were reportedly responsible for commenting on and approving the text from the production team end. The covers were designed by Lee Binding.

The three novels are not numbered. While the composite picture on their spines would seem to suggest that the order in which they should be read is *Another Life* first, *Border Princes* second and *Slow Decay* third, the order actually intended by the editorial team was apparently *Another Life*, *Slow Decay*, *Border Princes*, and this is therefore the order in which the books are detailed below.

Those who have not yet read the books may wish to note that the following guide contains plot spoilers.

1: ANOTHER LIFE
AUTHOR: Peter Anghelides

PLOT: A Bruydac spaceship crashes part-way through the rift, underwater in Cardiff Bay, killing all on board except for one badly-injured warrior. Three scuba divers come across the ship and are captured. The warrior has control devices implanted in their necks before releasing them, then proceeds to possess each of them in turn as it attempts to obtain the nuclear fuel it needs in order to repair its ship and get back home. There are just two problems: first, the possessed subjects need to murder people and feast off their brainstem fluid in order to survive, attracting the attention of Torchwood; secondly, the spaceship is still forcing its way through the rift, causing freak storm weather and flooding in Cardiff. Jack eventually tricks the warrior into possessing him, then drowns himself in the submerged spaceship. The warrior is killed, but Jack revives once back in the Hub.

DOCTOR WHO REFERENCES

- There are numerous references to the Blaidd Drwg (English translation: Bad Wolf) nuclear research facility that formed part of the plot of the *Doctor Who* story 'Boom Town' – now, hopefully, working to a less catastrophic business plan!

- Toshiko mentions that Jack asked her to check UK hospital reports of examinations and autopsies over the past three years for 'info about binary vascular system', presumably in the hope of tracking down the double-hearted Doctor. This check has come up blank.

- One of the medical instruments in the Hub is said to be made of duralinium, a rare mineral sought by miners in the 1971 *Doctor Who* story 'Colony in Space'.

ALIEN TECH

- Owen uses a hand-held Bekaran scanner device, which enables the user to see inside a person's body through layers of clothes and skin, like a kind of advanced MRI scanner.

- The crashed Bruydac spaceship features prominently in the story. It has an escape pod that functions like a submarine. Inside the main control area of the spaceship is a cylindrical life-support chamber that holds the original body of the Bruydac warrior. There are also a number of cage-like chambers that can implant small metal control devices into the necks of those held within them.

- Ianto has an alien stun device, rescued from the remains of Torchwood One.

CONTINUITY POINTS

- Gwen has been with Torchwood for around two months. She has not yet begun her affair with Owen. Ianto is engaged in mysterious activities in the basement of the Hub, suggesting that the events of 'Cyberwoman' have yet to take place. *Another Life* is thus probably set at some point between the TV stories 'Ghost Machine' and 'Cyberwoman'.

- Gwen's former police colleague PC Andy makes a further appearance, and is here given a surname: Davidson.

- Toshiko at one point sets up an offline version of the Second Reality computer game in the Hub, transforming areas of the base into a virtual reality environment.

- Owen attempts to get his former girlfriend Megan Tegg to join Torchwood, which suggests that he has the authority to recruit additional members.

- Gwen has not previously been inside an alien spaceship, although all the other team members clearly have.

- An earlier Torchwood operation known as Operation Goldenrod is mentioned; this is also referred to in both of the other novels released at this time.

'BLOOD AND SNOGGING'

- Tony Bee, Guy Wildman and Sandra Applegate, under the alien's influence, murder a number of people – mostly vagrants – by biting through their necks and into their spinal columns. Bee is shot after shooting one of his fellow soldiers, Wildman commits suicide by allowing himself to fall from scaffolding at a construction site and Applegate is shot in the shoulder by Jack and later dies from her wounds. Megan Tegg is the next to be taken over, and is shot dead by Jack.

- Sandra Applegate recalls being in bed with Tony Bee when they were having an affair.

- Jack tangles with a large, starfish-like creature in a bathtub and sustains a bloody wound to his arm, which quickly heals. Smaller versions of this creature are vomited up by the possessed humans and are able to digest organic matter.

- Owen has sex with Megan Tegg at her maisonette.

- Gwen is attacked by the possessed Owen and suffers a cut to her head – but fortunately only a graze to the back of her neck.

- Jack kills the alien form of the Bruydac warrior with a harpoon.

REVIEW

Although perhaps a little more inclined toward straight science-fiction, *Another Life* captures very well the gritty, urban style of the TV series. It also reproduces very faithfully the environment of the Hub and the characters of the five regular team members, with only the interaction between Owen and Toshiko seeming a little different from how it appears on screen. These achievements are all the more remarkable when one considers that Peter Anghelides – like the authors of the other two novels – had to embark on writing his manuscript before the series had even been transmitted, and so presumably had only some scripts to refer to, at least initially. There are certain passages that seem to have been inspired in part by the sequences of the Weevil hunt at the start of 'Combat', suggesting that this must have been one of the scripts he had access to. The narrative cleverly juxtaposes Owen's role-playing in the Second Reality game – clearly inspired by the genuine Second Life virtual world at www.secondlife.com – with the Bruydac warrior's adoption of a succession of 'other lives' through its control devices, making some interesting points about the attractions and dangers of living life vicariously over the internet. The novel also scores highly in sustaining an excellent oppressive atmosphere, with some vivid descriptions of the constant downpour and rising water levels from the storm over Cardiff, and in placing the Torchwood team in a situation that, perhaps rather surprisingly, they have yet to encounter in the series itself: specifically, having to venture beneath the surface of Cardiff Bay to deal with an underwater threat. Another plus point is the very good and imaginative use made, at the end of the story, of the fact that Jack cannot be killed. A highly enjoyable read.

2: SLOW DECAY

AUTHOR: Andy Lane

PLOT: The Scotus Clinic has come up with a revolutionary new slimming treatment: just one pill to 'Start', and another to 'Stop' when the desired weight-loss has been achieved. The downside is that the patient develops an insatiable appetite – even to the point of cannibalism. Each 'Start' pill is actually an alien egg, from which develops a worm-like creature that lodges in the patient's gut and consume the nutrients from his or her food. The worm eventually develops into a winged creature, which implants further eggs in a new, secondary host, which then dies and is consumed by predators, and the whole cycle starts over again. Dr Scotus has been kidnapping his patients in order to set up a profitable 'production line' of the alien eggs, but the Torchwood team track him down and put a stop to his operation.

DOCTOR WHO REFERENCES

- The jar containing the Doctor's severed hand is mentioned.

ALIEN TECH

- An alien device found at a nightclub crime scene picks up, amplifies and transmits emotions. Its appearance marks it out as one of a set, of which others are already held in storage in the Hub. When scanned, the circuitry within each device forms an image of an alien creature. If the images from the set are viewed in sequence, they seem to tell the creature's life story.

- In the basement of the Hub is an aquarium that, through alien technology, is able to reproduce the extreme pressures and temperatures of a deep ocean environment, sustaining the exotic fish that live within it.

- Toshiko's gun fires bullets made of an alien alloy.

- Torchwood have alien hand clamps made of a flexible metal that seals tight and turns rigid when they are applied, and can be loosened again by applying low-level microwave radiation.

- Owen has a supply of a powerful alien tranquiliser administered by injection through the skin.

- The Bekaran scanner device introduced in *Another Life* is featured again here. Toshiko is said to have made some modifications to it to improve its function.

CONTINUITY POINTS

- This novel is set at around the same time as *Another Life*.

- A typed report found by Toshiko in a box in the Hub's archive is signed by Jack and dated 1955, suggesting that he has been head of Torchwood Three since at least that time.

- The Torchwood SUV can be driven into the Hub via a concealed entrance in the basement of Bute Place car park.

- The flat that Gwen and Rhys share is in the up-market Riverside area.

'BLOOD AND SNOGGING'

- Five young men have killed each other in a brief but vicious fight at the nightclub, having been influenced by the alien emotion amplifier.

- A Weevil is found dead in an empty church, having suffered numerous bite marks and had its blood drained.

- Rhys punches a thug who tries to kidnap his friend Lucy Sobel, giving him a bloody nose.

- Toshiko is attacked by a Scotus Clinic patient named Marianne Till and sustains a cut to the back of her head, but escapes being eaten when Owen tranquillises the young woman. Later, in a cell in the Hub, Marianne chews the skin off her own fingers and attacks Owen. She is subdued by Jack and Toshiko hitting her on the back with a fire extinguisher. She eventually dies from blood loss after she manages, despite being restrained, to bite off her own arm.

- The hunger-crazed Lucy bites Rhys on the cheek, causing it to bleed profusely. She later kills her heroin addict boyfriend Ricky and eats parts of his body, soaking the surrounding area and herself in his blood. She attacks Gwen too, but Gwen hits her on the head with her gun and then with a discarded shoe, causing her to fall back against a door and thus rendering her unconscious.

- Dr Scotus's receptionist dies when one of the worm-creatures bursts free of her body.

- Dr Scotus dies himself when he is given one of the 'Stop' pills to kill the creature within him, the tendrils of which prove to have been too closely intertwined with his brain and internal organs for him to survive this.

OOPS!

- It is stated here that Toshiko has no medical training, which is at odds with what is seen in the *Doctor Who* episode 'Aliens of London' and in a number of *Torchwood* episodes, including 'Small Worlds', in the latter of which she carries out a medical examination of a body.

REVIEW

Less densely plotted than *Another Life*, Andy Lane's *Slow Decay* is a strongly character-driven novel. Gwen and Rhys come to the forefront here, and the reader learns a lot about the state of their relationship and their feelings toward each other at this point, prior to the start of Gwen's affair with Owen. Rhys certainly gets a bigger slice of the action in this story than in any of the televised episodes, pointing up the fact that this has been something of a missed opportunity in the series to date. The reader also gains some new insights into Owen's character and background, particularly in the passages where he opens up to the young girl Marianne while she is being held in a cell at the Hub, and when he is left distraught by her subsequent death. Despite the strong focus on characterisation, there is still plenty of action and suspense within the story, and some exceptionally gory deaths. The Weevils also feature quite prominently. The overall style is thus somewhat similar to that of 'Combat', again leading the reader to suspect that the script of that episode is one to which the author had access while writing his manuscript. The first two-thirds of the novel are superb, but the final third sees it faltering just a little, the earlier strong characterisation giving way to some more action-orientated and exposition-heavy chapters as the life-cycle of the alien creature is expounded upon and the story moves toward its slightly over-elaborate denouement. It nevertheless remains a very well-written and enjoyable book.

3: BORDER PRINCES

AUTHOR: Dan Abnett

PLOT: James Mayer is a new member of Torchwood … but as far as the others are concerned, he is a long-standing colleague and friend. It transpires that he is actually a human construct placed on Earth as a 'training exercise' prior to assuming his hereditary role as a Border Prince watching over the rift on an alien planet. His programming having been disrupted, he is no longer capable of understanding his true nature, and so is perturbed to realise that in times of danger he is liable to demonstrate superhuman strength and agility. Jack and the others discover that their perceptions have been altered to make them accept James as one of their number. Two shadowy alien 'watchers' stationed on Earth to protect James – or, as they know him, the Principal – take him back to his own planet.

DOCTOR WHO REFERENCES

- None.

ALIEN TECH

- The Amok is a multi-dimensional alien puzzle device that can disorientate and even kill humans who come into contact with it.

- The Bekaran scanner is again used by Owen.

- World War Two veteran Davey 'Taff' Morgan digs up a robot on a neighbour's allotment. Jack recognises it as a Serial G – one of a troop of ruthless artificial soldiers constructed by the Melkene race to enable them to win a war against a rival species. The Serial G is destroyed by one of the Principal's 'watchers', known in human form as Mr Dine, although both Jack and James suffer minor injuries in the conflict.

CONTINUITY POINTS

- This novel opens on a Thursday evening in mid-October – presumably October 2007 – which would place it at around the same time as, or possibly a little earlier than, *Another Life* and *Slow Decay*.

'BLOOD AND SNOGGING'

- The Torchwood team encounter a crowd of locals rendered zombie-like by the effects of the Amok. There is much blood spilt; at least three deaths occur; and all the team sustain minor injuries.

- Gwen has an affair with James, and they make love at his home on several occasions.

- Davey Morgan is attacked by a group of yobs, leaving him with an injured leg, a bloody nose and a bruised cheek. The yobs are subsequently killed and their body parts strewn over the allotment by the Serial G robot, which has an empathic connection with Davey as a fellow soldier.

OOPS!

- James indicates that the Hub's computer system is of human design, whereas it is strongly implied in the TV series, and stated as a fact on the official Torchwood Institute System Interface website, that it is of alien origin.

REVIEW

Dan Abnett is known primarily for his work in comics, and his prose writing has a sharp, fast-paced, visually-evocative style that conveys something of the feel of a graphic novel. Rather like the Amok device featured in its early chapters, *Border Princes* is a clever puzzle: for much of its length, it keeps the reader perplexed as to why Torchwood has an additional member, James, who has not featured in the TV series but is apparently a familiar colleague to Jack and the others – even to the point that Gwen temporarily splits from Rhys and goes to live with him. James comes across as a very likeable person, and by the end of the story it actually seems a real pity that he *isn't* a regular character. This is a very astute and original piece of writing by Abnett, and makes *Border Princes* seem quite different from the other *Torchwood* stories; an impression compounded by the fact that there is, for once, no single 'problem of the week' facing Jack's team, but instead a rapid succession of quite different problems. The disadvantage of this latter approach is that, leaving aside the mystery over James's presence in the Hub, it makes the story seem a little lacking in substance, as each of the problems is set up and dealt with relatively quickly, albeit not without difficulty and danger. All things considered, though, *Border Princes* is well up to the standard of *Another Life* and *Slow Decay*, rounding off a very impressive opening trio of novels.

APPENDIX C – TORCHWOOD DECLASSIFIED

With the exception of the 'Preview' episode, each *Torchwood Declassified* mini-documentary focused on one particular episode of *Torchwood* and made its on-air debut on BBC Three in the early hours of the morning following that episode's first transmission. From the same day onwards, it was also available to view – by those in the UK – on the *Torchwood* official website. The 'Preview' episode was made accessible online before *Torchwood* began, and had its first broadcast – in heavily re-edited and extended form – at a later date, as indicated in the episode guide below.

Although shorter, and thus necessarily less detailed, than the similar *Doctor Who Confidential* documentaries, these *Torchwood Declassified* programmes nevertheless gave an excellent insight into many aspects of the making of *Torchwood*, and became increasingly well-assembled and informative as the series progressed. For each episode of an ongoing series to be accorded its own mini-documentary in this way remains a very rare occurrence, and this is a clear indication of the importance placed on *Torchwood* by the BBC.

Additional material from interviews recorded for these purposes was utilised in features on the *Torchwood* official website and extras on the series' DVD releases.

SERIES CREDITS

PRODUCTION TEAM[117, 118]

DV Director: Geoff Evans (1.05, 1.06, 1.07, 1.08, 1.09, 1.10, 1.11, 1.12, 1.13)
Camera: Aled Jenkins (1.00, 1.01, 1.02), Eric Huyton (1.00, 1.01, 1.02), Stuart Brereton (1.03, 1.11)
Sound: Kevin Meredith (1.00, 1.01, 1.02, 1.03), John McCombie (1.11)
Cyfle Trainee: Olivia Mills (1.03, 1.05)
Production Runner: Robert Wootton, Olivia Mills (1.02, 1.04)
Edit Assistant: Rhian Arwel
Researcher: Cat Chappell (1.00, 1.01, 1.04, 1.05), Lucy Lutman (1.00, 1.01, 1.02, 1.03, 1.04, 1.05, 1.11), Jamie Lynch (1.06, 1.07, 1.08, 1.09, 1.10, 1.11, 1.12, 1.13)
Assistant Producers: Geoff Evans (1.00, 1.01, 1.02, 1.03), Laura Hayes, Donovan Keogh
Production Team Assistants: Catrin Honeybill, Claire Jones, Alexandra Gibbs (1.02, 1.03, 1.04, 1.05, 1.06, 1.07, 1.08, 1.09, 1.11)
Production Co-ordinator: Rhiannon Cooper (1.00, 1.01, 1.02), Clare Rutteman (1.02, 1.03, 1.04. 1.05, 1.06, 1.07, 1.08, 1.09, 1.10, 1.11, 1.12, 1.13)
Senior Production Co-ordinator: Rhiannon Cooper (1.03, 1.04, 1.05, 1.06, 1.07, 1.08)
Production Manager: Natalie Street
Editor: James Brailsford (1.00, 1.01), Simon Abrahams (1.00), Alex Boyle (1.10)
Offline Editor: Sven Brooks (1.02), James Brailsford (1.03, 1.12), Fiona Pandelus (1.04, 1.06, 1.11), Rob Franz (1.05), Simon Abrahams (1.07, 1.09, 1.13), Lizzie Minnion (1.08)
Online Editor: Rob Franz (1.00, 1.01, 1.03), James Brailsford (1.02), Adam Mitchell (1.04), Marius Grose (1.05, 1.06, 1.07, 1.08), Alex Boyle (1.09, 1.11, 1.12, 1.13)

117 Where an episode number (or more than one) appears in brackets after a person's name in the listing, this means that they were credited only on the episode (or episodes) indicated. Otherwise, the person concerned was credited on all 14 episodes.

118 In this listing, the credits for 1.00 are taken from the broadcast version of the episode, rather than the website version.

Original Music: Murray Gold (1.00), (1.01), (1.02), (1.03)
Dubbing: Cranc
Graphics: Lee Hallett
Technical Project Manager: Rhys Williams
New Media Producer: Anwen Aspden
Senior Interactive Producer: Jo Pearce

Executive Producers for *Torchwood*: Russell T Davies, Julie Gardner
Executive Producer: Mark Cossey

Series Producer: Gillane Seaborne
Producer and Director: Mark Procter

A BBC Wales production for BBC Three

EPISODE GUIDE

Apart from in the case of the 'Preview' episode, the durations quoted below are for the website versions rather than the BBC Three transmissions. The latter were generally a couple of seconds shorter, as each episode tended to be cut into very slightly by the preceding and/or following continuity caption and announcement.

1.00 – PREVIEW

DEBUT TRANSMISSION DETAILS

BBC Three
Date: 31 October 2006. Time: 7.45 pm.

Duration: 13' 00"

INTERVIEWEES (IN ORDER OF APPEARANCE)

Russell T Davies, Julie Gardner, John Barrowman, Burn Gorman, Naoko Mori, Gareth David-Lloyd, Eve Myles, Chris Chibnall, Richard Stokes, Edward Thomas.

SUMMARY

A general introduction to *Torchwood*.

1.01 – JACK'S BACK

DEBUT TRANSMISSION DETAILS

BBC Three
Date: 23 October 2006. Time: 2.40 am.

Duration: 8' 07"

INTERVIEWEES (IN ORDER OF APPEARANCE)

Naoko Mori, John Barrowman, Eve Myles, Russell T Davies, Brian Kelly, Julie Gardner, Richard Stokes.

SUMMARY

A discussion of 'Everything Changes'; behind-the-scenes details of the Weevils; and a preview of 'Day One'.

1.02 – BAD DAY AT THE OFFICE

DEBUT TRANSMISSION DETAILS

BBC Three
Date: 23 October 2006. Time: 2.50 am.

Duration: 9' 08"

INTERVIEWEES (IN ORDER OF APPEARANCE)

Eve Myles, John Barrowman, Burn Gorman, Russell T Davies, Julie Gardner, Chris Chibnall, Ben Austin, Richard Stokes, Edward Thomas, Brian Kelly.

SUMMARY

A discussion of Gwen's role and integration into the Torchwood team, in particular in 'Day One'; details of the design of the Hub; and a preview of 'Ghost Machine'.

1.03 – LIVING HISTORY

DEBUT TRANSMISSION DETAILS

BBC Three
Date: 30 October 2006. Time: 1.10 am.

Duration: 9' 12"

INTERVIEWEES (IN ORDER OF APPEARANCE)

Burn Gorman, Naoko Mori, Julie Gardner, Russell T Davies, Colin Teague, John Barrowman, Helen Raynor, Richard Stokes, Gareth David-Lloyd.

SUMMARY

A discussion of 'Ghost Machine'; comment on the use of Cardiff as a location; details of the recording of the episode's chase sequences; and a preview of 'Cyberwoman'.

1.04 – GIRL TROUBLE

DEBUT TRANSMISSION DETAILS

BBC Three
Date: 6 November 2006. Time: 2.40 am.

Duration: 10' 18"

INTERVIEWEES (IN ORDER OF APPEARANCE)

Russell T Davies, John Barrowman, Eve Myles, Naoko Mori, Gareth David-Lloyd, James Strong, Chris Chibnall, Burn Gorman, Neill Gorton, Caroline Chikezie.

SUMMARY

Comment on 'Cyberwoman', focusing on the character development of Ianto; behind-the-scenes details relating to the Cyberwoman, including the creation of its 'sexy' costume, the challenges of playing the role and the shooting of the green-screen work for the fight with the pterodactyl; and a preview of 'Small Worlds'.

1.05 – AWAY WITH THE FAIRIES

DEBUT TRANSMISSION DETAILS

BBC Three
Date: 13 November 2006. Time: 2.40 am.

Duration: 10' 10"

INTERVIEWEES (IN ORDER OF APPEARANCE)

Russell T Davies, Julie Gardner, Eve Myles, Peter J Hammond, John Barrowman, Alice Troughton, Lara Phillipart[119], Burn Gorman, Naoko Mori, Paul Bennett[120], Will Travis, Nick Rae.

SUMMARY

Behind-the-scenes on 'Small Worlds', including background to the fairy characters, the role of Jasmine, location recording at the school, the mystery of Jack's past, the character of Roy and location recording of the climactic party scene; and a preview of 'Countryside'.

---

119 Surname misspelt here as 'Philippart'.

120 3rd Assistant Director, uncredited on 'Small Worlds' itself. Surname misspelt 'Bennet' on screen in 'Away with the Fairies'.

1.06 – THE COUNTRY CLUB

DEBUT TRANSMISSION DETAILS

BBC Three
Date: 20 November 2006. Time: 1.10 am.

Duration: 10' 25"

INTERVIEWEES (IN ORDER OF APPEARANCE)

Russell T Davies, John Barrowman, Eve Myles, Chris Chibnall, Burn Gorman, Andy Goddard, Naoko Mori, Richard Stokes, Neill Gorton.

SUMMARY

Comment on the dark and horrific tone of 'Countrycide', the atypical setting of the Brecon Beacons and the developing relationship between Gwen and Owen; a description of the making of the gory body parts representing the cannibals' victims; a discussion of the style of direction of Jack's dramatic rescue of his team at the end of the episode; and a preview of 'Greeks Bearing Gifts'.

1.07 – THERE'S SOMETHING ABOUT MARY

DEBUT TRANSMISSION DETAILS

BBC Three
Date: 27 November 2006. Time: 1.40 am.

Duration: 10' 36"

INTERVIEWEES (IN ORDER OF APPEARANCE)

Richard Stokes, Eve Myles, Naoko Mori, Russell T Davies, Burn Gorman, John Barrowman, Colin Teague, Daniela Denby-Ashe.

SUMMARY

A discussion of Toshiko's character, how it develops in 'Greeks Bearing Gifts' and her relationship with Mary; love and sex in *Torchwood*; the design and creation of the 'fire angel' creature; the ability of the Torchwood team members to survive extraordinary situations; and a preview of 'They Keep Killing Suzie'.

1.08 – BEYOND THE GRAVE

DEBUT TRANSMISSION DETAILS

BBC Three
Date: 4 December 2006. Time: 1.10 am.

Duration: 10' 52"

INTERVIEWEES (IN ORDER OF APPEARANCE)
Russell T Davies, Richard Stokes, John Barrowman, Burn Gorman, Gareth David-Lloyd, James Strong, Naoko Mori, Eve Myles, Paul Chequer.

SUMMARY
Consideration of the dark nature of 'They Keep Killing Suzie', including the return of Suzie, the links to 'Everything Changes', the resurrection glove and the emotional journey that Gwen experiences; the direction of the episode; the 'emotional heart' of the story being the scene of Gwen and Suzie driving through the night in a car; and a preview of 'Random Shoes'.

1.09 – DEAD MAN WALKING

DEBUT TRANSMISSION DETAILS
BBC Three
Date: 11 December 2006. Time: 2.05 am.

Duration: 10' 30"

INTERVIEWEES (IN ORDER OF APPEARANCE)
Eve Myles, Julie Gardner, Paul Chequer, James Erskine, Richard Stokes, Rob Woodruff, Russell T Davies, John Barrowman.

SUMMARY
The story of Eugene Jones is discussed, including the difficulties of realising an 'invisible' character from both production and performance perspectives; the execution of the stunt scene of Eugene's hit-and-run death; and a preview of 'Out of Time'.

1.10 – TIME FLIES

DEBUT TRANSMISSION DETAILS
BBC Three
Date: 18 December 2006. Time: 2.05 am.

Duration: 10' 42"

INTERVIEWEES (IN ORDER OF APPEARANCE)
John Barrowman, Mark Lewis Jones, Russell T Davies, Richard Stokes, Catherine Tregenna, Alice Troughton, Olivia Hallinan, Eve Myles, Kai Owen, Burn Gorman.

SUMMARY
A discussion of the atypical nature of the 'Out of Time' storyline, featuring no science-fiction elements other than the time displacement of the three 1950s characters; the portrayal of these three characters, and the difficulties they face in coming to terms with life in the 21st Century; the shooting of the suicide sequence utilising a cut-down car rig; the interaction between

Gwen and Emma; Kai Owen's nude scene; the changing relationship between Gwen and Rhys; the development of Owen's character, and his relationship with Diane; and a preview of 'Combat'.

1.11 – WEEVIL FIGHT CLUB

DEBUT TRANSMISSION DETAILS

BBC Three
Date: 25 December 2006. Time: 4.00 am.

Duration: 10' 36"

INTERVIEWEES (IN ORDER OF APPEARANCE)

John Barrowman, Burn Gorman, Julie Gardner, Andy Goddard, Richard Stokes, Russell T Davies, Eve Myles, Alex Hassell, Jason Hujan[121], Tom Lucy.

SUMMARY

Comment on the violent content of 'Combat', the characterisation of Owen and his connection with the fight club members; the realisation of the stunt fight sequences; the recording of the climatic fight scenes with the cage; and a discussion of the Weevils, and of how Owen may have been affected by being bitten by one.

1.12 – BLAST FROM THE PAST

DEBUT TRANSMISSION DETAILS

BBC Three
Date: 2 January 2007. Time:2.40 am.

Duration: 10' 18"

INTERVIEWEES (IN ORDER OF APPEARANCE)

John Barrowman, Matt Rippy, Julie Gardner, Naoko Mori, Richard Stokes, Russell T Davies, Ashley Way, Marie Doris, Keith Dunne, Carol Perry[122], Gavin Brocker, Catherine Tregenna.

SUMMARY

Reflections on the character of Torchwood's Captain Jack; the design aspects and direction of the 1940s sequences; rehearsals for Naoko Mori's dancing sequence; and the love story – and kiss – between the two Captain Jacks.

---

121 An uncredited stuntman on 'Combat'.

122 Uncredited dance instructor on 'Captain Jack Harkness'.

1.13 – TO THE END

DEBUT TRANSMISSION DETAILS

BBC Three
Date: 2 January 2007. Time: 2.50 am.

Duration: 10' 25"

INTERVIEWEES (IN ORDER OF APPEARANCE)

John Barrowman, Burn Gorman, Naoko Mori, Murray Melvin, Richard Stokes, Russell T Davies, Eve Myles, Julie Gardner, Barney Curnow, Andy Guest[123], Neil Roche[124], Gareth David-Lloyd.

SUMMARY

Discussion of the apocalyptic quality of 'End of Days'; the sinister Bilis Manger and his evil, manipulative plot to release Abaddon; the apparent death of Rhys, and its effect on Gwen; the links between 'Captain Jack Harkness' and 'End of Days'; the climactic finale of Abaddon emerging from the time rift and striding over Cardiff, while the Torchwood team falls apart; the effects work involved in realising Abaddon; and the apparent death and resurrection of Captain Jack.

123 Credited here as 'Technical Director', but on 'End of Days' itself as '3D Artist'.

124 Credited here as '3D Animator', but on 'End of Days' itself as '3D Artist'.

APPENDIX D – RATINGS AND RANKINGS

Assessing a programme's popularity by reference to its official viewing figures has never been an entirely straightforward matter – prior to the late 1970s, the UK didn't even have a single set of agreed figures, but two competing sets produced for the BBC and the rival ITV network respectively. A programme's ratings can also be affected by factors such as seasonal variations – the total TV audience tending to be lower in the summer, when people are more frequently out and about – and by circumstances specific to the day of transmission, such as it coinciding with a public holiday or a major sporting event. The pulling-power of the programmes scheduled in the same time-slot on other channels is also, of course, an important consideration.

One thing that can be said with absolute certainty, though, is that – however one looks at it – the first series of *Torchwood* was a spectacular hit with the general viewing public. The heavily-publicised debut transmission of the 'Everything Changes'/'Day One' double-bill on BBC Three broke the record for the most-watched non-sport programme ever on a UK digital channel[125], and although – as is generally the case for any series – the figures then dropped for subsequent episodes, *Torchwood* still ended up taking nine of the top 15 places in the chart of the highest individual audiences for programmes broadcast on BBC Three during 2006[126], making it by far the most successful show ever to be screened on the channel. On BBC Two as well, the series got very strong viewing figures indeed, usually being amongst the channel's highest-rated programmes each Wednesday and within its top 30 for the week of transmission.

The number of viewers tuning in for a show is not, of course, the only measure of its success. Also important is the extent to which those viewers enjoyed it; and a measure of this is provided by the Appreciation Index (AI). In this respect, too, the first series of *Torchwood* performed extraordinary well. The average AI figure for a drama programme broadcast by the BBC or ITV is 77, but every single episode of *Torchwood*, both on BBC Three and on BBC Two, scored higher than that. The average figure on BBC Three was 84, with a still-excellent low of 82 for the season opener 'Everything Changes' and an astonishing high of 86 for the closing double-bill of 'Captain Jack Harkness'/'End of Days'; the average on BBC Two was 81, with a low of 78 for both 'Ghost Machine' and 'Random Shoes' and a high of 84 for the closing double-bill. So not only were the figures all higher than the average for drama, they were also remarkably consistent, the difference between the lowest and highest being only four points on BBC Three and six points on BBC Two.

The relatively low AI figure for 'Everything Changes' on BBC Three may well have been due to its relatively high viewing figure; this is a commonly-witnessed phenomenon, attributable to the fact that a proportion of those who tune in for the first episode of a series just to see what it is like will inevitably find that it is not to their taste; they are then less likely to watch subsequent episodes, hence the viewing figure falls while – as those who remain are more favourably-disposed toward the series – the AI rises. The average difference of three points between the figures for the BBC Three transmissions and those for the equivalent BBC Two transmissions is probably also due to the fact that the audiences for the latter were higher than those for the former, and thus more likely to include a proportion of casual viewers who would not class themselves as particular admirers of the series. Even so, these AI figures are still exceptionally good.

125 On 17 December 2006, the record was broken again, by the first episode of the Sky One adaptation of Terry Pratchett's *Hogfather*.

126 Had 'Captain Jack Harkness' and 'End of Days' been transmitted a day earlier, rather than on 1 January 2007, they would have made it into this chart as well, giving *Torchwood* ten of the top 15 places (with 'Random Shoes' knocked down to number 16.)

APPENDIX D – RATINGS AND RANKINGS

The table below shows, for the BBC Three and BBC Two debut transmissions of each of the 13 episodes: the estimated total number of viewers aged four and over (adjusted to include those who recorded the episode to watch within the week following transmission) in millions (RATING); percentage share of total TV audience at that time (SHARE); position in that week's chart of programmes on the channel of transmission (C); position in that week's chart of programmes on all digital channels (not applicable – N/A – in the case of the BBC Two transmissions) (MC); and the audience appreciation index as a percentage (AI). The two entries marked n/a are not available.

EPISODE	CHANNEL	RATING	SHARE	C	MC	AI*
'Everything Changes'	BBC Three	2.52 m	13%	1st	1st	82
	BBC Two	3.03 m	14%	3rd	N/A	80
'Day One'	BBC Three	2.50 m	14%	2nd	2nd	83
	BBC Two[127]	3.03 m	14%	3rd	N/A	80
'Ghost Machine'	BBC Three	1.77 m	11%	1st	1st	84
	BBC Two	2.49 m	11%	14th	N/A	78
'Cyberwoman'	BBC Three	1.39 m	8%	1st	2nd	84
	BBC Two	2.16 m	10%	24th	N/A	80
'Small Worlds'	BBC Three	1.26 m	7%	1st	2nd	85
	BBC Two	2.36 m	10%	17th	N/A	81
'Countrycide'	BBC Three	1.22 m	7%	1st	3rd	83
	BBC Two	2.29 m	10%	18th	N/A	80
'Greeks Bearing Gifts'	BBC Three	1.31 m	8%	1st	2nd	83
	BBC Two	1.80 m	8%	n/a	N/A	81
'They Keep Killing Suzie'	BBC Three	1.12 m	7%	1st	2nd	85
	BBC Two	1.86 m	8%	30th	N/A	82
'Random Shoes'	BBC Three	1.08 m	6%	1st	4th	83
	BBC Two	2.26 m	10%	21st	N/A	78
'Out of Time'	BBC Three	1.03 m	6%	1st	6th	80
	BBC Two	2.16 m	9%	n/a	N/A	79
'Combat'	BBC Three	0.83 m	4%	1st	10th	85
	BBC Two	1.98 m	9%	24th	N/A	81
'Captain Jack Harkness'	BBC Three	1.23 m	6%	1st	2nd	86
	BBC Two	2.14 m	8%	21st	N/A	84
'End of Days'	BBC Three	1.23 m	6%	1st	2nd	86
	BBC Two[128]	2.14 m	8%	21st	N/A	84

Source for viewing figures: Broadcasters' Audience Research Board (BARB)

* AI figures not sourced from BARB

127 The opening double bill of 'Everything Changes' and 'Day One' was treated as a single programme on BBC Two for ratings purposes, so the figures are the same for both episodes.

128 The closing double bill of 'Captain Jack Harkness' and 'End of Days' was treated as a single programme on both BBC Three and BBC Two for ratings purposes, so the figures are the same for both episodes.

A quick perusal of the above table would seem to indicate that after the initial 'Everything Changes'/'Day One' double-bill gained its huge audiences of around two and a half million viewers on BBC Three and around three million viewers on BBC Two, the figures then went into a slow but fairly steady decline over the course of the series, to around one million on BBC Three and a little below two million on BBC Two – a fall of around 60% in the former case and around 40% in the latter case – before rallying slightly for the 'Captain Jack Harkness'/'End of Days' finale. This, though, is by no means the full story. Unlike in years gone by, when any given programme would generally have just a single initial transmission and then not be repeated until weeks or even months later, if at all, it is now the norm for shows on digital channels such as BBC Three to be repeated multiple times within the week of their debut airing. *Torchwood* was, of course, no exception to this rule, and some of its BBC Three repeats – particularly the regular Tuesday evening one – picked up significant numbers of additional viewers in their own right.[129] In most cases where the rating for the debut transmission dipped, there was a noticeable rise in the figures for the repeats (including the one on BBC Two), suggesting that at least a proportion of those who missed seeing – or recording – the episode at the first opportunity made sure to catch it later on, perhaps at a more convenient time for them. A more meaningful picture of how the ratings varied over the course of the series can thus be gained by adding together the figures for all the various transmissions of each episode, including repeats, on both BBC Three and BBC Two.[130] The combined totals thus arrived at are set out in the table below.

EPISODE	TOTAL AUDIENCE
'Everything Changes'	6.61 m
'Day One'	6.51 m
'Ghost Machine'	5.18 m
'Cyberwoman'	4.32 m
'Small Worlds'	4.22 m
'Countrycide'	4.37 m
'Greeks Bearing Gifts'	3.81 m
'They Keep Killing Suzie'	3.87 m
'Random Shoes'	4.26 m
'Out of Time'	4.22 m
'Combat'	3.78 m
'Captain Jack Harkness'	4.37 m
'End of Days'	4.49 m

From this it can be seen that – leaving aside the higher figures for the first three episodes, which benefited from the series' novelty value and the heavy advance publicity – the total

129 General research into viewing figures has shown that the great majority of viewers who tune in for such repeats are additional, i.e. that they have not already seen the programme on one or more of its earlier transmissions. Some sources suggest that the figure is as high as 90 percent.

130 Some of the late night BBC Three repeats were watched by too few viewers to be recorded in the BARB statistics; the totals quoted therefore omit figures for those repeats, but this of course makes no significant difference.

audience actually remained remarkably constant over the course of the run, with just a small mid-series dip. The lower-than-usual figure for 'Combat' can be accounted for by the fact that it was transmitted over the Christmas holiday season, with its BBC Three debut coming in an earlier-than-usual slot on Christmas Eve, when many people's minds would no doubt have been on other things than watching television.

The series-average viewing audience per episode, based on the figures in the table above, was 4.62 million – which would be a very respectable tally for a (single-screening) BBC One drama, let alone a BBC Three one.

Torchwood was naturally never going to rival *Doctor Who* in terms of viewing numbers, being aimed at a smaller, exclusively adult audience, made with a considerably lower budget and transmitted in a late evening slot on a digital channel; but, judged on its own terms, the spin-off had arguably proved just as remarkable a ratings triumph as the parent series.

An indication of the relative merits of the episodes from the point of view of fans – or, at least, of *Doctor Who* fans, who, as discussed in the Series Overview in Part Six, may not necessarily be *Torchwood* fans as well – can be gleaned from the online episode polls conducted in the forum of the Outpost Gallifrey *Doctor Who* website. Between around 1,000 and 2,000 voters participated in these polls, in which each episode was given a mark of between one and five, with five being the highest. The percentages in the table below have been calculated by adding together the total number of marks received by each episode (as of 19 January 2007) and dividing by the maximum that could have been achieved if everyone who voted had given the episode a five.

EPISODE	FAN RATING
'Everything Changes'	76.60%
'Day One'	69.40%
'Ghost Machine'	76.60%
'Cyberwoman'	70.90%
'Small Worlds'	79.80%
'Countrycide'	73.80%
'Greeks Bearing Gifts'	76.00%
'They Keep Killing Suzie'	81.10%
'Random Shoes'	69.70%
'Out of Time'	76.80%
'Combat'	76.70%
'Captain Jack Harkness'	82.60%
'End of Days'	81.10%

Based on these figures, the fans' order of preference, working downwards from favourite to least favourite, would thus seem to have been:

1. 'Captain Jack Harkness'
2. = 'They Keep Killing Suzie'
2. = 'End of Days'
4. 'Small Worlds'

5. 'Out of Time'
6. 'Combat'
7. = 'Everything Changes'
7. = 'Ghost Machine'
9. 'Greeks Bearing Gifts'
10. 'Countrycide'
11. 'Cyberwoman'
12. 'Random Shoes'
13. 'Day One'

This ranking corresponds quite well with that suggested by the AI figures for the general viewing population, perhaps the main difference being that the latter obviously rated 'Cyberwoman' much more highly than the fans. Another point worth noting here is that the spread of these figures – from a low of 69.7 percent to a high of 82.6 percent – is considerably less than in the equivalent polls for *Doctor Who*'s first two series – which went from a low of 68 percent ('Boom Town') to a high of 93 percent ('Dalek') and from a low of 65 percent ('Fear Her') to a high of 93 percent ('Doomsday') respectively. This would seem to suggest that, as far as *Doctor Who* fans were concerned, the spin-off neither rose to the same heights nor sank to quite the same depths as the parent series. (It should be noted, however, that roughly twice as many people voted in the *Doctor Who* polls.)

Finally, for what it's worth, below is this author's own ranking of the episodes, again working downwards from favourite to least favourite – although I should perhaps add two things here: first, my views on this tend to change from time to time; and, secondly, as mentioned previously, I actually loved the whole series!

1. 'Combat'
2. 'Countrycide'
3. 'They Keep Killing Suzie'
4. 'Out of Time'
5. 'Greeks Bearing Gifts'
6. 'Ghost Machine'
7. 'Everything Changes'
8. 'Day One'
9. 'Cyberwoman'
10. 'End of Days'
11. 'Captain Jack Harkness'
12. 'Small Worlds'
13. 'Random Shoes'

APPENDIX E – WEBWATCH[131]

Like many popular TV series, particularly those with a science-fiction basis and/or cult following, *Torchwood* has a very strong presence on the internet.

Two must-see websites for any *Torchwood* fan are the official BBC ones – the programme website at www.bbc.co.uk/torchwood and the Torchwood Institute System Interface at www.torchwood.org.uk – both of which have a wealth of well-presented, high-quality content. The former concentrates mainly on behind-the-scenes information, making available not only all 14 *Torchwood Declassified* mini-documentaries complete and unedited (save for the preview episode, which is a different, slightly shorter edit than the version eventually transmitted) but also numerous additional video interviews, a virtual tour of the Hub, a certain amount of textual information and a large number of photographs. The Torchwood Institute System Interface – referred to as the Torchwood External Hub Interface in its simpler HTML version – is presented as if it were the website of a real-life Torchwood organisation, and contains files – or 'Nodes' – on each of the 13 episodes, each of the six regular characters (including Suzie) and the Torchwood SUV, plus a 'Welcome to Torchwood' overview. Within these files can be found numerous (fictional) case reports, PDF documents, transcripts of instant messenger and e-mail exchanges, photographs and even a few video and audio files. For rights reasons, not all the content of these two websites is officially accessible by those outside the UK.

BBC Wales also has its own, relatively basic, *Torchwood* website. This is to be found at www.bbc.co.uk/wales/southeast/sites/torchwood. Another site recommended for anyone simply wanting factual information about the series – or, indeed, about just about anything else! – is the Wikipedia encyclopaedia at www.wikipedia.org. This has to be treated with a certain amount of caution, however, as the principle on which it operates is that its contents may be amended by any user, and this leaves open the possibility of inaccuracies being introduced from time to time, and even of deliberate sabotage, though those who administer and monitor the site are usually quick to correct anything that goes against the policies under which it is run.

The great majority of *Torchwood* websites, though, are unofficial fan-produced ones. One of the most impressive of these is Torchwood.TV at www.torchwoodtv.blogspot.com, which is probably the best place on the internet to pick up breaking *Torchwood* news and also features a short section of user comment on each episode, a tag board and even a chat room. Another contender for the title of best fan site is Torchwood Guide at www.torchwoodguide.co.uk, which, as the name suggests, takes the form of an episode guide to the series, and a very good one at that. Also a must-see is The Torchwood Institute at www.community.livejournal.com/torch_wood, a LiveJournal community that forms a repository of highly stimulating *Torchwood* discussion and debate, and is probably the best jumping-off point for the large amount of other *Torchwood*-related material on LiveJournal – click on the 'User Info' or 'Torchwood Communities' links on the front page to find a list of all the relevant communities, which number over 50 at the time of writing. A fair number of these communities are devoted to fan fiction, much of which is well worth a read, although – as is generally the case with such

131 Please note that neither Telos Publishing Ltd nor the author has any connection with, or can take any responsibility for the content of, any of the websites mentioned in this Appendix. The use of appropriate anti-virus and firewall software is always recommended for anyone accessing the internet.

things – the writers often seem preoccupied with telling stories in which the regular team members indulge in all manner of sexual activity with outsiders, each other and even occasionally themselves, placing these very much in the 'not for the easily shocked' category.

Two other nicely-produced websites are Torchwood Online at www.torchwood-online.co.uk – notable for its unique feature of regular *Torchwood*-themed podcasts by its editors – and The Institute at http://torchwood.time-and-space.co.uk – another site with a tag-board for those wishing to leave comments. A lively *Torchwood* message board is to be found at http://p097.ezboard.com/btimelord. Any fans in Holland can meanwhile check out a very good Dutch-language site at www.sfseries.nl/content.php?id=263.

Those wishing to know more about the places in Cardiff where *Torchwood* location recording has taken place should check out Torchwood Locations at www.torchwoodlocations.com. Further information on the same subject, along with a very useful annotated map, can be found on the official Cardiff tourist information website, which has a dedicated Torchwood section at www.visitcardiff.com/torchwood.html.

Sites with rather more basic – and in some cases, at the time of writing, out-of-date and/or under development – content are TTIG at www.groups.msn.com/TTIG/_whatsnew.msnw, The Torchwood Archives at www.loony-archivist.com/torchwood, The Torchwood Files at www.ttv.simonswebsite.co.uk/torchwood and Torchwood at www.sylvestermccoy.com/torchwood.

A number of fan-produced *Doctor Who* websites have *Torchwood* content that is well worth checking out. First and foremost amongst these is Shaun Lyon's phenomenal Outpost Gallifrey at www.gallifreyone.com, which includes *Torchwood* amongst its unparalleled *Doctor Who* news coverage, has a *Torchwood* section in its extremely popular forum, and – for those wishing to delve even further into the world of *Doctor Who*/*Torchwood* online fandom, offers 'The Web Guide to *Doctor Who*', a mind-bogglingly extensive and comprehensive listing of relevant links. Others include DoctorWhoTV – see www.doctorwhotv.co.uk/torchwood.htm – A Brief History of Time (Travel) – which provides a useful basic guide at www.shannonsullivan.com/drwho/torchwood.html – and, particularly good for reviews, Kasterborous – see www.kasterborous.com – and Behind the Sofa – see www.tachyontv.typepad.com/waiting_for_christopher.

Last, but certainly not least, John Barrowman has his own official website, which naturally offers a considerable amount of *Torchwood* content, at www.johnbarrowman.com.

AFTERWORD

I signed up to write this book several months before *Torchwood* was even transmitted, which was obviously a risk on my part. I might, after all, have found that I hated the series, in which case producing these 125,000-odd words of text on it would probably have become a nightmarish chore. It wasn't *that* much of a risk though. As mentioned in the Introduction, I suspected right from the word go that it was going to be my kind of series; and, happily, it turned out that I was right.

I very much hope that my enthusiasm for *Torchwood* has come across loud and clear over the course of the preceding chapters. I expect the vast majority of you who are reading this will have shared that enthusiasm even before you bought the book (or borrowed it from your library or whatever) – just on the general principle that people tend not to pick up books on subjects they have no interest in – but I hope that I have managed to give some fresh insights and deepen your appreciation of the series. And if there *are* any people reading this who didn't actually like *Torchwood* to start with, or were perhaps ambivalent about it, well I hope I have managed to convince you that it really is well worth watching!

All being well, I will be back in about 18 months' time with a similar book on *Torchwood*'s second series, and we can all venture inside the Hub again!

Stephen James Walker

ABOUT THE AUTHOR

Stephen James Walker became hooked on *Doctor Who* as a young boy, right from its debut season in 1963/64, and has been a dedicated fan ever since. He first got involved in the series' fandom in the early 1970s, when he became a member of the original *Doctor Who* Fan Club (DWFC). He joined the *Doctor Who* Appreciation Society (DWAS) immediately on its formation in May 1976, and was an attendee and steward at the first ever *Doctor Who* convention in August 1977. He soon began to contribute articles to fanzines, and in the 1980s was editor of the seminal reference work *Doctor Who - An Adventure in Space and Time* and its sister publication *The Data-File Project*. He also became a frequent writer for the official *Doctor Who Magazine*. Between 1987 and 1993 he was co-editor and publisher, with David J Howe and Mark Stammers, of the leading *Doctor Who* fanzine *The Frame*. Since that time, he has gone on to write, co-write and edit numerous *Doctor Who* articles and books - including *Doctor Who: The Sixties*, *Doctor Who: The Seventies*, *Doctor Who: The Eighties*, *The Doctor Who Yearbook 1996*, *The Handbook* (originally published in seven separate volumes), *The Television Companion*, and the three-volume *Talkback* interview compilation - and he is now widely acknowledged as one of the foremost chroniclers of the series' history. He was the initiator and, for the first two volumes, co-editor of Virgin Publishing's *Decalog* books - the first ever *Doctor Who* short story anthology range. He has a BSc (Hons) degree in Applied Physics from University College London, and his many other interests include cult TV, film noir, vintage crime fiction, Laurel and Hardy and an eclectic mix of soul, jazz, R&B and other popular music. Between July 1983 and March 2005 he acted as an adviser to successive Governments, latterly at senior assistant director level, responsible for policy on a range of issues relating mainly to individual employment rights. Most of his working time is now taken up with his role as co-owner and director of Telos Publishing Ltd. He lives in Kent with his wife and family.

Other *Doctor Who* Telos Titles Available

BACK TO THE VORTEX: THE UNOFFICIAL AND UNAUTHORISED GUIDE TO DOCTOR WHO 2005 by J SHAUN LYON

Complete guide to the 2005 series of Doctor Who starring Christopher Eccleston as the Doctor

£12.99 (+ £2.50 UK p&p) Standard p/b ISBN: 1-903889-78-2
£30.00 (+ £2.50 UK p&p) Deluxe h/b ISBN: 1-903889-79-0

SECOND FLIGHT: THE UNOFFICIAL AND UNAUTHORISED GUIDE TO DOCTOR WHO 2006 by J SHAUN LYON

Complete guide to the 2006 series of Doctor Who starring David Tennant as the Doctor

£12.99 (+ £2.50 UK p&p) Standard p/b ISBN: 1-84583-008-3
£30.00 (+ £2.50 UK p&p) Deluxe h/b ISBN: 1-84583-009-1

Other Telos Titles Available

TIME HUNTER

A range of high-quality, original paperback and limited edition hardback novellas featuring the adventures in time of Honoré Lechasseur. Part mystery, part detective story, part dark fantasy, part science fiction … these books are guaranteed to enthral fans of good fiction everywhere, and are in the spirit of our acclaimed range of *Doctor Who* Novellas.

THE WINNING SIDE by LANCE PARKIN

Emily is dead! Killed by an unknown assailant. Honoré and Emily find themselves caught up in a plot reaching from the future to their past, and with their very existence, not to mention the future of the entire world, at stake, can they unravel the mystery before it is too late?
An adventure in time and space.
£7.99 (+ £1.50 UK p&p) Standard p/b ISBN 1-903889-35-9 (pb)

THE TUNNEL AT THE END OF THE LIGHT by STEFAN PETRUCHA

In the heart of post-war London, a bomb is discovered lodged at a disused station between Green Park and Hyde Park Corner. The bomb detonates, and as the dust clears, it becomes apparent that *something* has been awakened. Strange half-human creatures attack the workers at the site, hungrily searching for anything containing sugar …
Meanwhile, Honoré and Emily are contacted by eccentric poet Randolph Crest, who believes himself to be the target of these subterranean creatures. The ensuing investigation brings Honoré and Emily up against a terrifying force from deep beneath the earth, and one which even with their combined powers, they may have trouble stopping.
An adventure in time and space.
£7.99 (+ £1.50 UK p&p) Standard p/b ISBN 1-903889-37-5 (pb)
£25.00 (+ £1.50 UK p&p) Deluxe h/b ISBN 1-903889-38-3 (hb)

THE CLOCKWORK WOMAN by CLAIRE BOTT

Honoré and Emily find themselves imprisoned in the 19th Century by a celebrated inventor … but help comes from an unexpected source – a humanoid automaton created by and to give pleasure to its owner. As the trio escape to London, they are unprepared for what awaits them, and at every turn it seems impossible to avert what fate may have in store for the Clockwork Woman.
An adventure in time and space.
£7.99 (+ £1.50 UK p&p) Standard p/b ISBN 1-903889-39-1 (pb)
£25.00 (+ £1.50 UK p&p) Deluxe h/b ISBN 1-903889-40-5 (hb)

KITSUNE by JOHN PAUL CATTON

In the year 2020, Honoré and Emily find themselves thrown into a mystery, as an ice spirit – *Yuki-Onna* – wreaks havoc during the Kyoto Festival, and a haunted funhouse proves to contain more than just paper lanterns and wax dummies. But what does all this have to do with the elegant owner of the Hide and Chic fashion

chain … and to the legendary Chinese fox-spirits, the Kitsune?
An adventure in time and space.
£7.99 (+ £1.50 UK p&p) Standard p/b ISBN 1-903889-41-3 (pb)
£25.00 (+ £1.50 UK p&p) Deluxe h/b ISBN 1-903889-42-1 (hb)

THE SEVERED MAN by GEORGE MANN

What links a clutch of sinister murders in Victorian London, an angel appearing in a Staffordshire village in the 1920s and a small boy running loose around the capital in 1950? When Honoré and Emily encounter a man who appears to have been cut out of time, they think they have the answer. But soon enough they discover that the mystery is only just beginning and that nightmares can turn into reality.
An adventure in time and space.
£7.99 (+ £1.50 UK p&p) Standard p/b ISBN 1-903889-43-X (pb)
£25.00 (+ £1.50 UK p&p) Deluxe h/b ISBN 1-903889-44-8 (hb)

ECHOES by IAIN MCLAUGHLIN & CLAIRE BARTLETT

Echoes of the past … echoes of the future. Honoré Lechasseur can see the threads that bind the two together, however when he and Emily Blandish find themselves outside the imposing tower-block headquarters of Dragon Industry, both can sense something is wrong. There are ghosts in the building, and images and echoes of all times pervade the structure. But what is behind this massive contradiction in time, and can Honoré and Emily figure it out before they become trapped themselves …?
An adventure in time and space.
£7.99 (+ £1.50 UK p&p) Standard p/b ISBN 1-903889-45-6 (pb)
£25.00 (+ £1.50 UK p&p) Deluxe h/b ISBN 1-903889-46-4 (hb)

PECULIAR LIVES by PHILIP PURSER-HALLARD

Once a celebrated author of 'scientific romances', Erik Clevedon is an old man now. But his fiction conceals a dangerous truth, as Honoré Lechasseur and Emily Blandish discover after a chance encounter with a strangely gifted young pickpocket. Born between the Wars, the superhuman children known as 'the Peculiar' are reaching adulthood – and they believe that humanity is making a poor job of looking after the world they plan to inherit …
An adventure in time and space.
£7.99 (+ £1.50 UK p&p) Standard p/b ISBN 1-903889-47-2 (pb)
£25.00 (+ £1.50 UK p&p) Deluxe h/b ISBN 1-903889-48-0 (hb)

DEUS LE VOLT by JON DE BURGH MILLER

'Deus Le Volt!'…'God Wills It!' The cry of the first Crusade in 1098, despatched by Pope Urban to free Jerusalem from the Turks. Honoré and Emily are plunged into the middle of the conflict on the trail of what appears to be a time travelling knight. As the siege of Antioch draws to a close, so death haunts the blood-soaked streets … and the Fendahl – a creature that feeds on life itself – is summoned. Honoré and Emily find themselves facing angels and demons in a battle to survive their latest adventure.
An adventure in time and space.
£7.99 (+ £1.50 UK p&p) Standard p/b ISBN 1-903889-49-9 (pb)
£25.00 (+ £1.50 UK p&p) Deluxe h/b ISBN 1-903889-97-9 (hb)

THE ALBINO'S DANCER by DALE SMITH

'Goodbye, little Emily.'

April 1938, and a shadowy figure attends an impromptu burial in Shoreditch, London. His name is Honoré Lechasseur. After a chance encounter with the mysterious Catherine Howkins, he's had advance warning that his friend Emily Blandish was going to die. But is forewarned necessarily forearmed? And just how far is he willing to go to save Emily's life?

Because Honoré isn't the only person taking an interest in Emily Blandish – she's come to the attention of the Albino, one of the new breed of gangsters surfacing in post-rationing London. And the only life he cares about is his own.

An adventure in time and space.

£7.99 (+ £1.50 UK p&p) Standard p/b ISBN 1-84583-100-4 (pb)
£25.00 (+ £1.50 UK p&p) Deluxe h/b ISBN 1-84583-101-2 (hb)

THE SIDEWAYS DOOR by R J CARTER & TROY RISER

Honoré and Emily find themselves in a parallel timestream where their alternate selves think nothing of changing history to improve the quality of life – especially their own. Honoré has been recently haunted by the death of his mother, an event which happened in his childhood, but now there seems to be a way to reverse that event … but at what cost?

When faced with two of the most dangerous people they have ever encountered, Honoré and Emily must make some decisions with far-reaching consequences.

An adventure in time and space.

£7.99 (+ £1.50 UK p&p) Standard p/b ISBN 1-84583-102-0 (pb)
£25.00 (+ £1.50 UK p&p) Deluxe h/b ISBN 1-84583-103-9 (hb)

COMING SOON:
CHILD OF TIME by GEORGE MANN

When Honoré and Emily investigate the bones of a dead child in the ruins of a collapsed house, they are thrown into a thrilling adventure that takes them from London in 1951 to Venice in 1586 and then forward a thousand years, to the terrifying, devastated London of 2586, ruled over by the sinister Sodality. What is the terrible truth about Emily's forgotten past? What demonic power are the Sodality plotting to reawaken? And who is the mysterious Dr Smith? All will be revealed in the stunning conclusion to the acclaimed *Time Hunter* series. Coming in 2007.

An adventure in time and space.

£7.99 (+ £1.50 UK p&p) Standard p/b ISBN 978-1-84583-104-2 (pb)
£25.00 (+ £1.50 UK p&p) Deluxe h/b ISBN 978-1-84583-105-9 (hb)

TIME HUNTER FILM

DAEMOS RISING by DAVID J HOWE, DIRECTED BY KEITH BARNFATHER

Daemos Rising is a sequel to both the *Doctor Who* adventure *The Daemons* and to *Downtime*, an earlier drama featuring the Yeti. It is also a prequel of sorts to Telos Publishing's *Time Hunter* series. It stars Miles Richardson as ex-UNIT operative Douglas Cavendish, and Beverley Cressman as Brigadier Lethbridge-Stewart's daughter Kate. Trapped in an isolated cottage, Cavendish thinks he is seeing ghosts. The only person who might understand and help is Kate Lethbridge-Stewart … but when she arrives, she realises that Cavendish is key in a plot to summon the Daemons back to the Earth. With time running out, Kate discovers that sometimes even the familiar can turn out to be your worst nightmare. Also starring Andrew Wisher, and featuring Ian Richardson as the Narrator.
An adventure in time and space.
£14.00 (+ £2.50 UK p&p) PAL format R4 DVD
Order direct from Reeltime Pictures, PO Box 23435, London SE26 5WU

HORROR/FANTASY

CAPE WRATH by PAUL FINCH

Death and horror on a deserted Scottish island as an ancient Viking warrior chief returns to life.
£8.00 (+ £1.50 UK p&p) Standard p/b ISBN: 1-903889-60-X

KING OF ALL THE DEAD by STEVE LOCKLEY & PAUL LEWIS

The king of all the dead will have what is his.
£8.00 (+ £1.50 UK p&p) Standard p/b ISBN: 1-903889-61-8

ASPECTS OF A PSYCHOPATH by ALASTAIR LANGSTON

The twisted diary of a serial killer.
£8.00 (+ £1.50 UK p&p) Standard p/b ISBN: 1-903889-63-4

GUARDIAN ANGEL by STEPHANIE BEDWELL-GRIME

Devilish fun as Guardian Angel Porsche Winter loses a soul to the devil …
£9.99 (+ £2.50 UK p&p) Standard p/b ISBN: 1-903889-62-6

FALLEN ANGEL by STEPHANIE BEDWELL-GRIME

Porsche Winter battles she devils on Earth …
£9.99 (+ £2.50 UK p&p) Standard p/b ISBN: 1-903889-69-3

SPECTRE by STEPHEN LAWS

The inseparable Byker Chapter: six boys, one girl, growing up together in the back streets of Newcastle. Now memories are all that Richard Eden has left, and one treasured photograph. But suddenly, inexplicably, the images of his companions start to fade, and as they vanish, so his friends are found dead and mutilated.

Something is stalking the Chapter, picking them off one by one, something connected with their past, and with the girl they used to know.
£9.99 (+ £2.50 UK p&p) Standard p/b ISBN: 1-903889-72-3

THE HUMAN ABSTRACT by GEORGE MANN
A future tale of private detectives, AIs, Nanobots, love and death.
£7.99 (+ £1.50 UK p&p) Standard p/b ISBN: 1-903889-65-0

BREATHE by CHRISTOPHER FOWLER
The Office meets *Night of the Living Dead.*
£7.99 (+ £1.50 UK p&p) Standard p/b ISBN: 1-903889-67-7
£25.00 (+ £1.50 UK p&p) Deluxe h/b ISBN: 1-903889-68-5

HOUDINI'S LAST ILLUSION by STEVE SAVILE
Can master illusionist Harry Houdini outwit the dead shades of his past?
£7.99 (+ £1.50 UK p&p) Standard p/b ISBN: 1-903889-66-9

ALICE'S JOURNEY BEYOND THE MOON by R J CARTER
A sequel to the classic Lewis Carroll tales.
£6.99 (+ £1.50 UK p&p) Standard p/b ISBN: 1-903889-76-6
£30.00 (+ £1.50 UK p&p) Deluxe h/b ISBN: 1-903889-77-4

APPROACHING OMEGA by ERIC BROWN
A colonisation mission to Earth runs into problems.
£7.99 (+ £1.50 UK p&p) Standard p/b ISBN: 1-903889-98-7
£30.00 (+ £1.50 UK p&p) Deluxe h/b ISBN: 1-903889-99-5

VALLEY OF LIGHTS by STEPHEN GALLAGHER
A cop comes up against a body-hopping murderer ...
£9.99 (+ £2.50 UK p&p) Standard p/b ISBN: 1-903889-74-X
£30.00 (+ £2.50 UK p&p) Deluxe h/b ISBN: 1-903889-75-8

PARISH DAMNED by LEE THOMAS
Vampires attack an American fishing town.
£7.99 (+ £1.50 UK p&p) Standard p/b ISBN: 1-84583-040-7

MORE THAN LIFE ITSELF by JOE NASSISE
What would you do to save the life of someone you love?
£7.99 (+ £1.50 UK p&p) Standard p/b ISBN: 1-84583-042-3

PRETTY YOUNG THINGS by DOMINIC MCDONAGH
A nest of lesbian rave bunny vampires is at large in Manchester. When Chelsey's ex-boyfriend is taken as food, Chelsey has to get out fast.
£7.99 (+ £1.50 UK p&p) Standard p/b ISBN: 1-84583-045-8

A MANHATTAN GHOST STORY by T M WRIGHT

Do you see ghosts? A classic tale of love and the supernatural.
£9.99 (+ £2.50 UK p&p) Standard p/b ISBN: 1-84583-048-2

SHROUDED BY DARKNESS: TALES OF TERROR edited by ALISON L R DAVIES

An anthology of tales guaranteed to bring a chill to the spine. This collection has been published to raise money for DebRA, a national charity working on behalf of people with the genetic skin blistering condition, Epidermolysis Bullosa (EB). Featuring stories by: Debbie Bennett, Poppy Z Brite, Simon Clark, Storm Constantine, Peter Crowther, Alison L R Davies, Paul Finch, Christopher Fowler, Neil Gaiman, Gary Greenwood, David J Howe, Dawn Knox, Tim Lebbon, Charles de Lint, Steven Lockley & Paul Lewis, James Lovegrove, Graham Masterton, Richard Christian Matheson, Justina Robson, Mark Samuels, Darren Shan and Michael Marshall Smith. With a frontispiece by Clive Barker and a foreword by Stephen Jones. Deluxe hardback cover by Simon Marsden.
£12.99 (+ £2.50 UK p&p) Standard p/b ISBN: 1-84583-046-6
£50.00 (+ £2.50 UK p&p) Deluxe h/b ISBN: 978-1-84583-047-2

BLACK TIDE by DEL STONE JR

A college professor and his students find themselves trapped by an encroaching hoarde of zombies following a waste spillage.
£7.99 (+ £1.50 UK p&p) Standard p/b ISBN: 978-1-84583-043-4

TV/FILM GUIDES

DOCTOR WHO

THE TELEVISION COMPANION: THE UNOFFICIAL AND UNAUTHORISED GUIDE TO DOCTOR WHO by DAVID J HOWE & STEPHEN JAMES WALKER

Complete episode guide (1963–1996) to the popular TV show.
£14.99 (+ £4.75 UK p&p) Standard p/b ISBN: 1-903889-51-0

THE HANDBOOK: THE UNOFFICIAL AND UNAUTHORISED GUIDE TO THE PRODUCTION OF DOCTOR WHO by DAVID J HOWE, STEPHEN JAMES WALKER and MARK STAMMERS

Complete guide to the making of Doctor Who (1963 – 1996).
£14.99 (+ £4.75 UK p&p) Standard p/b ISBN: 1-903889-59-6
£30.00 (+ £4.75 UK p&p) Deluxe h/b ISBN: 1-903889-96-0

WHOGRAPHS: THEMED AUTOGRAPH BOOK

80 page autograph book with an SF theme
£4.50 (+ £1.50 UK p&p) Standard p/b ISBN: 1-84583-110-1

TALKBACK: THE UNOFFICIAL AND UNAUTHORISED DOCTOR WHO INTERVIEW BOOK: VOLUME 1: THE SIXTIES edited by STEPHEN JAMES WALKER

Interviews with behind the scenes crew who worked on Doctor Who in the sixties
£12.99 (+ £2.50 UK p&p) Standard p/b ISBN: 1-84583-006-7
£30.00 (+ £2.50 UK p&p) Deluxe h/b ISBN: 1-84583-007-5

TALKBACK: THE UNOFFICIAL AND UNAUTHORISED DOCTOR WHO INTERVIEW BOOK: VOLUME 2: THE SEVENTIES edited by STEPHEN JAMES WALKER

Interviews with behind the scenes crew who worked on Doctor Who in the seventies
£12.99 (+ £2.50 UK p&p) Standard p/b ISBN: 1-84583-010-5
£30.00 (+ £2.50 UK p&p) Deluxe h/b ISBN: 1-84583-011-3

TALKBACK: THE UNOFFICIAL AND UNAUTHORISED DOCTOR WHO INTERVIEW BOOK: VOLUME 3: THE EIGHTIES edited by STEPHEN JAMES WALKER

Interviews with behind the scenes crew who worked on Doctor Who in the eighties
£12.99 (+ £2.50 UK p&p) Standard p/b ISBN: 978-1-84583-014-4
£30.00 (+ £2.50 UK p&p) Deluxe h/b ISBN: 978-1-84583-015-1

HOWE'S TRANSCENDENTAL TOYBOX: SECOND EDITION by DAVID J HOWE & ARNOLD T BLUMBERG

Complete guide to *Doctor Who* Merchandise 1963-2002.
£25.00 (+ £4.75 UK p&p) Standard p/b ISBN: 1-903889-56-1

HOWE'S TRANSCENDENTAL TOYBOX: UPDATE NO. 1: 2003 by DAVID J HOWE & ARNOLD T BLUMBERG

Complete guide to *Doctor Who* Merchandise released in 2003.
£7.99 (+ £1.50 UK p&p) Standard p/b ISBN: 1-903889-57-X

HOWE'S TRANSCENDENTAL TOYBOX: UPDATE NO. 2: 2004-2005 by DAVID J HOWE & ARNOLD T BLUMBERG

Complete guide to *Doctor Who* Merchandise released in 2004 and 2005.
£7.99 (+ £1.50 UK p&p) Standard p/b ISBN: 1-84583-012-1

TORCHWOOD

INSIDE THE HUB: THE UNOFFICIAL AND UNAUTHORISED GUIDE TO TORCHWOOD by STEPHEN JAMES WALKER

Complete guide to the 2006 series of *Torchwood*, starring John Barrowman as Captain Jack Harkness.
£12.99 (+ £2.50 UK p&p) Standard p/b ISBN: 978-1-84583-013-7

BLAKE'S 7

LIBERATION: THE UNOFFICIAL AND UNAUTHORISED GUIDE TO BLAKE'S 7 by ALAN STEVENS & FIONA MOORE

Complete episode guide to the popular TV show.
Featuring a foreword by David Maloney
£9.99 (+ £2.50 UK p&p) Standard p/b ISBN: 1-903889-54-5

SURVIVORS

THE END OF THE WORLD?: THE UNOFFICIAL AND UNAUTHORISED GUIDE TO SURVIVORS by ANDY PRIESTNER & RICH CROSS

Complete guide to Terry Nation's *Survivors*
£12.99 (+ £2.50 UK p&p) Standard p/b ISBN: 1-84583-001-6

CHARMED

TRIQUETRA: THE UNOFFICIAL AND UNAUTHORISED GUIDE TO CHARMED by KEITH TOPPING

Complete guide to *Charmed*
£12.99 (+ £2.50 UK p&p) Standard p/b ISBN: 1-84583-002-4

24

A DAY IN THE LIFE: THE UNOFFICIAL AND UNAUTHORISED GUIDE TO 24 by KEITH TOPPING

Complete episode guide to the first season of the popular TV show.
£9.99 (+ £2.50 p&p) Standard p/b ISBN: 1-903889-53-7

FILMS

A VAULT OF HORROR by KEITH TOPPING

A guide to 80 classic (and not so classic) British Horror Films.
£12.99 (+ £4.75 UK p&p) Standard p/b ISBN: 1-903889-58-8

BEAUTIFUL MONSTERS: THE UNOFFICIAL AND UNAUTHORISED GUIDE TO THE ALIEN AND PREDATOR FILMS by DAVID McINTEE

A guide to the *Alien* and *Predator* films.
£9.99 (+ £2.50 UK p&p) Standard p/b ISBN: 1-903889-94-4

ZOMBIEMANIA: 80 FILMS TO DIE FOR by DR ARNOLD T BLUMBERG & ANDREW HERSHBERGER

A guide to 80 classic zombie films, along with an extensive filmography of over 500 additional titles.
£12.99 (+ £2.50 UK p&p) Standard p/b ISBN: 1-84583-003-2

CRIME

THE LONG, BIG KISS GOODBYE

Hardboiled thrills as Jack Sharp gets involved with a dame called Kitty.
£7.99 (+ £1.50 UK p&p) Standard p/b ISBN: 978-1-84583-109-7

MIKE RIPLEY

The first three titles in Mike Ripley's acclaimed 'Angel' series of comic crime novels.

JUST ANOTHER ANGEL by MIKE RIPLEY
£9.99 (+ £1.50 UK p&p) Standard p/b ISBN: 1-84583-106-3
ANGEL TOUCH by MIKE RIPLEY
£9.99 (+ £1.50 UK p&p) Standard p/b ISBN: 1-84583-107-1
ANGEL HUNT by MIKE RIPLEY
£9.99 (+ £1.50 UK p&p) Standard p/b ISBN: 1-84583-108-X

HANK JANSON

Classic pulp crime thrillers from the 1940s and 1950s.

TORMENT by HANK JANSON
£9.99 (+ £1.50 UK p&p) Standard p/b ISBN: 1-903889-80-4
WOMEN HATE TILL DEATH by HANK JANSON
£9.99 (+ £1.50 UK p&p) Standard p/b ISBN: 1-903889-81-2
SOME LOOK BETTER DEAD by HANK JANSON
£9.99 (+ £1.50 UK p&p) Standard p/b ISBN: 1-903889-82-0
SKIRTS BRING ME SORROW by HANK JANSON
£9.99 (+ £1.50 UK p&p) Standard p/b ISBN: 1-903889-83-9
WHEN DAMES GET TOUGH by HANK JANSON
£9.99 (+ £1.50 UK p&p) Standard p/b ISBN: 1-903889-85-5
ACCUSED by HANK JANSON
£9.99 (+ £1.50 UK p&p) Standard p/b ISBN: 1-903889-86-3
KILLER by HANK JANSON
£9.99 (+ £1.50 UK p&p) Standard p/b ISBN: 1-903889-87-1
FRAILS CAN BE SO TOUGH by HANK JANSON
£9.99 (+ £1.50 UK p&p) Standard p/b ISBN: 1-903889-88-X
BROADS DON'T SCARE EASY by HANK JANSON
£9.99 (+ £1.50 UK p&p) Standard p/b ISBN: 1-903889-89-8
KILL HER IF YOU CAN by HANK JANSON
£9.99 (+ £1.50 UK p&p) Standard p/b ISBN: 1-903889-90-1
LILIES FOR MY LOVELY by HANK JANSON
£9.99 (+ £1.50 UK p&p) Standard p/b ISBN: 1-903889-91-X
BLONDE ON THE SPOT by HANK JANSON
£9.99 (+ £1.50 UK p&p) Standard p/b ISBN: 1-903889-92-8

Non-fiction:
THE TRIALS OF HANK JANSON by STEVE HOLLAND
£12.99 (+ £2.50 UK p&p) Standard p/b ISBN: 1-903889-84-7

The prices shown are correct at time of going to press. However, the publishers reserve the right to increase prices from those previously advertised without prior notice.

TELOS PUBLISHING
c/o Beech House, Chapel Lane, Moulton, Cheshire, CW9 8PQ, England
Email: orders@telos.co.uk
Web: www.telos.co.uk

To order copies of any Telos books, please visit our website where there are full details of all titles and facilities for worldwide credit card online ordering, or send a cheque or postal order (UK only) for the appropriate amount (including postage and packing), together with details of the book(s) you require, plus your name and address to the above address. Overseas readers please send two international reply coupons for details of prices and postage rates.